The Faber Book of Mexican Cinema

Jason Wood is a curator, film-maker and writer whose previous books for Faber include *The Faber Book of Mexican Cinema* (first edition), *Nick* ~~Broomfield Documenting Icons and New British Cinema~~ *rom* Submarine ~~~~ so written *100* ~~~~ BFI. He holds a

The Faber Book of
Mexican Cinema

Jason Wood

faber

First published in 2006
by Faber & Faber Ltd
Bloomsbury House
74–77 Great Russell Street
London WC1B 3DA
This new edition published in 2021
First published in the USA in 2021

Typeset by Faber & Faber Ltd
Printed and bound by CPI Group (UK) Ltd, Croydon CR0 4YY

A CIP record for this book is available from the British Library

ISBN 978–0–571–35377–4

2 4 6 8 10 9 7 5 3 1

Contents

PART TWO

Illustrations

Interviews

Carlos Reygadas, Director: 17 August 2002, London
Alfonso Cuarón, Director: 21 November 2002, London
Carlos Cuarón, Writer/Director: 8 August 2003, Mexico
Emmanuel Lubezki, Cinematographer: 14 July 2003, Mexico
Bertha Navarro, Producer: 30 September 2003, Mexico City
Ángeles Castro, Director of the Centro de Capacitación Cinematográfica:
    1 October 2003, Mexico City
Laura Imperiale, Producer: 2 October 2003, Mexico City
Guillermo Arriaga, Writer: 2 October 2003, Mexico City
Francisco González Compeán, Producer: 3 October 2003, Mexico City
Alfredo Joskowicz, Director of IMCINE: 3 October 2003, Mexico City
Martha Sosa, Producer: 4 October 2003, Mexico City
Carlos Carrera, Director: 4 October 2003, Mexico City
Leonardo García Tsao, Critic/Academic: 15 October 2003, Mexico City
Alejandro González Iñárritu, Director: 1 November 2003, London
Rosa Bosch, Producer: 7 November 2003, London
Juan Carlos Rulfo, Director: 8 November 2003, Mexico City
Brigitte Broch, Production Designer: 8 November 2003, New York
Daniel Birman, Producer: 21 November 2003, Mexico City
Guillermo del Toro, Director: 24 November 2003 Los Angeles
Rodrigo Prieto, Cinematographer: 14 December 2003, London
Salvador Carrasco, Director: 15 December 2003, Los Angeles
Martín Salinas, Writer: 29 December 2003, Buenos Aires
Hugo Rodríguez, Director: 13 January 2004
Gael García Bernal, Actor: 14 January 2004, New York
José Luis García Agraz, Director: 20 January 2004, Mexico City

Lila Avilés: 2019, Manchester/Mexico
Natalia Beristáin: 2019, Manchester/Mexico
Mariana Chenillo: 2019, Manchester/Mexico
Alfonso Cuarón: 2019, London (updated interview from the 2006 edition)

Interviews

Jonás Cuarón: 2007, London
Fernando Eimbcke: 2008, London
Amat Escalante: 2019, Manchester/Mexico
Michel Franco: 2019, Manchester/Mexico
Cary Joji Fukunaga: 2009, London
Everardo González: 2019, Manchester/Mexico
Daniel Graham: 2019, Manchester/London
Jorge Michel Grau: 2019, Manchester/Mexico
Alejandro González Iñárritu: 2019, Toronto/Los Angeles/New York
    (updated interview from the 2006 edition)
Gerardo Naranjo: 2019, Manchester/Mexico
Nicolás Pereda: 2019, Manchester/Mexico
Carlos Reygadas: London/Manchester/Mexico (updated interview from
    the 2006 edition)
Alonso Ruizpalacios: 2019, Manchester/Mexico
Guillermo del Toro: 2020, Manchester/Los Angeles (updated interview
    from the 2006 edition)
David Zonana: 2019, Manchester/Mexico

Foreword

I think the bottom line is that in Mexico – where you don't receive too much good news – any reports of a success, especially on an international level, is going to be in some ways inspiring. It would be disingenuous to think that the government supports and then directly helps the emergence of great art. It has a responsibility to art but art and artistic movements are created by people, and usually by new generations that are fearless. I am not going to defend or attack the films that Carlos, Alejandro, Guillermo or myself have made but we have perhaps been an inspiration for younger people to say, 'Oh shit. It's possible.' Guillermo and I were more connected to the film-makers of the previous generation than Alejandro or Carlos. We were part of the industry before we started directing our films. Pretty much the message you used to receive as an aspiring film-maker is that it's impossible. There was an entire psychology like this. So when we began to have our success, even the people that may not have liked our films may have thought that perhaps it can be done after all. Of course, I am not saying that there have not been good government initiatives but we have to remember that these initiatives were often pushed for by film-makers who held government or academic positions. All the good government policies in Mexican cinema were crafted by film-makers and we have to be very grateful to the film-makers and producers such as Jorge Sánchez who, once they became bureaucrats, used their position and their power to make a difference. There is also a tremendous sense of solidarity amongst the Mexican film community.

Alfonso Cuarón
London, November 2019

PART ONE

Introduction

It's chemistry, alchemy, pieces falling together at the same time. How can you effectively explain other essential moments in film history, like the German New Wave? Sometimes these things are just moments in time, linked to specific political, social or cultural situations. It's not only that there were a bunch of film-makers. There were also actors, cinematographers, production designers, producers . . .

Rosa Bosch, producer, *The Devil's Backbone*

Enjoying phenomenal critical and commercial success in quick succession, *Amores Perros* and *Y tu mamá también* alerted the eyes of the world to the riches to be found in Mexican cinema. The former marked the audacious directorial debut of Alejandro González Iñárritu; the latter was the work of Alfonso Cuarón, a more experienced film-maker returning home for a personal project, after a fruitful Hollywood excursion. Both films featured the poster-boy looks and electrifying screen presence of Gael García Bernal; each was confident, stylishly shot and structurally complex. Moreover, these films were thematically provocative in their treatment of prescient social issues, and thrillingly forthright in their willingness to address the ills afflicting contemporary Mexican society.

The global media, ever eager to pinpoint a new trend, wasted little time in devoting many column inches to predicting an exciting new wave, or *buena onda*, and Mexican cinema immediately became its darling. However, a more informed assessment of film production in Mexico, largely through the pages of industry periodicals such as *Screen International* and *Variety*, soon revealed a harsher and somewhat paradoxical reality; and in turn the headlines just as quickly became epitaphs. Attention shifted to Argentina – a country reeling from economic collapse – and yet still able to sustain a profitable cinema industry and nurture the careers of emerging talents such as Pablo Trapero (*El Bonaerense*, 2002, and *Familia Rodante*, 2006) and Lucrecia Martel (*La Ciénaga*, 2001, and *La Niña Santa*, 2004).

On the one hand there existed an undeniable surplus of young, formally daring creative talent, whose rise to prominence coincided with an emerging generation of Mexican cinema-goers thirsting for intelligent, identity-affirming, locally made product. Having endured a period of relative famine throughout the 1980s and for much of the early 1990s, Mexican audiences had, for the most part, given up on Mexican cinema, preferring instead to pay to see the numerous American productions that were filling the screens at the increasingly popular multiplex cinemas springing up throughout the country. Now, though, they once more had a national cinema to be optimistic about, one that matched if not bettered the films imported from across the border; a cinema with its own stars, its own high production values, and its own characters and concerns. These Mexican audiences were once again able to recognize themselves, their hopes, aspirations and troubles, on screen.

Facilitating the aspirations of film-makers and audiences alike was a new entrepreneurial spirit among private investors and producers, a good number of whom had valiantly struggled under the closed-shop mentality of previous administrations, taking the crumbs that fell occasionally from the table of the state-controlled industry. Prepared to invest time, energy and money on unconventional projects that were not, in the majority of instances, mere local variations on American genre pictures, they soon understood that financial autonomy from the existing government institutions also accorded formal and ideological liberty. No subject was taboo, no narrative too complex, in the continued search for an authentic means of expression and the need to address directly the ever-present issue of what it meant to be Mexican.

Conversely, and severely undermining these outwardly fertile conditions, was the unfavourable distribution of the peso at the box office, a distribution that made recouping costs for private producers almost impossible. Without government-initiated tax incentives, and confronted by escalating production costs and prints and advertising budgets, private producers faced an arduous task even getting an independent feature off the ground. With the eyes of the world looking on, it became all too apparent that the Mexican cinema industry was beset by structural problems so deep rooted and irreparable that they threatened to place a foot to the throat of what had briefly been a tantalizing renaissance.

This book – compounded of extensive interviews with a rich diversity of leading lights and industry professionals, edited into a narrative interspersed with linking prose – is an attempt to offer a clear perspective on the current aesthetic and economic climate, while also contextualizing contemporary

Mexican cinema in relation to its own frequently brilliant but equally troubled past. By the same token, a film such as *Amores Perros* did not emerge from a vacuum and so it is essential that *Contemporary Mexican Cinema* touch on some of its key antecedents and the social, political, technical and individual and collective creative forces that helped give birth to it.

A constantly shifting environment confronts today's Mexican film industry professionals. The clearest and most alarming example of this is the now thwarted plans of Mexican President, Vicente Fox, to extinguish state involvement in cinema by closing the Mexican Film Institute (imcine), calling time on Mexico's leading film school, the Centro de Capacitación Cinematográfica (the institution that trained many of the people with whom I spoke), and selling off for real-estate-development purposes the legendary Studios Churubusco.

The howls of outrage that greeted Fox's proposals – proposals that were perceived as direct attacks on culture and identity and that would remove the last barriers to American cultural domination – is evidence of the strength of spirit and the feeling of community within the Mexican cinema fraternity. Just as González Iñárritu, Alfonso Cuarón and Guillermo del Toro – the directors perhaps most popularly associated with recent Mexican cinema, whose high profiles have seen them assume ambassadorial roles – are all close friends and frequent advisers on each other's works. This sense of kinship, encouragement and responsibility has helped to sustain Mexican cinema in times both good and bad.

Viva México!

Jason Wood

'Golden Age', *El Grupo Nuevo Cine*, Boom and Bust

ALFONSO CUARÓN *director*: Remember what Claude Chabrol said: 'There is no wave, there is only the ocean.' I am not purely interested in 'Mexican cinema', I am interested in cinema. And when you start using these words like 'wave', it's a way of creating an identity for certain films, but it also becomes an aspect of marketing. You know, the common identity of the films people are describing as part of this 'Mexican wave' is that they are from Mexico, but the only other thing they have in common is that they are cinema. And that is the reason these films are seen everywhere and why they have been embraced everywhere. But people are also disregarding Mexican film-makers who have been making films for the last thirty years – people like Arturo Ripstein. You have to remember that there have been lots of Mexican film directors, but that doesn't make a 'wave' – it's not as if we have all shared a particular aesthetic.

HUGO RODRÍGUEZ *director*: Let's not forget that Mexico has a long film-making tradition, which started almost at the same time as the international film industry was born. We have films that date back to the early 1900s, and the historical relationship with Hollywood has meant that our technicians are highly trained.

One of the belle époque*'s success stories, Mexico was prosperous and politically stable in the 1890s. It should come as little surprise, then, that the movie projectors and early films produced by the Lumière Brothers should appear there shortly after they became popular in Europe. Mexican audiences greeted the new form of entertainment just as enthusiastically as had their European counterparts; and, while it is not well documented, there was certainly a 'silent-film era' in Mexico, with the origins of cinema there linked to Salvador Toscano Barragán, an engineering student who opened the first Mexican movie salon and began to create some of the country's first film productions. By 1900 the popularity of cinema within Mexico – and particularly Mexico City – was well established, with new salons opening and new equipment being imported.*

*In this formative period the majority of 'entertainments' were locally pro-
duced documentations of momentous national events, such as the opening
of new railway lines and presidential excursions. However, in 1908 one of
the first major films to be produced from a script was completed: Felipe de
Jesús's* El Grito de Dolores. *After a period of boom, there followed one of
decline in the 1920s as Hollywood established itself as the dominant force in
film-making. With audiences turning increasingly to imported newsreels
originating from America, film production in Mexico – which was not
supported by the state – suffered a rapid downturn, while the more sophisticated Hollywood films successfully offered fantasy and escape. This rejection of localized product would repeat itself many times. Moreover, such
Mexican film artists as had established themselves were not adverse to
overtures from the north, and so figures such as Delores del Río and Lupita
Tovar set sail for pastures new.*

*It was the coming of sound that allowed Mexico to regain ground as a
film-making entity, and although in 1932 (a few years after the important
arrival of Sergei Eisenstein in the country) only six films were produced, two
were by directors who would make a valuable contribution to the country's
cinema: Fernando de Fuentes* (El anónimo) *and Soviet émigré Arcady
Boytler* (Mano a mano). *Buoyed by renewed private investment (for
example, wealthy distributor Juan de la Cruz Alarcón formed the Compañía
Nacional Productora de Películas), Mexican cinema was once again at the
forefront of Spanish-language film production by 1933.*

LEONARDO GARCÍA TSAO *critic/academic*: 'The History of Mexican Cinema'
is a course I have not yet taught and, to be honest, it's not something that
I would really enjoy teaching – although there are some Mexican films that I
enjoy very much, by the likes of Emilio Fernández and Fernando de Fuentes.

*A former actor who in the 1920s found work in the United States, Emilio
Fernández returned to Mexico and leading-man status with roles in Carlos
Navarro's* Janitzio (1934) *and Rafael E. Portas's* Adiós Nicanor (1937). *In
1941 Fernández made his directorial debut with* La isla de la pasión. *Two
years later Fernández teamed up with actors Delores del Río and Pedro
Armendáriz on projects such as* Flor Silvestre *and* María Candelaria.
*Winning numerous festival prizes and bringing Mexican cinema to wider
international attention, Fernández directed well into the 1970s, completing
his final work,* Erótica, *in 1978.*

*Fernando de Fuentes began his career as a cinema manager, and would
later use his experience in this regard to challenge the existing exhibition*

monopoly of the 1940s. He became arguably the most important figure in the Mexican cinema of the 1930s because of his trilogy of films about the Revolution: El prisionere trece *(1933)*, El compadre Mendoza *(1933) and* Vámonos con Pancho Villa *(1934)*.

Emerging from this period is what is termed 'The Golden Age of Mexican Cinema', or 'El Cine de Oro'. It coincided with the administration of Miguel Alemán between the years 1946 and 1952, and was inextricably linked to unprecedented economic growth and prosperity, proving to be a high point both in terms of production (quantity as well as quality) and of profits. A major contributing factor to Mexico's film-making status at this time was the courting of Mexico as a valuable ally against Axis countries by the US. Increased revenue and access to technology became widely available. Similarly, the period saw an increased attention to film-making by the state as it sought to protect what was becoming a valuable cultural and economic asset. Thus, in 1942, the Banco Nacional Cinematográfica was founded to facilitate the funding of film production. A law was also passed in 1946 that protected the film industry from income tax: 'Thriving in the shade of the state's protection and subsidization, Mexican cinema found itself in the midst of a Golden Age, an era of quality films and high output that continued into the late 1950s.'[1] *It was also through these movies that a romanticized and idealized view of Mexico was projected on to movie screens across Latin America, giving Mexico a dominance in this market second only to Hollywood.*

Though born in Spain, Luis Buñuel – widely credited as the founder of surrealist cinema with films such as Un Chien andalou *(made with Salvador Dalí, 1929) and* L'Age d'Or *(1930) – is inextricably linked to the development of Mexican cinema and remains one of its most prominent and influential figures. Emerging at the tail end of the 'Cine de Oro' period, the director arguably provides a lineage with the subsequent 'Grupo Nuevo Cine', and – through his unsentimental consideration of themes of poverty and social injustice, allied with his formal experimentation and ability to work creatively with limited resources – to the prominent Mexican directors who would emerge on the cusp of the twenty-first century.*

Having, like many Spanish artists and intellectuals, relocated to Mexico in 1946 following the Spanish Civil War (becoming a Mexican citizen in 1949), Buñuel embarked on Gran Casino *(also known as* En el viejo Tampico, *1947), his first directorial project since 1933's* Las Hurdes.

[1] Berg, *Cinema of Solitude*, p. 15.

Working extensively with producer Óscar Dancigers, Buñuel would go on to produce a number of Mexican films including Los olvidados *(1950),* El *(1953),* Ensayo de un crimen *(1955) and* Nazarín *(1959) and* Viridiana *(1961). That last picture once again garnered him international attention and acclaim, precipitating a return to international productions such as* Belle du Jour *(1967) and* Tristana *(1970). Though working mostly in France during the latter part of his career, Buñuel would return frequently to his adopted Mexican homeland, eventually dying in Mexico City in 1983.*

GUILLERMO DEL TORO *director*: Goya is one of my favourite painters, and I think that Goya didn't really come to be until the last days of his life when he produced his 'Black Paintings'.[2] That is the ultimate expression of him. The same with Alfred Hitchcock – I think that the only real glimpse of the very dark and very complex man that Alfred Hitchcock was comes with watching *Frenzy* (1972). To my mind the opposite happened with Buñuel. I think that Buñuel did some of his best work very early on, and then went to read what the critics had to say about him and started to make movies that were a little too hermetic. I maintain that his Mexican period is his best period.

LEONARDO GARCÍA TSAO: There were one or two good Mexican films in the 1960s but, with the exception of Buñuel, the movie scene was pretty poor then. So people of that generation developed and sustained a prejudice against Mexican films. It was a class thing. The upper-middle classes deemed that watching Mexican movies didn't befit their social position: they felt that only the lower classes would go to see such films. I remember, when I was a kid, my father would resolutely say, 'No way! We are *not* going to see a Mexican movie!'

Identified in 1960 after a series of concerts attended by leftists critics, scholars and film-makers including Buñuel, El Grupo Nuevo Cine published the magazine Nuevo Cine *from April 1960 to August 1962. A manifesto criticizing the state of the Mexican film industry,* Nuevo Cine *demanded a number of sweeping reforms, including the formation of an institution to teach film-making, and increased exhibition and production of independent films.*

---

[2] Goya's 'Black Paintings' were completed while the artist was living in seclusion outside of Madrid. Extremely personal in style – and executed on his walls – the fourteen paintings gave expression to his deepest and darkest visions.

LEONARDO GARCÍA TSAO: From the *Nuevo Cine* magazine came the idea that Mexican cinema really had to change, and so they organized an experimental film contest.

In part a response to declining production levels, but also as a response to calls from young university-based cineastes, the leading Mexican film union, the Sindicato de Trabajadores de la Producción Cinematográfica, announced the First Contest of Experimental Cinema in 1964. Founded in 1919 as the Unión de Empleados Confederados del Cinematográfica, the STPC was the union that by 1944 came to represent all film workers.

The entries were judged in July 1965 by a thirteen-person panel, representing the industry, critics and cultural institutions. First prize was awarded to Rubén Gámez's La fórmula secreta *(The Secret Formula, 1965), a surrealistic work dealing with Mexico's search for identity. Second prize was awarded to Alberto Isaac's* En este pueblo no hay ladrones *(In This Town There Are No Thieves, 1964).*

JUAN CARLOS RULFO *director*: Rubén Gámez, for whom I worked as assistant director, I regard as the most inventive film director Mexico has had in the last forty years, and the one who has taken the most risks. His films *Megueyes* (1962), *La fórmula secreta* (*The Secret Formula*, 1965), and *Tequila* (1992), among others, are points of reference for anyone wishing to talk about the roots of Mexican and experimental cinema.

JOSÉ LUIS GARCÍA AGRAZ *director*: At sixteen, I wanted to be a professional footballer, a guitarist in a rock band, a poet, a cartoonist, and a heroic guerrilla fighter. That was 1968, and the government was brutally putting down any attempt to make society more democratic. Teachers, doctors and railway workers were murdered, put in prison; it was a period that ended with the cruel suppression of the student movement on 2 October in Tlatelolco to the north of Mexico City, which was a place of Aztec sacrifice before the arrival of the Spanish in the sixteenth century; then a shunting yard in the 1920s, and a middle-class housing project in the early 1970s.

Following mass outbreaks of anti-government demonstrations across the country during the summer of 1968, some six thousand students and non-student protestors (including women and children) gathered on 2 October 1968 at the Plaza of the Three Cultures in Tlatelolco. Government troops opened fire on the protestors (the government was to later protest that students had fired first), killing an estimated two hundred people and wounding hundreds more.

The generation that cut their teeth in 1968 duly rose to the forefront in the 1970s and collectively brought about an important cinematic movement.

LEONARDO GARCÍA TSAO: The 1970s brought a slight change, with Felipe Cazals and Arturo Ripstein. I was a student at university then, and this was the time when I started to get interested in watching Mexican films. I remember that in class we would all decide to go see the new film by Cazals or Ripstein.

Born in France, Felipe Cazals had lived in Mexico since early childhood. Originally working in Mexican television and later on a number of short films for the film department of Belles Artes, Cazals directed his first feature in 1968, the independently produced La manzana de la discordia *(The Apple of Discord). As a reaction against the difficulties of breaking into the national film industry, in 1969 Cazals collaborated with Arturo Ripstein, Rafael Castenado and Pedro F. Miret to create the influential if short-lived Cine Independiente de Mexico group. Subsequently working with state funding on numerous high-scale productions (*El Jardín de tía Isabel, 1971, *and* Aquellos años, 1972, *among them), Cazals began to focus more and more on projects concerned with highlighting the social and ethnic problems affecting Mexico. 1975's* Canoa *(written by Tomás Perez Turrent), a documentary-style examination of a 1968 uprising by a Mexico City student movement, is perhaps his best-known work.*

ALFONSO CUARÓN: When I was growing up and realized I wanted to make films, there were directors who showed me there were other approaches to the cheesy sex comedies that were being produced in Mexico. A very important film for me was *Canoa* by Felipe Cazals.

The winner of a Special Jury Prize at the Berlin Film Festival, Canoa *re-creates the real-life events of 1968 in which four employees of the University of Puebla were lynched by the townspeople of San Miguel de Canoa. Based on a script by film critic Tomás Pérez Turrent,* Canoa's *documentary aesthetic was much imitated and the film is widely regarded as a classic of the national cinema.*

Cazals was subsequently to fall in and out of favour with the national cinema industry and his post–1970s output is largely made up of less personal projects and generic pictures undertaken on commission.

Born in Mexico City in 1943, Arturo Ripstein, son of producer Alfredo Ripstein jnr, had been involved in the Mexican film industry since childhood. After appearing in supporting roles in the 1960s, Ripstein worked as an assistant to Luis Buñuel on The Exterminating Angel *(1962). At the age of twenty-one Ripstein adapted a script by Gabriel García Márquez to make his feature debut,* Tiempo de Morir *(1965). A director of truly international standing whose work has been celebrated at festivals worldwide, Ripstein's key films include* El castillo de la pureza *(1972);* El Santo oficio *(1973); and* El lugar sin límites *(1977).*

*Two other substantive film-makers of the 1970s were Jorge Fons and Alfredo Joskowicz. Fons, part of the first graduation class of the Centro Universatario de Estudios Cinematográficos (*CUEC*), was initially an assistant director to Arturo Ripstein before moving into directing 'telenovelas' on Mexican television and establishing his own directorial career. Fons's early work includes the* Caridad *segment of* Fe, esperanza y caridad *(1972) and* Los albañiles *(1976).*

Beginning his film-making career with 1968's La Manda, *Alfredo Joskowicz is widely considered to have made two of the finest Mexican films of the early 1970s in* Crates *(1970) and* El Cambio *(The Change, 1971). Made in the wake of the massacre at Tlatelolco, both films echoed an acute disillusionment with Mexican society.*

*An institutional strength was added to Mexican cinema in the 1970s through the presidency (sexenio) of Luis Echeverría Álvarez. Coming to power in 1970, Institutional Revolutionary Party (*PRI*) candidate Echeverría regarded cinema as a tool through which Mexico could be promoted throughout the world. Throughout his sexenio (1970–76) Echevarría was extremely supportive of cinema, offering a state level of financial and infrastructural backing that provided an exciting opportunity for emerging film-makers.*

ALFREDO JOSKOWICZ, *film-maker/Director,* IMCINE: At the beginning of the 1970s there was a very new look to Mexican cinema, but this arose from the decision of the government to make film-making more democratic. Previously, the Banco Nacional Cinematográfico had given money for film production only to a very narrow and business-orientated band of independent film producers, and Echeverría abolished this system. He installed his brother Rodolfo[3] as the head of the BNC and sanctioned the establishing of

---

[3] A former president of Asociación Nacional de Actores (ANDA), Rodolfo Echeverría (screen name Rodolfo Landa) was a well-known actor in Mexican cinema.

three state-formed production companies: CONACINE, CONACITE I and CONACITE II. To ensure a consistency of quality, the state became the major film producer in Mexico. But it was not a conservative film-making environment – the opposite, in fact, it was a time of liberal ideological reform.

Echeverría also ensured that the two major films studios, including Estudios America and Estudios Churubusco – where I also worked for the last four years before coming to IMCINE – became the base for Mexican film production. Echeverría also created the Centro de Capacitación Cinematográfica and generally ensured a heightened commitment to exhibiting and distributing locally produced cinema. Cinema was very almost – but not quite totally – an entirely state-funded and controlled industry. So the state effectively held control of production, distribution and exhibition.

Echeverría established a relaxed and liberating film-making environment where the emphasis was not on turning a quick buck by churning out production after production but rather on quality, diversity and freedom of speech. An explosion of internationally acclaimed film-making ensued, in which directors such as Cazals, Ripstein, Miguel Littín, Jaime Humberto Hermosillo, and Paul Leduc – considered part of the New Cinema movement – rose to prominence.

After studying film-making at IDHEC in Paris, Mexico City-born Paul Leduc returned to Mexico in 1967 and directed seventeen documentary shorts for the Olympic Committee with Cine 70, a group he had helped found alongside Rafael Castanedo, Alexis Grivas and Bertha Navarro.

BERTHA NAVARRO *producer*: I directed theatre productions at university when I was younger and then I graduated to directing short films. I originally studied anthropology and was going to become an anthropologist, but then I became enraptured by documentary cinema and decided to get involved. I met Paul Leduc and cinematographer Alexis Grivas; both had studied at IDHEC in Paris and had just come back to Mexico and so we decided to work together. Then came the Olympic Games and we had a lot of work, so I started to help out even more by producing and even editing some of the films.

Leduc's work would be characterized by a high degree of political commitment, and he truly came to prominence with Reed: México Insurgente *(Reed: Insurgent Mexico, 1973), a historical work with the aesthetics of a documentary, based on American journalist John Reed's account of the Mexican Revolution.*

BERTHA NAVARRO: Paul and I did our first feature film together, *Reed: México Insurgente*, when I was twenty-six. I acted in the film and also produced it. It was an independent film and a huge adventure. The industry and the unions were so closed that they wouldn't let anybody new in, and so we were forced to take the independent route. I've worked in different moments of this industry, and it has *always* been about challenging and breaking the structures that don't allow you to do things.

We were called 'pirates'. We were a young generation trying to do new things within the older structure of the Mexican film industry. *Reed: México Insurgente* was actually promoted by the official industry institutions, who sent it to numerous international festivals. We also had a huge amount of backing from intellectuals and the cultural community within Mexico – Carlos Fuentes cited it as one of the best films he'd seen. With all this backing and support the existing structures tried to integrate us into their system, and we went to Cannes, where the film was selected for the Directors' Fortnight. It made a big impact, and so we decided to take our 16 mm print and have it blown up to 35 mm. This was also done with the help of the industry officials. It was a good start for us, but after the film nothing really changed, because the industry officials didn't wish to help us make another project, and they certainly weren't going to provide any financial aid.

LEONARDO GARCÍA TSAO: The 1970s, the Echeverría period, saw the cinematic fruits of the Nuevo Cine group, which in the 1960s had been purely theoretical.

ALFREDO JOSKOWICZ: It's a very long list of film-makers who flourished but one that would certainly include Jaime Humberto Hermosillo, Alfonso Arau, Gonzalo Martínez and Alberto Isaac. I was the previous generation: we were aggressive, but the industry was completely closed to us.

A student of the Centro Universatario de Estudios Cinematográficos (CUEC), Jaime Humberto Hermosillo made his full-feature commercial debut with La verdarera vocación de Magdalena *(1971). His subsequent career alternated between highly personal projects that examine issues of class, gender and sexuality, and more lacklustre, overtly commercial fare. In the 1980s, generally considered to be Hermosillo's weakest period, his films garnered a cult international following, specifically* Doña Herlinda y su hijo *(Doña Herlinda and Her Son, 1984), regarded as the first openly gay film in the history of Mexican cinema.*

Alfonso Arau's films include: El Águila descalza *(The Barefoot Eagle,*

1969), Calzonzin Inspector *(*Inspector Calzonzin, *1973),* Mojado Power *(1979) and, most famously,* Como agua para chocolate *(*Like Water for Chocolate, *1992).*

After working in documentary, Gonzalo Martínez made his feature debut with Tú, yo, nosotros *(1970), co-directed with Juan Manuel Torres and Jorge Fons.* El Principio *(1972) won numerous awards. He was prolific in film and documentary until his death in 1998.*

Alberto Isaac was a member of the Nuevo Cine group and later the first Director of IMCINE, *after having been previously blacklisted by Margarita López Portillo for publicly criticizing Mexico's investment of approximately half a million dollars in* Superman *(1978); his other credits include:* Las visitaciones del diablo *(1967);* Fútbol México *(1970);* Tívoli *(1974);* Tiempo de lobos *(1981) and* ¡Maten a Chinto! *(1989).*

For all its obvious virtues, President Echeverría's emphasis on quality inevitably led to a decline in the number of films produced annually. In 1970, the start of his presidency, eighty-two films were produced. In 1976, at its end, the number had dropped to just thirty-five.

ALFREDO JOSKOWICZ: And now we enter the tragic story of Mexican cinema. The amount of films made by private producers was decreasing while the amount of films produced by the state was increasing. The privately funded films were shot in two or three weeks, and were of extremely low quality. Remember also that in Mexico, for a very long time, the price of admittance was 40 cents, whereas in America it was about $2.50. So these privately made films were exported to the Mexican communities living in America, so that the producers could make more money.

At the end of the Echeverría period, cinema suffered a massive devaluation. The private producers said that they had to make fifty-two films per year, and they did this with the guarantee of the state that these films, though not state-funded, would be exhibited in the government-owned exhibition chain. At the beginning of 1979 the Banco Nacional Cinematográfico closed, and CONACITE I was also abolished. As a result, there began the retreat of the state from film production, and the return to prominence of the private producer.

When José López Portillo assumed power in 1976 he quickly labelled his predecessor's term a disaster, taking the view that 'fewer films meant fewer profits'.[4] Reversing many of Echeverría's advancements and policies

[4] Berg, *Cinema of Solitude,* p. 15.

(including dissolving CONACITE I, *reintroducing a stricter censorship, and encouraging the return of private investment and fat-cat producers to reduce the involvement of the state in the industry), Portillo's sexenio (1976–82) did once again see annual production levels rise (ninety-four features in 1981) but it also led to 'lowered production values and an intensified suppression of films dealing with difficult social themes'.*

*His sister Margarita López Portillo was made the Head of the Directorate of Radio, Television, and Cinema (*RTC*), a new government agency established to oversee all state-owned electronic mass media production. Preferring the term supervision to censorship, Margarita López Portillo oversaw the return to a more cautious and conservative climate.*

ALFREDO JOSKOWICZ: I was Director at the Centro de Capacitación Cinematográfia (CCC) for six years during the worst period of Margarita López Portillo. Every day Margarita was trying to close the school . . .

LEONARDO GARCÍA TSAO: The Echeverría presidency had really helped a lot of young film-makers. After Echeverría, things went really bad and people again began to stay away from the cinema. I remember Paul Leduc's *Frida* (1984) coming out and nobody going to see it. A great shame – it's much better than the Hollywood film directed by Julie Taymor.

After 1976, the generation of 1968 became marginalized. But during 1981, the penultimate year of López Portillo's sexenio, ninety-four feature length films were produced in Mexico. Despite the conservative nature of the majority of these films (resulting from a state-supervised return to a more cautious cinema) and the fact that the bulk of them are now considered to be of variable technical quality, Mexico had attained its highest level of production since the 1950s. Margarita López Portillo was arguably justified in her claim that the administration of López Portillo had 'resurrected' Mexican film-making.

LAURA IMPERIALE *producer*: In those days, the reality of Mexican cinema was completely different from what it is today. Production was dominated by the old-school producers and the cinematographic labour unions. In order to show a film you needed to have a film licence, and this licence was granted by the union as long as you had worked in accordance with its rules, and used its affiliates and numerous staff. The films produced were basically *gringo* films – we provided production services – and very poor quality both in terms of story and technically speaking; except for the honourable exceptions of films produced by the state for directors such as Felipe Cazals, Arturo Ripstein, Jorge Fons and a few others.

As a result of this situation there was a strong independent cinema movement, which differed from the 'industry' of the time in the subject-matter of its stories and in the way they tried to produce films. Out of this came what would later be known as the 'New Mexican Cinema'. Several of these productions were made by co-operatives and shot in Super–16, which was the way to get round the union rules.

ALFREDO JOSKOWICZ: There would almost always be something good happening still, even with the decreased amount of films produced by the state, because the ambitions were so different. The state-produced films were certainly less interested in commerce, but they were also more *outré*, if you like. You therefore had a very schizophrenic situation, as we had a handful of good films with very low commercial success and a lot of bad films that were commercially successful.

At the end of López Portillo's *sexenio* and the beginning of Miguel de la Madrid Hurtado's presidency, there was another massive devaluation of cinema. The state maintained some involvement, but only a very small amount of money was given to production and it was the export market that was privileged over any attempt to satisfy the demands of domestic cinema-goers. Films were being made at an average cost of between $100,000 and $200,000, and so the quality of the films was generally extremely poor. The films of this period were being shot and completed in as little of two weeks.

In March 1983, Alberto Isaac was named the first Head of the newly created Mexican Film Institute (IMCINE), under the presidency of Miguel de la Madrid. IMCINE's task was seen by Isaac to 'rebuild a ruined cinema in a ruined country'.[5]

With the national cinema dramatically impoverished it was decided by the newly elected president that the state would need to once again become a cultural arbiter. As well as fulfilling this role, IMCINE would also be the structure through which various other much needed sweeping reforms would be implemented and upheld. Such reforms included the dispersal of newly available state funds to film-makers; the continued insurance of prolonged employment for the country's many technicians (the privately produced films made under López Portillo might have been dreadful but they did ensure that an industry continued to exist); the encouragement of a

[5] Mora, *Mexican Cinema: Reflections of Society*, p. 149.

wider diversity of film product in both political and aesthetic terms, and an attention to ways in which television and the mass audience it commanded might act as a facilitating organ vis-à-vis the production of more highly crafted and stimulating cinematic product.

IMCINE *would prove that the state was serious about getting its cinema industry back on track and would be the body through which a new vision for Mexican cinema could be first implemented and then sustained. Like other national cinema bodies, it would not merely exist as a bank through which grants and funding would be dispersed (though it would oversee the* FOPROCINE *(Fondo de Fomento a la Producción Cinematográfica) and* FIDECINE *funding schemes) but would be the infrastructure through which Mexican film would be able to exist once again at the interface of art, commerce, and popular entertainment.*

The selection of Alberto Isaac was a shrewd one. A much respected veteran director who had been blacklisted by the previous administration, Isaac offered the film industry hope that the state's intentions were true. Under Isaac's stewardship, there was hope among the film community that Mexican cinema – if freed from the suffocating red tape of bureaucracy that had stifled previous governmental 'interference' in localized cinema production – could once again establish its identity and reflect the culture of its people once more in cinema theatres in Mexico and throughout the world.

In this transitional moment, the 1980s did not produce a considerable yield of leading new Mexican directors. Best known among those who did emerge was Luis Mandoki from Mexico City, who made a name in his homeland before answering overtures to work in the US.

ALFONSO CUARÓN: Luis Mandoki is of a slightly different generation from myself, the one right after Arturo Ripstein. I was an assistant to Luis for many years – he's perhaps my mentor. In a way, Luis was the first Mexican director who was very comfortable working in Hollywood.

LEONARDO GARCÍA TSAO: Mandoki had really made only shorter pieces in Mexico such as *El secreto* (1980), *Mundo mágico* and *Papaloapan* (1982) before making *Motel* (1984). After that he did *Gaby* (1987), which was in English and a co-production, and basically a Hollywood film. To be honest, I must say that I think that Mandoki is a hack. I'm not a fan of his work, which I find to be bland and lacking in personality and style.

ALFONSO CUARÓN: For someone like Luis, it was very difficult to make a film in Mexico because of the humiliations with the government, and difficulties with IMCINE. Luis was also one of the first ones to say, 'I want to make a film, and I'm not embarrassed about saying that this movie is going to cost this much to make, and so it's going to have to make this much to recoup the money.' He was a survivalist in that sense. And then when he did it, and was very successful with *Gaby*, he found the comfort in Hollywood after the spurning and humiliation in Mexico.

An English-language drama, Gaby: A True Story *tells the tale of Gaby Brimer (Rachel Chagall), a physically handicapped woman whose desire to succeed as a student causes her to triumph against adversity. Invariably and favourably compared to* My Left Foot *(1989), the film also features Liv Ullmann and Robert Loggia.*

MARTÍN SALINAS *screenwriter:* Luis and I had been living just a few blocks away from each other for couple of years in Mexico City, but we didn't meet until I attended the Havana Film Festival. Luis and a Mexican producer called Abraham Cherem and Luciana Cabarga, who was the godmother of that project, were looking for a screenwriter for Luis's project based on Gaby Brimer's real story. Luis had already worked on several attempts to adapt Gaby's life and was obsessed with the project. There was very little money, but a lot of enthusiasm. And there was the real Gaby Brimer, who had written hundreds of pages about herself and her tremendous struggle against her extreme physical limitations. I refused to read previous treatments and drafts of that project and just read what Gaby had written about herself. And what made me want to write the script was to try and tell a story about someone who struggles against her own limitations, tries to surpass them, crashes against those ones she definitely cannot, and can continue moving forward and getting involved in new challenges only when she accepts those limitations and learns to live with them. Which is how I feel about my own life . . .

I then got locked away in a house with an amazing view in Cuernavaca. Luis and Abraham would bring me the mail and the food and their notes – the perfect scenario in which to write. It took me six months to get to a serious first draft. I almost got divorced for that. But when we finished that first reading, we all knew that we did have a film there. Luis got it translated into English by Michael James Love, who came up with a few notes, which I obviously hated at first. Then we came to terms and we finally ended up writing the final version of *Gaby: A True Story* together. The script was translated in order to test the waters all over the world regarding possible producers and European actors to play Gaby's parents. I always thought I was going to get it made in Spanish, but the producers who were interested spoke only English. *Gaby* took Luis and us to the Hollywood arena from one day to another. Alfonso Cuarón had been the first assistant director. From there on, Michael and I became writing partners for almost ten years in Hollywood's 'development hell'. But that's another story . . .

Meanwhile the 1980s also saw further fruits from the establishment of vocational film education in Mexico. Founded in 1963 and 1976 respectively, the Centro Universitario de Estudios Cinematográficos (CUEC) and the Centro de Capacitación Cinematográfica (CCC) collectively and individually represented the fulfilment of a much cherished dream of Mexican cineastes since the silent-film era. As the testimonies below attest, the value and function of the two schools cannot be overstated. They provided artistic life-blood for the industry even during some of its darkest hours. The schools can claim credit for the existence of almost every single Mexican director, editor, cinematography and actor to have emerged in recent decades.

ROSA BOSCH *producer*: Almost all of the key writers, cinematographers, production designers and directors have come out of CCC or CUEC. It's

The Centro de Capacitación Cinematográfica (CCC)

obvious that the film schools have been essential in terms of nurturing, sustaining and producing a fresh influx of talent. They have also taught people to take their talents seriously, and to approach their various disciplines as a craft.

JOSÉ LUIS GARCÍA AGRAZ: I started to work for a left-wing magazine, at the same time as deciding to study economics so that I could 'serve my country once the forces of the proletariat and the *campesinos* had seized power' (*sic*). But things don't always turn out how you expect: I found I didn't like economics and my brother Carlos, who is a year younger than me and who'd had a vocation for cinema from a very early age, encouraged me to go to the only film school there was at that time in Mexico, the CUEC at the National Autonomous University of Mexico, to study film-making so that I could do the photography on his films. The CUEC turned out to be a place where I had wonderful teachers, with whom I'm still friends, such as the great Polish-born theatre director Ludwik Margules, Alfredo Joskowicz, and the director José Estrada, who is no longer with us. It was there I discovered some of the enormous artistic and expressive possibilities that cinema offers, and my love of film-making.

In a country where the film-production sector comes second to the cinema chains and to the distributors, the film schools have the difficult task of being centres of technical and artistic learning, as well as that of resisting the globalizing intentions of governments which for over twenty years have been pursuing the demise of Mexican producers with the too obvious question: 'Why make films here when so many are already being made in Hollywood?'

The film schools – for all their limitations – have become production companies for shorts; where young people have the complete freedom to make the films they choose – a freedom that, as we well know, brings with it many other political and philosophical demands. However, it's almost impossible to create a national film sector on the basis of film schools. Budgets are very small, relations with the outside world are weak, and nor do film schools represent the totality of a country's artistic expression. What they are, though, is a breeding ground for young film-makers. Unfortunately, later faced with so many obstacles and a lack of opportunities to develop their artistic expression, many of these young film-makers go on to work in the world of television – which in Mexico is profoundly stupid – or advertising.

JUAN CARLOS RULFO: In itself, I don't think that film school teaches you how to go about things. It's you, in a particular context – all the people you meet or don't meet, all your fears and frustrations – that's what pushes you to look for projects. It was at film school that I decided I wanted to become a director; although before that I had wanted to write and, years earlier, I had wanted to be a photographer. Maybe film school was the place where it all came together and allowed me to understand what I wanted to do. But it had to happen then, it couldn't have been earlier.

MARTÍN SALINAS: I first graduated and worked as an architect in Argentina. My first step into film-making was by making animated films with an independent group of film-makers. Argentina was then suffering the most cruel and bloody military dictatorship in our country ever, so we ended up having to leave and go to Mexico. The solidarity of people like Bertha Navarro, Jorge Sánchez, Alfredo Joskowicz and many, many other Mexican film-makers and friends made it possible for us to continue with our projects as a group (Grupo Cine Sur). I wrote and co-directed several animated independent short films in Mexico and Nicaragua. But as I moved forward, I felt more and more that – at least to me – drawings were not enough; that there were many things about human beings, and their nature, that I wanted to explore, for which real human performers were needed. So I applied and was admitted to the CCC to study screenwriting.

I have no doubt that film schools in Latin America have played a key role in what has happened with Latin American films along the last ten years or so. Especially in Mexico, Argentina and Cuba. With their ups and downs, those film schools have been the actual place where older generations of Latin American film-makers who – especially in Mexico – had managed to reach the highest standards with their films in the late 1960s, early and mid–1970s, were able to pass the torch and the craft to the following generations. In countries in which the film industry as such practically does not exist, in countries where the distribution business is completely dominated by Hollywood productions (with bullying, dumping, corruption and uneven practices), the continuity between generations is always in danger.

Again, from a less epic point of view, I tend to think there's always a teacher who makes a difference in everyone's life. In my case, the CCC was not only a great chance to meet some wonderful teachers, but also a sort of point of departure to get my first jobs as a screenwriter. But if I have to mention a teacher, Ludwik Margules, who taught Dramatic Literature, was probably the one who really led me into a new level of understanding of what drama was about. Screenwriter Tomás Perez Turrent, who had written several very powerful scripts for Felipe Cazals and had been around Luis Buñuel, was also a bridge between that older generation and mine. Film school to me was not only about just learning the technical aspects of the craft, but about all the other things that no manual can teach.

17

HUGO RODRÍGUEZ: The CCC was my entry into cinema. Before that, I'd done some animation and lit a few shorts. But at CCC I decided I wanted to become a director, even though I graduated as a cinematographer. Film school was a place rich in ideas and in friendships. I remember my teacher, the Mexican documentary-maker Eduardo Maldonado, who taught me the importance of fully immersing yourself in a project. He used to say, 'When you're completely absorbed in what you're doing, things will happen in front of the camera almost without you realizing it.' And for that to happen, you need to be rigorous. Again, he said, 'Rigour is not the same as effort. You can spend weeks working non-stop, but if you don't put the will in the right place, it's a waste of time.'

My generation of graduates, friends and colleagues with whom I developed my vocation for the cinema, today is bearing fruit: Carlos Carrera, Ignacio Ortiz, Francisco Athié, Alfonso Cuarón, Luis Estrada, Salvador Aguirre and others.

EMMANUEL LUBEZKI *cinematographer*: I wanted to be a stills photographer from a very early age, and the two options in Mexico were the art school or the film school. I decided to go to the film school and after one week I realized that I was hooked on film and was going to shoot cinema.

The biggest influence was my not liking Mexican films, and I couldn't begin to understand why. I thought that something was wrong with me but, as far as I was concerned, they really didn't *look* good. There was something in the tone of most of the movies, in terms of acting or the fact that in most cases the sound was awful that just made them very hard to watch. There was the so-called 'Golden Era', which I personally feel is a little overrated. However, one can be more forgiving there, because it was a long time ago. What really bothered me were the movies from the 1970s. There wasn't really an industry, but there were films being made. They were mainly tiny, low-budget movies and in these films the women were invariably all prosti-tutes and the men were inevitably macho. These films were so horrendously lit. In fact, the acting, the themes, everything was horrible. And I didn't really love what the Mexican Film Institute was doing, which was favouring intellectual directors.

In film school we realized that we were never going to be able to shoot film, as all the films being made at this time were mainly to satisfy a demand for Spanish-language cinema in certain communities in America. Our idea was to start our own company while we were in film school and make a little money by also making a film for this market. So one night we went to a coffee shop and wrote the worse script ever. We decided to shoot *Camino largo a Tijuana* (1991) on video and sell it and use the money we made from it to shoot the kind of movie we really wanted to make. I ended up producing the film and convincing Luis Estrada, a film-school colleague, to become the director. Because his father was a famous director before him, he had a pool of actors and people who became interested in helping us. So suddenly this little tiny movie grew into something bigger.

Estrada's film was indeed respectfully received and marked Emmanuel Lubezki's feature-producing debut in 1991. It was not as a producer but as a director of photography, however, that he poised to begin a sensational professional ascent.

2

Another 'New Mexican Cinema': 1989–94

After years of drought, the early 1990s witnessed the feature-film debuts of several directors who would thereafter become international names. A new generation was on the brink of making itself heard, and these directors were conscious that something of a break from the past would be necessary if they were to assert their own identities.

GUILLERMO DEL TORO *director*: If you look at the films of the 1970s, some Mexican directors were actually very successful: [Arturo] Ripstein, [Felipe] Cazals. In their time, movies like *Canoa* or *El castillo de la pureza* were very commercial. Now the times have changed, and the audiences have changed. Many technical aspects have also changed. But many movies in Mexico remained shipwrecked in the 1970s, for almost twenty years. In those twenty years the style of photography, the style of sound design and the style of story-telling completely changed, except in this little time-capsule that is the Mexican film industry, and specifically the Mexican 'art film'. All of a sudden things changed abruptly when our generation entered. And some people just very simply didn't like this. Others are very generous and serve as a link for the new generation – in my case, [Jaime Humberto] Hermosillo and Arturo Ripstein were both incredibly generous with me when I was starting. But some others really resented it.

Some feel that the works of Alejandro [González Iñárritu], Alfonso [Cuarón] and I are among the early modern films in Mexico – they felt that finally, in film terms, we were approaching the twenty-first century. And I just feel that there are a lot of people in the Mexican industry who lived their heyday in the 1970s and wished that this decade were still all the rage. Unfortunately it's not, and, for better and for worse, time moves on. These people resent what we do. They qualify our work as being superficial or polished in an inconsequential way.

I can remember exactly the moment this happened. It happened with *Como agua para chocolate* and it happened with *Sólo con tu pareja*, and it was to do with the fact that these films were making money. I remember that a director – who shall have to remain unnamed – said to me, 'Money doesn't matter. Movies should never concern themselves with making money.' I said, 'You are absolutely right from an artistic point of view. But what you don't realize is that you are killing the industry.'

Film is an art *and* an industry. Unfortunately film is also one of the few arts that require millions of dollars to be made. A painter may require only a few hundred dollars for a canvas and some paint, but a film-maker requires a couple of million dollars. The director who said this obviously didn't realize that he was on something of an ego-trip and had forgotten one of his main responsibilities is to maintain the industry. Many cinemas like France, Italy and other European counties make perfectly valid artistic films with an eye towards the box office.

Two key directors made feature debuts in 1991. The first of these, twenty-eight-year-old Carlos Carrera, had been animating since childhood, and was still in his teens when he directed the live-action documentary short Un vestidito blanco como la leche nido *(1989). He studied at the* CCC, *and in 1991 made* La mujer de Benjamín *(Benjamin's Woman). Benjamín (Lopez Rojas) an old bachelor, still living with his sister, is distracted from the childish company of his older friends when he falls for Natividad (Arcelia Ramirez), a beautiful younger woman, and after an unsuccessful campaign of love letters, he and his friends plan to abduct her in order that she can fall in love with him.*

CARLOS CARRERA *director*: I had always felt a need to tell stories with images since I was very young. I drew comic strips before even learning to write. I then started to paint and even managed to sell a few paintings, which enabled me to buy my first Super-8 camera. I then started to work on animation. I started to develop stories with Claymation and drawings around twelve or thirteen years old. I made several animation shorts before buying a Bolex 16 mm camera and then completed a number of short films. I then attended the CCC. One of my teachers there was Ludwik Margules, a very important theatre director. I worked with him as an assistant director in theatre where I learned how to deal with actors. During this time I continued to make my animation shorts and to learn many of the other aspects of film-making. You learn to shoot, edit, write. When I finished the school I had four animation shorts, two fiction shorts and a documentary about a psychiatric institution for women in Mexico titled *Un vestidito blanco como la leche nido*. In the film they talk very much about love and being lonely. At the end of film school there was a contest in which you submit a project to make your first feature film. Fortunately I won and so was able to make *La mujer de Benjamín*. I was very lucky.

HUGO RODRÍGUEZ *director: La mujer de Benjamín* was the second full-length feature made as part of the CCC's 'First Work' programme, of which I am now Executive Producer. Rather than having a teacher–student relationship, Carlos and I were – and still are – colleagues of the same generation. As one of the students with the most professional experience, I tried to lend support wherever I could. At the preparation stage, I drew up the budget, trying to fit the 'foot' into the 'shoe' of our tiny budget. During filming I worked closely with Carlos as his personal assistant, and several times had to step in as unit manager in order to help the shooting run more smoothly. I even edited the film's final sequence – the fight, the robbery and the main character's escape – all intercut – and I took charge of the post-production, which we had to bring forward in time for the Berlin Film Festival to which we had been invited.

Twenty-nine-year-old Alfonso Cuarón meanwhile came up with Sólo con tu pareja *(Love in the Time of Hysteria). Juan Carlos Rulfo, then twenty-six years old and soon to direct himself, assisted on the production side of Cuarón's picture just as he had for Carrera's.*

JOSÉ LUIS GARCÍA AGRAZ *director*: I've known and loved Alfonso Cuarón for twenty-three years. He's my friend, my teacher; he's like a brother. I saw his work when I was a student at the CUEC and I was lucky enough to have him as my assistant on my first full-length feature, *Nocaut*, in 1982, as well as on several subsequent features. I've seen him take his first steps in cinema, and I've been close to him and followed his career ever since. He's very intelligent and possesses a vast knowledge of cinema – which, together with a love of hard work and his clear principles, makes him one of the most powerful directors around today. That his work, so rich in filmic values, can be based on a narrative skill that is at once original, direct, agile and fresh is no coincidence. His talent and versatility as a director mean that he can make a film as beautiful as *A Little Princess*, then switch to one for a young audience like the fun, edgy *Y tu mamá también* and from there move on to the third Harry Potter film.

Written by Alfonso's brother Carlos, Sólo con tu pareja *concerns a yuppie womanizer (Giménez Cacho) who contemplates suicide when a jealous girlfriend tricks him into thinking he has Aids. Initially seeking a rapid exit from the world, Tomas falls in love with Claudia (Claudia Ramírez), a beautiful stewardess herself suicidal after learning of her lover's infidelity.*

CARLOS CUARÓN *screenwriter/director: Sólo con tu pareja* was my first collaboration with Alfonso in film. We did some things previously in television, a programme much like a Mexican version of *The Twilight Zone*. It was a very low-budget production; in fact Alfonso used to call it 'The Toilet Zone' . . .

The film also signalled the beginning of Cuarón's collaborations with two men who would become the leading directors of photography of their generation.

EMMANUEL LUBEZKI *cinematographer*: I met Alfonso a long time before film school. I used to bump into him at parties and hang around in the same slightly hippy, slightly left-wing, upper-middle-class intellectual circles. We also liked the same music and the same movies, and we used to go to a movie house where they showed the best cinema from around the world – Tarkovsky, Pasolini, Antonioni. I've never found any movie theatre like that in Los Angeles. We weren't friends yet at that time, but I would see him going in and out every week, usually with a different girl . . .

I then started to work for him after we met in film school, and we simply became a team. It's hard to explain, because it happened very naturally. We like and dislike the same things and are attracted to the same stories. We also have very similar motivations. Sometimes when we work we don't have to talk about the concept of the project, that is how in tune we are.

Rodrigo Prieto and I worked together on *Sólo con tu pareja*. I knew from the moment I met Rodrigo that he was going to be a great cinematographer, much better than myself.

RODRIGO PRIETO *cinematographer*: I was actually still at CCC when I worked on Alfonso's film. Alfonso and Emmanuel saw some of the films that I was working on, and asked me to do the second unit. I jumped at the chance as I loved their work, especially *Bandidos* (1991), which Emmanuel had shot shortly before. I did *Sólo con tu pareja* for free, and I loved the experience. What I had to do was match Lubezki's lighting and, in a way, this was easy because I really liked his approach. I was on my own with a camera assistant, begging for a lens, and was allowed to do lots of insert shots, of condoms or airplanes passing. Thankfully it was a very small second unit. Shortly after, I did my first and second features, but this experience gave me

23

the confidence to know that I could light scenes and that they would work. If my work could be put together next to the work of Lubezki's . . . Yes, it certainly helped.

As a teenager I shot little Super-8 science-fiction and horror movies and I knew immediately that I wanted to do film, I guess in whatever capacity. I applied to the CCC and took the very extensive three-stage exams. The first time, I was not admitted on the last stage. That was pretty depressing at first, but it actually became a good thing because I started working with a stills photographer that year and that's where I started to get more and more interested in the image and in lighting and composition. When I applied again to the school the following year I knew that I was more interested in photography and so likely to follow cinematography. The first time I had applied I had thought I wanted to be a director. When I was finally admitted I had that year of experience to my advantage, that under-standing of lighting. During my first year, we all directed a short movie and performed roles on the films of others. I then realized that I was much more excited by being a cameraman on the shorts that I had shot than I was about the film that I'd directed. That was the moment I realized that this was what I wanted to do.

At that time I was specifically interested in the work of Néstor Almendros, Sven Nykvist, Jeff Cronenweth, and Vittorio Storaro. They all had very different styles. Almendros and Nykvist are very subtle and realistic while Storaro and Cronenweth are much more stylized. I was interested in both ways and so tried to find a method by which I could get a little bit of all of them in what I was doing. I had a lot of chance to practise among my group of twelve fellow students, as I was the only one who wanted to be a cinema-tographer. In my first year I shot six shorts and in my second year another six or seven. Another director did later decide to become a cinematographer but in the beginning I was the only one and so I got to shoot a lot.

It's hard to explain, but in cultures such as Mexico things are very visual and dramatic. This sticks to you in a way. With my generation there was also a friendly sense of competition. We were all checking out what the other was doing and hoping to do at least as well as the other or perhaps even better. There was a sense of camaraderie and competition really egging us on. This was certainly true in my case as I looked up to these people, some of whom had started slightly before me. For example, I was a camera assistant to Carlos Marcovich on a couple of episodes of a television series called *Hora narcada*. This series, which was mainly horror tales and very similar to *The Twilight Zone*, stopped when I was about to start shooting some of them but I did at least get to be a camera assistant. It was fun and exciting and this was the way many of us started. I think Guillermo del Toro directed some episodes, as did Alfonso Cuarón.

ALFONSO CUARÓN *director*: In Mexico until the late 1980s everything was controlled by the unions, so if you wanted to be a cinematographer you had to go through all the scales of the union and they wouldn't admit new cinematographers, it became a closed shop. The younger cinematographers were all doing commercials because it was the only work they could get that was connected to the film industry. I personally feel, though I believe in the concept of a union, that in Mexico the unions nearly destroyed the film industry. What Emmanuel and I were doing was a big reaction to that, and to the ugly-looking films that were being produced as a result.

The production designer of Sólo con tu pareja *was German-born Brigitte Broch, who had found her way to Mexico and studied dance and theatre before meeting Luis Mandoki and accepting work as a production manager on* Los Mazatecos *(1980), his documentary about an Indian tribe in Vera Cruz. The pull of theatre remained strong, but she eventually found her métier.*

BRIGITTE BROCH *production designer*: In 1987 I was offered the job of doing the art direction for *Los caminos de Graham Greene*, a docudrama for Mexican Television. That was a revelation; I loved it and never stopped doing it. To be honest, I was highly inexperienced at the time of *Sólo*, so the design was much more a result of the teamwork between Alfonso, El Chivo [Lubezki], costume designer María Estela Fernández and myself. In our discussions, our imaginations flew high. We just played with the gag, though I was also reticent to over-satirize. And visually it just built up and boomed.

Actually, *Sólo con tu pareja* had very little distribution in Mexico, the copy was pretty bad and Alfonso went to the US with it and, as you know, started an incredible career.

GAEL GARCÍA BERNAL *actor*: It was great to see a film like *Sólo con tu pareja* coming from *anywhere* in Latin America. You'd see films that left you unsatisfied, as films do, and keep on doing. And what Mexican ones there were didn't make the grade – they tried so hard to be American films that they ended up not even looking like films at all. But *Sólo con tu pareja* portrayed a reality that wasn't necessarily portrayed in films coming out of the United States. It also had a very subtle sense of humour. If I had to name one person at this point about whom I said, 'Yeah, I want to work with him', it would have to be Alfonso Cuarón.

Alfonso Arau's Como agua para chocolate *(Like Water for Chocolate, 1992) was a watershed moment for more recent Mexican cinema, particularly on an international level. It was adapted from the novel by Laura Esquivel, Arau's wife at the time, and told of the sorrows and joys of a young woman called Tita who loses her sweetheart in marriage to her older sister, since their mother insists it is the duty of the younger daughter to be homebound. But Tita's magical culinary skills help her to save the day.*

First published in 1989, the book was a massive bestseller in Mexico (it also remained on the New York Times *bestseller list for over a year) and went on to be translated into twenty-nine languages. For his film adaptation Arau hired Emmanuel Lubezki as cinematographer.*

EMMANUEL LUBEZKI: At the time, I honestly had no real idea how to photograph a movie. I just had this instinct that told me what I *didn't* like. With *Como agua para chocolate* I tried to do a movie that I myself could watch, but I didn't have the tools or, to be frank, the craft. People obviously talk about the movie in connection with the Mexican strand of magical realism, but I think that's because of the theme of the film and the original novel, as opposed to my cinematography. Of course, the theme and characters of the film were viewed as exotic and embraced all over the world, especially in Europe. It's completely stylized and presents a very unrealistic view of Mexico. You can call it magical if you want – but people certainly loved it outside of Mexico.

LEONARDO GARCÍA TSAO *critic/academic*: I think that *Como agua para chocolate* is absolutely regressive in its representations. It's a Mexican film for tourists, one that presents a backwards notion of Mexico populated by revolutionaries and women cooking. I really hate the film. There are merits to be found in the original novel by Laura Esquivel – that offered quite a witty notion of someone falling in love with somebody who cooks. Unfortunately this became the entire basis for the film. The cinematography by Emmanuel Lubezki is also good but, that aside, this film offers a very conservative view of Mexico and the fact that it was so successful was much to my chagrin. People would come up to me at international festivals and when I would tell them that I was from Mexico that would tell me how much they loved *Como agua para chocolate* in an attempt to break the ice. It had the exact opposite effect . . .

Nevertheless Arau's film was the most commercially successful Mexican production of the 1990s and the highest-grossing foreign-language release of 1993 in the United States. It also won eighteen international awards.

EMMANUEL LUBEZKI: *Como agua para chocolate* certainly opened doors for me, at least the combination of that movie and Alfonso's *Sólo con tu pareja*. These two movies were the ones that meant that I almost immediately had agents and directors calling me from Los Angeles asking if I wanted to work there.

In terms of proximity, Mexico is close to the United States; and besides, American directors have always been attracted to cinematographers from other countries.

It was exciting. I always liked English and American movies. And I think I speak not only for myself but also for the people who I was in film school with when I say that this is what we *all* wanted to do. We loved Martin Scorsese and Francis Ford Coppola without knowing that not all American movies necessarily corresponded to this level of quality. We didn't know that there were a whole bunch of other crappy movies and that the industry was very hard. I simply had a fantasy that I was going to the land where Coppola was directing movies . . .

* * *

BERTHA NAVARRO *producer*: Guillermo [del Toro] says he deals with monsters because there is a monster part present in his own character, and he would rather it emerge in his films than in his life. I must say, I've never seen this monstrous aspect to his personality. He's the most good-natured guy I have ever met. He does have his obsessions, and I think a director *should* have obsessions. I think in the end that good directors are to an extent always making the same film.

GUILLERMO DEL TORO: Most people may remember an altered version of their childhood, but for me my childhood was the most brutal and frightening period of my life. I think that children react very naturally to horror, perhaps in a more natural and pure way to adults, and are very much exposed to it. Horror comes from the unknown and you react with horror only to things that you don't know.

Why is horror so popular? It's a morbid fascination that is part of human nature; we still secrete this fascination. It's not in *everyone*, but certainly within most people. I think that there's a thrill in seeing the worst possible outcome of anything: there's certainly a reassurance to our wellbeing to be able to witness vicariously the misfortune of someone else. It makes us, I believe, more human, to be in contact with our darker side. And it's a fact that there was a time when early civilizations believed that the world was created and destroyed every day and every night. This is how strong our fear of the dark is. The other power of the genre is that there is no other that generates images that stay embedded in your mind so strongly. For example, there are millions of people in the world who still won't go in the water because of *Jaws* or pick up a hitchhiker because of *The Texas Chainsaw Massacre*.

I used to stay up late without my parents' permission to watch *The Outer Limits*. I remember my brother and I were watching an episode called *The Mutant*; I got very scared by the make-up Warren Oates was wearing in this episode and I went to my crib really scared. My older brother put two plastic fried eggs over his face and my mother's stockings over his headband, and crept into my room. I was so scared. After that, I started waking up at night and I'd see monsters all around my room. The patterns in the shaggy 1960s carpet became, for me, a waving ocean of green fingers. I'd get so scared that I would need to pee but I was too scared to go the toilet so I ended up peeing in my bed. Of course I was punished for this, so I finally said to the monsters that if they allowed me to go to the toilet in the night then I would become their friend. Since this time, I've had a very intimate relationship to creatures.

I'd also say that, being in Mexico, I was exposed to a lot of very brutal images and situations. I saw my first corpse at the age of four. It was a highway accident. We were coming back from Lake Chapala and a red car went zooming by us and I remember my father saying very clearly, 'They're going to *kill* themselves.' And a few miles later the same car was overturned and there was a guy crying and bleeding on the side of the road. He had a bottle of Tequila in his hand. There was another guy with his butt exposed, and no head. You could see his head two metres away, dangling in the barbed-wire fence. That, plus the very gory religious imagery we have in Mexico, combined to give me a very intimate relationship with death at a very early age.

The fact is that I have a very active imagination. I lived with my grand-mother for many weeks in a row and I used to sleep in an old bedroom at the end of a long corridor, and at night I would see in a super-slow-motion manner a hand come from behind a closet and then the face of a goat. I could *see* it – it might have been in my mind but it was incredibly real to me.

I still to this day don't know how to be alone. When I met my wife, I was for the first time in my life able to sleep in peace. Before that I was an insomniac. But since she has been with me, it's been twenty years of peaceful sleeping. It still takes only for me to be alone for my imagination to go into overdrive.

In terms of movies, I actually started to get excited by horror-movie stars. I wasn't conscious of the director, but of the type of movie they were. My three favourite actors as a child were Boris Karloff, Vincent Price and Peter Cushing. I would look for them in movies, because I didn't know anything about directors. I would just seek out the movies that they were in, as I knew that this guaranteed me being in for some horror.

JOSÉ LUIS GARCÍA AGRAZ: I've known Guillermo del Toro since his early beginnings; I know his short films, and I'm amazed by his narrative instinct and the passion he has for 'gore' and the horror genre. He, like Alfonso Cuarón, has become someone I'm continually learning from – I have him to thank for bringing me up to date with the world of comics. Years ago del Toro wrote a book about the cinema of Alfred Hitchcock which showed not only his deep knowledge of the art of cinema but also contained a vein of humour which has never left him – hence his ability to make horror films in which the timing and the technical perfection could be the work of any one of the great masters of the past, such as Hitch himself. Del Toro is one of those artists who is born 'already knowing': all that such artists require in order to produce work that is brilliant and full of invention are time and resources.

Del Toro took writing classes with Jaime Humberto Hermosillo but then really began his career in special effects and make-up.

GUILLERMO DEL TORO: Doing my short Super-8 films in Guadalajara I didn't have anybody to do effects for me. In fact, I didn't have anybody to do *anything* for me. I was doing the catering, the lighting, the post-sound – just everything. Little by little other people began to ask me to do the effects for their movies. I was involved in a motorcycle accident with my wife that put me in bed for several weeks. I decided then to try to learn the craft professionally in order to gain a little bit of an edge for myself and start preparing for *Cronos*. *Cronos* took me eight years to do and one of the first obstacles that I found when talking to producers was being asked, 'Well, who's going to do the effects for this movie?' When I replied, 'Me!', they expressed their lack of confidence in my being able to do this level of effects yet. I applied to a course run by Dick Smith[1] and during my bedridden days I proceeded to do

[1] One of cinema's foremost make-up and effects artists. See *Little Big Man* (1970), *The Godfather* (1972), *The Exorcist* (1973). He won an Academy Award for his work on *Amadeus* (1984).

a series of pencil and pen sketches and some very crude make-up effects. Dick Smith told me that he liked my draughtsmanship but not the sculpting or the appliances. He thought that his course would help me make my movie and so agreed to let me try it. I literally got the course and then got a job at the same time.

You met with Dick in New York and then you had to practise in Guadalajara. Then you had to meet again for an evaluation after a few months. Anyway, I would meet with producers and agree to do the job for x amount of money which was always just barely enough to pay for the materials and barely enough to re-invest in buying a little more equipment and materials. Eventually, when *Cronos* started, my special effects company – Necropia – had twenty people, offices and the whole thing was run as a great enterprise but we closed it at the start of *Cronos* because it had served its purpose. To this day, Necropia is a name that I own because I like it; it's my childhood.

I had written *The Devil's Backbone* with the intention of having this script as my thesis for Humberto Hermosillo. But Hermosillo was very strict on presentation, and he didn't like the way the script was formatted. He took it and threw it in the garbage, telling me that he will not read it until I learn to present my stuff more cleanly. Back in those days only the very rich writers had word-processors, and I had typed my screenplay on my IBM electric typewriter. I was so angry and so disappointed that I thought, 'Screw it, I'm going to write something else rather than go back and rewrite the same script just because the *margins* weren't right . . .' Looking back, it was not such a big loss because *The Devil's Backbone* evolved into a better movie.

Anyway, I told Hermosillo that I was going to write a story in which a young girl gives her grandfather a vampire as a pet. The very first thing that generated the idea was a paragraph in a treatise about vampires, where they say that in Europe the vampire first comes to a house and vampirizes the family, then goes out to the world. My first impulse, which is not there so much in the movie, was to make a critique of the Mexican family in which the father figure returns and sucks them all dry. I started writing this version but found it too dogmatic, as if the thesis was overwhelming both the genre and the feeling of the movie. So I thought, 'What if I make it a kind of love story between the granddaughter and the grandfather, and very much a story of acceptance?' At that moment my grandmother was dying very slowly, and I had come to accept and love her despite all our differences and the Catholic fears she had instilled in me as a child. *Cronos* is actually dedicated to her. I started to use the movie quite literally to heal – and I do think that movies can have a cathartic effect.

The absence of the father was clearer in the screenplay. The movie was about thirty minutes longer, and in these minutes the origin of the missing parents is explained. That segment was really interesting.

Cronos *begins with the legend of a Spanish alchemist who invented a small elegant device in the shape of a mechanized scarab beetle, capable of sinking its golden claws into a man and injecting a substance that bestows immortality, and a vampire's craving for blood. Centuries later, this 'Cronos Device' falls into the hands of old antiques dealer Jesús Gris (Federico Luppi), who suffers its bite. But the device is coveted by ailing industrialist Dieter de la Guardia (Claudio Brook), who sets his violent American nephew Angel (Ron Perlman) on its tail. And meanwhile, Gris's new-found urges endanger his own beloved granddaughter, Aurora (Tamara Shanath).*

GUILLERMO DEL TORO: I was doing storyboards for an action sequence in a Mexican movie called *Morir en el golfo* (1990) and Guillermo Navarro was the director of photography. Guillermo was famous in Mexico for being ill-tempered, and when I arrived on the set everybody told me that he was in a really bad mood and I shouldn't provoke him. Well, I am famous for being imprudent, so I stood next to the camera and suggested that he change the lens for this shot. He was looking through the eye-piece but stopped to turn to me and said, 'Listen, kid, do you even have any fucking idea what the lens is looking at?' I got immediately red-faced and said, 'I'll show you what this fucking lens is looking at', and walked right in front of it. Guillermo smiled and said, 'I like you.' From that moment on we have rarely had a bad day . . .

Guillermo also led me to my long-time producer, his sister Bertha Navarro. He suggested that Bertha produce *Cronos*. We met and she hired me to do indigenous make-up and effects for *Cabeza de Vaca* (1991). I said, 'How much work is it?' and she said, 'On the very worst of days you will be making up anything up to two hundred extras.' I said, 'Can I hire an assistant?'

After originally studying music Nicolás Echevarría founded the composers group Quanta in 1970. He began his career in film with a number of short documentaries, and continued to make documentary films throughout the 1970s and 1980s – frequently working on video – with his work often bearing witness to the cultural, religious and artistic experiences of indigenous Mexicans.

Cabeza de Vaca *was among the most important Mexican films to emerge*

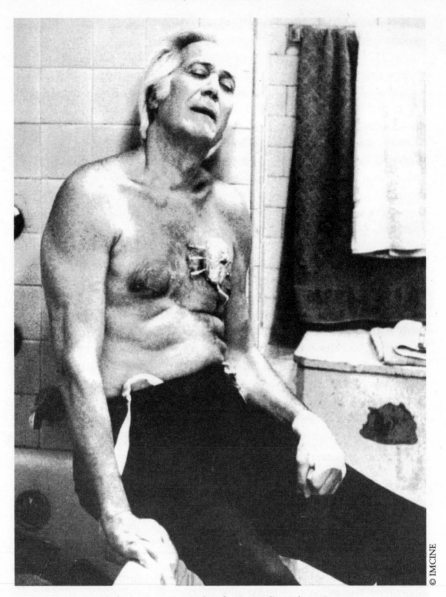

© IMCINE

Federico Luppi searches for eternal youth in *Cronos*

in the 1990s. Set during the early days of the Conquest, the film is based on the writings of Alvar Núñez Cebeza da Vaca (played by Juan Diego), a treasurer on Pánfilo Narváez's shipwrecked expedition to Florida. Combining ethnography and autobiography, the film offers a fascinating portrayal of Spanish–American conflict while also offering an appreciation of the mystical reality of native peoples.

BERTHA NAVARRO: I thought that Echevarría's vision of the new world in *Cabeza de Vaca* was so amazing and gave us an opportunity to touch upon the subject of the Conquest. It took a huge effort to make this film at the time. Again, Nicolás had this passion for the story and to touch that moment of our history was special. So much of the imagery of this film is iconic, especially the image of the cross at the end of the film.

GUILLERMO DEL TORO: I did the entire movie – a huge enterprise – with one assistant, and my wife. Bertha recognized how crazy I was in terms of commitment and loved that and offered to read my screenplay.

BERTHA NAVARRO: My brother recommended I read del Toro's script, and so I asked him to bring it to me. He was quite shy. I read the script and thought it was so different from anything happening in Mexican cinema. It was in a world of its own and, to me, quite magical. Del Toro is not just horror and gore; he has real tenderness, depth and humour. I immediately decided to do his first film.

GUILLERMO DEL TORO: Just as I say Guillermo is a brother, I feel that Bertha is one of those mothers that you also find along the way. I really love Bertha and I will never forget that Bertha believed in me, a twenty-something kid from Guadalajara who wanted to make this massive vampire project.

Guillermo Navarro and I trust each other implicitly. I only second-guessed him once, very early on during *Cronos*. He said, 'OK, I am going to do it the way you want it and then we'll see it on the dailies.' We saw his way and then my way and his way was infinitely better. We both have no ego problems and understand that collaboration is collaboration and so we are free to suggest things to each other. To this day, he understands that I am not territorial but that I do my compositions and my planning of camera moves so far in advance that if you bring another idea it has to be a very well-thought one. In terms of light I can tell him what I want only in terms of how much darkness and how much light and then leave the execution entirely to him. I really trust Guillermo completely.

Cronos is the perfect example of the feeling that your first movie will also be your last. You try to put everything that you have ever wanted to say about a particular subject in it. I wanted to show the vampiric relationship between the nephew and the uncle, and, of course, the vampiric relationship between Mexico and the United States. This is why the date in the movie –

which we see on a newspaper – is 1997, even though the film was made in 1993. I wanted it to be set in a post-NAFTA Mexico.[2]

Ultimately I think that it was very accurate in terms of what happened. That is why all the signs that you see in the street are in Chinese, English and Russian. I made a fictional Mexico that was much more cosmopolitan.

To me, the movie also explores on numerous levels the relationship that characters have with time and age and death. You have the grandmother who refuses to age by trying to fit into the same dress that fitted her last year; you have the millionaire who does nothing but shit and piss all day, living like a recluse in his room like Howard Hughes but wanting to live together just out of sheer greed. And you have the nephew who wants to change his flesh to become more handsome. The only truly mortal character in the film is the daughter, who does not care about time and is immune to the concept of death. By the same token, I wanted to show a vampiric chain that went all the way to the insect locked within the device. That's the ultimate vampire and the ultimate victim. It is locked there like a living filter and is at the same time the master and the slave.

BRIGITTE BROCH: *Cronos* was a wonderful experience, because del Toro knew exactly what he wanted. He's not only a director but also a special-effects expert and make-up artist. He created the ingenious Cronos device, and the original archangel statue.

GUILLERMO DEL TORO: The outside of the device was designed with a painter friend of mine. We sat down together and I explained that I wanted it to be like a Fabergé egg. This is obviously pertinent, because the egg is the symbol of immortality and of eternity. We filled the film with such images – for example, the serpent that bites its own tail, which in early cultures symbolized immortality. The very shape of the device was intended to remind of a scarab, also a symbol of eternity.

There was a time when the producers refused to pay for the construction of the device, and I said, 'But we absolutely need it! It's the focal point of the movie. If you don't have the inside, then you don't have the movie.' I sold my own van and personally paid for the construction of the interior of the device, which I designed completely. It was intended to look like a big factory. Microscopic drama has always intrigued me and as a child I would lie on my belly on the patio and watch ants for hours. This entomological fascination goes all the way to the inside of the device, as I wanted to have the point of view of the insect. The insect is based on a prehistoric tick. It

[2] See p. 39.

Cronos: Claudio Brook

was very elegantly designed. I sculpted the tail and my father-in-law mechanized the tail and all the interior pieces. Incidentally, most of the mechanical parts that you see were wind-up devices extracted from toys. It took us over a year to build the devices. We built thirteen of them and every single one of them got stolen at the end of the shoot. I actually like this fact – someone at some point may have opened the case full of these devices and mistaken them for the real thing . . .

Cronos also meditates on the ancient history of Mexico with the device originally being brought to Mexico by an exiled alchemist.

GUILLERMO DEL TORO: I was actually more interested in opening the movie like a Hollywood movie. Open it as if you are about to see a super-expensive production but then this production lasts only three minutes. Then you go in to meet the most boring guy on earth. This is what I was attracted to. It's like beginning with a Mexican version of *The War of the Worlds* with all of the spaceships arriving and then cutting to a Mexican family working in their fields on their cows and seeing the invasion from their perspective. It's really about the everyday-guy perspective of a Hollywood premise.

The image that better represents *Cronos* for me is that of the guy licking the blood from the nosebleed on the toilet floor. There were so many walkouts during this scene. What a waste; it was an extremely beautiful bathroom. There is, however, something about this shot that gets to the very root of revulsion.

Another iconic moment is the police discovery of the body being bled in the alchemist's apartment.

GUILLERMO DEL TORO: I also wanted this scene to comment on the rather sad nature of the alchemist's life. During the hundreds of years that he lived, he became a recluse – his only company was a hanging corpse. I do think that the hanging-corpse shot in particular is influenced by Hammer, and the sense that you sometimes got from their Dracula movies that it can be very lonely to be immortal.

I wish on *Cronos* that I had had a little more experience and a little more budget, and then some of the stuff would have had more clarity. That said, I am very happy with some of the images in the film, and that one is certainly one of them.

I really hate it when Hollywood shows Mexicans or Latin Americans as sweaty villains with a big moustache. I wanted to do that to the American characters. I was very conscious that they should be like comic-book villains. Ron Perlman was exactly right to bring a bit of colour and a little bit of a flourish to his character. I told him that his character was a big guy, but his nose was his Achilles heel. If you observe the movie carefully, you see him constantly smelling everything and paying attention to his nose. It's with great pride that I say that Jean-Pierre Jeunet and Marc Caro cast Ron in *The City of Lost Children* after seeing him in *Cronos* while they were jurors at a film festival.

I should point out that like most of my films, and this is something that I will do again and again, I did not set *Cronos* in any real world, I don't try to represent reality exactly as it is. I always try to take it a couple of notches above. The Spanish Civil War in *The Devil's Backbone* looks like a Sergio Leone western, except at night where it looks like a Mario Bava[3] movie. The New York in *Mimic* doesn't bear any resemblance to the real New York. Except maybe for the cockroach problem.

The production design and use of location marked del Toro's work out immediately.

BERTHA NAVARRO: We were in many ways very lucky with the team on *Cronos* but in other ways one of the real skills of producing is getting the very best people for that director. This is especially important for a first-time director – you nourish them by surrounding them with the very best people. Tolita Figuero and Brigitte Broch did the production design. *Cronos* was mainly filmed in an astonishing house in Condesa, central Mexico City. It was like a set for us, because we had the whole house to ourselves. Many of the other locations were also shot in this house – the crematorium sequence, for example. We also had a remarkable derelict factory in the south of the Mexico City [where the industrialist resides], which has since been pulled down and made into a shopping mall.

GUILLERMO DEL TORO: When I was finishing *Cronos* I was really desperate, because the first cut was horrible. I showed it to Alfonso Cuarón and he asked if I had edited the first part. I told him that another editor had done it, and he recommended that I do it myself. We tried it right there, and took out a lot of hot air in a single afternoon. He literally changed the movie.

So when Alfonso was starting *Harry Potter* [in 2003] and asked me if I

[3] Italian director/cinematographer of sumptuously styled films such as *La maschera del demonio* (1960), *I tre volti della paura* (1963) and *Sei donna per l'assassino* (1964) who inspired a wave of Gothic Italian horror films, later known as *giallos*.

would recommend some creature designers. I recommended a few that he then proceeded to use . . .

I was never the darling of Mexican cinema. The story of *Cronos* and the Mexican institutions is not a very happy one. When I first presented the film to IMCINE, they complained that it wasn't an art movie, it was a vampire film, and that I should go and get some private money. I disagreed, I said it *was* an art film and horror can also be art. They invited me to go away and storyboard the movie and come back. I did that, then they said that they wanted to see the device in a drawing. After the drawing, they wanted to see it physically, because they wanted proof that I could create it. In the end it took us almost three years to get the financing secured from IMCINE.

When we showed them the finished film, they said, 'This is a horror movie and it's not going to go to any festivals, it isn't going to win any prizes.' They felt that nobody was ever going to see the movie and that they had wasted their money. Our entire budget for *Cronos* in Cannes was ten posters and a roll of Scotch tape. All the producers, my wife and myself slept in a one-bedroom apartment. I thought that IMCINE's attitude would change after *Cronos* won twenty-five international awards and after it became one of the most celebrated films from Mexico in many years. It didn't change.

Cronos's impressive haul of over nineteen international awards includes eight Ariels (including Best Direction); a Silver Raven award at the 1994 Brussels International Festival of Fantasy Film; a DICINE award at Guadalajara; a Mercedes-Benz award at Cannes 1994 and the Audience Jury award at the 1994 Fantasporto.

BERTHA NAVARRO: *Cronos* went to Cannes and screened in the Critics' Week, and we had fantastic press. This gave us international distribution. In Spain it became a cult film and played in theatres for more than a year. It did well in England too. In Mexico, it had the worst distribution possible. The state had sold everything and we didn't have the small theatres so we had to open in competition with a huge Hollywood star-driven picture in huge theatres. That was a catastrophe. But the critical reaction was very positive. I was slightly amazed by this, because I thought that some critics might perceive the film as not dealing with issues specifically relating to Mexico. I actually think that there is something *very* Mexican about the film and about Guillermo's films in general. There is always very strong religious imagery that relates to the fact that he had a very strict Catholic grandmother, and he equates many of these terrifying images to his childhood.

LEONARDO GARCÍA TSAO: I think that *Cronos* really adds something to the vampire genre. I also think that with this film del Toro demonstrated that he has a unique vision and that he is also able to change the rules subtly. In some ways the picture has proved to be quite prophetic . . . The film takes place in Mexico but it is a given that everybody speaks English in a normal way.

BERTHA NAVARRO: I also feel that *Cronos* was very much a film for film-makers. I remember James Cameron seeing the film in Los Angeles and being really impressed by it. What *Cronos* did obviously do was to trigger del Toro's career. It also became apparent that his imagination and special effects required more financing than Mexico could provide. In Mexico it is virtually impossible to make films that cost over $2 million. *Cronos* made it clear, even to del Toro, that he needed another structure to bring his visions to the screen.

*   *   *

In a bid to reduce the public debt and encourage private investment, President Carlos Salinas de Gortari pushed through the North American Free Trade Area (NAFTA) in September 1993, creating a free market between Canada, the US and Mexico. Intended to allow the Mexican economy to expand to the extent that it could enter the 'first world', in actuality NAFTA led to the exploitation of Mexico's cheap labour and US companies out-sourcing certain polluting industries.

ALFREDO JOSKOWICZ *film-maker/Director,* IMCINE: The *sexenio* of Carlos Salinas de Gortari [1988–94] had been a disastrous period, during which many of the state production companies were terminated. Conversely, private production continued to flourish. At this time, there were around fifteen private companies and all of their films were distributed by Películas Nacionales. The films were exhibited on Compañía Operadora de Teatros (COTSA), the state-owned exhibition circuit, which was very advantageous tax-wise for the private producers. However, in 1991, for different reasons and for various motives, this arrangement was terminated and in 1993 the state sold COTSA. It was an important moment of this period under President Salinas that in 1993 Mexico entered NAFTA.

BERTHA NAVARRO: The landscape really changed after NAFTA was signed. Before NAFTA, we were able to produce a decent number of films annually. Quality-wise, the films were a mixture of the good, the bad and the ugly, but we *were* able to produce them. After NAFTA we produced, I believe, just eight films. It had a massive impact on the industry. Prior to NAFTA it was largely state production – something with which I have never been involved – but after NAFTA it was completely the opposite, a totally open market, with nothing in between and no period of transition. Now we have different rules to the game.

GUILLERMO DEL TORO: I remember at the time that I felt that NAFTA was so ill-planned, because it was passed without getting any consensus from the world of culture as to how best to protect the industry and the local culture. We were raided and invaded by media companies and there was nothing there to protect us.

ALFREDO JOSKOWICZ: Prior to joining NAFTA there was a very important law – albeit one seldom respected – dictating that Mexican cinemas had to show a certain minimum percentage of locally produced films. In the first three years of joining NAFTA, this percentage was reduced to 30 per cent, then to 20 per cent, and then to just 10 per cent. However, NAFTA did have an important effect on exhibition in Mexico, because it allowed exhibitors to increase ticket prices. With this came the proliferation of the American-style – and frequently American-owned – multiplex screens that did bring much improved screening facilities and improved technical specifications.

You also have to take into account the new freedom of choice Mexican audiences faced. Previously the cinema would have two, maybe three screens. Now they had eight. Of course, if you wanted to see spectacular special effects and big stars then you would invariably pay to see an American film. But if you wanted to view a representation of your identity then you would choose to see the Mexican film. That is, if the film was good. If it wasn't, why would you pay to see it?

This is perhaps the beginning of a new story: because, from an industry on the point of collapse, there finally came signs of regeneration.

3

Adventures in Hollywood, and More Generational Stirrings

In 1994 Alfonso Cuarón took up his first Hollywood engagement, directing an adaptation (scripted by Richard LaGravenese) of Frances Hodgson Burnett's A Little Princess *for Warner Bros. Updating its action to the First World War, the film tells the tale of ten-year-old Sara Crewe (Liesel Matthews), raised by her father in India until he heeds the call to war, and so places Sara in a magnificent New York private school run by the stern Miss Minchin (Eleanor Bron), where Sara introduces the other girls to the joys of make-believe and makes a spirited adjustment when her circumstances suddenly and tragically become straitened. Enthusiastically greeted on release, the film was praised as a formally audacious, sensitive and humanist rites-of-passage story. It won Cuarón a New Generation Award at the 1995 Los Angeles Film Critics Awards and also saw Emmanuel Lubezki nominated for an Academy Award for his cinematography.*

JOSÉ LUIS GARCÍA AGRAZ *director*: Alfonso Cuarón and Guillermo del Toro understood that if they wanted to find fulfilment in their chosen profession, they'd need adequate resources in order have continuity and development, which is why they emigrated to Hollywood. I suppose many other filmmakers have had the same idea – although not everyone possesses the 99 per cent of artistic rigour and 1 per cent of holiness that these two have.

ALFONSO CUARÓN *director*: I ended up in Hollywood not because I wanted to; I ended up in Hollywood because I didn't have any *choice*. When I did my first film I burned my bridges with the government, and I knew that if I were going to go back, the way of doing films in Mexico or the ways *I* knew of doing films in Mexico would have to change. Most films had a big percentage in terms of input from the government; my first film had 40 per cent. To survive as a film-maker in Mexico you had to sustain yourself by doing lots of work that had nothing to do with cinema – stuff like commercials. I didn't want to go from being an assistant director with Luis Mandoki to making commercials. *Sólo con tu pareja* premiered at the Toronto Film Festival and I knew I had a choice: I was completely in debt but immediately started getting offers of work from Hollywood. There was an open door and I went to pursue that open door and I'm very thankful.

I don't see Hollywood as the 'dark side'. Again, it's all about film, and in this regard the idea of working in Hollywood is irrelevant. Paul Thomas Anderson works for studios but so what? For me, independence has nothing to do with budget – and this is where many mediocre film-makers shelter themselves. There are people who do amazing masterpieces for nothing and at the same time there are people who make crappy films for nothing. My point is that Hollywood is what it is: it's an industry, and I don't feel that the mission of Hollywood is to corrupt film-makers. There are talented people working in that industry and mostly, yes, there are mediocre people who don't care about cinema but do care about power and money. But I can't classify things as simply as: 'This is a Hollywood film: it's bad. This is a Mexican film: it's good. And this is an Iranian film: so it's good. And this is a big-budget French movie: it *must* be bad . . .'

Guillermo del Toro had been having a tough time finding the means to follow up Cronos *– at least, until a Hollywood studio came calling.*

GUILLERMO DEL TORO *director*: Four years passed between *Cronos* and *Mimic*, and they passed because I didn't know then what I know now. At the end of *Cronos* I was in incredible personal debt, to the tune of a quarter of a million dollars; I may have made a career on the film, but I certainly didn't make any money. And I was desperate, because I was in no position to have that kind of debt. My father helped, he told me he would assume the debt, but that he wanted to be paid back in dollars. Then I watched in horror as the value of the dollar rose . . .

Then, out of the blue, came an offer to meet with Universal Studios to discuss the possibility of a project. They explained that they would pay me $125,000 for writing a screenplay. I was immediately interested, but I told them I would do it only if the screenplay were something I really wanted to do. And so I wrote *Spanky*, based on the novel by Christopher Fowler. I really think it's one of the best things I've ever written. Perhaps because of that, it was rejected by the studios, who said it was too dark, and unlike any other movie in that it sounded like a comedy but ended up as a tough horror film. I said, 'Exactly! That's the whole spirit.' I lost about a year on that one . . .

Then I started developing a period project, and Universal told me they didn't do period movies. Lo and behold, a few years later – *The Mummy*.

But after two years came the chance of doing *Mimic* as a short film – part of an anthology movie. At the same time I was also developing *The Devil's Backbone* but we were finding very little support in Mexico. So I was trying to do a Mexican film and I couldn't; I was trying to do an American film and I couldn't. When I pitched the *Mimic* short to Bob Weinstein at Miramax's Dimension outfit, he loved the story and said, 'Why not make it into a feature?' I must say, my first response was, 'It's a perfect short but is there enough here for a feature?' But it had been three years since I'd made a film, so I said yes to it. I learned a lot after that . . .

Mimic *proposes a classic horror plot. After a disease carried by the common cockroach has reached epidemic proportions in Manhattan, entomologist Dr Susan Tyler (Mira Sorvino) genetically engineers a mutant species of insect that can exterminate the roaches before dying out itself. The venture is a seeming success but a handful of years later Susan learns that people are disappearing and corpses turning up in and around the Manhattan subway. The mutant species has proved more durable and adaptable than she intended and so alongside her colleague and partner Peter Mann (Jeremy Northam) and reluctant New York subway cop Leonard (Charles S. Dutton) Susan sets out to destroy the mutant race she has unwittingly unleashed. Ostensibly a subterranean sci-fi thriller,* Mimic *is also a convincing allegory about genetic manipulation and, a recurring del Toro preoccupation, how the ghosts from the past come back to haunt us.*

GUILLERMO DEL TORO: *Mimic* remains the hardest shooting experience of my life – it's still right up there, pricking at my pain threshold. There were many reasons. Back then, it was the most expensive movie Dimension had made and also by far the most expensive movie I'd ever done. I experienced many hardships with it. I sustain the belief that you learn through pain, and I certainly learned a hell of a lot. One of the main things I learned, and which I cherish to this day, is that you are *always* making two movies. You are making the movie that the screenplay is telling, and you are making a movie that is pure image, pure cinema. Cinema has a kinship to theatre and other forms of drama in that it needs a narrative, characters and an arc, but in fact a film may also remain full of memorable images in spite of the screenplay not being completely there, or screwed with by the powers-that-be. And that is the most intimate part of the movie and the part that nobody should be able to take away from you. That was a revelation, almost like an out-of-body experience. To this day I can see this being the case with film-makers such as Dario Argento and Lucio Fulci. Sometimes their films can be

43

completely incoherent but out of this mass of incoherence a beautiful and absolutely powerful image arises.

As well as being hard for me, it was also a hard movie for Miramax to make and I didn't make it any easier on them. At the end of the day, with a cold head and a cool heart, I see that they wanted to do *Alien* and I wanted to do *Mimic*, and so we ended up with *Alien 3-and-a-half* . . .

American films seldom show child characters coming to harm, but Mimic *surprises us in a scene where a child who breaks into a basement is first terrorized and then mercilessly killed.*

GUILLERMO DEL TORO: Horror is an extension of the fairy tale and in fairy tales ogres and wolves eat children and I think that it goes to the roots of story-telling to have children as vulnerable. It's something I really take very seriously when I make movies. To me it's more dangerous to show kids in a movie about giant dinosaurs, and pretend like the dinosaurs won't eat them. In reality, they would. I think it's best to show that, should a child ever encounter danger, then he or she should act cautiously. Children don't necessarily need to fear what they know – such as the granddaughter in *Cronos*. But they do need to show caution towards that which they don't know. If they don't, just like adults, they are apt to pay the consequences.

I shot that basement scene very slowly over a single day, paying very careful attention to pull back and show the final moments from a wide angle. That was for fear of censorship. With every frame I shot, I feared that it would never be included in the final movie. Thankfully it is, and it remains not only my favourite scene from the film but I think among the very best things I have done. I don't like *Mimic* as a whole, but that scene, and the scene of Mira Sorvino being abducted on a subway platform, are two of the best scenes I have ever shot.

There was some stuff shot by the second unit that I detest. I refuse to shoot fake scares, and *Mimic* has a couple of them. One is the girl leaving the building with her bicycle; that sequence is absolutely ridiculous. The other is of the boys finding a derelict under a plastic bag. I really hate 'jump' scares. I can safely say to this day that I have never shot one of those. There are also things on the first unit that weren't done by me, and I really find them very defective. They lessen the movie. I still love the moments I mentioned, and I still love the stuff in the abandoned subway. Actually, the scene where Charles S. Dutton's character meets his death was a sequence that they wanted to give to the second unit and Charles and I stood united and said,

'Screw that.' I love that death. It's an unexceptionally beautiful death that we took a great pride in shooting.

One of the ways in which del Toro responded to his troubles on Mimic *was in the formation of the production company Tequila Gang, in which he was joined by Laura Esquivel, Bertha Navarro, Rosa Bosch and Alejandra Moreno Toscano.*

BERTHA NAVARRO *producer*: All Guillermo's Spanish-language films and projects are done through Tequila Gang. Guillermo also wants to help other people so that they can have the same break that he did, and this is another function of Tequila Gang.

Spanish-born Rosa Bosch moved to Los Angeles and began working at Filmex, the American Film Institute Film Festival in LA. In the early 1980s she attended the Havana Film Festival, a force that brought all of Latin America together in large numbers.

ROSA BOSCH *producer*: When I went to Havana I discovered that there was an incredible heritage of Latin American film-making that I knew very little about. It gripped me in a very passionate way, a little like falling in love. In Havana I not only met some great people but was privileged enough to watch a lot of films that are very difficult to access, particularly films of the third cinema, the ground-breaking political cinema from the 1960s which was a major force at the Festival and in the international arena. Then I began to go back even further, exploring the Brazilian cinema of the 1940s, the silent cinema of Mexico and Argentina, the Mexican cinema of the 1940s, the so-called 'Golden Era'.

The whole boom has always been celebrated as a Spanish–Latin American thing but the attitude of the Spaniards until recently was always very condescending. At that time in Havana there were actually very few Spaniards running around. Then came the celebration of five hundred years since the discovery of Latin America, and out of that came quite a change in attitude.

I was then appointed Deputy Director of the National Film Theatre in London and of the London Film Festival. Sheila Whitaker, the Director at the time, was extremely interested in Latin American cinema. I was given a fantastic opportunity to do a huge number of seasons focusing on national cinemas from Brazil, Mexico, Argentina and Central America. At the end of my time in London I took something of a semi-sabbatical but remained on the Committee of the San Sebastián Film Festival. It was around this time, while on a trip to Mexico, that Bertha Navarro mentioned to me that she and Guillermo del Toro were thinking of setting up a production company. This was Tequila Gang. Bertha was the driving force and we went into it full force and full of enthusiasm, even though we had no backing for the venture. It was a very good mix of personalities. Bertha and Guillermo were already very close. Bertha, of course, is historically a very important figure in Mexican cinema. Having me on board to look after some of the business aspects of the company and the launching of the projects just seemed to make perfect sense.

Because we all have to eat, we also started handling films from other people and other production companies. This increased on a greater scale after I worked with Wim Wenders on *Buena Vista Social Club* (1999), which provided a key link into Cuban cinema and Cuban culture.

From the beginning we presented ourselves as people who understood the business, and wanted to *do* business. We also helped unite film-makers in a desire to be seen, and to be commercial. Unlike the film-makers of the 1960s, most of whom were driven by a purely artistic or political force but despised the business side of the industry, Guillermo del Toro, Alfonso Cuarón and Alejandro González Iñárritu, the guys we have emerged alongside, all understand the business side of film-making. Instead of sitting around and bitching – 'We're on the other side of the world and nobody's interested in the films we're making' – they have really gone out and shaken up film-making and grabbed the interest of the world. It's similar to what later happened with the Argentinian group. They want to be in the world and for their films and culture to be visible. What brought about the change, I think, was primarily their analyses of and frustrations at what had come before. All of these film-makers are very ciné-literate, highly educated and very savvy both technically and artistically. In a business sense they are all very confident and competent.

This is the driving force; the desire to have a place in the market. They are also aware that as a film-maker you really have artistic freedom and space only if you also have box-office success. One often generates the other. Freedom is not given to you; it has to be earned. They have also watched the previous generation of film-makers grow quite bitter and angry and have made a resolution that this is not going to happen to them.

The film-makers were of a new generation, with an age range of late twenties to early forties. Of this generation I think that Cuarón is the oldest but he is still relatively young. *Como agua para chocolate* was directed by an older director; Alfonso Arau is now in his mid-sixties. There is a big difference. Arau also came out of a very different milieu. The newer generation of directors we are talking about are well travelled, very cosmopolitan and emerged in a very different cultural moment in time.

* * *

After completing the short films Un muy cortometraje *(1988),* Malayerba nunca muerde *(1988) and* Amada *(1990) Carlos Carrera – who began making short animations aged only twelve – attended the Centro de Capacitación Cinematográfica (CCC), studying under important theatre director Ludwik Margules. Carrera's first feature, the multi-Ariel-nominated* La mujer de Benjamín *(Benjamin's Woman) (1991) was followed by the comedy-crime hybrid* La Vida conyugal *(1993). This was a project beset by financial difficulties and Carrera put the experience behind him with his third feature,* Un Embrujo *(1997). The film is set on the Yucatán peninsula in 1928. Eliseo (Daniel Acuña) is the son of a violent stevedore, and faring poorly at school. But his teacher Felipa (Blanca Guerra) takes an interest in him and, though she is in love with a sailor, winds up having a sexual encounter with the boy, which inevitably stirs up gossip and trouble, not to say local superstition.*

BERTHA NAVARRO: Carrera had done those two films prior to *Un Embrujo* and, quite simply, I liked him very much. I was also impressed by his animation work. What's very clear is that the film I made with Carlos was his most personal. He has covered other subjects and worked from other scripts that were given to him, but I think that even above his first film, *Un Embrujo* is the one that meant the most to him. I liked the fact that Carlos had a passion for the project, felt that it was a story that had to be told. As a producer I need that passion from the director – I don't believe in compromises. In Mexico we have so few film-making opportunities that when we do make them we should always try to make jewels. There's no room for mediocrity.

CARLOS CARRERA *director*: It took us about ten years to make *Un Embrujo* and it was originally supposed to be my second film. It is based on a book by a good friend, Marcel Sisniega, who had written down the stories as told to him by a very old man. I found the material fascinating and very original. It was also very Mexican. It happened in a region that has very seldom been portrayed on film. We also placed the story in a period that had not been shown on film before, a very interesting time in Mexico's history. When I started working with Bertha Navarro I also met Martín Salinas.

MARTÍN SALINAS *screenwriter*: After several years of mostly 'development hell' and writing in English, with no directors attached to the projects in

47

most cases, or not meeting with them at all along the whole development process, teaming up with Carlos Carrera and Bertha Navarro for *Un Embrujo* was a blessing. Not only did I have a director to talk to, but one whose favourite drama teacher at CCC was the same as mine. What he had on paper were a series of wonderful, powerful moments in the life of a man who Marcel Sisniega had interviewed over several months, written as a series of vignettes. The story started in Yucatán around 1923, and spanned several years, with no dramatic structure at all. He had been trying to turn these pearls into a screenplay and needed someone to build a story with what he had. He told me he didn't want the story to concentrate on just a childhood story, but to try to give the feeling of a life going by, to span several years of Eliseo's life – from childhood to adulthood but with a clear dramatic unity. I agreed because that was the kind of thing you felt when you read all of those fragments. The other thing that we wanted to keep and strengthen was this amazing cultural mix of conservative Catholicism, Marxism and Mayan pre-Columbian cultural background that prevailed in Yucatán in those days – sometimes even within the same character.

We first talked for days about the characters and what the father–son aspects in those fragments suggested to us. Then we worked together on a first tentative structure. I then flew back to Argentina – where I had returned to live – and worked on my own until I was able to send Carlos a first storyline and outline. He liked it and we continued working until we got to what we felt was the main storyline: the story of the son of this idealist union fighter at the docks who deals with frustration by drinking too much, a mischievous kid who has this dream of living a very different life to the one his father lived, and doesn't want to follow in his steps. The romance with his teacher is a possible way for him to find this way out of that world. But it is obviously an impossible dream and as he grows up he can't help finding himself in his father's place and has to cope with this until he is pushed by circumstances to take some decisions as an adult. We all have been involved in a father–son story in our lives. I felt I knew what I was writing about and that we had a very clear common denominator with Carlos on that, without needing to say a word about own father–son personal stories. Once we had this storyline clear, we travelled to Yucatán on a research trip and found lots of very original stuff and events in the newspapers of those days and stories told by the older people in Puerto Progreso, to build the plot.

RODRIGO PRIETO *cinematographer*: Originally *La mujer de Benjamín* was going to be Carlos's thesis project at CCC and I was going to work on it, but Carlos had the opportunity to turn it into a feature and I couldn't work on it because I had not yet finished my studies. You wouldn't *believe* how disappointed I was. That said, Xavier Pérez Grobet did a truly wonderful job on it. I had always wanted to work with Carlos and so we began to discuss another movie that also sadly never happened. Then, at last *Un Embrujo*. The film was very different from anything I had done before, and Carlos was worried that I was into only very stylized and sleek movies when in fact I just thought that this style was what was best suited to some of these movies. Carlos wanted something much more subdued and realistic and I was also very eager to also explore this avenue. *Un Embrujo* was the perfect opportunity to do it. The style of the film is very simple and I really enjoyed working with a naturalistic type of lighting. Carlos is also very visual: he draws incredible storyboards but he is not stuck on the visual side as his emphasis is on the drama, the narrative and the characters. He was very good to work with. He let me do my thing while also encouraging me to try doing less.

On the evidence of Un Embrujo *it was obviously very important to Carrera that he relate stories and places that connect specifically to Mexico and Mexican history. From an early stage he was viewed as one of the leading voices in contemporary Mexican cinema.*

CARLOS CARRERA: I didn't, and still don't, pay much attention to that. I want only to make the films and to tell the stories I like – that is, stories about common people in common situations. I really don't care too much about such things; I also don't pay any attention to box-office results. It's the stories I believe in. I feel comfortable with the stories I know. I am not a nationalist but I like the stories that I know better.

*   *   *

FRANCISCO GONZÁLEZ COMPEÁN *producer*: You know, everyone talks about 'New Mexican Cinema' and many see *Amores Perros* at the forefront of this boom, but for me it all started with an earlier film that was not as successful as *Amores Perros* – Salvador Carrasco's *La Otra conquista* (*The Other Conquest*). It was very well marketed by Twentieth Century-Fox and it opened well on what was for Mexico a large number of screens.

Carrasco's film takes place one year after Hernán Cortés's arrival in Mexico, and opens with the infamous massacre of the Aztecs at the Great Temple. The lone Aztec survivor of the massacre is a young Indian scribe, Topiltzin (Damián Delgado), illegitimate son of Montezuma. Spanish friar Diego

49

The American poster for *The Other Conquest*

(José Carlos Rodríguez) has been charged with converting the native 'savages' into civilized Christians, but naturally finds Topiltzin to be a tough assignment.

SALVADOR CARRASCO *director*: My sisters had a lot to do with my passion for cinema. As a teenager they would take me to art houses in Mexico to see films that marked me for ever. Then it became a ritual for me to go on my own. My approach to some of these films was almost religious, treating them as cultural icons that transcended everyday existence and made me feel, think and learn things I hadn't experienced before. Intimate films with universal dimensions. Some personal favourites that always come to mind are Lelouch's *Les Misérables* (1995), Saura's *Cría cuervos* (1976), Wenders's *Wings of Desire* (1987), Teshigahara's *Woman of the Dunes* (1964), Scola's *Le Bal* (1982), Kieslowski's *The Double Life of Veronique* (1991), Tarkovsky's *Nostalgia* (1983), Kurosawa's *Ran* (1985), Claire Denis's *Chocolat* (1988) and Buñuel's *Los olvidados* (1950).

My producer Alvaro Domingo and I met in the first week of college and immediately we hit it off. Although we come from different worlds, we share many artistic objectives, and thus complement each other very well. *The Other Conquest* is a quintessentially independent film in that, in order to do it our way, we took seven years to make it, from 1992 to 1999. As an exemplary producer, Alvaro carried it through from beginning to end. His faith in the project was unfaltering, and there is no question that this film would never have happened without his commitment, perseverance, loyalty, hard work and, ultimately, an unconditional respect for the integrity of my vision as the writer–director of this film.

The first seed, so to speak, came to life on 13 August 1991. I remember the date so distinctly because it was the four hundred and seventieth anniversary of the fall of Mexico-Tenochtitlan, I was in New York, thinking about my country's origins – the sort of thing one does more often when abroad. And I felt like reading something about that historic day, which is how I came upon Vasconcelos's *Brief History of Mexico*.

One of Mexico's leading philanthropists and businessmen, Manuel Arango, had generously granted me a scholarship to attend college, and after my graduation from New York University, we discussed the possibility of making a short film about the Conquest for the Expo '92 in Seville. In October 1991, I presented him a treatment of the film, which was then called *The Absolved Vision*. Fortunately he liked it very much, and that is how the seed money came about. Then over some *tacos de cochinita pibil* in a restaurant in Coyoacán, I suggested to Alvaro, with whom I had made a couple of short films at NYU, that we join forces, he as producer and I as writer–director, to make this short film together. He read the treatment, fell in love with it, and we resolved to create our own company, Carrasco & Domingo Films, as a framework to take the big plunge together.

It wasn't long before Alvaro and I saw in the story the potential to turn it into a feature film. Neither he nor I then knew exactly what we were getting into, so our primary motivational drive has always remained to tell Topiltzin's story as best as we could. We both believed there's something in this story about resistance and preserving one's identity and beliefs that would be appealing to different kinds of people, just as he and I were originally drawn to it for different reasons.

So I worked on the feature screenplay. Alvaro showed it to his father, Plácido Domingo, who was able to read it on a plane from Europe to New York, and was very moved by it. Needless to say, Mr Domingo himself embodies the best possible form of syncretism between Spain and Mexico. Once he agreed to participate as a co-producer, the fundraising odyssey had officially begun. Mr Domingo also sings the aria 'Mater aeterna', composed by Samuel Zyman originally for the film, in the end credits. Another significant co-producer who later came into the project was Enrique González Torres SJ, who is currently the Dean of the Iberoamerican University in Mexico. Mr González's faith in the film has been a continuous source of inspiration for us. He believes that, bottom line, *The Other Conquest* helps remind everyone that Indians are an intrinsic part of Mexican history and contemporary society. At the time of the film's narrative, the 1520s, there was an ongoing debate in the courts of Europe about whether Indians had a soul or not.

In August 1992 we decided to shoot some sequences in order to generate credibility and dispel a certain notion that this film couldn't be made. We obviously didn't have enough money to shoot the whole feature yet, so we shot as much as we could, until the money ran out, and we were not able to resume until June 1995.

I should also point out that at Bard College I took a wonderful literature course with Mary McCarthy, with whom I developed a friendly relationship. Among other things, she was kind enough to bring a collection of poems of mine to the attention of Octavio Paz and Carlos Fuentes. One day she urged me to read a short story she believed would affect me profoundly: Vsevolod Garshin's *The Scarlet Flower*, about a man who in the most adverse of circumstances – such as being confined in a mental asylum – becomes obsessed with the idea of stealing a flower that embodies all evil; thus he would redeem mankind. The premise resonated deeply within me, perhaps because of its Don Quixote-like connotations, but also because it embodies a simple truth: life makes more sense if you have something to fight for.

In fact, that story couldn't be further away from the subject-matter of *The Other Conquest*, but an interesting turn of fate happened. A few months later, I was reading a book my father gave me, the aforementioned *Brief History of Mexico*, and it occurred to me that at the time of the Spanish

Conquest of Mexico, an Indian who had been deprived of everything might have tried to conquer, so as to possess and absorb, the powers of a statue of the Virgin Mary – in whose name questionable things were being done – in order to redeem himself and his people. The twist was that 'to conquer' would not imply destruction, but to regain his own Aztec Mother Goddess through the Virgin Mary, the utmost symbol of the invaders. In Topiltzin's and in Friar Diego's minds, the Virgin Mary and the Mother Goddess become one and the same. Ultimately, I think the film is a parable about cultural tolerance.

The main thing was to tell that particular story in a context that had always fascinated me for its complexities and ambiguities, its poetry and its harsh brutality. Just to imagine those encounters, the misperceptions – Moctezuma believing Cortés was the God Quetzalcoatl; the friars believing conversion could happen overnight; the mere idea of 'conquering', the will to resist expressed in mysterious ways, the religious fervour, the other-worldly sounds . . . anywhere you turn you find movie material. I'm just surprised there aren't many more films out there about the Conquest. One of the most significant contributions of our film has been to heighten interest in a topic so vast and complex that it deserves to be treated with a multiplicity of voices, stories, and points of view.

We raised the money mostly through private investors and rather symbolic contributions from Mexican institutions that support the arts and culture. There were hundreds of phone calls, letters, and appointments throughout the years. It was a painstaking process, with many ups and downs, countless disappointments and a few occasional breakthroughs that made it possible in the end. I am in complete awe of Alvaro as a producer for pulling this through, for not only was the subject-matter and scope of the project regarded with scepticism by many people, but he was also trusting a first-time, ambitious, completely unknown twenty-four-year-old writer–director.

Damián Delgado was undoubtedly the best casting for Topiltzin. At the time he was dancing in a brilliant company called Ballet Teatro del Espacio. He was a first-time actor. Subsequently, he was one of the leads in John Sayles's *Men with Guns*, among others. I was looking through the video camera during Damián's casting session, and when he said the line 'Hicieron cenizas de mi pueblo; ahí quedó hecha humo nuestra verdad de las cosas . . .' ('You turned my people into ashes; our truth went up in smoke . . .'), it became very clear to me that he was not acting, as he knew what those words meant. He was Topiltzin. Incidentally, during the shoot people never called him by his real name.

We had a first-time writer–director and editor, first-time producer, first-time lead actor, first-time production designer, first-time composer. But our art director was Brigitte Broch, who went on to win an Oscar for her superb work in Baz Luhrmann's *Moulin Rouge*.

BRIGITTE BROCH *production designer*: I read of the period through books and novels set during this era to help me get the feel of mood and time. I tried to use colour not only from an aesthetic point of view but also in connection with its symbolism and relation to the state of mind of the characters and their spiritual voyage. I prepared a Zapata project for Alfonso Arau – a film that fell through then – but had the great fortune to work briefly on two occasions with Vittorio Storaro. His colour theories have embedded themselves in me and I try to be aware, to use colours with utmost care as to their significance. So, *The Other Conquest* was really no more difficult than any of the other movies I have worked on. It involved research, locations that don't betray the period and detail to the spaces in order to make them believable.

SALVADOR CARRASCO: I went to every possible archaeological site within a three-hundred-kilometre radius surrounding Mexico City, where the production was based. I was looking for an intimate setting far away from the metropolis, where clandestine rituals would still be taking place without the Spaniards immediately realizing ... though of course, eventually they would, like in the film. What we see in the film is not, and did not ever attempt to be, the great Mexico-Tenochtitlan that Bernal Díaz del Castillo described. It is a post-Conquest look, since the present time of the film begins in 1526, five years after the fall of Mexico-Tenochtitlan.

Other sets include sixteenth-century monasteries, underground caves, colonial plazas, etc., which one still finds in Mexico. Of course we had to make up and retouch them for authenticity. Slight architectural licence was taken for the sake of spectacle, but we always remained true to an internal aesthetic coherence.

In terms of location permits, the real breakthrough took place when Alvaro pitched the film to the Director of the National Anthropology and History Institute, who told Alvaro that she had always envisioned a serious, committed, Kurosawa-like approach to this subject, and that here was the opportunity to fulfil that.

The logistical challenges could be summed up in an unforgettable phrase that my first assistant director once told me: 'The problem with you, Salvador, is that you're trying to make a first-world film with third-world resources.' I am convinced that the biggest asset of this film was that most of the people who worked in it genuinely believed they were doing something worthwhile, something about a subject we all carried in our veins and yet were regrettably ignorant about, since many of the issues raised by the film are still taboo in Mexico. And yet, the film had an incredibly positive response in Mexico, becoming the highest-grossing Mexican film ever when it opened in 1999.

The opening sequence at the aftermath of the Great Temple Massacre was filmed in the archaeological site of Tenayuca, which is situated in the heart of Mexico City. The camera placements had to be carefully chosen, for moving the camera an inch in any direction would have revealed the local market, buses, phone cables, etc. The rain hoses weren't powerful enough, so we had to spend many hours fixing them versus a few hours shooting one of the main events in Mexican history! That was my first day of professional 35 mm shooting ever. But I was hooked.

The shot of the Spaniards discovering the clandestine ritual was filmed in 1992. The reversal of the Indians reacting to their arrival was shot three years later. Thanks to our ingenious production designer, you don't notice the difference. In the process, actors aged, even disappeared, and the sacrificed princess was now dripping milk from breast feeding, which was a beautiful metaphor for the idea of rebirth through sacrifice.

The title has three levels. First it refers to the religious or spiritual conquest that followed the military conquest of Mexico; second, to the Conquest of Mexico focused on an 'other', an indigenous protagonist – the Aztec scribe Topiltzin, illegitimate son of the Emperor Moctezuma; and third to the 'conquest' carried out by the indigenous peoples themselves, who appropriated European religious forms, and made them their own. The Virgin of Guadalupe, which combines the Aztec cult of the Mother Goddess with the Catholic veneration of the Virgin Mary, is perhaps the best example of this 'reverse conquest'.

My goal was to narrate a passionate story, one based on a careful imaginary reconstruction of what things might have been like during the decade between the fall of Mexico-Tenochtitlan, capital of the Aztec Empire, in 1521, and the alleged apparitions of the Virgin of Guadalupe to the Indian Juan Diego in 1531. This decade constitutes what we might call the gestation period of the contemporary Mexican nation; it is a period fraught with complexities and ambiguities which are still relevant today, five hundred years later.

Frequently, when the indigenous peoples of the time of the Conquest are portrayed, they come across as entirely passive, as if they had just simply and unquestioningly accepted the things imposed on them by the Spaniards. *The*

Other Conquest depicts a creative and critical indigenous culture which, despite all sorts of losses and setbacks, makes an effort to assume an active role in the shaping of its own destiny. The characters in the film show us that, even under the most adverse circumstances, people will strive to carry out their own 'conquests'.

In other parts of the world, the 'encounter' between European and 'native' peoples was resolved by the outright annihilation of the indigenous groups. The social consequences of the Conquest of Mexico are especially profound, in that in Mexico the indigenous peoples, through their violent and partial incorporation into the official and religious life of New Spain, managed to survive.

The new, hybrid, *mestizo* race which is Mexico was certainly not the result of a tidy and idyllic process of harmonious interaction. Still, I don't think that it's a good idea to adopt a facile Manichaean point of view, that sees history as a black-and-white story with good guys and bad guys. *The Other Conquest* explores different levels of the Spanish Conquest of Mexico, a remarkable historical process whose relevance has in no way been diminished by the passing of five centuries.

This picture is not just about Aztecs and Spaniards; the topics it explores are relevant to all ethnic or national identities that were formed in the crucible of colonization, conversion, and syncretism. *The Other Conquest* is an invitation to dialogue, an opportunity to reflect on our origins and respect our differences.

La Otra conquista *opened in Mexico on 4 April 1999. Released on twenty-seven screens, by the end of the film's first week the film had grossed $216,038 with a high screen average of $8,001. Expanding over the subsequent three weeks to a maximum of seventy-two screens, the film grossed an impressive $1,507.306. Opening in seventy-four screens in Los Angeles on 19 April, the film dominated industry headlines, grossing $400,000 on its opening weekend alone. It went on to finish among the highest-grossing foreign-language films of the year in America.*

* * *

Juan Rulfo is widely regarded as one of the greatest writers in the history of Mexican literature. An exponent of magic realism, perhaps his best known work is Pedro Páramo, *in which the book's narrator, at the behest of his dying mother, visits the deserted village haunted by the memory of his patriarchal father.*

After working on both La mujer de Benjamín *and then* Sólo con tu pareja,

Rulfo's son, Juan Carlos Rulfo, emerged as a singular film-making talent in his own right during the mid-1990s: first with El Abuelo Cheno y otras historias *(Grandfather Cheno and Other Stories), then with* Del olvido al no me acuerdo *(I Forgot, I Don't Remember).*

JUAN CARLOS RULFO *director*: *El Abuelo Cheno* came about as a result of ignorance and ingenuousness. I had wanted to tell a story that moved me deeply, but I was worried that a story personal to me would not be interesting for the spectator. Yet, at the same time, I was sure there was something in it that could justify making a film. Curiously enough, the only thing I'd done before then was a 'Making of' documentary of Carlos Carrera's first full-length film, as well as a lot of interviews with a bunch of old men. I wasn't concerned – I'm still not – by the formal and/or conceptual distinctions between fiction and documentary. *El Abuelo Cheno* represented the discovery that the personal can have value as narrative, and that you can learn from that. You could say that what I achieved in the film was achieved unwittingly, although I was learning along the way.

My father did have an influence, of course. But it was to do with discovering the process of introspection that an author has to go through in his work. Rather than being close to my father in the sense of reinterpreting his work, I think it's something more intimate and personal: a son learning from the steps and the paths taken by the father – which, in a mysterious way, have an existence very close to mine. The part of his work that I feel closest to is his photography. It's there that you see his attitude to things. The way he framed a photograph, the atmosphere, the feeling it imparts – all comes together perfectly, allowing an apprentice like me to fathom from it an approach to life that, doubtless, will be with me for ever.

When talking about *Del olvido*, it's important to bear in mind *El Abuelo Cheno*, which tells the story of the tales surrounding the death of a character called Cheno – my grandfather. Originally, however, I'd been trying to find people who had known my father, who had lived in the same region. I didn't find anything out about my father, but, on the other hand, I did discover all these real characters who led me into a fascinating world full of stories and sensations I just couldn't ignore. That's why I came up with the structure of the death of the grandfather – to provide myself with a pretext for telling all the other stories. *El Abuelo* is basically a short told in a circular structure, without taking too many risks. It was my answer to what had seemed the failure of not finding what I had been looking for: my father.

Later on I decided to keep on looking, but making use of the seeming failure of the non-meeting, basing myself on the things people had forgotten, in order to continue telling their stories. Let me add that it's these stories that attract me the most, much more so than the direct testimonies concerning my father, which, although I did get them, didn't offer as much, in filmic terms, as the other characters. *Del olvido* is a work full of loose ends, in which the themes of memory and the transitory nature of life allow me to play with very evocative atmospheres and film time. Memory and the fleeting nature of things are both very cinematographic.

It's perfectly normal for people to feel uncomfortable in front of a camera. We can take that as a given. It's really a question of not treating people as though they were material for a news report. You need a great deal of time, and they do too. If you expect to get everything on a first take, then think again. In this particular case, the working plan stated that the most important thing was to get right up close to daily life, to the pace of life there, and to listen. All the crew, cameraman and sound recordist, knew exactly when to turn on their equipment; they'd learned to sense when the words we needed were approaching.

The film was well received, although I think the results could have been much better. Critics and producers, who reckon they know about these things, want me to accept the numbers. They argue that it was enough that a documentary of such a personal nature was even able to enter the big-screen battle of midsummer 2000. Ten prints went out, compared to 250 for *The Perfect Storm*, 250 for the *Flintstones in Viva Rock Vegas*, and 250 for *Amores Perros*. It remained in cinemas for over eight weeks and for a similar length of time on video and in video shops and clubs.

All this, it should be said, was achieved despite the total scepticism of the distributor, who invested very little in promoting the film – still the case today now that a DVD version has been edited and has yet to be released. *Del olvido al no me acuerdo* remains in circulation thanks to word of mouth, which has gradually become the film's real promoter. In this sense I'd go as far as to say that it's a film that, over time, has become more powerful.

4

The Making of *Amores Perros*

In turning to the impact of what became the signature film of the New Mexican Wave, it is necessary first to consider certain trends in Mexican film exhibition during the 1990s, together with the domestic success of a 1999 picture entitled Sexo, pudor y lágrimas *(Sex, Shame and Tears).*

ALFONSO CUARÓN *director*: What happened is that, for many years, the Mexican people stopped going to the movie theatres, because the theatres were so lousy. First they stopped going to Mexican films, then they stopped going to films in general. Most of these films were financed and released by the government. IMCINE couldn't really have cared less; its function was political, in that they had to state that they made twenty films per year. These were films that nobody saw. Though, I must add, there are now some good people at IMCINE . . .

FRANCISCO GONZÁLEZ COMPEÁN *producer*: The cinema ticket price was controlled by the government, so there wasn't much money coming back to the producers, and the quality of the films declined to that point that people finally stopped going to see them. Then in 1995 the price controls were terminated, and bigger exhibition chains started to flourish. We not only got a lot of screens, but better quality too. These new theatres also cultivated a new audience, the more affluent classes who had previously avoided the cinema because it was such a low-grade, shabby experience.

ALFONSO CUARÓN: In the mid-1990s, there were new chains of cinemas, multiplexes. When you walked into one of these, it was no different from being in a cinema in the US, right down to the concessions stand. My memory of cinema from childhood is related to Mexican candies, now it was all Hersheys . . .

FRANCISCO GONZÁLEZ COMPEÁN: So, now we had all these lovely cinemas – but they were completely filled with American films because Mexico was not producing any films of its own.

ALFONSO CUARÓN: When the middle classes started going back, there was a film called *Sexo, pudor y lágrimas* by Antonio Serrano.

Serrano's comedy drama concerned a pair of young couples in Mexico City: Ana (Susana Zabaleta) is starved for love by her intellectual husband Carlos (Victor Huggo Martin) at the point when their friend Tomas (Demián Bichir) returns from many years of foreign travel. Over the street, promiscuous executive Miguel (Jorge Salinas) and his unhappy wife Andrea (Cecilia Suárez) are visited by old friend María (Mónica Dionne). Inevitably, the two visitors stir up the marital relations of their respective hosts.

Released on 16 August 1999 on 138 prints by Fox, Sex pudor y lágrimas became at the time the highest-grossing locally produced film at the Mexican box office.

ALFONSO CUARÓN: What was interesting was that it didn't open particularly big – but on its second week, when most Mexican films throw in the towel, instead of dropping it did a little better. The third week it did even better. And it just kept on escalating. People in the industry began to say that there was an audience for this film – which had proved more popular than many contemporary American films – and so they decided to distribute Mexican

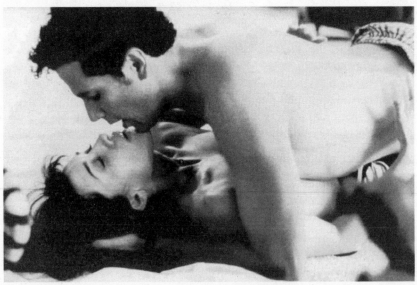

Bringing Mexican audiences back: *Sexo, pudor y lágrimas*

films again. Not enough to regenerate Mexican productions, but enough to ensure that films such as this began to be seen.

ALFREDO JOSKOWICZ *film-maker/Director,* IMCINE: In 1997 Mexico produced only nine feature films, the lowest number since 1932 so the government was compelled to help; FOPROCINE (Fondo de Fomento a la Producción Cinematográfica) was created to assist quality films.

In the last five years, we have used FOPROCINE funds to assist forty-seven films. The government put $13.5 million into FOPROCINE, a fund that was responsible for *Sexo, pudor y lágrimas*, a film that attracted an audience of 5.3 million people. *El crimen del padre Amaro*, another FOPROCINE-assisted film, also achieved in advance of 5 million viewers in Mexico and has gone on to be the most successful Mexican film in our history. Unfortunately, even with these successes, the fund is not enough, and the $13.5 million has not been recouped.

JOSÉ LUIS GARCÍA AGRAZ *director*: FOPROCINE has a committee of senior figures who can award your project, if selected – you need to submit your script, budget, plan of financing, etc. – up to $700,000. Even in Mexico a film nowadays costs around $2 million. In other words you're going to need at least as much again in order to start filming.

BERTHA NAVARRO *producer*: The release of *Sexo* marked an interesting moment, because it was one of the first big local successes in a long time and was also, I think, the first time that a major company had distributed a Mexican film. It's also a very open, fresh and sexually frank work that the young people in Mexico identified with – it was not moralistic. But it was quite a broad comedy of the kind that has been done many times in Europe, so for audiences outside of Mexico it wasn't really able to offer anything new. To all intents and purposes, it was *Amores Perros* that served notice or gave affirmation of the fact that we in Mexico can make films that compete with any made anywhere in the world.

GAEL GARCÍA BERNAL *actor*: There are four key aspects to *Amores Perros*. The first was the attention paid to the film from those people in the industry who supported it. The second was the quality of the film itself. Third was the fact that it was a big box-office hit in Mexico and claimed a place in the market. Fourth, and the basis of all this, is that it was a privately owned film. I must also tell you that the amount of work that Alejandro [Iñárritu] and the producers put in to make sure that this film was seen was *unbelievable*.

* * *

AltaVista Films, the Mexican production outlet that would nurture Amores Perros, was originally set up as a joint venture between Corporación Interamericana de Entretenimiento (CIE), Latin America's leading live-entertainment provider, and investment capitalist Sinca Inbursa. The creative team at AltaVista had funds, but not so much experience: Francisco González Compeán came from advertising, while Martha Sosa was a former television journalist.

MARTHA SOSA *producer*: Alejandro Soberón [chief executive of CIE] was the crazy visionary who said, 'Let's make a production and distribution company to do the films that we want to do.' My job at AltaVista was to look for those films and for that talent. This was also the job of Francisco González Compeán, the director general of the company.

Previously I'd had a long career as a journalist in radio and television. I also owned a very successful television production company with my husband, but I'd grown tired of this career. I'd always been a film buff, and many of my friends were film-makers. Being a film-maker then was not as it is now. It was extremely difficult, and not made easier by the fact that many film-makers simply didn't care about audiences. They would claim that they wanted their films to be widely seen, but they were often elitist in their approach. I think that this is a major difference between many of the film-makers at work today in Mexico and those who were operating in the late 1970s and 1980s.

FRANCISCO GONZÁLEZ COMPEÁN: My father is a lawyer and a politician – so there was surprise, on my part as well as my parents', that film was the career I chose. In fact, I went to business school first, but in retrospect that was a smart move because very few people at film school actually care about or understand the business side. Then I was about to enter Columbia University in New York to study Public Administration, but I began to have doubts. I'd taken some screenwriting classes at NYU and realized this was something I wanted to get further into. So, I took a Masters in Media Studies, specializing in film production. And I loved it, because whenever a teacher talked about financing or the contract details of a production, I was the only one paying attention – everybody else wanted to get their hands on a camera and get the hell out of the room. Nobody wanted to be a producer. But I came to the conclusion that's what I wanted to be.

Before going to the US I had worked in advertising, and when I returned to Mexico I had some bills to pay off so I got back into the strategic planning area of advertising. That really helped a lot in terms of finding a system for connecting with people. So, I had a business background, a little advertising background, and a little film background. And when students ask me what they need to become a producer, those are the three disciplines I recommend.

After a year or so in Mexico, Martha Sosa, Monica Lozano Serrano, Yissel Ibarra and I started toying with the idea of film production. It all came together when Alejandro Soberón, the President of CIE, who had started in film, pledged his allegiance to us, then we put together a business plan for AltaVista Films. AltaVista also spawned a sister distribution company, NuVisión, for Mexico and Latin America. At that time in Mexico, 1998, just having a business plan was a first, because everyone approached film on a single-film basis – the industry was completely devastated, there was simply no production. In the mid-1980s there would be maybe a hundred films produced per year, very low-quality, cheesy productions, but there were lots of them. And 450 million tickets would be sold a year. By 1998, ticket sales were closer to 80 million, and only four or five films were shot that year. We were at rock bottom.

At that time, you had two kinds of producers. First there were those making low-budget exploitation films, and for a number of reasons – the ticket price, the falling audiences – they were running out of gas. The second kind of producer was the art-house type who wasn't concerned with anything but getting the film made and maybe taking it to a couple of festivals. Frequently these films weren't even released in Mexico. Or if they were, they were released on very few screens. They didn't really care about the movie being seen by lots of people, in fact they *frowned* on films that were seen by lots of people and so created this very elitist little clique, because they made their money out of actually producing the film, not through selling tickets.

To have a huge bank and a huge entertainment company backing film production was shocking. When we announced the formation of AltaVista and NuVisión, we had to choose our words very wisely. We couldn't say that we wanted to make commercial films, because then we would be labelled as anti-culture. So, we came up with the statement that we wanted to make films that a lot of people would want to see. This wasn't received so badly . . . but it's absurd that we had to be so careful. Surely the aim of making a film is to make something that a lot of people are going to want to go and see?

We started to develop. We said, 'We can't pay for stars' – which, at any rate, we didn't have at this time in Mexico – 'and we can't pay for special effects. So this has to be a story-driven studio. Director-centred, and story-driven.'

The first film AltaVista made was *Todo el poder* (*Gimme the Power*,

2000). It was a comedy, and very local, but it also says some very strong things, so much so that some of the executives at the company were slightly worried by it. It directly deals with a theme very close to that of *Amores Perros*, the insecurity that comes from living in the city. It was very successful, and great fun to produce and market. It didn't do well outside of Mexico, but it was exactly the kind of film that we wanted to make.

Thanks to my marketing background, I proposed the idea of market research, and that was another first. What it revealed was that people didn't mind happy endings; they also liked romantic endings – but what they *really* wanted was to be able to recognize themselves on the screen. Film is about reality, and film constructs reality. We always called it 'the little mirror'. So we really wanted to make provocative films in which the Mexican people could recognize themselves. And the moment that people in Mexican films started to look and speak like real Mexican people, they went crazy.

* * *

BERTHA NAVARRO: González Iñárritu wasn't from the film community, and in some ways he was like del Toro – a guy who seemingly came out of the blue, but was pure talent.

ALEJANDRO GONZÁLEZ IÑÁRRITU *director*: First of all, I am an autodidact and a kid from the streets. I lived in a neighbourhood very similar to that of Octavio and Susana in *Amores Perros*. The green mosaic on the front of Octavio's house is an *hommage* to my house in the Narvarte neighbourhood.

I grew up with parents who taught me love and education as my main tools, but with three sisters and one brother it was a very, *very* limited economic situation. Because we were five I didn't get that much attention, therefore I was very free-spirited, growing up and learning about life on the streets from the time I was eight years old. At sixteen I escaped, hitchhiking, with my girlfriend, in search of myself, selling jewellery on Mexican beaches.

Twice – first at seventeen, then at nineteen – I boarded a cargo ship crossing the Atlantic: once from Vera Cruz and another time from Coatzacoalcos. On the first trip I spent three or four months. The second time, I remained in Europe, surviving for one year on a thousand dollars. I did every kind of job to survive, including picking grapes with the gypsies in Spain and dancing in a swimsuit in the pool of a discothèque. I think these two experiences taught me more than any university.

Then I returned to Mexico to create a rock band, to be a serious musician – and a film-maker, after seeing the film *Yol* (1982). I had started to study

Communications when suddenly a friend of mine, Mariana Garcia Barcena, offered me an opportunity to be a DJ, because she liked my voice. So I had a three-hour show where I could play, say and create anything that I wanted. I learned to entertain people with my favourite music, my characters and ideas, and my bizarre imagination. I then became the director of the station at twenty-two years of age, and was listened to by millions of people in the biggest city in the world.

After five years, I thought that I had completely cracked radio and considered myself a master of the medium – so I suddenly felt poor. I quit when WFM was the most important and influential radio station in the country because I realized that I wanted to make films, and communicate through a visual medium. To do this I had to learn how to work with images. I was lucky. After the huge success of the radio station, I received the opportunity and support from Miguel Aleman – my former WFM boss – to create the corporate image of a huge TV corporation. With my partner, Raul Olvera, I started to write, produce, direct, edit, post-produce and sell approximately eighty commercials a year, this for the next five years. It was crazy, but this was the first time that I went on a set as a director. My only experiences had been with a Super-8 camera when I was eleven – that, and having been the assistant director and composer for a short film taken from a story by Julio Cortazar directed by Pelayo Gutiérrez during university.

I have learned skills by doing them. I learned film on sets, doing horrible things, experiments, failing and spending more time on them than in my own house. Also important to my development was my theatre studies with Ludwik Margules, a great teacher who strengthened and expanded my concept of directing. But it was the commercials that gave me the opportunity to play with all the tools, to understand the mechanics, to create and explore in thirty or sixty seconds, different genres, tones, beats, rhythms – and, most importantly, to have a camera, a couple of actors and tell a story and say something through images and sounds. All of the things that I have directed were written and produced from the beginning to end by me so that gave me the best education in the world, the freedom and the tools to make anything happen.

The problem with the commercials was that they filled your pocket but emptied your brain and soul. It was not a wise interchange. So after five years I decided to quit, and I wrote and produced with Pelayo a thirty-minute pilot, *Behind the Money*, for TV, with Miguel Bose as the star. It was a great exercise to confirm to myself, before making a feature film, that I could direct something larger than thirty seconds. My goal was to have at least one good scene, just one would have been enough for me – and there is one scene that I still like today. With the next step, *Amores Perros*, I thought, 'Should I? Can I?' Now, today, I know that I can.

Pelayo Gutiérrez helped me produce *Behind the Money*. But I was desperate because they loved the pilot, but it was never accepted as a TV series – it was too expensive to shoot. I was developing an idea about a family from Guerrero and their two young sons who began to involve themselves in the guerrillas of Chiapas with Subcommandante Marcos and the consequences of that. And I wanted a writer to help me, so I wanted to read scripts. Pelayo sent me a very good one that was fluid and extremely well written. I said, 'Who is this guy?' It was Guillermo Arriaga.

GUILLERMO ARRIAGA *writer*: I have always been interested in writing, and I think this was because when I was about twelve years old I was very shy; I was incapable of saying to a beautiful girl, 'I like you.' So I wrote thousands and thousands of words to say it. And there is still a shyness inside of me.

I was finally able to go to a very good school called the Mexican-American School, after having been in schools from which I was expelled; I have Attention-Deficit Disorder so it was always easy for me to lose concentration and get distracted. At the Mexican-American School there was a course where we were given the opportunity to work in theatre, writing, directing and working with actors, and here I discovered Shakespeare and a lot of writers of the Spanish 'Golden Age'. At sixteen I wrote, produced and directed a play, and it transpired that the cast didn't like the ending. They said that if I didn't change the ending they wouldn't perform it. I said, 'No way.' The day before the play was due to be performed, it was cancelled. I then began writing a story for a children's supplement in a newspaper.

It was at about this time that I became seriously interested in politics, and became of the belief that revolution was much more important than writing. But I then went back to it, because I became ill and found out that I had developed an infection in my heart. The doctor treating me disclosed that he had good news and bad news: the good news was that I was not, after all, a hypochondriac; the bad news was that I risked dying because my heart was so swollen. I was told to remain in bed for three months. During this period I read Jorge Luis Borges for the first time, decided that I wanted to be a writer, and began to write short stories. Then nothing happened, I became a little bit despondent, feeling like I had no talent.

A last throw of the dice was my applying for a writing scholarship at the National Institute of Fine Arts, which I won. I subsequently wrote a novel in approximately ten days – wrote it as if possessed. I entered the novel into a writing contest, which it didn't win. Fortunately, Laura Esquivel read it, liked it and recommended it to her publisher who decided to publish me. The novel was *Relato de los esplendores y miserias del Escuadrón Guillotina y de cómo participó en la leyenda de Francisco Villa*. After this came my second novel, *A Sweet Scent of Death*; my third, *The Night's Buffalo*, and a collection of short stories, *Retorno 201*. I was approached by Gabriel Retes who had read and admired *A Sweet Scent of Death* and wanted to make it into a film. The finished film is one that I absolutely dislike. It wasn't a pleasant experience and if it were possible I would take my name off of it. At one time Alfonso Cuarón was going to do it but ... [*pretends to cry*] he didn't.

I had written previous screenplays, *Amores Perros* was just the first to be filmed. It is really the second film in a trilogy that began with a screenplay called *Upon Open Sky*, which has yet to be filmed. I have the option to direct it. *Upon Open Sky* begins also with a car accident. I have experience of this. Once there were seven of us in a jeep returning at six in the morning from a hunting trip in the north of Mexico. The passenger in the front seat somehow distracted the driver, and we went down a deep cliff. Suddenly I was in the middle of breaking glass and twisted metal. It was especially horrifying for me because I was sleeping in the back seat when it happened. But miraculously we survived because we were carrying huge metal coolers on the roof. Then suddenly people I didn't know and wouldn't ordinarily come into contact with surrounded us ... I became obsessed with what happens before, during and after an accident.

I was teaching at the university in Mexico City. A mutual friend heard that Alejandro had read *Upon Open Sky* and liked it and so set up a meeting between us. We went to a restaurant, where I asked him two very personal questions. I cannot reveal to you either the questions or his answers, but his responses demonstrated that he was a very interesting, complex and profound man, and somebody that I wanted to know.

ALEJANDRO GONZÁLEZ IÑÁRRITU: Guillermo has been a teacher all his life, and I had previously made some declarations about how bad my teachers were and expressed my belief that cinema could not be taught in classrooms, that cinema was outside, in real life.

GUILLERMO ARRIAGA: I of course ribbed him about being the fucking guy who had gone around telling everybody that the university was no good when there were professors there killing themselves in order to ensure that they were doing a good job ...

ALEJANDRO GONZÁLEZ IÑÁRRITU: Guillermo was initially so mad at me, like,

'Who do you think you are?' But I think that deep down he thought I was right.

I told him that I was developing a project and I would love for him to write it. We started to work, but ten days later he called me back and said that for personal reasons he couldn't continue with it.

GUILLERMO ARRIAGA: It was basically a comedy. After more meetings and four or five attempts I had to say to him, 'Listen Alejandro, I'm not one to commit the ideas of others to paper, I can only write personal stuff.' So I suggested that he and Carlos Cuarón work together on the comedy, since Carlos is a brilliant comedy writer. After I had said goodbye, I immediately thought, 'Shit!' So I told him about the screenplay I was writing that involved three parallel stories. And I told him it was very dark. But he was adamant that he was interested.

ALEJANDRO GONZÁLEZ IÑÁRRITU: We started working together based on that idea and it all fell into place from there. As he was writing the film, I was already directing it in my mind. Sometimes I discussed the blocking of the actors that I had in my mind with Guillermo, so that he could translate that in the script. Every book, every song, every smell and everything that I absorbed over three years helped me to know and reveal the characters, and then to be able to share that with Guillermo. I participated very closely in the idea, concept and design. But it was Guillermo who wrote, solved and conceived the thing, and who I consider one of the best screenwriters in the world.

GUILLERMO ARRIAGA: Alejandro is a perfectionist and he is also very obsessive. He considers every angle of human condition. He also has a brilliant sense of humour; you should see his commercials. He is a man who has big thoughts and is not afraid to reflect on life. We have a constant dialogue throughout both the screenwriting and the film-making process. We are living proof of the myth that the writer and the director are adversaries. There is an absolute mutual respect.

* * *

GUILLERMO ARRIAGA: For me, the epitome of the human condition is contradiction. The more contradictory the character, the more human and interesting they are. I personally avoid making characters likeable; I want to make interesting characters, not likeable ones. Some of my characters are despicable but rather than the audience liking them I want them to understand and perhaps recognize them.

Mexico City is very complex, very interesting and very difficult to understand. It is a strong presence within itself, and, as the biggest city in the world, it's an anthropological experiment – there's no way it could not be a character in the script. I think that there are cities in the world that can be there or not – Mexico City has far too much power for that. I cannot escape it when I write.

I think that my major influence is perhaps the street. I want the films I write to look real; and I would hope that anyone watching *Amores Perros* would say, 'The guy who wrote this, he was *there*.'

Arriaga's screenplay for Amores Perros *was finally structured as a triptych of overlapping and intersecting narratives, exploring the lives of disparate characters who are catapulted into unforeseen dramatic situations, instigated by the seemingly inconsequential destiny of a dog named Cofi.*

GUILLERMO ARRIAGA: In terms of the structure, my Attention Disorder helped me. When I was at school it made some of my teachers think that I was mentally retarded, but this chaotic thinking actually works for me in film. Things go back and forth and stories mingle. Faulkner is without a doubt my major literary influence: *The Sound and the Fury; The Wild Palms; Absalom Absalom!* and *Light in August.*

The three male characters represent an archetype divided into three different stages: a guy under twenty; a guy in his forties and a guy in his sixties. In a certain way these represent who I am. So the film is autobiographical, absolutely.

I was the owner of the real Cofi. When I was eight years old, everyone in my neighbourhood had a dog. Cofi was an ugly dog, a mixed-breed combination of a Labrador and a Weimaraner. When I was nine I was watching television and there was a knock on the door, and I was called to be told that Cofi had killed the champion of the neighbourhood. My neighbours took my dog and they fought him against the dogs of opposing neighbourhoods; Cofi became a champion. He was so fierce that sometimes he arrived home with small dogs still in his jaws . . .

In Story No. 1, Octavio (Gael García Bernal), Cofi's teenage handler, enters the dog into brutal fighting contests, hoping to win enough money so that he can elope with Susana (Vanessa Bauche), the appealing young wife of his aggressive brother Ramiro (Marco Pérez). A near-fatal injury to Cofi prompts a reckless car chase that ends violently in a dreadful crash.

GUILLERMO ARRIAGA: The hardest and most problematic for me was the first story. Remember, this has lots of characters and mainly takes place on the outside. The second story has mainly two characters, trapped on the inside. The first was riskier for me as a writer. Then again, I like to take risks.

We can see my characters as like Adam and Eve, they are often on their own and they don't have a society that will comfort them and give them space. The only thing that sustains two lovers is love itself. There is nothing else. This is why forbidden love for me is very important.

In Story No. 2, middle-aged businessman Daniel (Alvaro Guerrero) discovers that dreams can become nightmares, after he abandons his family to set up house with a beautiful young model, Valeria (Goya Toledo), who will then be severely injured by the car crash and ultimately lose a leg.

Initially Valeria is presented as the kind of shallow media creature who appears on TV to announce to the delighted audience that she is dating a movie star, and dotes on a small dog called Richi. After Daniel installs her in a part-finished apartment, the dog disappears down a hole in the floorboards.

GUILLERMO ARRIAGA: I did want to show the stupid superficiality and the obsession with celebrity. I wanted to make a very strong point about the superficiality within the media and show how this superficiality can suddenly and very quickly lead to hell.

Daniel is really in love with Valeria and makes sacrifices for her, accepting her as she now is after the crash. I think also that sympathy for Valeria is harder won, because she's much younger than him.

I had the story of a woman with her little poodle – I hate women who use pooches in this way – but I didn't have the link until Alejandro told me the story of a woman who had lost her poodle under the floorboards.

I love dogs and think they represent the kind of person you are and so in *Amores Perros* I did want them to represent their owners but I also wanted to use them to make a wider point about the human condition. In the first story you have an innocent boy who slowly becomes a murderer, just as you have an innocent dog slowly becoming a murderer. Then you have a beautiful dog with a beautiful owner who loses everything and slips into a living hell, just as the dog is also trapped in a living hell. Finally, you have a hit man who meets his canine counterpart.

In Story No. 3, El Chivo (Emilio Echevarría), a revolutionary-turned-assassin, witnesses the accident and finds that it leads him to a life-changing

*moral epiphany. Not least, he also becomes the adoptive owner and guardian
of Octavio's dog, Cofi.*

*The final shot of El Chivo heading into the horizon allows for a certain
ambiguity.*

GUILLERMO ARRIAGA: Many people ask me why he is leaving and I always
say that he is going to review his life and come back when he is better. I
wanted there to be room for optimism.

* * *

ROSA BOSCH *producer*: Remember, on paper a film such as *Amores Perros*
would have frightened even many private companies. For a start, it was
long, it had dog-fighting, and a very complex narrative structure. But still, it
could only have been made privately. IMCINE would never have been able
to finance it fully. The average cost of a film in Mexico is $1.5 million
dollars. If IMCINE gives you half a million dollars, how are you going to get
the rest?

GUILLERMO ARRIAGA: I must stress that I am not against state-funded cinema. I think there are some films that *have* to be state-produced, but what
happened in Mexico was that suddenly the state was the *only* producer of
films – so it wasn't the good film-makers who got to make films, but the ones
who had the best contacts within the government. What Alejandro and I are
both critical of is the friends-in-high-places scenario. I also take exception to
those directors who said 'I am going to make this movie and I don't care if
anyone goes to see it or not.' With the cost of one film you could build a
number of schools. So I think that the film-maker does have a certain
amount of responsibility. Personally, I want my work to be seen as widely as
possible – England, France, Vietnam – not just Mexico. This doesn't mean
that you have to be purely commercially minded and make endless
concessions.

Alejandro had been very successful at everything he'd done, and was
already very well known within Mexico. I also had been published. So the
moment that we went out into the market AltaVista films and Martha Sosa
were very keen. I want the input of Martha Sosa to be fully recognized
because she was the one that pushed this film to be made.

The only problem we had was with audiences and the commercial potential of the project because, as other producers were quick to tell us, Mexican
audiences were largely used to broad romantic comedies, not a brutal,
urban film involving dog-fighting. Martha was not concerned only with the

commercial potential of the film, she was determined to make it whether it was commercial or not.

MARTHA SOSA: I had admired Guillermo and Alejandro for a long time – Guillermo, incidentally, was also one of my professors in Communications Theory at university. During my years as a journalist I hosted a radio show dedicated to cinema – and not just Mexican cinema, because there wasn't enough of that. But I wanted to introduce to the new audiences what newer Mexican cinema was about, because there was such a prejudice at the time, the common consensus being, 'If it's a Mexican film then it must be really bad.' I started inviting directors on to the show to talk about their work, mainly younger directors who were just starting out and who had perhaps made only shorts. But I interviewed Alejandro when he made *Behind the Money*. And that show would be the only filmed piece I had on which to sell Alejandro to investors. I didn't show investors his commercials, because everybody knew that they were very good but also very expensive . . .

I felt I could bring interesting and positive aspects to the project, starting with convincing investors to become involved. But also I'm the kind of producer who does get involved on a very personal level. And that's what happened with Guillermo and Alejandro – I knew immediately on reading the script that there was something very powerful dragging me into it.

I wasn't sure at that moment exactly what needed to be done to it, but I did recognize that it wasn't quite the finished article. It was certainly too long, and it also had some elements that were in their minds but hadn't translated so well to the page. For example, in the original script it wasn't clear to whom the dog Cofi belonged.

I had to also work out the dynamics of the relationship between Alejandro and Guillermo, because I hadn't seen a writer–director association like it before. They were very close and yet polar opposites. Because of this I was aware that there would be no room for a threesome, and that if I was going to work with them I would have to accept that I would be slightly on the outside. I can only describe the experience as being a little like working with two directors.

Francisco was initially a little apprehensive about my passion for the project, because he's much more practical than I am, and carried a huge responsibility at AltaVista in terms of the finances of the company. Both Francisco and I were quite young in relation to the amount of responsibility we had to assume on *Amores Perros* and I think Alejandro and Guillermo recognized this and were tolerant of it. Equally, Francisco and I were very tolerant of Alejandro and Guillermo through the creative process.

Alejandro Soberón read Guillermo's script and, despite being blown away by it, was also concerned that it was too long. At the very beginning we decided that we were going to have to cut it and also made it clear that we were not going to start shooting until we were sure that we were not going to be shooting copious amounts of material that would be surplus to the finished picture. We couldn't take this risk.

FRANCISCO GONZÁLEZ COMPEÁN: The first draft of Guillermo Arriaga's script was 148 or so pages long. We read the script and we loved it and so we started to work on it with Guillermo and Alejandro González Iñárritu and this was quite a long process. We were very respectful of the talent and this was essential to us because one of our company mission statements was to work with only the best talent possible.

Alejandro Soberón was a little bit doubtful, but we had sold Alejandro to our money people on the strength of his background as a DJ and commercials director, convincing them of his huge ability to connect with people. We were convinced that we should do this film but it was a risk because it was an expensive film; the initial budget started at $1.4 million and it escalated from there. Anyway, I gave Alejandro Soberón a copy of the script to read one night and the next morning he told me that he had gone to sleep at 4 a.m. because he had not been able to stop reading it. He loved it and was adamant that we make it. In this, Alejandro González Iñárritu was quite lucky.

I would be dishonest if I said that the financial department was not worried all the way through the project but they were very supportive of the story and of Alejandro.

MARTHA SOSA: The structure was the one of the things that was really thrilling for us at AltaVista. I got it and I love William Faulkner, one of Arriaga's primary influences.

The main thing, however, at least for me, were the characters – and this came from listening to how Alejandro spoke so passionately about each one. Alejandro really wears his heart on his sleeve and so listening to him describe the characters was a beautiful experience. It was also important that Alejandro was a DJ and so used to speaking to people and making his thoughts and passions very clear. He is very convincing.

Of course, Alejandro's ambition was to establish himself as a director. Francisco's and my main responsibility was to the budget because we knew that Alejandro was difficult to handle in this regard and we didn't want to have any problems with him or with the investors. The investors had made it very clear that we could not go a single peso over $2 million. For a Mexican film this was a lot of money. Prior to *Amores Perros* the traditional budget of a Mexican film was between \$1.2 and \$1.5 million so this was quite a leap and a gigantic risk for AltaVista. Remember, after *Todo el poder* this was only the second film AltaVista had produced and *Todo el poder* was a very different film to *Amores Perros*. As a company AltaVista was also still very much an un-established outsider. Everybody was like: 'So they're going to start making films without knowing a thing about it?'

Francisco and I made it very clear to Alejandro and Guillermo that we felt that we could learn from them and slowly gained their confidence. It was not easy and initially they did give us quite a hard time. Remember, for the project of their lives, Alejandro and Guillermo were also taking a risk and expressing a mutual trust in believing in producers who were not as experienced as some in Mexico.

FRANCISCO GONZÁLEZ COMPEÁN: Alejandro was an outsider who came from commercials and AltaVista were also outsiders and this appalled some people. When we started doing films there was a lot of jealousy because one of our financial partners previously funded other films and other production companies, and so we were seen as cutting off a potential financial source.

ALEJANDRO GONZÁLEZ IÑÁRRITU: There was some resentment, yes, and I think that sadly this a basic emotion of human nature. It is a very destructive and terrible feeling. However, I think that there was more of a feeling of surprise because, as well as coming from the wrong side of the tracks, I also lacked academic credentials. People thought, 'Who does this guy think he is? He comes from the world of commercials? Oh my god! Let's put a cross on him!' I was breaking the rules and *Amores Perros* raised a lot of questions about the system. But a lot of institutions and ways of thinking were shaken, and that was a very positive after-effect of the film.

*   *   *

FRANCISCO GONZÁLEZ COMPEÁN: Alejandro always wanted to cast Gael García Bernal as Octavio. I had seen him in Antonio Urrutia's Academy Award-nominated short film *De tripas, corazón*, and I knew that this guy glowed like a star and should be in movies.

ALEJANDRO GONZÁLEZ IÑÁRRITU: I knew that he was the one for the part. I had worked with Gael a couple of years ago on a commercial and I have nothing but praise for him. So one of the first and most crucial decisions that a director makes in a film was to my advantage because of that. Gael didn't have any feature-film experience, but he was studying theatre in London and had acted in some TV soap operas when he was a child, because he's the son of two talented actors.[1]

GAEL GARCÍA BERNAL: Acting was the obvious pathway for me. When I was very little I used to think that I was meant to be an actor, so my parents must be actors. Of course, it's the other way around . . . But it does feel as if I was born into this, in a way. I started acting in plays when I was ten or eleven, with the knowledge that it was what I wanted to do. And I acted in plays and plays and plays . . . But films seemed a very faraway destination, just because of the lack of films being made in Mexico. Also, film-making is a very special club, in Mexico and in any country, and a very difficult club to gain entry to. As theatre actors, my parents weren't members of that club.

Then I did *El Abuelo y yo* (1992), my first – and last – soap opera. But it was great fun and a good way to start: I made lots of friends, some very good actors that I still work with. It was after seeing this that Antonio Urrutia called me up to work in *De tripas, corazón* in Guadalajara – where he and I are both from, and it was a film about a town near Guadalajara, so we knew exactly what we were talking about. It was incredible to be able to work in film, and from that moment on I knew it was what I wanted to do. But there

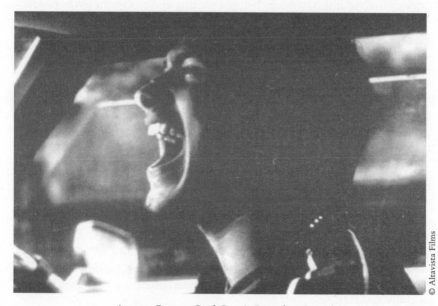

© Altavista Films

Amores Perros: Gael García Bernal as Octavio

[1] Patricia Bernal and José Ángel García.

still wasn't any real film industry to speak of, so I still thought that I would work in theatre and that would be it. It wasn't until *Amores Perros* came along that I started to see that there were some great opportunities.

When I first got the script I read it so quickly. The intensity that you see in the film right from the very beginning was also there in the writing. I was totally mesmerized by it and shocked by the pace of it. And it was well written and extremely moving and I just savoured each page. At that point I'd read maybe four film scripts – now I receive about a hundred a day; most of which are terrible. But *Amores Perros* had a magic that I can only compare to when you are a little kid and you go to watch a movie in a cinema and it feels like a really big deal. And I knew I wanted to be involved.

Alejandro has a talent for telling stories and when he tells something he really seduces you into it. You trust him instantly and there is no question of whether or not he will be able to pull it off. I cannot really nail it in words – but there is something about him that inspires confidence.

I loved the fact that there were so many ambiguities to Octavio, but this was also one of the scariest aspects, the fact that there was so much complexity. I remember initially feeling overwhelmed with all the possibilities of the character and feared that I would not be able to capture the different tones. I arrived just two weeks before shooting and so came into the production very cold and on the outside. Vanessa Bauche [Susana] and Marco Pérez [Ramiro] had already been rehearsing together for months. Vanessa, Marco and indeed Alejandro were incredibly supportive of me. It was this support and understanding that helped me understand the complexities.

ALEJANDRO GONZÁLEZ IÑÁRRITU: I was initially worried, because when we first started rehearsing Gael didn't seem to have much idea about who his character was. I remember that when he arrived on location he asked me if I thought that his character would play tennis in the afternoons and I remember saying, 'What are you thinking? This guy is from the lower class!'

Gael was a little lost because we had been communicating mainly by telephone and because of school commitments he arrived on location later than many of the other actors. I was worried. But then, he went out for one or two nights with a few guys and then he got it just like that. He began to talk with the right kind of slightly vulgar accent and underwent something of a surprise and almost instant metamorphosis. He was and is a natural and I was fascinated since the first day by the supernatural relation between him and the camera.

GAEL GARCÍA BERNAL: I went to those places and did a lot of fieldwork. But what was pivotal and cathartic in terms of my grasping the character was working with dogs. I trained with guard dogs and also with ex-fighting dogs and, man, at times I was shitting myself. What you see in the film is us grabbing the dogs by the cheeks to stop them fighting with the other dogs and this really was all we had as a means of controlling them. In some scenes they were muzzled, but not all and I can tell you that the dogs would go absolutely mad. It was shooting these scenes that I gained an understanding as to why such contests as dog-fighting and even bull-fighting exist. This is not to say that I agree or disagree with them, but these experiences taught me that these situations are not human control against beast, it is beast against beast and the power of instinct. You lose it in there for a nanosecond and you are gone. This served as a really strong metaphor for me to do the film and to get the character. It had to be instinctive otherwise it would explode and become a horrendous melodrama. It was pivotal to get this edge, to capture the essence of the fact that the choices this character makes may decide whether or not he lives.

* * *

ALEJANDRO GONZÁLEZ IÑÁRRITU: With regards to the visual style of *Amores Perros*, it was something that I was experimenting with long before the movie through some exercises that I did in my commercials. Rodrigo Prieto, Brigitte Broch and Martín Hernández have been working with me as a team and developing different explorations together for several years, so we understand each other almost telepathically. They know exactly what I like or don't like and what I'm interested in.

RODRIGO PRIETO *cinematographer*: I first met Alejandro when he was directing commercials. I got a call to go into his office to show him my demo reel. He liked it and we began to work together on television commercials. We developed a very good working relationship and also a very good friendship. I loved his way of working, his intensity and really thought that his visual sense was just incredible. I remember one day telling him that I wanted to be considered when he made his first feature film.

While he was finishing working on the script for *Amores Perros* he sent me a copy and I was completely shocked. After all the stylish commercials we had shot, I wasn't expecting a script that was so hard and dramatic. My first reaction was: 'Man, are people going to like this?' But Alejandro is known for that. He always takes these huge risks, which I guess is the secret of his success. To be honest, whatever the script had been, with Alejandro directing I would have done it. Again, Alejandro had his own preconception about me. He thought that I was only into beautiful images and that I wouldn't want to do something as gritty as *Amores Perros*. In fact, I was precisely ready for it; it was *exactly* what I wanted to do.

MARTHA SOSA: Alejandro and Rodrigo Prieto can read each other's minds and trust each other completely. Alejandro is a great talker whereas Rodrigo is much quieter because he always knows exactly what Alejandro is thinking. Anyway, the first day Rodrigo met with Alejandro after having read the script and before they had even begun to discuss their ideas of what the film should look like, they both appeared at the meeting with a Nan Goldin book. Without knowing it, they both were thinking along exactly the same lines. In fact Brigitte Broch, the production designer, made up a book with photographs by Nan Goldin plus some photographs taken during the location scouting by her and Alejandro.

BRIGITTE BROCH *production designer*: I had worked with Alejandro for years off and on doing commercials, so we knew each other quite well. However, doing the movie with him and Rodrigo Prieto opened up a world for me that I did not know: the way a team can work, the way three passions can converge and create together with each of us putting a new idea into the cooking pot that eventually stewed up the raw look of the film.

Nan Goldin's photography was a suggestion from Alejandro and Rodrigo and I totally fell for her work. In addition I used photo references from Mexican photographers, including Pablo Ortiz Monasterio who had edited *La ultima ciudad*. There was a lot of field research, where Alejandro personally participated. In front of Chivo's location we found a makeshift hut of an old man who went out with his cart to collect trash. We ended up using his backyard for the burning of the dogs. That is how close we were to our characters' realities. None of us was afraid of getting too close to these worlds that seem so shocking, even though once we were assaulted by a gang of kids with real pistols sticking in our faces. We just lived in the movie. I must say, it is a rewarding feeling to be able to share passion on a project – it is a bonding for life.

Mexico City is a melting pot and all extremes inhabit it. We just presented what we personally lived and researched. I am sure that being a foreigner, even after thirty-five years of living in this country, helps me to always have a fresh and astounding view on situations, people, details, colours and smells And yes, I exploit this.

RODRIGO PRIETO: We used other movies in terms of the visual look that we wanted, I remember that we were particularly blown away by Wong Kar-Wai's *Happy Together*.

ALEJANDRO GONZÁLEZ IÑÁRRITU: Rodrigo and I made a commercial together for a bank in which we really explored the potentials of the hand-held camera and the bleach-bypass process. We love this commercial. The bleach-bypass really captured the light of Mexico City, especially given that we shot the commercial on a very grey and overcast day. Commercials for me were always exercises, a way of exploring methods and approaches that I could use in a feature film later.

The bleach-bypass process I find has a spiritual quality that I relate to and really love.

RODRIGO PRIETO: I was looking to have a different texture to each one of the stories, so when we were doing our testing I played around with every procedure you can imagine – bleach-bypass, cross-process, dirty-dupe printing. In the end we decided not to be so obvious in the difference. I particularly wanted to do El Chivo's story in cross-process and maybe do Valeria's story in a more normal style and use bleach-bypass for Octavio. Alejandro felt that it would look like three different movies and I think that he was right. We decided to go for the whole movie with the bleach-bypass, as we liked the way that the intense colours reproduced a little bit less intense but still kept their basic intensity. We also liked the contrasts and the way that the skin tones became a little bit more bleached. We also liked the way that the grain was enhanced. So, we decided to separate the stories in more subtle ways, with lens choice, camera movement and style. I think that the way we shot each story in terms of the choice of lenses represented the greatest difference.

What happens in bleach-bypass is that when the negative is developed, one of the last steps that it goes through is bleaching to clean the excess silver off the film. Then you fix it and you have your negative. In this case we skipped that bleaching process so that the negative retains the excess silver. This is what creates the contrast and grain enhancement. The silver highlight element is retained. It is not that you are ruining the negative itself, though I do remember that this was a major concern of the studio behind *Amores Perros*. They were very concerned because at that time the process was relatively experimental and Kodak wouldn't guarantee that the negative would sustain the process. When we were preparing to do it I had to call all sorts of people who were doing it at the time to make sure that we weren't going to ruin the negative. I think David O. Russell's *Three Kings* was one such production. Alejandro, again being a risk-taker, always thought that we should go for it and that the risk element would be worth it.

*　*　*

ALEJANDRO GONZÁLEZ IÑÁRRITU: The second segment was difficult to shoot, mainly because it took us into other genres apart from drama. I mean, it has moments of comedy and also of surreal farce. The whole thing seems absurd, even when it was a real story that happened to a friend of mine when we were eleven years old. In the real story, things were worse, because the apartment began to smell terrible and the puppy was dead. To tell you the truth, this segment was in its entirety one hour and fifty-eight minutes, and as a stand-alone piece worked perfectly. However, as part of the whole it jarred.

RODRIGO PRIETO: Logistically the shoot was often a nightmare. For example, for the car-crash scene we had to close off a street for three consecutive Sundays. It was also very tricky because we didn't have the budget to do the accident twice; we just had one take with nine cameras. On the day that we were preparing for it, it started to rain and the road became very slippery. During one of the rehearsals the car actually struck another car when we weren't shooting. We had to repair the car, all the while very aware that the light was fading. We also had a man who refused to move his taxi out of the street and just left it there. Of course, when the crash happened, one of the cars just went straight into the taxi.

ALEJANDRO GONZÁLEZ IÑÁRRITU: It was very hard. I had to shoot the car chase in just one day, and the car crash in half of a day. We were pulling the car using electric power and the people were furious in the streets. The police were there to help, but were not really helping us. The day we shot the crash we had nine cameras and the sun was beginning to go down and the whole situation was becoming very dangerous. The video assist projecting the nine cameras was off because of a technical problem. Rodrigo Prieto and I were running from one angle to another like crazy. That same day in the morning we shot the scene of the bank robbery and we were exhausted. The car that was hit travelled a hundred metres without control and people were desperate to see what was happening despite our pleas for them to stay clear and keep out of the way. The car was travelling at a hundred kilometres per hour and ended up accidentally hitting a taxi that was parked near by and nearly killing a hundred people that were two metres from that taxi without security. It was insane. I will never forget the sound of that crash and the braveness of Emilio Echevarría ('the goat') who knew the danger he was running being in front of that car where nobody knew exactly what would happen after the other car hit it at forty miles per hour. You would never see this kind of car crash on film in the United States. The shot and the whole set-up were very risky which also makes it feel so real.

RODRIGO PRIETO: The sequence where Octavio has Cofi bleeding on his back seat was very uncomfortable, particularly as I was crouched right next to a dog that was asleep and covered in blood. It was very sticky and extremely hot. It may not look like it but I had a lot of lighting in there to bring the levels up and to ensure that we could still see outside of the car and still see the other car following. Also, to be able to see the black dog with the bleach-bypass process I had to really pump a lot of light into the car. I was there sweating with a camera covered in blood and myself getting very smelly.

ALEJANDRO GONZÁLEZ IÑÁRRITU: People say that *Amores Perros* is very stylish but I do not think that this is true. You and I and every human being see the world in hand-held. In other words, we look and move our heads. My head and eyes have never been mounted on a crane, a dolly or a tripod. Those things are stylish and unnatural to our relationship with the world. The approach is both more intimate and more real.

RODRIGO PRIETO: Absolutely all of the film is shot hand-held. Even when El Chivo calls his daughter and leaves a message on her answerphone. I was inside a closet with the camera on my knee and I was looking through the finder. It was very difficult to operate. The camera is static, but it breathes. This was our philosophy behind a lot of the movie because there are other static shots where the camera is either on my shoulder or on my knee. There are certain shots where we placed the camera on a sandbag but we always wanted it to be slightly moving, as if it were breathing. We wanted to give a sense of witnessing things.

That particular scene with El Chivo I couldn't stop crying myself because I have two daughters and it was very emotional. He was talking about leaving his daughter and with my line of work I am often away from home for long periods and feel so much guilt for being away and seemingly abandoning my family. At this moment it really got to me and I was even starting to fog up the viewfinder. I could hardly keep myself from sobbing.

The same thing happened to me on *21 Grams* – twice in fact. Alejandro has this capacity and really does go straight to the heart.

There are several moments that stay in mind as very characteristic of *Amores Perros*. One is the scene where Octavio and Susana are talking and she confesses that she is pregnant again, and Octavio offers to run away with her. There is a close up of Gael that when we were filming Gael went way past the mark where he was expected to go and came so close to the camera that it went out of focus. As he passed the camera I panned to follow him. Technically the scene is wrong – in the movie you can actually see a stand from some equipment – but emotionally it is so charged. I love this shot and never for one moment did I dare say, 'We have to do this again.' The fact that it went out of focus because he went out of focus and caught us off guard gives it more power. It is exciting for me to see things happen that I didn't expect and then just let them be.

I try more and more to allow the actors to do their thing. I try not to put very specific marks on the floor and give them exact directions. I prefer it when a movie has more emotional impact; the photography is often better as well, even if sometimes it may have technical defects. I have obviously worked on movies where everything is compositionally exact and I hate it when people say to me, 'You know, the movie wasn't very good but the photography is great.' My reaction is that if that's the case then it wasn't worth it. I don't care to do beautiful photography on bad movies.

It was very scary being in a little arena amongst these dogs operating a hand-held camera. There were trainers, who were out of shot of course, and apart from the Rottweilers the other dogs, I was told, would attack only other dogs and not a human. However, I still decided to wear a security blanket. It was frightening but I think that the danger in the finished film comes across as a result of the sound and the editing. The dogs were muzzled so that they could not open their mouths when they were actually fighting but of course in the film there are all these shots of the dogs barking and baring their teeth. There is a kind of montage mêlée of this barking that goes on for something like fifteen frames that is very disquieting. We did go to actual dogfights on scouting missions to get a sense of the atmosphere and the ambience and I can tell you that it was upsetting and really horrible. The fights are slow and take a long time but the dogs are not allowed to kill each other. The fight ends when one dog gives up.

*　　*　　*

ALEJANDRO GONZÁLEZ IÑÁRRITU: The film changed a lot in post-production because it had to. It was always changing. I believe that film is very much a living thing and should always be susceptible to even the subtlest of changes. If water doesn't run, it smells bad . . .

MARTHA SOSA: You are probably going to hear several versions about this because nobody can agree . . .

First of all, Francisco and myself were inexperienced producers, scared to death because we had gone over budget. Our investors had made a number of key stipulations, including that Alejandro stick to the script, that the film have a strong contemporary soundtrack – and that Alejandro remain on budget. Should he go over budget, the investors made it a point of contract that he would have to pay for it personally. They also insisted on retaining final cut, so, despite what you may hear to the contrary, Alejandro did not have final cut on *Amores Perros*. We happened to agree with almost all of the creative decisions that Alejandro and Guillermo made. It was after we went over budget that things started to get a little complicated, and I think that Alejandro felt that our belief in him was starting to waver. I couldn't make the investors change their mind, though I tried very hard, so as not to make Alejandro pay for the over-budget. It was too painful. It was like having my heart broken, because on the one hand I could see something really magical happening with the film he was making, but on the other hand I realized that when he was on Take 20 of a scene this could seriously affect the whole production and was outside of our agreement. I can't tell you how hard it was. I wanted to see what he was looking for, and often Take 20 was the best one. The thing about working with a genius is that there is a high price to pay, but it's also so unbelievable what he can achieve.

I think the film, perhaps out of a sense of growing insecurity, was then screened to too many people to get advice. Some of those willing to offer advice really cared for Alejandro and for his film, while others were simply envious and so apt to offer counsel that was destructive. It was at this time that Alejandro asked if he could edit the film in his home, because he hadn't seen his children for so long. I was so touched by this request, despite the fact that others saw it as his means of effectively kidnapping the film.

Guillermo del Toro then offered his assistance and expertise.

GUILLERMO DEL TORO *director*: I didn't know Alejandro back then but Alfonso Cuarón had told me that I should see *Amores Perros*. I saw it and called Alejandro to tell him that he had made a masterpiece but that it was twenty minutes too long . . .

ALEJANDRO GONZÁLEZ IÑÁRRITU: We began a series of intense telephone conversations, with him calling me every day at 7 a.m. He had a lot of very radical ideas, including taking out the majority of the second story, to which I replied, 'Fuck you, who do you think you are?' At this time del Toro was in Spain during the production of *The Devil's Backbone*. He flew to Mexico and knocked on my door. I opened it and he said, 'Hi, I'm Guillermo del Toro', and then he spent three days with me working on the film and sleeping on my floor. He also ate everything that he found in my house.

By that time, I had already spent seven months editing the film alone in my house and even when I was really happy and very, very close, I knew that I should cut it a little bit more but didn't know how. During this time we had a lot of discussions as, at the time, the film was almost two hours and forty minutes long. Guillermo really helped me to pare it down another seven minutes, and encouraged me and told me not to be afraid. I really appreciated this, as there are times when as the director you can begin to lose your perspective. Guillermo has the mind of a producer too, and I really believe in him. I don't always believe producers and always tend to produce my own things, but the fact that he is also a director meant that I was able to trust him. He and Carlos Bolado helped me at the end to reduce the fat that is so often simply left in films.

FRANCISCO GONZÁLEZ COMPEÁN: I remember thinking that the film needed cutting but Alejandro felt that he had reached a dead end with it so we did a test screening – something which was at the time rarely done in Mexico – and after seeing it with an audience Alejandro and Guillermo Arriaga emerged and admitted that it still needed cutting just a little more. When you are sitting with a hundred strangers watching your film you immediately know if it is too long. And Alejandro saw how the film played and naturally came to the conclusion that he needed to trim it a little more.

MARTHA SOSA: The most important thing to me was not the running time; it was the ending. In the script and in Alejandro's original ending, the film concludes on two gunshots heard outside El Chivo's house. I felt that this ending was very unfair and quite false, as it didn't reflect any possibility of hope. Also, the two corrupt brothers, the Cain and Abel of the story, are not main characters and, in their selfishness and willingness to kill each other, very difficult to care about. I felt that it was very important to finish on two of the main characters of the film, El Chivo and Cofi, the dog that had so dramatically changed the course of his life. I wasn't the one who was able to convince Alejandro to make the change, but I was one of those obsessed with the ending. Actually, I think that we have to thank Alejandro's wife Maria Eladia for the concluding glimpse of salvation, because she had a similar response to Alejandro's original conclusion and quietly suggested to Alejandro that perhaps he ought to at least contemplate other possibilities.

ALEJANDRO GONZÁLEZ IÑÁRRITU: Guillermo visited me during the shoot with his family for a week or so. Then he saw the final cut. Fortunately, even with some of the changes and scenes that I had to take out or move around, he froze for a couple of hours, but then he seemed to like it.

MARTHA SOSA: Cannes was very important because it gave us the opportunity to launch the film very successfully in Mexico. This may seem something of a paradox, but a very tough, two-and-a-half-hour film had to be

© Altavista Films

Amores Perros: Emilio Echevarría as political assassin El chivo

accompanied by something extraordinary, especially as we weren't in the Official Selection but the Critics' Week. So we created something extraordinary, spinning an aura around the film and its Cannes experience, to make it seem much bigger than it actually was. From a Mexican perspective we made it look as if we'd won the World Cup. You have to remember that at this time we were trying to grab new audiences and were asking people to give us the opportunity to show them that we could make good films that they could identify with and be proud of. We needed to create a lot of noise and you cannot do that with advertising alone.

We also had very good reflexes. Alejandro Soberón and Federico may not have had a long track record in terms of producing an international film such as *Amores Perros* but they knew that they had to profit from the moment. NuVisión, the Mexican distributor of the film and so the company responsible for deciding how much would be put into the film's prints and advertising campaign, just really didn't get it. On seeing *Amores Perros* before it screened in Cannes, NuVisión said that they felt that the film was well made but needed more cutting, especially the middle story. They also outlined their plans to release the film in Mexico on forty prints. As soon as I heard these comments I knew that we were going to have a very big fight. Fortunately, Alejandro Soberón and Federico knew that the distributor was wrong, and after winning the Critics' Week Grand Prize in Cannes were able to successfully argue against releasing the film in August, NuVisión's original plan, and insisted on it being released in June, as a big summer picture. Post Cannes, *Amores Perros* was released on over two hundred prints.[2] So, in terms of luck, strategy and prestige, Cannes was a very good moment.

I believe that the audiences, and especially the younger ones, were eager to see something different. I also believe that Alejandro has the ability to turn everything he touches into gold. I also consider him one of the best salesmen you will ever meet and the work that he did to publicize the film in terms of giving interviews and doing Q&As was phenomenal; even the media were seduced by this.

You have to remember that when Alejandro made the film he was already very successful. If you are a successful person in Mexico and you offer a portrayal of poor people and the way they live their life there will be a certain amount of resentment. What Alejandro did very intelligently point out was that he was not born rich; that his father worked hard for a living and that he grew up in a so-so neighbourhood. Alejandro has made no secret of the fact that he has climbed the social ladder but he did not begin at the top of it. Arriaga is the same. They were both forced to justify their right to offer these representations and talk about the poor and to their credit they did it.

What is important is that the film appeared in a very specific moment and we were lucky. We are good at marketing ... but not geniuses. At the moment the film appeared, every single young person in Mexico was thinking about the kind of changes they wanted to see in Mexico and the ways in which they could make a difference. Once *Amores Perros* was launched you could see two things very clearly throughout the city: the *Amores Perros* marketing campaign and Vicente Fox's political campaign.

FRANCISCO GONZÁLEZ COMPEÁN: Remember that Alejandro is a partner in a very important advertising agency, and so put his entire advertising infrastructure together with ours. We had a great team including Richard Ham

---

[2] Released on 215 prints on 16 August 2000 by NuVisión, a sister company of AltaVista, *Amores Perros* grossed approximately $8.8 million at the Mexican box office. This currently makes it the fourth-highest-grossing Mexican film in Mexico of all time.

who was the head of marketing for Fox Latin America and really put his all into *Amores Perros*. Alejandro was personally involved in making the trailers, which often led to very lively discussions but with teamwork we got there in the end.

It's important to note that the typical publicity and advertising budget for a film in Mexico was $50–$70,000 at most. With *Amores Perros* we spent $1.1 million. It's all about competing and getting the film out there and making sure that everybody knows about it. This is the aspect that I am very closely involved with.

MARTHA SOSA: I think that *Amores Perros* has become a very focal point of reference. I mean this in many ways, mainly in the quality of the film. It has also undeniably become a point of reference in the whole question of how a film is manufactured, marketed and then launched.

FRANCISCO GONZÁLEZ COMPEÁN: A lot of the research and thinking we conducted did address the question of how we could make our films fly outside of Mexico. There are two ways to do this. One is to give a false impression, as in *Como agua para chocolate* (1991). People saw that film and thought of Mexico as so romantic and so passionate and full of magical food and love. The other way to do it is to shock them, be different, play with the structure and be formally audacious. *Amores Perros* is completely daring, fresh and different and when people saw it they went, 'Wow!'

ALEJANDRO GONZÁLEZ IÑÁRRITU: I was completely surprised. That said, when I was editing the film during seven months in my house I knew I had something that had the capacity to touch the hearts of people and I knew that it captured life. But, I never imagined how people would react to it. I also was surprised by the reaction to the film outside of Mexico because at this time I had no idea of the bigger picture of cinema. I hadn't been to festivals and wasn't a cineaste; I was just a guy who happened to like films. I had no perception of the film within the world so it was overwhelming for me when *Amores Perros* took the place that it did within the cinema world.

MARTHA SOSA: One of the things I adore about living in Mexico City is the huge contrast. But it's hard and painful. *Amores Perros* certainly captures Mexico City as a place of contrast in a time of change but perhaps reflects only a belief as to what Mexico is like as opposed to depicting the reality of what it is like.

ALEJANDRO GONZÁLEZ IÑÁRRITU: It is a very Mexican film. I avoid showing the city and show very few landmarks. There is nothing that you can recognize from Mexico City and yet it captures the smell and essence of the city. Without pointing a political finger, the film is also through its characters and their situations a very political film and is inherently Mexican. I feel very proud of that. I travel everywhere and when people ask me where I am from and I say Mexico, without knowing that I am the director they say that they have seen *Amores Perros*, a film that for them crystallizes Mexico and three or four years after lives in their minds. It has become synonymous with Mexico. To me this is fucking unbelievable. I wanted to portray a fascinating and complex place without wishing to patronize, diminish or insult it. Unfortunately, there were some Mexican cultural ambassadors who felt that *Amores Perros* degraded Mexico throughout the world. This was the case with the Mexican cultural attaché in Japan who refused to screen my film even after I won Best Director and Best Film for the first time in the history of the Tokyo Film Festival. That's the classical Mexican political stupidity.

ÁNGELES CASTRO *Director,* CCC: I believe that maybe because of the overwhelming influence of American cinema, and because of the influence of the 'Golden Age' of Mexican cinema, it has become very difficult to look at ourselves now. It seems that if the films were not filled with Mexican cowboys or singers, then from the 1960s there were only isolated examples of films that seemed to work in terms of offering an authentic representation. *Amores Perros* reveals a reality, but it reveals only an urban reality. This reality is of course not the same across the whole country. The fact that *Amores Perros* was set in a city was, I believe, integral to its international success. Cities can be treated in a very universal way and urban themes and concerns can be very easily transmitted to other cultures.

GAEL GARCÍA BERNAL: I think Mexico City has never before been so alive on film before and that even just a single frame of that film says so much about society and social status and also about lives and loves and passions. It makes you embark on a journey. I am also moved by the energy and blunt uncompromising nature of the film. It speaks volumes about a film-maker doing what he wants and is also a very abrupt example of the value of teamwork in the film-making process.

I suppose that people react in a positive way to something that is good, especially when it is something from their own country and so a source from which they can take pride. What you must also consider besides the obvious quality of the film was that it was so refreshing to have a Mexican film that did not treat the Mexican audience like idiots. In Mexico we love to watch films and I personally really love to watch films but I don't need marketing gimmicks to tell me what is good and what is valuable. I myself and people in general in Mexico forged a real connection with this film. They became a part of it and came to feel almost as if they owned their own small piece of it.

Outside Mexico it is perhaps a little easier to explain. The success of the film at festivals was very important, as was the fact that it more or less came from nowhere, or rather from a place that for the previous few years had not had any kind of cinematic spark. It was highly recommended at festivals, Cannes especially, and I think that when people did see it after numerous recommendations they were pleasantly surprised.

I remember arriving in Cannes for the film. I hadn't at that point seen it and like many of us from the film who had made the trip, I didn't even have a hotel room. It was also for many of us our first film experience. The whole trip was crazy, going to parties and meeting people, but from the moment that the film won,[3] our lives changed. I mean of course the lives of those involved in the film but I also refer to those involved in the Mexican film industry.

GUILLERMO ARRIAGA: When they released *Amores Perros* in Mexico, Alejandro and I would often turn up unannounced at the theatres and ask the managers if we could go up and talk to the audiences afterwards. We would listen to the opinions of the audiences and they would all thank us for the film because they were sick of being fed stupid urban comedies. They appreciated the fact that they were able to see themselves on screen.

I think that *Amores Perros* taught film-makers and producers to take bigger risks and to show more respect for the audiences. I think that film-makers are no longer scared of touching on these more realistic themes. It is also a film that played well to audiences of all age and classes. Despite the prohibitive cost of going to the cinema in Mexico, almost everyone went to see it. People had a reconciliation with Mexican cinema. It is also a very contradictory film, it shows Mexico and Mexicans as ugly but sometimes we are and we are also tired of trying to live up to the fantasy of a soap-opera world.

BERTHA NAVARRO: González Iñárritu brought to the project a vast knowledge of film-making. It certainly doesn't look like a first film.

CARLOS CUARÓN *screenwriter/director*: The first time I saw *Amores Perros* I had to bow to Alejandro. I saw it in the editing stage and I thought, 'Wow, this is new!'

---

[3] At the 2000 Cannes Film Festival *Amores Perros* won the Critics' Week Grand Prize and was awarded the Young Critics' Award for Best Feature.

LEONARDO GARCÍA TSAO *critic/academic*: I think that what was perhaps most interesting about *Amores Perros* was that it was privately funded. Stylistically, yes, it took some risks but not too many. The Jorge Fons film *Midaq Alley* (1994) had a very similar structure. It starts with one action, the playing of dominoes, and then moves on to encounter different characters and narratives in that way. *Amores Perros* is certainly more indebted to this film than to *Pulp Fiction*, which everybody was so quick to compare it to. Arriaga, I think, really used *Midaq Alley* as a model in terms of structure.

Don't get me wrong, *Amores Perros* is extremely well done, and it is amazing that a first film can have such energy and drive. It creates a potent sense of atmosphere and is a really important film for capturing the characteristics of Mexico City at the turn of the century. It avoids stereotypes, and moves through many social classes, never marginalizing either the working or middle classes. I thought that it was also important to show the former guerrilla fighter who is now completely on the margins of society but, because of his daughter, is torn by the notion of trying to find his way back. That was very telling of the moment.

I think its success was a combination of the film appealing to a younger demographic; its visual panache and its ability to capture the Zeitgeist in terms of a general dissatisfaction with the social and political situation in Mexico. It certainly came out at the right moment and it had an unprecedented advertising campaign. I can think of few films before this that had such a huge advertising campaign. It was on every billboard and on the side of every bus. There was also heavy support from the media in general, specifically television and radio. It was impossible to miss it. Audiences in Mexico are very fickle and unpredictable. But it was a film that built huge expectations and somehow managed to fulfil them.

At the same time I know that, although it broke even, *Amores Perros* didn't turn a profit. They had spent so much that the box-office earnings barely covered it. It's a very high-risk game and the stakes are getting so high that it is becoming ridiculous.

Amores Perros *is the winner of over thirty international awards and is among the most decorated films in the history of Mexican cinema. Nominated in the best Foreign Film category at both the Golden Globes and the Academy Awards, the film won the Cannes Critics' Week prize; a* BAFTA *for Best Film not in the English Language and a New Directors Award at the Edinburgh International Film Festival. At the Ariels (the prestigious Mexican equivalent of the Academy Awards), the film triumphed in a brace*

of categories including Best Director, Best Actor (Gael García Bernal), Best
Cinematography and Best Editing. The film was also presented with the
Golden Ariel.

GUILLERMO DEL TORO: I think that audiences are incredibly hungry to see
themselves in movies that go beyond what they were previously used to, the
dumb comedies, the soaps and the like. They want to see themselves in that
car wreck in *Amores Perros*. For better or for worse there is a level of
excitement that Alejandro gives to his images, and a level of excitement
among audiences in saying, 'That's the street where I work!' or 'There's the
street where I live!' And there's certainly a level of excitement in recognizing
yourself in a genre situation. Beyond the social exploration of *Amores
Perros*, the foremost characteristic of that movie is the sheer level of adrena-
lin. It's a non-stop ride in your hometown that gives such a high. Why do all
the chases have to happen in Manhattan? Why do all the exciting things
have to happen in America? Why can we not have exciting things happen
here in Mexico?

ROSA BOSCH: There is a theory, and I'm not necessarily saying that I sub-
scribe to it, that the popularity boom experienced in the last ten years or so
of the soap opera or *telenovela* has rekindled in Mexico the appetite for local
stories. I think there is a young generation who want to see local stuff.

ALFREDO JOSKOWICZ: In art, you have no moral conclusions. If it works, it
gives you a strong emotion and that's it . . . It is very complicated; we are
very proud of the new democracy we have, but we still do not have a clear
national patriotic direction. Feelings are intricate, and the newer directors
and producers are looking to feed into this and give a stronger emotion.
There is also a new phenomenon in the arts generally, and especially I feel in
cinema, in that the author or the director now feels that they can really say
whatever it is that they want to say. They can do this even if they have
received financial assistance or help from the state. There is a feeling of
liberation.

ROSA BOSCH: I also think there's a certain element of backlash against
Hollywood. Mexico now has its own stars, and I'm thinking specifically here
of Gael and Diego. So why should Mexicans go and see only films with run-
of-the-mill American stars? There is also a sense of a renewed pride in our
national product. For many years, and this is also the case in Spain, local
films were considered inferior, they were perhaps not well made, certainly
cheaply made, and they didn't have any 'hip' factor. It certainly wasn't hip to

take your girlfriend on a Friday night to see a Mexican film. Now, this is exactly what you would do.

FRANCISCO GONZÁLEZ COMPEÁN: There have been a lot of repercussions from *Amores Perros*. It showed Mexican film-makers and producers that you could make a very strong, daring film, and still be successful at the box office. Another major repercussion was that it showed our Mexican directors working in the US that they could come back to Mexico and still make a challenging and successful personal project. I am, of course, directly referring to Alfonso Cuarón and *Y tu mamá también*; and indirectly to Guillermo del Toro and *The Devil's Backbone*. I'm not saying that Alfonso decided to do *Y tu mamá también* only after seeing *Amores Perros*. But it must have helped . . .

5

Y tu mamá también and *The Devil's Backbone*

In 2000 the Mexican political landscape changed once more, with repercussions in due course for the national cinema. For seventy years Mexican politics had been dominated by the Institutional Revolutionary Party (PRI), but the 1997 parliamentary elections saw the combined opposition win more support, thus breaking what was in effect a one-party system with a democratic façade. The 2000 presidential elections confirmed the development, as Vicente Fox of the National Action Party (PAN) beat the PRI candidate by more than 6 per cent of the vote.

Sensing Fox's impending victory and a potential for change, democracy and reform, Mexicans had been swept along on a euphoric wave of optimism. Fox assumed the presidency in December, following a high-profile and extensive media campaign aimed at attracting younger voters. He promised sweeping reforms, including better distribution of income in Mexico and an overhaul of state institutions.

Alfredo Joskowicz was appointed Director of the Mexican Film Institute (IMCINE) in December 2000, and immediately had to get to grips with administering a budget that included much coveted production funds.

ALFREDO JOSKOWICZ *film-maker/Director*, IMCINE: I took up my position in January 2001. It's very hard work. I'm fighting. But I think my background has been very important, because I understand all the difficulties of the sector.

IMCINE has two substantial areas: the direction of support towards production, and the promotion of Mexican cinema both in Mexico and throughout the world. Promotion is the significant area, and annually we have a national contest for aspiring and developing writers. We invite projects and make a selection of those to which we can give financial assistance for development. We also have a national contest for short films, and we are able to place the winners on the front of commercial features, so that they can play in theatres. It also makes the films easier to position at international festivals and we receive a lot of recognition and prizes for our shorts. We don't receive any extra subsidies for this, but our aim is to put into position and nurture new actors, writers, directors etc. With regard to feature films, we have two government funds. The first, FIDECINE received $7 million in 2000, around 70 million pesos. This money was received at the end of 2000 so was used towards features being made in 2001. At the end of 2001 another $7 million was made available, this will go to features being produced in 2002. With these FIDECINE funds we supported sixteen films in two years.

We have another older fund that was created in 1998 because in this year local feature production was very low. In 1997 Mexico produced only nine feature films, the lowest number since 1932 so the government was compelled to help; FOPROCINE was created to assist quality films. In the last five years, we have used FOPROCINE funds to assist forty-seven films in the last five years. The government put $13.5 million into FOPROCINE, a fund that was responsible for *Sexo, pudor y lágrimas* (1999), a film that attracted an audience of 5.3 million people. *El crimen del padre Amaro* (2002), another FOPROCINE-assisted film also achieved over 5 million viewers in Mexico and has gone on to be the most successful Mexican film in our history. Unfortunately, even with these successes the fund is not enough and the $13.5 million has not been recouped. The FOPROCINE fund comes to an end in 2003 so from 2004 FIDECINE is the only fund that will exist.

To be relatively proportionate you cannot give all of the money to one or two films so the FIDECINE rules dictate that you can give only a maximum of $700,000 per film or 49 per cent of the total budget. Private producers therefore have to provide 51 per cent of the budget. If we consider the fact that the average cost of a film in Mexico is now $1.5 million, then even with FIDECINE funding of $700,000, the private producer still has to raise $800,000, which is very difficult. People say that this is market forces but this doesn't take into account the distribution of the peso at the Mexican box office. Fifteen cents is tax. Fifty-one cents is for the exhibitor. Thirty-four cents goes to the distributor. From this the distributor will recoup the cost of prints and advertising. After recouping these costs the distributor gives to the producer thirteen cents and retains twenty-nine cents. The producer, the one who raises the finance for the film and takes all the risks, is right at the very end of the chain. This is a major problem and not only in Mexico but throughout Latin American countries. What the governments in other Latin American territories have done is instigate tax incentives and channelled money from television and video distribution back into cinema production. Argentina, for example, raised $25 million dollars last year in this way and can now produce fifty to sixty films annually. We must remember that they are doing this despite a period of severe economic depression. In Mexico we do not have such taxes for cinema.

JOSÉ LUIS GARCÍA AGRAZ *director*: A producer can't receive money from both funds; it's either one or the other. In this second fund there are fewer dignitaries and the committee comprises representatives of sectors such as distribution, the cinema owners and the trade unions – this committee is supposed to have a more 'commercial' vision.

The truth of the matter is that it's not enough, and that you do have to look for co-producers among the 'Anglospoken' – the US, the UK, Australia, Canada – among whom the hardest to find are the Americans . . .

* * *

CARLOS CUARÓN *writer/director*: In 1997 I started directing short films I had written,[1] and in 2000 I was going to make my first feature but the production collapsed. In hindsight I'm grateful, because I wasn't ready to direct it – the script wasn't ready; the producers weren't ready. And because of that, I sat down with Alfonso and wrote *Y tu mamá también*.

ALFONSO CUARÓN *director*: My son was in New York and we'd go to movies together all the time; sometimes I would choose the movie, and other times he would. And basically I had to see a lot of crap, and a lot of teen comedies. The problem with the teen comedies is that there's something really interesting at their core: they're so moralistic and they have a phoney and overly respectful sense of character. You don't have to make fun of the characters or invent clever plots to humiliate one or the other, or have them sticking their dicks into a pie. I was lucky, because when my son was ten I made *A Little Princess*, which, in a way, was a film for me; and then I wanted to do a teen movie for him because of course he ended up being a teen. This movie was *Y tu mamá* and in many ways I used my son as an adviser. Ultimately my son is very Mexican – even living in New York he's very Mexican and he sees that the fundamentals and the emotions between teens – most of his friends are American – are basically the same. The politics may be different but the human experience is ultimately the same, they are all insecure, they all want to bed women and they are all in love with the girl who loves the other guy.

Carlos and I had talked about the ideas of *Y tu mamá* even before *Sólo con tu pareja*. We were looking for a low-budget film to do before my first film. Lubezki suggested a road trip to the beach, and Carlos loved the idea of two

---

[1] Perhaps the best known of these, *Me la debes* (*You Owe Me*), is included on the UK DVD of *Y tu mamá también*.

boys and one girl. For various reasons we moved on into *Sólo con tu pareja*. But, every couple of years, Carlos and I would return to it before putting it back in the drawer. It was in this way that it evolved.

Directors are really perhaps only as good as the projects they choose. And choices can be dangerous, because you can lose sight of what you really want to do. What happened to me was that I was choosing so many projects that I forgot that I could write. And that was part of the beauty of *Y tu mamá*.

EMMANUEL LUBEZKI *cinematographer*: I remember when Alfonso and I were working on *Great Expectations* and we were both so fed up and having trouble finding the energy and enthusiasm to like our work any more. We both felt that *Y tu mamá también* was a way of reinventing ourselves.

GUILLERMO DEL TORO *director*: I think that a career is a learning curve. Alfonso and I have discussed this many times. I remember Alfonso being revered as a visionary when *A Little Princess* came out and maligned as a

© Focus Features

Y tu mamá también: Dirty Dancing – Diego Luna, Maribel Verdú,
Gael García Bernal

hack when *Great Expectations* emerged. I went through similar stuff with *Cronos* and *Mimic,* and I said to Alfonso, 'People seem to think that you are making a definitive last statement with every movie. It's not the case; you are searching, in the way that a painter may experiment with a blue period or a green period.

ALFONSO CUARÓN: I didn't do *Y tu mamá* to go 'back home'; I did the film in Mexico because I always wanted to make it. I never really intended to go to Hollywood, and I don't regard it as the Mecca of cinema. For many directors, Mexican or otherwise, it's a goal; for some others it is just part of a journey. For me, personally, it's the latter. I want to do films elsewhere and everywhere.

Some film-makers don't need to touch Hollywood. Guillermo del Toro is clear: when he does his Hollywood movies, he isn't pretending to do his smaller movies, and vice versa; they are two different approaches and two different beasts.

When I did *Y tu mamá* I did feel that I had perhaps started to lose some of my identity and that I needed to reconnect with my roots – not bullshit nationalistic roots but creative roots. I wanted to make the film I was going to make before I went to film school, and that was always going to be a film in Spanish, and a road movie involving a journey to the beach. All the rest, Mexico versus the big Hollywood giants, is ideology. I have very eclectic tastes in terms of film, and I want to explore these.

Great Expectations, if it was successful or not is not for me to say, but it's obviously a completely different film to *Y tu mamá*; it has an entirely different point of view. The same with *A Little Princess* – I was following the point of view of the main character. Our approach, mine and Lubezki's, on these films was not to see the world the way it is, but the way it is perceived by the protagonists – to give a heightened reality, almost. On *Y tu mamá* we wanted to do the opposite: an objective approach to our reality, just to keep our distance and observe things happening.

Carlos and I didn't find a way into the film until around 2000, when we decided that the context was as important as character and that we wanted a very objective and in some ways *distant* approach to the story. We didn't want to take a nostalgic approach.

Abandoned by their girlfriends for the summer, the well-heeled Tenoch (Diego Luna) and barrio boy Julio (Gael García Bernal) meet beautiful, thirtyish Luisa (Maribel Verdú) at a wedding. Luisa's marriage to Tenoch's cousin is in bad shape. The teenagers seek to impress her by boasting that

97

they are about to embark on a road trip to an idyllic but barely known beach called Boca del Cielo ('Heaven's Mouth'). They are surprised when Luisa asks if she can accompany them, and soon the unlikely trio are headed out of Mexico City. The journey (widely seen as an allegory as well as a literal excursion) brings sexual gratification and rivalry for the boys and a lesson in Mexico's geography, as well as its socio-economic context, for the viewer.

CARLOS CUARÓN: We were kind of blocked in the writing and got ourselves stuck with a narrator. He doesn't actually narrate that much; rather, he contextualizes. And we decided that context – in this case, Mexico, as a country – was character. When we discovered this early structuring, we decided that it was a parallel trip. The woman's journey is also important, because she too is finding her own identity, perhaps in a much more Spanish way. But, yeah, the two guys are searching for an identity. And I still feel that Mexico is still a teenage society. The difference, I believe, is that the society is much more mature than the government. We are sixteen, seventeen, and pimply and in the middle of the teenage years. And my feeling is that the government is about thirteen and just starting with the hormonal thing . . .

EMMANUEL LUBEZKI: It couldn't be just a coming-of-age story and nothing else. The context is so important, and it's actually a very complex movie told in quite a simple way – that's what really blew me away. A friend of us who lived with us in Mexico when we were growing up but then moved back to Uruguay wrote to me to say that the film really helped him understand who we were, and how sex was so important to us that, despite our leftist sympathies, it blinded us to the situations that were going on around us. Sadly, Mexico is now such a complex country that if you and a girl were to head to the interstate in a car the chances are that you would be robbed and raped.

ALFONSO CUARÓN: The story wasn't autobiographical, but there are elements from when Carlos and I were growing up. The nanny in the film is played by our nanny in real life, and one of the destinations the trio go through is her town in real life; Carlos and I went to a wedding in the same place where you see the wedding in the film, and the President of the time was present and everybody was more interested in the President than the newlyweds. We also had a car like the one in the film and there is a town the trio visit that is also the name of the street where we grew up. The character of Diego 'Saba' Madero, the friend of Julio and Tenoch, is a character that we know. Of course, we both also had trips to the beach and the incident with the pigs in the tent happened to my cinematographer, Emmanuel Lubezki. There's lots of incidental stuff like that. I think that both Carlos and I are in between

Julio and Tenoch – leaning more towards Julio, I guess, socially speaking. What we really wanted to do was convey a universe and an atmosphere that we really knew first hand.

CARLOS CUARÓN: It was mainly drawn upon our energy as teenagers and the adolescence I had. It's not autobiographical, except for the scene where Diego questions Gael about how he fucked his girlfriend in the hotel. This actually happened to me when I was playing for a football team, and it involved someone who was then a very close friend. It wasn't difficult for me to write this scene, because I already had the dialogue. There are specific things that only very close people would know. For example, our family had a car with the same name as that in the film,[2] and our mother in Mexico City lives in a street after which we named a town in the film.

EMMANUEL LUBEZKI: I was so happy when I read it – because it was so close to us and to our lives. It was a story that we had talked about for many years, mainly while getting drunk in bars while eulogizing our love of road movies. We would talk about this crazy idea of a road movie with two guys and a girl. To then suddenly see all this stuff written down by Alfonso and his brother Carlos was amazing. The film offered portraits of people that we know and captured them so well. I immediately told them that I had to shoot the movie.

GAEL GARCÍA BERNAL *actor*: I think that this film has a real edge to it and also a lot of depth. I also have to say that I think it's the best script I've ever read. I was laughing from the first paragraph, and really enjoying it so much. The characters and the situations were so alive but also full of subtleties. The depth of the film is perhaps surprising, because it really comes from a very clichéd story. I mean, two guys taking a road trip with a woman – how B-movie is that? It's *Porky's* meets *Dude, Where's my Car?* But Y *tu mamá* had a genuine reason to exist and a connection to real kids who were experiencing the loss of innocence.

EMMANUEL LUBEZKI: It was also important, and perhaps not unconnected, that the film was independently financed. One of the reasons that film was slow to evolve in Mexico was that the directors had to wait for the government to fund them. I have to say that through a combination of luck, charm – he is the most charming – and judgement, he met Jorge Vergara. Now Jorge is hooked on movies. I had dinner with him last week and he told me

---

[2] The car is called Betsabé. In the booklet that accompanies the aforementioned DVD there is a whole chapter devoted to the car and its history.

Y tu mamá también: Alfonso Cuarón (far right) huddles with his actors

he was fucked. I asked him why and he said, 'Because I love making movies so much.'

ALFONSO CUARÓN: In Julio's room there's a poster for *Harold and Maude* (1971). I wanted to put Godard's *Masculin-Féminin* (1966) in because that was the only conscious reference Carlos and I had when writing the script. But it's probably for the best that the poster didn't arrive. Character-wise *Harold and Maude* probably has more to do with my film in terms of the relationship between male and female. It's also a beautiful film.

CARLOS CUARÓN: Alfonso and I wanted to make a very realistic movie that would be like a candid camera. Chilango, generically speaking, is what we use in Mexico City. It's the language that all Chilangos and all Mexicans would understand. What we did, and what is original, is that we used hard-core Chilango, and you rarely see this in movies. You see it more maybe now as it's become slightly standardized. In *Amores Perros* they also speak Chilango but it's not hardcore Chilango. We were the first to do it with that freedom, that freshness if you will, and it played very well.

EMMANUEL LUBEZKI: I love the fact that the style that we found to shoot in really suited the movie. When we started work, we weren't cutting and we were shooting without covering, which is quite a risky thing to do. I remember Alejandro González Iñárritu coming to the set and telling us that we were insane, that we were ruining the rhythm of our movie because we didn't have anywhere to go. Because he's our friend and because we rate his work, we panicked – for one night. Then we watched what we had shot, and decided it was still the way that we were going to do it. And I really think that this was the best way to tell the story.

The entire movie is shot hand-held. This all goes back to our original idea of fifteen years ago, in which we would do a low-budget road movie that would allow us to go with some young actors and semi-improvise scenes and have a bare storyline but not be afraid of adding things as we went. We also wanted to work with a lot less equipment, because we felt that the last two movies we had done together in Hollywood before this one had both had a little bit too much. Everything was so slow because everyone was trying to make their work the best possible and everything was so expensive and there was a crew of something like a hundred and thirty people and this can really rob the project of momentum. This also robs you of the liberty to experiment. By consciously making *Y tu mamá* smaller and by working in *a cappella* fashion we could move faster and really let the actors go.

In its entirety it is the movie that I am most proud of, full-stop. I see other movies that I have shot and I often like moments from them but I have never liked a whole movie, except for this one. I love the story, I love the actors and I love the surroundings.

Gael García Bernal and Diego Luna acted together in El Abuelo y yo *and indeed were friends since early childhood.*

GAEL GARCÍA BERNAL: It almost seemed as if we had spent twenty years in rehearsal for the film . . . Diego and I were twenty when we were doing the film, playing characters who were supposed to be sixteen, so it was fun to make fun of that, but it also contributed to the evolution of our friendship. We became partners in crime, but in a much more serious way. It was great to work with Diego again. I grew up with him and, to use a football metaphor, we played very well together – because when one of us was about to pass the ball, the other instinctively knew where it was going. We were also able to share in each other's goals. Isn't football wonderful to use as a metaphor?

Making the film was incredible, one of the happiest experiences I have had. I would reduce it all to the seven-minute take at the end of the film when the characters are drunkenly talking and dancing in the bar.

Visions of Light: Emmanuel Lubezki at work on Y *tu mamá también*

Everything was really precise and synchronized, all the crew having at least six tasks to perform, and yet through teamwork and spirit it all came together perfectly. I also think that this scene reveals Alfonso's true qualities as a director. He would arrive at the location and talk through with the actors and block the scene and then think about where to put the camera. It is the good directors who do this. They work around the story, the actors and the life of the film.

I have many favourite scenes. I love the scenes where Tenoch and Julio fight, and I also love all the car scenes where they are talking.

It would have been much easier if the guy I had to kiss weren't my best friend in real life! That was like jumping into cold water. But you just have to go for it. And in terms of my career it was very liberating, because after that I was no longer able to be pigeon-holed. I was able to do what I wanted.

There were obviously instances of men who completely disagreed with it. It must have touched a very raw nerve inside them. On the other hand, the majority really went for it and understood it. I was at screenings where people were clapping. This is another aspect of the *Y tu mamá* experience that I really savoured, seeing how deeply involved people became when watching it. I'm also not specifically referring to Mexico but also abroad, and especially in England where people also shouted and clapped. People became very passionate about it. Which is surprising.

Released in Mexico by Fox, Y tu mamá también *grossed over $9.5 million dollars. In the UK, where it was released by Icon, the film took £1.6 million, and in the US, with* IFC *as its distributor, $13.6 million. The box-office performance was equally impressive throughout Europe and other key territories.*

CARLOS CUARÓN: I was surprised by the success. We have a huge young population in Mexico, and we knew it, but we weren't pre-determined about it. We made the movie we wanted and didn't give a fuck about marketing or how to sell it.

I have my own thermometer when writing, and with this specific script I was laughing a lot, even though it's not a comedy. I had a feeling it was going to work, but perhaps not as well as it did. In the first place, with these things, you can never tell. In the second place, when I work, whether it's with Alfonso or whoever else, I'm not thinking in terms of box office or festivals and awards. I just want to do my thing.

ALFONSO CUARÓN: The film, ultimately, is about themes that are very

Cooling off: Gael García Bernal and Diego Luna in Y *tu mamá también*

Y *tu mamá también*: Gael García Bernal

universal. It's about the experience of searching for identity: and that breaks boundaries of country, class, sex and race. It's also an on-going process. As Freud remarked, this search for identity doesn't stop until you're dead. Also, happily for me and for the film, we touched a chord with a lot of people. We also saw a reality in Mexico that a lot of people were completely unaware of. But if we had made a documentary then a lot of people wouldn't have cared and consequently wouldn't have seen the film.

The journey that Tenoch and Julio take subtly reveals a lot about the country itself. Voice-over narration (a device sparingly used throughout the film) reveals that a migrant worker is killed in an accident because of a poorly located pedestrian crossing and a fisherman loses his livelihood to the economically lucrative tourism industry.

CARLOS CUARÓN: Those moments were certainly spotted by critics abroad. In Mexico, many of the critics didn't see it, perhaps because it's their reality and for them was nothing new. This is not true for all critics. The reviews were 80 per cent positive; the other 20 per cent totally missed it.

LEONARDO GARCÍA TSAO *critic/academic*: Mine was one of the few negative reviews it got. I think that it is very well made and I think that Alfonso is technically a very skilled film-maker. I also think however that he is very superficial. He is perfect for Hollywood. I thought the narration was a ploy to imbue the film with a false depth.

ALFONSO CUARÓN: I was in Venice when the film opened there – and it went on to win two prizes in the writing and acting categories – and at the press conference a journalist described the film as reactionary and bourgeois and how dare I, in a country filled with many social and economic problems, do a stupid film about some kids who want to get laid. My answer to him was that I thought he was racist. Why is it that they can accept a European film-maker dealing with things in a middle-class or universal context, but Latin Americans are put in a box where we have to make social-realist ideological films? In the 1960s Mexico and Latin America were part of this very ideo-logical movement of film-making; and I think that these overtly political films are so important and it's great that they exist. But it's like saying that Mexican artists have to continue to produce murals because Diego Rivera[3]

[3] Born in Guanajuato in 1886, Rivera is thought the greatest Mexican painter of the twentieth century, credited with the reintroduction of fresco into modern art and archi-tecture, famed also for radical political views and his romance with Frida Kahlo.

was a muralist and so politically aware. My approach and the criticisms the film suffered were also in part due to the fact that, for good or for bad, I have been living outside of Mexico for twelve years now but going all the time back to Mexico so that I can comprehensively follow the social events that are going on.

A lot of the things that I represent in the film have social connotations, but for Carlos and me what was more important was the human dynamic. Part of the point was how oblivious Julio and Tenoch are to the world around them. Yes, they're trying to get laid, and for them their biggest problem turns out to be the fact that they have betrayed each other with their respective girlfriends. But around them an entire culture is being stripped right in front of their eyes.

GUILLERMO ARRIAGA *writer*: I think that *Y tu mamá también* is among my five favourite films of the last five years. I didn't go to the premiere; I paid my money and went to see it in a very small rural Mexican city where the audience was quite macho. You cannot imagine the silence when Gael and Diego kiss. I was absolutely thrilled, and very moved by it. I called Carlos the moment I left the cinema to tell him that I viewed it as a major moment for Mexican cinema in an international sense.

GAEL GARCÍA BERNAL: Well, it certainly doesn't patronize or ridicule its characters; it respects them. This struck a chord all over the world because it was a very universal film despite being set in a specific location with a specific social strata.

There was widespread surprise when the film was rated '18' within Mexico, thus prohibiting a teenage audience – who might perhaps prove most receptive to seeing their loves and the challenges they face presented on screen – from actually seeing it.

CARLOS CUARÓN: The rating thing is very stupid. Alfonso and I were the first to charge the ratings system in Mexico as being illegal because it goes against the freedom of a parent to raise their child. The film was given a certificate that restricted it to only those of eighteen years of age and older. As a responsible parent, I should be allowed to bring my kid. We criticized the fact that the ratings system in Mexico is controlled by the Department of State. We want it to be an autonomous entity, just like the Electoral Institute in Mexico or the Commission of Human Rights in Mexico. Starting from that, we wanted the whole ratings system changed. In the light of all the fuss that we made when our movie was released, the new administration claimed that they reviewed the whole thing when patently they didn't. We are still against the members of the board deciding whether or not I am responsible enough to bring my kid to the movie.

GAEL GARCÍA BERNAL: The decision was shameful. It was, once again, the government depriving Mexican people of respect. It was complete censorship. In other places that we went to, such as Chile, Argentina and Spain, the film was given a less prohibitive certificate, which encouraged parental guidance. The Mexican government never grows tired of ridiculing people. In Mexico there are some laws and restrictions relating to cinema that are almost avant-garde and quite cool, but on the other hand we have these faceless bureaucrats who establish by their own paradigms and parameters what a film is and who it should be seen by.

People have claimed that the controversy generated by the film was beneficial to it but I don't think that's true. Without its restrictive certificate, many more people would have seen it. Mexico is a young country – 50 per cent of the population is under thirty – and so many more young kids would have been able to see the film. Those that did had to break the law to do so, thus creating a really fucked-up double moral standard.

ALFONSO CUARÓN: We sued the ratings board . . .

It's one of the many ways in which the Institutional Revolutionary Party (PRI) was very clever in disguising censorship with civic and democratic masks. There is an organization called RTC – Directorate of Radio, Television, and Cinema – and they are the ones who control the airwaves. There is a case to be made in terms of legislation to prevent the guys from the big corporations from completely taking over, but we are talking about a corrupt country. In terms of censorship, every single film that is released in Mexico has to go through a ratings board. I am all for ratings except this ratings board is controlled by the government, so it is political censorship. The person running this bureau has been the same person for the last twenty years, and so everything depends on the humour and taste of this person. This person feels himself to be a liberal and often overrules his advisers and has made comments such as: 'My colleagues felt this should be an "18" but I think this is an important film so I am giving it a "15".' So whoa! It is this one person who decides.

I am all for ratings, but I also believe in parents being empowered in terms of making decisions as to what their kids can and cannot see. I think it is important to make people responsible but I also believe in freedom and I think that freedom and responsibility are very similar. That was part of our plea; more involvement from parents.

The most important thing is to take the ratings system away from the government, to create a board that is independent of government and of any private group. In this group you would have representation of people made up of different religions, races, political persuasions, etc., and that would be, in my view, a better way to proceed. Obviously the government would be involved but they would not be in control. Our campaign revealed that the ratings system is illegal and that it contravenes a lot of fundamental legal rights in Mexico. The government is responding basically by ignoring us and hoping we will go away, but we still have the legal action in place. The government felt the necessity to show that they were the good guys and created a congress to define new ways of rating but it is typical of the government that I could not attend but Carlos was invited and went and listened to a series of speeches. It felt like a preliminary thing but the next day in the papers it was reported as the sitting of a panel in which people such as Carlos Cuarón supported and agreed with everything that was said. I mean, he was just present; he didn't even open his mouth or anything!

You have the same problem in the UK; I'm thinking of the furore around the language in Ken Loach's *Sweet Sixteen* (2002). Kids speak like this, but if they want to see a film about themselves they have to see one that shows how a censor would like them to speak. Why are they so afraid of kids seeing themselves the way they are? By censoring it you are not going to stop kids speaking like this. By censoring a movie in which kids have sex you are not going to stop them. With *Y tu mamá* there were a lot of parents and sexual educators who were promoting the film to be seen by the parents and by the kids and for them to have conversations about it.

Then the board said it wasn't about the sex, it was about the drugs. We realized that *Almost Famous* (2000) by Cameron Crowe had a much higher use of drugs but that was rated a 'B', the equivalent of a '15'. This is also a Mexican-film and an American-film thing. Their attitude is that you can see Americans using drugs but not Mexicans because, hey, we don't use drugs.

We were also very pissed off with Fox, our distributor, when we began legal proceedings because they made it clear that they didn't want any part of it. It's sad that a country that is supposedly going through democratic change still has an institute in which the same guy is still in power.

LEONARDO GARCÍA TSAO: It pandered. That's why Alfonso and Carlos were so outraged that the film got a restricted rating. It was a publicity ploy to claim that they had been censored. In Mexico anyone can get into the cinema once they have paid for their ticket. There's no real control. The Cuarón brothers are very smart.

Y tu mamá también: Verdú and Luna

ALFONSO CUARÓN: I consider *Y tu mamá* a cousin to *Amores Perros* and I think that this is true for audiences in Mexico too. For many years in the 'Golden Age' of Mexican cinemas there were melodramas and a romanticized idea of reality, and you would be aware of class difference but it was so romanticized that you would always fall for the idea of the servant marrying the rich guy. This romanticized reality was taken over by the soap operas. And what happens now is that audiences in Mexico want to see something that is very direct and which presents reality as it is. They want to recognize themselves; they don't want a romanticization of their lives. In that sense I think that *Y tu mamá* and *Amores Perros* are cousins, because both deal with a society that is fractured by class.

GUILLERMO DEL TORO: What is wrong in doing *Y tu mamá*, a film described by some Mexican critics as *Beavis and Butthead*, as a sex comedy/road movie in which we recognize our social identity? This film took a proven generic mould and turned it on its head. Where is the sin in that? This is what makes it good.

* * *

Another Mexican success of 2001 saw the return of Guillermo del Toro to Mexico for the purposes of a long-cherished endeavour.

BERTHA NAVARRO *producer*: Guillermo had done *Mimic*, and it was very tough. He tried to make a personal film in impossible circumstances. The end of *Mimic* actually has nothing to do with del Toro, and he was very divided by the compromise. After that experience he wrote many scripts. And several projects, including *The Count of Monte Cristo* with Coppola, fell through. So we felt, 'Why not now make *The Devil's Backbone?*'

GUILLERMO DEL TORO: I had been trying to make the story fit with the Mexican Revolution for many years, and it just wasn't working. For one thing, I realized that the Mexican Revolution has never ended, and secondly it was a very complicated mess with factions being subdivided into other factions. There were a series of intestinal wars in Mexico that didn't stop until the 1930s or later. It was very dirty metaphorically, and I wanted the war to be a war that happened within a family, an intimate war where brothers killed brothers – and that was the Spanish Civil War. I wanted a war movie where you could have the war be geographically far away but also have it created within the walls of the orphanage in a very metaphorical way.

Del Toro's script is set in 1938, with Franco's forces poised to rout the Republicans. Ten-year-old Carlos (Fernando Tielve), son of a fallen Republican, is sent to a remote orphanage run by sympathetic leftists Carmen

Guillermo del Toro and 'kid' on the set of *The Devil's Backbone*

(Marisa Paredes) and Casares (Federico Luppi). But there is much there to unnerve him, from the attentions of bullies to an unexploded bomb in the courtyard; the ominous approach of Franco's troops to the orphanage's walls; teacher Conchita's (Irene Vicido) brooding boyfriend Jacinto (Eduardo Noriega), and the presence of the ghost of a boy called Santi, who ominously predicts, 'Many of you will die . . .'

GUILLERMO DEL TORO: You have Fascism represented by Eduardo Noriega's character Jacinto, and you have the people, represented by the children, and you have the old Republicans represented by Marisa Paredes [Carmen] and Federico Luppi [Casares]. All of them felt they were safe from the effects of the war when they were really re-enacting the war, bit by bit. I felt that the overwhelming image of the movie was the ghost looking at the bomb. It's a movie that doesn't say that everything ends up happily; it says that the bomb never exploded, the ghost never left the place and the only thing you have as a positive is that the children are going to march.

I have a very early drawing that I made when I finished *Cronos* that featured a man drowning in a pool with blood floating from his forehead. It was taken from below and I loved this image. All of a sudden I thought, 'What if a ghost of a guy that has been thrown into a pool with an injury to his head actually walked around with a trail of blood? I found this idea so compelling that I thought this would be the only terrifying thing about the ghost. The rest of it would be like a porcelain doll. It would actually be quite a sad ghost. The idea of showing it very early in the movie was my hope that the movie would eventually clarify for the audience that you shouldn't be afraid of a ghost – you should be afraid of the living. Never fear the dead, fear the living, they are the real danger.

BERTHA NAVARRO: Spain for him was great on *The Devil's Backbone*. It is still a relatively small film in terms of budget but I think that the film would have been difficult to make within Mexico.

Latin American co-production certainly opened up new possibilities for funding. This is especially true of co-productions with Spain; this has been a valuable source of finance. *The Devil's Backbone* was a very special thing. Pedro Almodóvar had seen *Cronos* and met Guillermo at a festival in Miami, and invited Guillermo to come to him if he ever felt that he had a project that could be made in Spain. Many years passed and we called them to say that we do have a project, and they said, 'Great!' They met up again at the Guadalajara Film Festival and the film happened very quickly after that.

GUILLERMO DEL TORO: I had a very happy experience on the film. Film has shown me over the years that you have to remain malleable when faced with financial problems. You have to find the positives under these circumstances. There was a very clear way for me to finance *The Devil's Backbone*, and I had already set it during the Spanish Civil War so I didn't have to make changes as financial considerations as I already was creatively engaged before talking to Pedro and Augustin Almodóvar. I also felt that I would benefit from the international cast and the international *experience*, and I was happy to open myself to it. I learned a lot from working in Europe – I especially loved the fact that they drink wine at their lunch break . . .

IMCINE's approach is very archaic and elitist. It's also a very classicist. It is almost a form of racism. When people ask me why I went to the States I tell them that I would have been perfectly happy to make movies in Mexico for the rest of my life but there was never an open door, you were always, every time, having to kick it open. Even as late as 2000 when we were trying to raise money for *The Devil's Backbone* I went to the head of IMCINE and asked what it was that I was doing wrong. I pointed out that my movies had made a lot of money internationally, had won a lot of prizes internationally and yet you refuse to support me. They said that they didn't think I needed their support. I replied that of course I need it. No. I didn't need it for a project like *Mimic* but this is me trying to do something else. It was a no-win relationship, and has continued like that.

Few people know this but Guillermo Navarro and I were meeting at my home in Austin to discuss the visuals of *The Devil's Backbone* while Guillermo was shooting *Spy Kids* for Robert Rodriguez. I was showing him some Hammer movies and some Mario Bava movies. He literally arrived at the set of *The Devil's Backbone* with only half a day of prep. He shot *Spy Kids* to a Friday, travelled on Saturday, prepped for half a day on Sunday and then began shooting on Monday. But we didn't feel rushed because we know each other so well. After we had tested different kinds of filters for the brown sepia tones, we knew exactly what we were doing from that moment on. Guillermo is one of those brothers that you are not given genetically but that you somehow find through life. We bought our house only because Guillermo lives near by.

The Spirit of the Beehive is a seminal movie for me. I even modelled the girl in *Cronos* exactly on Ana Torrent. That movie, along with the films of Buñuel and the films of Hitchcock, is almost a part of my genetic make-up, buried deep in my DNA. Visually, however, I tried to make *The Devil's Backbone* completely different from other Spanish Civil War movies. They normally texture it in a different way. I wanted to get the dryness of the landscape and the fact that the orphanage seemed to be almost out of a Mervyn Peake novel – a lonely building in a land of nothing.

One of the things that intrigued me about the Spanish Civil War – and indeed something that intrigued me about any war, even as a kid – was, 'Why don't they go away? Why don't they hide in a cave? How can you not see the oppressors coming?' All these little musings are because war is not really a purely geographical occurrence. It really permeates our everyday existence and every act that we do.

The American release of *The Devil's Backbone* was at a very unfortunate time – shortly after the events of September 11th. Seeing the film in a post–September 11th climate made me understand things in the movie that I hadn't understood before. It became more relevant. I also understood that when the worst possible situation occurs, you don't have to be near it – it comes to you.

There are a number of visual references to Alfred Hitchcock and Luis Buñuel in the film: for example, a wooden leg worn by the Marisa Paredes character, and a very Hitchcockian keyhole shot.

Something wicked this way comes: *The Devil's Backbone*

© Miguel Bracho (El Deseo/Tequila Gang)

Marisa Paredes as the Buñuellian Carmen in *The Devil's Backbone*

GUILLERMO DEL TORO: Both Hitchcock and Buñuel have great keyhole moments. There is a great one in *El* (1952) that involves a knitting needle ready to poke out somebody's eye. In order to get our shot we made an over-sized keyhole. I used to call it the Hitchcock keyhole because it was like one of the over-sized props that Hitchcock used to get depth of field in films such as *Dial M for Murder* (1953) or the cup of tea that Ingrid Bergman drinks in *Notorious* (1946). It's certainly a Hitchcockian–Buñuelian moment, and I dreamed for so long about this sequence and wanted so much for it to be successful. When I finally made it, I was filled with a childish sense of glee at being a little closer to my bastion of heroes . . .

6

Japón, El crimen del padre Amaro, Nicotina, and El Misterio del Trinidad

By the end of 2002 Mexico boasted the fifth-biggest international box office by admissions (154 million) and approximately three thousand screens, the largest number in Latin America. The total box office in Mexico had continued to rise (up by 8.4 per cent on 2001 with receipts of $483 million), as had the increased appetite for locally produced films among Mexican audiences (9 per cent of the total box office in 2002 compared with 8.2 per cent the previous year). In contrast, production levels had dramatically declined. In 2002 only fourteen films were produced within Mexico, down from twenty-one in 2001 and twenty-eight in 2000. Of these films, IMCINE, the state-backed film institute, produced just four, compared with seven in 2001 and seventeen in 2000.

ALFREDO JOSKOWICZ film-maker/Director, IMCINE: It's a paradoxical situation. Mexican cinema is growing and yet fewer films are being produced annually. But the films have improved immeasurably in terms of the sophistication of their narratives. They are beautifully shot and have skilful acting; their production values and technical details are generally much higher. Also, the films now deal with themes that appeal to Mexican audiences and are attracting younger audiences to the screens, something that has not happened in many years.

ÁNGELES CASTRO Director, CCC: Many Mexican films work well and win awards at festivals, but without a huge publicity machine it's very difficult for them to become as widely seen. For example, Japón by Carlos Reygadas won many awards and was well received at festivals, but it didn't necessarily do that well when released abroad.

Japón, released in 2002, concerns a man in his sixties (Alejandro Ferretis) who leaves Mexico City and heads to a remote mountainous region, intending to commit suicide. A group of hunters direct him toward a village overlooking a canyon, whereupon he finds lodging with a pious widow in her *eighties by the name of Ascen (Magdalena Flores), whose property is being coveted by a money-grubbing relative. As days go by in this strange environment, the visitor feels his suicidal tendencies recede while he becomes closer to his selfless host.*

ALFONSO CUARÓN *director*: There have been examples of recent Mexican product that has been made with the explicit intention of reaching audiences, and what happens is that the audiences don't give a shit. This is what happens when you try to second guess what audiences want. They're happy to tell you what they want to see, but then you make that movie, you show it to that audience and they're not surprised because they already know it. And it was probably better in their imagination. Audiences may say, 'Oh, I want to see another Bond movie.' They want to see what is already familiar to them. But every so often they also like to be surprised. There are many different kinds of audiences and I would hate that cinema becomes completely subservient to entertainment. A film that I consider one of the most remarkable to come from Mexico in the last thirteen years is *Japón*, and that is not a film that you could call entertainment, but it is an amazing piece of art: the use of sound, space and time is so rare and so strange. In terms of style *Japón* is very different to the films of Alejandro [Iñárritu], Guillermo [del Toro] or myself, and perhaps is more remarkable. I guess it belongs to what Paul Schrader would term a 'transcendental style'. For me, that's the most difficult to do, and I would love to be able to do this. I know that I can deal with expensive special effects but this I would really love to do.

With *Japón* my company tried to get distribution for the film in the States. I am not surprised that it hasn't got distribution because it's not a mainstream film. I relate very much to the work of Carlos Reygadas. People compared the film to Tarkovsky or Kiarostami but it reminded me more of Sokurov. Sokurov is one of my favourite film-makers right now; I also consider him to be one of the most important. For me, the idea of reaching audiences is not paramount; if you do then that's great. It terms of the industry that's a different thing and I think it's important to differentiate industry and cinema. It is also true that the healthier the industry you have, the more possibilities you have to take a shot at cinema.

CARLOS CUARÓN *writer/director*: Carlos Reygadas is doing his own thing, a very low-budget kind of thing, and he really doesn't want to tell a story – he is 'sculpting in time', to borrow from his beloved Tarkovsky.

CARLOS REYGADAS *director*: I was alone in Brussels studying law when I decided I wanted a career in cinema. I started going to the Museum of

© Lisa Roze (Artificial Eye)

Carlos Reygadas

Cinema, and saw perhaps three films a day. I like Roberto Rossellini very much, and the conditions in which he had to shoot with whatever was there. Rossellini was a master at using the world as it is to create everything he needed for his stories. For me, Dreyer is also great. *Ordet* is one of the most moving films I've ever seen in my life, a miracle of film. Bresson is also a master, especially in the way he works with actors and uses sound. *A Man Escaped* [1956] is a personal favourite. Tarkovsky was the one to really open my eyes. When I saw his films I realized that emotion could come directly out of the sound and the image, and not necessarily from the story-telling.

I realized that I had to go to film school to find the human team and the materials, to generally have *access* to things. While I was preparing for the exams I met Diego Martinez Vignatti, an Argentinian director of photography. It was Diego who persuaded me to do a short that I would be able to present as part of my entry credentials, and he also offered to provide me with access to a Super-8 camera and film stock. The next day, I had a storyboard and a completed scenario and had chosen the actors; in fact, everything was prepared. I had so many stories I wanted to tell and so many ideas in my head.

I then completed three further pieces in a similar way. Following that, I made another short film entirely by myself, because I wanted to learn and understand the whole process.

I then began working on the scenario for *Japón*. It was practical and relatively easy to make because it's set in an area I know well, close to Mexico City, and is also the house of my grandparents who live in the area. I worked with the team I had worked with on my shorts and we had to work very hard in an organized manner to make it. I prepared the script and the storyboards and decided that the film would have to be very practical and well prepared and consist of 300 shots. In fact it turned out to be 302 . . .

When I first saw Iranian films some years ago, I was struck by geographical, political and religious similarities, though Islam is perhaps more roughly applied there than Catholicism in Mexico – but socially the presence of religion is very similar. I was impressed by the work of Abbas Kiarostami and his decision to use very long takes with few cuts. I also appreciated that there was, in fact, lots happening within the scenes and within the little details. It's such details that I'm interested in. I'm not interested in the operations of MI5.

The lead actor in *Japón*, Alejandro Ferretis[1] is actually a friend of my parents, and has been for a very long time. I've known him since I was a very little boy, and he always appeared as special to me. He lived through the sixties in a very combative way; he reads voraciously and has a tremendous gift for languages. He was always asking me complex, stimulating questions,

---

[1] Ferretis committed suicide in March 2005.

often from a Marxist perspective, which we would then endlessly debate and discuss. So when I was writing the script I was always thinking of him, especially as he had often expressed his admiration for Arthur Koestler.[2] When we actually started shooting he started to glamorize himself a little bit, as if he thought we were shooting a French perfume ad. However, he soon learned that I didn't want any of that and that I actually wanted him to do very little, which reminds me again of my earlier point about Bresson. Alejandro had never acted before.

Magdalena Flores, who plays Ascen, had never acted either. In fact all the cast are non-actors. I wanted to work with pure, real matter, largely for the sake of authenticity. I can't imagine any actress in the world performing the role of Magdalena. This sense of authenticity was especially important for the sexual scene, in which Magdalena is really afraid and really modest but at the time has so great a sense of honour that she has to fulfil the promise that she made. This very real intellectual and spiritual fight she is having would have been impossible for an actress.

I did speak to professional actors, and most I met were sick with narcissism. One actress said that she would have done the nude scenes when she was younger but that an audience would vomit if they saw her naked now. I actually saw around three hundred women for the part, and there was always something more powerful about the peasant women I auditioned for the role. Magdalena was unaware of the fact that she wasn't beautiful because she is unaware of popular conceptions of beauty. It was an ethical and cultural problem concerning her nudity, which was overcome by mutual trust.

I had actually found another woman to play the part of Ascen and worked very closely with her, but one week into shooting she simply vanished, leaving a note saying that she had broken her hips. In Mexico this simply means that she was afraid so I didn't try to look for her in any hospital. We found Magdalena when we were shooting the slaughter of the pig as she had come to buy some meat and, of course, she initially said 'No' when approached about the part but finally consented after we went to see her family and developed the relationship naturally. Magdalena Flores is a very intelligent woman and did beautiful work. She didn't even have a script; she simply took direction on a scene-by-scene basis.

Shooting the sex scene was zero traumatic, and very simple. It's a bit like

---

[2] Koestler was a journalist who fought in the Spanish Civil War, renounced Communism after Stalin's show trials, and wrote *Darkness at Noon* (1941), about an ageing Bolshevik awaiting execution.

Alejandro Ferretis in *Japón*

Death is all around: *Japón*

virginity. Girls are told about sex and what is going to happen for years, then when it happens they think, 'All that shit for *this*?' Given Alejandro's liberal sensibilities I anticipated that he would have no problem with the scene, but as it often happens in life, at the hour of truth it was maybe harder for the man than for the woman. For Magdalena she had nightmares beforehand, but when the day came it was a very small, intimate crew and after some tequila she was very tranquil. I also kept the directions very simple to both Magdalena and Alejandro. And it was much like in the film; Alejandro was supposed to be in control but became more hesitant as he became nervous.

I showed the finished film to the people in the village but unfortunately I had to cut the sex scene because I was worried that Magdalena might suffer abuse and teasing; there is a saying, 'Little town, big hell.' You know, Mexico is a very special place; some of the population is Western and some of them are not. In terms of the cast, the only one with Western sensibilities was Alejandro so it's hard to really gauge what they feel and how they react. I know that they really laughed at the scene involving the screaming of the pig – in fact, anything involving animals prompted laughter, which is certainly not the reaction you will get in the UK. It's not even the reaction you might get in more highly populated cities in Mexico.

To me, titles are a necessary evil – ideally they wouldn't exist. Paintings, for example, don't always have titles. I wanted to do the same with my film and leave it untitled. I then thought about calling it 'Untitled' but that would just be pretentious. And we have to give it a name so that people can refer to it. I should have just called the film 'Magdalena and Alejandro in the Canyon' or 'Love at Last Sight' or something like that . . . I always wait until the end to find a title, so I wondered, 'What is this film about, after all?' For me it is partly about the cycle of light coming again after night. I was struck therefore by the notion of the sun rising which of course has connotations with Japan. I could have called it 'Korea' or 'Taiwan' but these countries are more closely associated with microchip technology. People also often associate other characteristics with Japan such as haiku poetry, a respect for the elderly and the repression of feelings. There is also the culture of the Samurai and in many ways Alejandro represents this with his veneer of toughness and the impression he gives that he is totally in control. Of course, all he really wants is to cry with his mother holding him. This is perhaps what most of us men really want.

There are also contradictory ideas in the film. People have interpreted Ascen's act differently. Some believe that she does what she does because there is a force that compels her to save him; other people believe that she does it because of ideas relating to Christian sacrifice. There are also those that interpret Ascen as simply realizing what may perhaps be her last opportunity to enjoy physical pleasure. All those things are and can be there.

Japón was shot on ordinary 16 mm, but in front of the primary lens a special anamorphic lens was introduced, so that the actual frame is a standard 1:37 ratio but the images are squeezed. The blow-up to 35 mm was a standard blow-up by photographical process. There are few 16 mm 'scope films, but it's actually quite a simple process that gives a very grainy look, which I like. I actually got the contact for the process after watching Gaspar

Noé's *I Stand Alone* (1998).[3] I had already decided that the film had to be in Cinemascope but if I hadn't shot it in the way I did, then I would have had to do it on 35 mm Panavision film and equipment which is both expensive and heavy.

Diego Martinez Vignatti has a very, very strong character and he understands films in the same way that I do. He also believes, pretentious though it may sound, that art is individual expression and so, prior to shooting, we talked at length about how the film was going to look in terms of the colour, the contrast and the texture. The framing we didn't talk about so much, because that is something I do completely by myself – for me framing is so basic and so important. Diego does make some very good suggestions but he also understands that suggestions are just suggestions and that they can be accepted or not accepted.

The music for the final shot revealing the tragedy is by Arvo Pärt[4] and it's an amazing piece of music. That piece of music in fact influenced very much the ending of the film and suggested the images and gave me the key and the clue regarding how to shoot the last shot. The sound in general is also very important and I sometimes believe that sound design is almost half of cinema, especially in terms of expression. Sound can be objective or subjective. I would say that Tarkovsky is a master of subjective sound and Kiarostami is a master of objective sound; I try to use both.

Each one of us chooses our own life. You are not 'more Mexican' as a filmmaker if you stay in Mexico and you are not a traitor if you create products in Iceland, for example. The only question is whether you're interested in product or in personal expression.

Hollywood probably wouldn't invite me but people don't believe me when I say that if they did I wouldn't want to go. That said, I don't want to say no to anything in life but really it's not my goal to shoot my next film with Tom Cruise. If I was in it for the money I should probably be doing another job. I love so much the images and the sounds that I have in my head. That's the reason I do it, no other.

*　*　*

[3] Photographed by Dominique Colin, Noé's *I Stand Alone* (*Seul contre tous*) has a bleached, grainy look that serves dramatically to heighten its intensity.

[4] Pärt was born in Paide, Estonia, and is a graduate of the Tallinn Conservatory. His significant early works include *Nekrolog*, Symphonie No. 1, Symphonie No. 2 and *Collage über BACH*. In 1968 Pärt's *Credo* was banned, leading him to undertake the first of what would become several periods of contemplative silence. Three 1977 pieces (*Fratres*, *Cantus In Memoriam Benjamin Britten* and *Tabula Rasa*) remain among his most highly regarded.

In 2002 *Carlos Carrera released his fourth and most successful feature,* El crimen del padre Amaro, *adapted and updated from the novel by Eça de Queiros. It concerns a recently ordained twenty-four-year-old priest (played by Gael García Bernal) who is sent to a small parish church to assist an ageing senior, Benito (Sancho Gracia). But Amaro is then challenged by his attraction to sixteen-year-old Amelia (Ana Claudia Talancón), whose mother has long since been dallying with Benito. And Amaro fast learns that the clerical life offers other temptations, once he has understood how deeply Benito is indebted to a local drug baron.*

Amid the success of privately funded films such as Amores Perros *and* Y tu mamá, El crimen *retained a much closer association with both* IMCINE *and the heritage of Mexican cinema. Actor Pedro Armendáriz – the son of one of Mexico's best-loved 'classic'-era stars – appeared in the picture. And the founder of the production company, Alameda Films, which oversaw the film is producer Daniel Birman, part of a formidable Ripstein dynasty: son of Arturo Ripstein, and grandson of legendary producer Alfredo Ripstein, a cornerstone of the Mexican film industry since* 1946.

A film-making dynasty: Daniel Birman (left) and his grandfather Alfredo Ripstein

DANIEL BIRMAN *producer*: I started studying law, but after two years I left the university to join my grandfather's company in 1991. I started there really knowing nothing – in fact, I didn't even get paid for a long time. But then my grandfather really became interested in my knowing more about the business, how he made films, and taking that experience, and adapting it to newer and more innovative techniques. He has also taught me that you never really finish learning – that there will always be new processes and situations to which you must adapt.

My role in the film actually came twenty-three years after it was initially conceived as a project. Alfredo Ripstein tried to do *El crimen* in 1970 but circumstances intervened. In 1995, after we shot *El Callejón de los milagros* (*Midaq Alley*), we decided it was time to do the film, and we called Carlos Carrera on board. It took us around six or seven years to get the funding, because nobody believed in the project. IMCINE was attached to it only at the very end.

Laura Imperiale is Argentinian by birth, but left the country in 1976. Initially interested in sound, she arrived in Brazil and found work as as an editing assistant for a commercials company. She reached Mexico in 1979, and starting producing documentaries for TV.

LAURA IMPERIALE *producer*: I met Arturo Ripstein and Paz Alicia at the Havana Festival in 1996. I think we made a good impression on each other straight away, but I only found out for sure the following year when I got a call from Arturo inviting me to work on the project he was preparing: *El Evangelio de las maravillas* (*Divine*, 1998). At that time I was working at Producciónes Amaranta with Jorge Sánchez. I suggested involving Jorge to Arturo. We then agreed to produce *El Evangelio* at Amaranta. After that, Jorge and I worked together on four of Arturo's films: *Divine*, *El Coronel no tiene quien le escriba* (*No One Writes to the Colonel*, 1999), *Así es la vida* (*Such is Life*, 2000) and *La perdición de los hombres* (*The Ruination of Men*, 2000). That period of work with Arturo and Jorge was my baptism of fire. On the one hand all the films were co-productions – Brazil, Argentina, Spain, France – on the other, although working with a director as experienced as Arturo presented certain demands, it was also a great apprenticeship. I was slightly apprehensive at first, given that Arturo had a reputation of being a tough person to work with, but I never had a cause for complaint. With Arturo we also made Mexico's first commercially released digital film, *Así es la vida*.

With *El crimen*, Daniel Birman and Alfredo Ripstein invited me to work with them because the project was to be made as a co-production with Spain and with support from Fondo Sur: they had no experience in either of these two areas – and I knew the Spanish co-producer, José María Morales of Wanda Vision, very well, having previously worked with him on several of Arturo's films. Part of my contribution to the production of *El crimen* was Cinecolor, an Argentinian company that was starting to work in Mexico too. What really made me excited about the project, though, was working with Carlos. Despite knowing each other well, we had never had an opportunity to work together.

CARLOS CARRERA *director*: There was also money from a French fund, Artcam, and an Argentinian laboratory, Videocolor. Co-production is an important new avenue. There is, however, also something about co-productions that I don't like at all. You make decisions depending on the co-production. For example you must hire a Spanish or Argentinian actor and adapt the script to fit. There are compromises that you have to make. As a director I am prepared to make them but I don't necessarily have to like them.

I like both rural and urban dramas. *Sin Remitente* (*No Return Address*) takes place in Mexico City. There is a problem in Mexico in that almost all the cultural life takes place in Mexico City. I grew up in Mexico City and I have spent almost all my life here, but my parents are from other places and my grandmother used to always tell me fascinating stories about the places they came from. There are many very other interesting stories to be told. We are a hundred million Mexicans, it's important to reflect our diversity.

The dramatic premise of impossible love almost always works, but I wasn't so interested in the forbidden love between a priest and a young girl. I was more interested in other aspects suggested by the novel: corruption, moral doubt and ethics. I felt there were lots of similarities with the behaviour of the priests in the novel and the priests of our days. There are many places where you can find human beings who as human beings make mistakes; they are as fallible as anyone. There are only two or three films that talk about the church in Mexico and almost 85 or 90 per cent of Mexican people are Catholic so I felt that it was very important to talk about what is going on in the Church. Most people are aware of the relationship between priests and drug dealers and crime lords. The Catholic Church is more of a political institution than it is a spiritual or religious one. Obviously I'm not saying that all priests are corrupt. This is the story of just one character. But we can easily find many more like him throughout our land.

Gael was making Y *tu mamá también* when he was cast. It took us four years to secure the financing to make *El crimen* so he had read the script some time before he became such a big star.

GAEL GARCÍA BERNAL *actor*: Carlos gave me the script and I really liked the idea of exploring the character of this priest who is riddled with moral complexities: someone who places the fear of God above anything else, and yet his personal ambitions and goals compromise this fear. It was great to investigate these themes and this type of story, especially in light of the American scripts that came my way and the parts that I was continually being offered after *Amores Perros*. These parts were all very stereotypical Latin lover types or the troubled boy from the *barrio*.

Like *Amores Perros* it felt absolutely necessary, but the decision to make it was perhaps less instinctive and more conscious and objective. Carlos's style is very different from either Alejandro [Iñárritu]'s or Alfonso [Cuarón]'s and this was also appealing. Having made a lot of films within Mexico I was also intrigued to see what Carlos would come up with next. The working atmosphere was also very different, more traditional if you like, but the film and its themes are very prescient.

CARLOS CARRERA: I tried to decide how to shoot the film in terms of the best way to tell the story and to communicate the central themes. Overall, I

© Columbia Pictures/IMCINE

Love in bad faith: Gael García Bernal and Ana Claudia Talancón in
El crimen del padre Amaro

would describe my style as very classic and, if you like, conventional. It is certainly more conventional than *Amores Perros*.

The violence I didn't want to focus on, but rather indicate that it is simply part of daily life. I think that the focus in this film should be more on the conflict between and within the characters, rather than showing the violence in our society. Mexico is a violent country with a violent culture and violence is a sad fact of everyday life.

Funded and fully supported by IMCINE, *released on an unprecedented 365 screens across Mexico on 8 August 2002 by Columbia Tri-Star,* El crimen del padre Amaro *earned 31 million pesos (approximately $2.8 million/£2 million) on its opening weekend. It has since gone on to gross over $15 million. This attendance ensured that the film, made on a budget of just 20 million pesos (£1.3 million) turned an immediate profit. It was released in the UK under its English-language title,* The Crime of Father Amaro, *by Columbia Tristar on 20 June 2003. Though largely well received, the film failed to attract large audiences and did not have the same controversial impact as it did in Mexico.*

LEONARDO GARCÍA TSAO *critic/academic:* I think that the film is very important in contradicting moral attitudes and the extreme-right Catholic thinking that has so far prevailed during the Vicente Fox regime. It was also important that it was shown with relatively little interference. Yes, there were protests but nobody tried actively to stop it from being exhibited. There was a huge coup, which in effect translated to massive publicity for free. The film was in all the papers and all the extreme-right groups took full-page ads in the papers urging people not to see the film but the ads had the exact opposite effect.

Carlos Carrera is a director who I rate very highly. He's much more academic and perhaps less risky as a film-maker, but I think he has an impressive way of capturing Mexican reality.

The middle classes were extremely attracted to a film that was critical of the Catholic Church. Working-class people in Mexico don't go to the cinema any more. It is too expensive. Each ticket costs on average $4, so if you go with someone that is $8. The working class waits for the pirate video.

GAEL GARCÍA BERNAL: I think that the controversy was expected. We didn't know how intense it would be but we did know that there would be repercussions relating to freedom of speech. The media actually defended the film a lot, pushing the spokespeople from right-wing Catholic groups to make really idiotic, ridiculous pronouncements. The media helped drive public opinion towards supporting the film. As a result, people that may have had no intention of seeing the film went to see it just to fuck these extremist groups over. In Mexico, whenever you are told not to do something, the immediate reaction is to do it.

DANIEL BIRMAN: The controversy that hit *El crimen* evolved in the manner of most speculation: nobody had seen it, and yet everybody was talking about it. Fortunately, alongside the speculation we also had a wonderful film that kept cinemas packed for months. Controversy might have made people attend initially but quality kept them coming back.

CARLOS CUARÓN: The huge success was in part due to the subject. It was also greatly helped by the Catholic Church trying to ban it. They were unable to do this because Mexican society has changed so much. Another huge factor of course is Gael, who's extremely popular. In formal terms *El crimen* is much more like the films of the 1970s, particularly early Ripstein. It was the combination of scandal, Mexican society and the Catholic Church and Gael. It tells you the story in a very linear fashion from A to Z and sometimes people like this.

BERTHA NAVARRO *producer*: It *is* very traditional. I think, when considering the success of the film and the fact that it did not correspond to the style of films like *Amores Perros*, one must factor in the presence of Gael García Bernal. He is a huge figure in Mexico. Box office in Mexico has nothing to do with directors: the Mexican public don't really know who the director is on a particular film. Well, some more knowledgeable ones do, but it's certainly not a key factor, even though in promotion and marketing you always say, 'A film by . . .' Names of directors can sometimes ring a bell but actors are more important. The phenomenon of Gael is beyond importance; he is a huge success.

Secondly, Mexico is a very Catholic country, but the public in Mexico does not like being told what to do. Once the Church and the state told them not to go and see the movie, of course the public was going to do exactly the opposite.

CARLOS CARRERA: I thought that in these times, with this new government, it would be harder to find a strong reaction against the movie. I thought, incorrectly, that we were living in more liberal times.

What saddens me most is that, because of these very conservative groups, the whole world got the wrong idea of what Mexico is. I think that Mexico is the healthy reaction of the audiences that went to see the movie, not the hysterical reaction of these very conservative groups. Mexico appeared as a medieval and regressive country.

I was very amazed and surprised by the film's success. I certainly don't care about money but obviously I like my films to be seen. I like to tell my stories in a comprehensive language for everyone. I am aware at all times of the audience and I like my films to be liked by them.

* * *

Unfolding in 'real time', Nicotina is a highly stylized black comedy of coincidence about a techie geek, Lolo (Diego Luna), who accidentally gives the wrong computer disk to some Russian gangsters. As a result, the lives of nine highly diverse Mexico City inhabitants entwine in one tumultous night over the whereabouts of a small fortune in diamonds. Released with a size-able publicity and advertising campaign, the film arguably attempted to marry sophisticated story-telling, high production values and an undoubted star in Diego Luna to seize the moment and capture the renewed hunger for locally produced movies from Mexican audiences.

MARTHA SOSA *producer*: I think it's dangerous to attempt simply to repeat a formula. *Nicotina* for me has a very different approach both visually and

Diego Luna in the urban black comedy *Nicotina*

thematically. I believe that *Amores Perros* left many people seeking a relief from drama.

I also believe – and this is the reason I joined forces with Laura Imperiale to do it – that at this moment we really need this film. I always try to position myself in the place of the spectator and as a spectator I needed a little light refreshment. Yes, let's talk about reality and how and who we are but let's also not forget to laugh.

HUGO RODRÍGUEZ *director*: I met Martín Salinas when I arrived in Mexico City in 1981. He was a cartoonist and the director of an animation company called CineSur, where I started working, colouring in his drawing and doing some camera animation. In fact, it's largely thanks to him that I'm working in films today. Around that time I also met Laura Imperiale, who already knew Martín. So we've been friends for a long time now, but until then we had never worked together. It was Laura who, after many years of trying, managed to bring us together. For several years I had been trying unsuccessfully to get various projects off the ground, when Laura set about finding a script for me to direct. She made several attempts; she even bought some rights, but the projects didn't bear fruit and we couldn't get them going. On one of Martín's visits to Mexico – I think it was in August 2001 – Laura suggested that he write a script for me to direct. Martín mentioned he had three separate stories that he thought could be combined to make a full-length film. He went back to Argentina and e-mailed them to me, with a suggestion about how they could be joined together. Each in his own country, we started work and, within four months, we already had a presentable script.

MARTÍN SALINAS *screenwriter*: I had been writing fifteen one-hour scripts for a TV series in Argentina, ruled mainly by a production and genre premise: three-to-five characters at the most, one single location; it all had to happen in real time, with as much suspense as possible, and completely different casts and stories each time. The opposite to what happens with 'development hell' – every script I delivered got made, and the series was very successful in terms of rating and reviews, and lasted three seasons. *Nicotina* was born out of that experience. At the very beginning, it was made of these three different independent stories which dealt with the opposite to what you would call 'love stories'. The title I chose for the first version of that three-stories script doesn't translate well into English: *Desamores*.

Those three stories – Lolo and his neighbour Andrea, the pharmacists, and the hairdressers – were written at very different moments. The common denominator, besides the 'No love!' aspect was the conflict between our efforts to try to consciously take control of our lives and make decisions, and chance, misfortune, luck and coincidences, and also our silly attempts to control other people's lives and feelings. I wrote the pharmacists' storyline right after trying to help my wife figure out what was wrong with our bank balance. I guess I became quite mean in pointing out her mistakes. She said she would undoubtedly make more mistakes if I stood there waiting for her to make more mistakes ... It got worse and worse ... The hairdressers' story was inspired by real people I know who are not hairdressers, and would probably not end up like Carmen and Goyo if something like that happened to them. But you need only to open the crime section of any newspaper to realize that it is a plausible story.

Hugo read the stories and proposed that we try to find a way to connect them through these two gangsters who break into the pharmacy, while incorporating the diamonds aspect of the story. I tried it and it worked. Then we realized that the cigarettes that were mentioned in one of the stories were closely related to this conflict between cause and effect and the coincidences that I mentioned before. I'm not a smoker. But my wife is ...

LAURA IMPERIALE: From the moment we read Martín's proposal, we decided that this was the project we would make together. We exchanged ideas by e-mail until we had defined very precisely what the film was about, then Martín started work on the script, and he produced a first draft very quickly. From the outset we saw *Nicotina* as a project that belonged to the three of us, so our working relationship was always marked along those lines. Just over a year after our initial discussions, we were filming. Later on, Martha Sosa joined the original team on the production side. Yes, it really was a team effort, with each member committed to making the best film possible.

Nicotina *is a co-production between Mexico and Argentina. Such productions between Latin American and Spanish-speaking countries have become increasingly necessary in order for these films to make it to the production stage.*

LAURA IMPERIALE: All official co-productions – those made within the framework of agreements signed between governments – receive the nationality of the countries involved; on the basis of which, producers are then entitled to the benefits afforded them by the cinema laws of their respective countries. Tax incentives for the production, the distribution, etc. .... These agreements oblige you to comply with certain requirements such as having actors from both countries in lead roles, a minimum percentage of private investment, and the participation of heads of production from both countries. The last two points don't create any great difficulties, but the first is always the most difficult and is the one you have to consider very carefully.

Some stories lend themselves to the inclusion of characters from different backgrounds, but many don't. In the case of *Nicotina* we thought the inclusion of Argentinian characters did the story no harm and could even benefit it with the play on the different ways we speak.

Right now in Mexico City we all know someone who is Argentinian – a neighbour, a boyfriend, a colleague, a friend. It's completely believable. It's well known how much Latin Americans have moved throughout the world in recent years. In terms of finance, the money from a co-production is not fundamental but it does help to tie up the financing. Once you have a co-production you can also apply to other funds such as the Programa Ibermedia.

As well as this, it ensures that your film will be shown in cinemas and on television in the country of your co-producer. Despite the fact that at the present time our films don't do very well in the other countries of our region, we are gradually getting the public used to offerings that are not only American. Once they've seen a film they like, the next time they'll try another. I think it helps to grow the market. I think that although the co-production route is not the only one, it is a good method for continuing to produce in the future.

The film plays out largely in real time. A difficult conceit to achieve on screen.

MARTÍN SALINAS: Contrary to what I used to believe, I've found that real time can sometimes make it a lot easier than when you have the freedom to cut to several hours, days or months later. It can even help you have more time within certain scenes when you think of showing characters at a closer range. It does also help a lot when it comes up to building suspense. But, above all, it seems to be a matter of scale. When we first see Carmen, the barber's wife, she's already very angry with her husband. If the Russian guy had not shown up, nothing would have changed; she would have continued feeling angry day after day. But the arrival of the Russian gangster breaks this routine and ends up throwing Carmen and Goyo into a pressure-cooker dynamic in which real time is probably the best possible way to go. Decisions have to be taken right away; it is right now or never. Which is why she makes the first big mistake and gets obsessed with the wrong belly. Same thing with Clara, the pharmacist, or Lolo, the hacker. I think real time is what helps us follow their conflicts and urges us to take certain decisions, second after second. Real time is probably the trick that actually makes these crazy improbable stories look plausible.

HUGO RODRÍGUEZ: The people for whom it was more laborious were the actors. They had to maintain throughout a whole week the emotional continuity of a scene, which, on screen, lasts ten minutes. The nuances of their acting, they had to sustain for a whole day. In film, more than in any other dramatic art, the actor has to have full control over his emotional memory so as to carry forward the continuity of his character, especially as in general a film is not shot chronologically. What happens with a story that takes place in real time is that the acting is condensed. The character is introduced, externalizes his conflict, achieves catharsis, and reaches resolution in a shorter period of time. That was a challenge that I think we resolved well.

A black comedy, Nicotina *also concentrates on numerous social malaises, such as greed, jealousy and the corrupting nature of power and the dangers of increased technology.*

MARTÍN SALINAS: Someone told me that at certain moments *Nicotina* seemed to have been written by an enthusiastic pessimist. I don't think that's my case, but it is true that I enjoy telling funny stories that reveal the darkest side of human nature. Not out of pure nihilism. I just don't think that the world can be simply divided between good guys and bad guys or between good and evil. I find it very appealing to tell a story in which you suddenly find yourself identifying, even for a few seconds, with someone who eventually does something awful. The fact that the audience laughs louder when the film reaches the darkest peaks tells me that what they're watching sounds disturbingly familiar to them. How far would I go, if I knew that if I don't grab those twenty diamonds without actually hurting anybody, some corrupt cop would? I think comedy has this potential to catch people off guard.

When you live in a big city in which little kids beg on the streets for food, like they do in Buenos Aires, and you don't close your eyes to this, your angle on what is unpleasant or not is affected by this. The day I decided to take the script of *Nicotina* to the Sundance/Toscano Screenwriters' Lab for feedback, Argentina was on fire. Middle-class people marched on the streets banging pots and pans in fury because banks had closed their doors to them and their lifetime savings had just been practically confiscated. Thousands of unemployed people were breaking into supermarkets and food shops to grab whatever they could find in order to feed their children. Barbershops were losing their clients, as people would just cut their hair at home. And I remember thinking that there were probably hundreds of desperate Carmen-like men and women out there, ready to dig twenty diamonds in a dead Russian's guts if they had the chance, without batting an eyelid.

One day I called Laura and told her I had a name to suggest for our new production company: Cacerola Films.[5] Laura and Hugo, who were both also born in Buenos Aires, liked it right away.

Latin American readers of the script at the Screenwriters' Lab felt a woman like the barbershop wife was a somewhat familiar real-life type. The same thing with the cop who smuggles cigarettes into the pharmacy; they are a part of the local landscape. In fact, if you have two cops in a Latin American film, and you don't see some sort of crooked corrupt detail in at least one of them, your friends will point it out to you. Over here you think twice before calling the police if you're in trouble. In terms of tone and genre, our goal with *Nicotina* was to try to get people to laugh at things that ring true to them. And for this you need somehow to exaggerate certain cultural and idiosyncratic patterns. In Latin America this seems to lead you very easily to writing black comedy, if not blatant farce. I actually see this as the most challenging aspect of trying to write and produce comedy for the big screen in Latin America.

MARTÍN SALINAS: The Lolo in the draft we gave to Martha Sosa was a plump fat guy in his early thirties. So when they sent the script to Diego for the first time, Hugo wanted him to play Nene. I can't recall what the steps were, as I was in Argentina, but I think it was Martha who proposed to make Lolo younger so that Diego could play it. Diego, who totally belongs to the acting species, loved the idea of playing a character against type like that. I got worried. How could someone so charming and seductive play the character that I had in mind? The timid, plump guy in his early thirties was someone who (according to me) you could feel pity for and even like him despite what he does to his neighbour. The moment I joined Diego and Hugo for a reading, I had the answer.

Nicotina *utilizes the full lexicon of film language, playing with film speed, character point of view and using audacious camera movement.*

HUGO RODRÍGUEZ: Camera movements are a well-established part of film language. As always, the important thing to know is what it is we're telling

---

[5] *Cacerola* translates as 'pots and pans'.

and how we want to tell it. In the case of *Nicotina*, the decision to use camera movements was a conceptual one. *Nicotina* is a black comedy. A comedy because the characters upset their world in order to get what they want, and a *black* comedy because in the course of upsetting their world and in resolving their desires, violence and death come into play.

The themes we deal with are strong: voyeurism, family violence, exaggerated ambitions. In order for the spectator to reach catharsis, we decided to treat the whole story in a realistic fashion. The intention was (and I think we achieved it) for the audience to be able to relate to parts of the characters' lives – probably not to all of a life, but, yes, to some of each character's minor neuroses.

This had a direct impact on the tone of the acting, the lighting, the set design, the make-up and the wardrobe. I could feel that the realism worked. But . . . Although I knew we'd manage to get the audience to identify with the characters, I was worried that, as the story progressed, we'd gradually lose the potential for catharsis, so that by the time we reached the outburst of violence we wouldn't provoke laughter, because the density of the narrative wouldn't allow it. I didn't want to get to the point where a spectator was hesitant about laughing – I wanted him to laugh first, and then to ask himself what he was laughing about. In this sense, the camera movements allowed me to lighten the narrative. To wink at the spectator. To act as a reminder that there was a narrator and that, after all, we were telling a story.

I think these factors partly explain why we have a film that is popular with younger audiences, although I think what we succeeded in reaching was a good intelligent audience.

With regard to the genre and the tone of the acting, my point of reference was Joel Coen. He's a director who really knows how to use the various dramatic genres and so can distort them effectively. He moves with complete ease from tragedy to comedy (*Fargo*, 1995), from farce to melodrama (*Raising Arizona*, 1987) or from comedy to melodrama (*The Big Lebowski*, 1998). Similarly, he keeps the tone of the acting flirting from one genre to another; in general, he's playing with realism and farce. Strictly speaking, I used more TV references than film references: the formal resolution of series such as *CSI* (*Crime Scene Investigation*), *Witchblade*, or 24, together with the narrative style of Japanese cartoons like *Cowboy Bebop*, *Eat-man*, and *Aeon*.[6]

---

[6] *Cowboy Bebop* (*Tengoku no tobira*) was directed by Shinichirô Watanabe and Hiroyuki Okiura. The *Eat-Man* series was directed by Toshifumi Kawase. The *Aeon Flux* series was created by Peter Chung.

I'm interested in human weaknesses. Day by day, it's becoming easier to live in isolation. Our generation feels nostalgia for streets where you could stroll, for markets and small stores; our children are going to miss the malls because, after all, they're a place where you can socialize; and, in a few more years, it's very probable you'll be able to do everything without ever having to leave your home. Lolo is an expression of that situation, a young man who's in control of the virtual world but who is incapable of showing the girl in the next apartment the feelings he has for her. When he does, it's already too late.

But each one of the characters has a dark side. And that's what makes them real, accessible and, in part, likeable.

From the outset, given the people involved in the production (and the Mexican industry was quick to dub the film as being from the same stable as Amores Perros), the pressure to achieve commercial success was relatively intense.

MARTÍN SALINAS: From the script onwards, people were very favourable about the project, but it wasn't until the film was finished that expectations about doing well at the box office were raised. I'd meet friends and colleagues and the jokes and comments suggested that there was a chance the film could be a success. But this was when the creative process had already been completed and we were at the stage of launching the film.

Although there are people around who are mean-spirited, in general those of us who work in films in Mexico always want Mexican films to do well. That may sound very romantic, but actually it's very practical. We face a constant struggle against Hollywood, which monopolizes most of the box office. If a domestic film does well, it paves the way for people to go back to watching Mexican cinema. If not, and a couple of years go by without a domestic film being a box-office hit, everything becomes more difficult, from obtaining advertising space that helps to bring audiences into the cinemas to getting the financing for another project.

LAURA IMPERIALE: Although we may not have had the impact of *Amores Perros* and *Y tu mamá también*, *Nicotina* has done well internationally.[7] We see it as a success.

*   *   *

---

[7] *Nicotina* was released by Videocine on 230 prints, grossing $4.1 million.

LEONARDO GARCÍA TSAO: For me, one of the most under-estimated Mexican directors is José Luis García Agraz. He is being very under-used and should be making many more films. He makes only personal films; he's not a director for hire, and that can act as a limitation on him. *El Misterio del Trinidad*, his most recent film, I admire – but other people don't seem to be so interested in it. It's a family melodrama – a genre not in vogue, and it has none of the modern kicks. It is linear; it doesn't jump from one character to another and doesn't feature rock songs on its soundtrack. It is very traditional but still very well made and I hope it finds an audience.

The protagonist of Agraz's film is Juan (Eduardo Palomo), illegitimate son of Joaquin, an elderly engineer who spent his life obsessively diving in the waters of the Gulf of Mexico, searching for a sunken seventeenth-century Spanish galleon, the Santísima Trinidad. *On Joaquin's death, Juan (divorced and with a ten-year-old daughter, Ana, of whom he sees little) receives the title to the old man's boat, the* Meridiano, *in his will. However Joaquin's legal heirs did not know of Juan's existence and moreover desire the boat for themselves. Only Juan's half-sister Isabel, herself unhappily married, is sympathetic to Juan. But before the clan can lay hands on Juan, he sets off to find the galleon for himself. At his ex-wife's insistence, however, he is accompanied by Ana.*

JOSÉ LUIS GARCÍA AGRAZ *director*: When I finished *Desiertos mares* (*Desert Seas*, 1995) and bearing in mind the ambiguity of the character of the father at the end of that film, I felt the need to go more deeply into a father character in my *next* film; that's when I began to write the script. The figure of the father has a dominant place in many cultures, and in Mexico it's perhaps the touchstone through which we relate to the world – a paternal-istic culture in which it is the father who loves and punishes, gives and takes; only the attainment of maturity will enable us to live in a world without fathers and in which we ourselves are masters of our own destinies.

It was a long and complicated process: I attended the Sundance Screen-writers' Lab and rewrote the script with David Olguín, a brilliant playwright and theatre director. Various friends of mine read it, including Alfonso Cuarón, Guillermo Arriaga, El Negro and Carlos Cuarón. All of them brought good ideas, but it was Carlos Cuarón who saw with great clarity how to resolve the problems, and gave the script the clear, solid structure that allowed me to concentrate on the actors and the filming. Basically my script moved between three levels: one was the captain of a Spanish galleon in the seventeenth century, caught in a storm in the Gulf of Mexico, his

The Mexican poster for *El Misterio del Trinidad* by respected director
José Luis García Agraz

reflections and his prayers, his secret search for a son of his, lost in America. Another was the story of Juan Aguirre who faces up to his own life which is in turmoil, as well as his memories of his mother and father during his childhood in Veracruz. Carlos suggested telling the story in a linear fashion, without movements in time, in order to concentrate on the story of Juan, who, in the final version, became the core of the film. I wanted to create a story about fatherhood and forgiveness as a way of growing, maturing. The best adventures are, I think, the adventures of the heart.

Ana is a little girl who, very probably, has been raised in the absence as much of her mother as that of her father – a little girl who has gradually grown up by herself. Ana is both a reflection of what Isabel probably was, as well as the inheritor of the adventurer tradition of her dead grandfather, and, thanks to Juan's reconciliation with the memory of his father, Ana is the possibility of a better human being in the future.

Isabel is the mirror of Ana: beautiful but frustrated, intelligent but submissive to men – first her father, then her husband. She has ruled out the possibility of love and of motherhood. She has reached the edge by the time she meets Juan – who is her half-brother but also a reflection of her absent father. This double image of this man – and of her father – along with the possibility of seeing her childhood in Ana, provokes her 'inner torment', which will be sublimated through her incest, and the separation from a husband she doesn't love. She learns to grow late, but decides to grow in order to become herself. Her last steps in the film are the first towards her maturity.

I love genre films – distributors more so, because that way they avoid complex definitions. And I realize that in this case the mix of genres allowed me a greater range. The film starts out as a historical adventure, then becomes a melodrama with elements of comedy, and continues in this vein until it reaches the limits of tragedy, then becomes a contemporary adventure story, passes into Latin American magic realism and ends as all of one piece.

In Mexico it's very difficult to raise the initial funding to make a film, even more so if it's a personal project; so IMCINE's support was a basic requirement from the outset. However, in the course of five years, from the time I submitted my first treatment, IMCINE had five different Directors, and obviously that delayed the project. The film received approval under Alejandro Pelayo, predecessor to Alfredo Joskowicz, the present Director, but with much less funding – because money had run out under the previous administrations. So I began to look for other partners, and brought into the project anyone who could provide me with funds or contribute in kind. My creative independence was never compromised. In the end the co-production had many partners; and on the one hand IMCINE supported me with risk capital and, on the other, it lent me money at a preferential rate of interest – but that didn't make it any easier to pay the interest back.

One of the aspects of film-making I've loved ever since I was very young are the special effects created while filming, and miniatures. Good special effects are based on a key combination of trickery and calculated optical ratios. Obviously in Mexico such effects cost a fraction of what they cost in Hollywood, although it's also true that Hollywood can make an entire film out of special effects whereas we have to be very specific as to where they should be employed and to what extent they should be visible. There are limits beyond which effects can start to look cheap. My aim, therefore, right from the script stage, was to be very precise about the storms – i.e. to decide exactly what features they should have, and how they should be filmed to look as good as possible. I drew a very detailed storyboard for the storms as well as for the underwater shots.

The cabin of the galleon and almost all the interiors of the *Meridiano* were built at the Churubusco studios. The exteriors of the storm were filmed with the actors on the ship at anchor; some of the long shots were filmed at sea with a replica, others months later in a studio. It wasn't expensive, but it was laborious . . .

The film was nominated by the Spanish Academy of Art and Cinemato-graphic Sciences for a Goya Prize in the category of Best Foreign Film in Spanish. I won the prize for Best Director at the Thirty-second Festival of Naval and Sea Films in Cartagena, in Murcia [Spain]. And the film received ten nominations from the Mexican Academy of Cinematographic Arts and Sciences, including Best Film, Best Director and Best Script. However, the distributors took a different view. They never believed in the film, despite investing $300,000. The launch displayed an almost complete lack of pro-motional planning, and the film came out in October 2003 and met with little success. IMCINE, the majority partner, pressed for the film to be kept showing in some cinemas outside Mexico City, and the National Film Theatre has put it on twice. But that's not enough in a medium dominated by American productions which are the top priority for the distributors that work in Mexico – Fox, Warner, UIP, etc.

for this particular film, I wanted and needed to work with the very best actors in the world, and English was the universal language that would allow me this opportunity. I am not only talking about Americans, but French, Australians and Puerto-Ricans.

I decided that I did not want to shoot either in Los Angeles or New York because these cities have become like a set for me, I've seen them so many times on film that they're predictable. I needed a city that is not a 'movie city'. I also needed a city that I liked, that has a certain smell, a distinct personality and a unique quality. Thirdly, I needed a city far from Los Angeles and New York to get all these actors out of their houses and away from their wives and kids and friends. I wanted them to have no distractions from their work. I found all these things in Memphis. It also has a real history – a sadness that I guess is intrinsically linked with it being the birth-place of the blues.

I didn't show my project until it was completely finished, and when I say 'finished' I'm not talking about the script but *all* the other main decisions. That was because, as in *Amores Perros*, I didn't want anybody involved in the creative process more than Guillermo and myself. I financed the location scouting in several US territories, I started the casting process eight months in advance with Francine Maisler, and I got the three main actors attached to the project before any studio read a line from the script. That meant a lot to me as it meant that the actors were supporting me because they loved the script. They trusted me as a director and I considered them partners of the project. Ted Hope budgeted the film so when I presented the project to the five main studios I said to them, 'This is the script, these are the actors, these are the cities and this is the budget. I want complete creative control and final cut.'

Four of them were really interested in it and I just received support, respect and enthusiasm from all of them. In the end I went with Focus Features because some very good film-makers told me good things about David Linde and James Schamus. I was in total control of the creative process so I was as independent as on *Amores Perros* where I had a great experience with AltaVista films with Alejandro Soberón and Martha Sosa producing their first feature. I regard myself as an independent film-maker and when I work with a company I like to work with, not for, them because in that way the only beneficiary is the film itself.

GUILLERMO ARRIAGA: The idea of Paul's voice-over at the beginning and the end of the film came from an old unfinished novel I wrote when I was twenty-four and began with: 'So this is death, these ridiculous tubes, these needles ...' And that's the way Paul's monologue begins. I considered this could help tell the story better. The screenplay needed a more committed point of view, and this monologue helps convey what the film is about.

ALEJANDRO GONZÁLEZ IÑÁRRITU: I felt that it was necessary to have a point of view. I pay a great amount of attention when I am blocking a film, and at various moments I found myself asking, 'Whose point of view is this? Is it Paul's; is it Christina's?' I felt that it was important at the end of the film to present very clearly one point of view. At the end the film it is like a memory for Paul and how he remembers events. I needed one leader, the one who redeemed the other two.

GUILLERMO ARRIAGA: Mary's and Paul's relationship was over a long time ago. The sad thing was that they were together because both of them were sick. He has the heart disease that limited his life, and she had this loneliness that was consuming her. He needs care and she needs someone to be with her. They both accept this situation, but when Paul has overcome his bad health through a new heart, things go back to where they were in the beginning. There is no love between them, just a convenient relationship. Without Paul's disease, they can no longer be together, and both they know it.

© Focus Features

21 *Grams*: Sean Penn as Paul

Flaubert said, 'Madame Bovary, c'est moi . . .' All the characters have something to do with me. Jack is the English name for Santiago, my son's name; Marianne, his wife's character, is named after Mariana, my daughter, and Mary, Paul's wife, after my wife, María. Jack is maybe the one that fascinates me the most. As an atheist I am always surprised by religious fanaticism. How can someone be so much into God to the point that you lose absolute control of your life? I had a very close friend, an atheist also, who got married to a religious fanatic. She believed that anyone out of her sect was touched by the devil, so both of them decided not to relate to someone out of their religion. Suddenly my friend became a born-again Christian, obsessed with Jesus and God and the Devil. Jack also seduces me because he is the one who has been living with more pain. He is a character full of pain, not only after the accident, but also through all of his life. But I also have very strong links with Paul and Cristina. The three of them are obsessive, as I am.

My favourite moment in the screenplay is where Claudia shouts Christina's name, a moment we later learn to be the moment of the death of Christina's family. It represents all the strength of the tragedy, the moment when everything changes – it has this 'terribleness'. I couldn't avoid crying every time I wrote this scene. It really hurt me because it shows that tragedy is around us all the time, that it hides in the most unexpected places and it grabs you by the throat without any piety.

Christina is told 'Life goes on', and she refutes it, but this is the motif of the film and I wrote it on purpose; 21 *Grams* is about the power of life over the power of death. Life has an enormous strength and it goes on even in the worst circumstances. When my son Santiago was five he asked me, 'If I die, will you ever smile again? Can you play again?' I was speechless. But he asked this question because his two-year-old cousin drowned in a swimming pool. And two or three years later his mom, my sister-in-law, was again smiling. Santiago couldn't understand – how could she smile after such an unbearable pain? So I wrote this film trying to answer his question for him.

ALEJANDRO GONZÁLEZ IÑÁRRITU: I think that one of the problems with cinema, and also with screenwriters – and this is where Guillermo really excels – is that they ask you to judge the characters. I never judge the characters; I always feel tenderness for them, always. No matter what they do, no matter who they are, I personally feel emotionally attached. This is one of the things that I really work on in the script. In *Amores Perros* El Chivo is a killer, but one of my goals was to make people understand this guy as a human being. This is imperative for me. This is also true of 21 *Grams*.

21 Grams: Naomi Watts (Christina) and Alejandro González Iñárritu

You are emotionally drawn to the characters and want to follow them no matter who or what they are.

GUILLERMO ARRIAGA: Contradiction is for me the essence of human nature. The more contradictory someone is, the more human they appear to me. For example, Paul can look selfish in his relationship with Mary and absolutely generous with Christina. Jack is speaking of love all the time, and he mistreats his son. So I intended to avoid black-and-white characters in *21 Grams*. I don't believe in villains and heroes. I believe in the villain and in the hero that everyone has inside. I wanted the audience to feel compassion with Jack, the 'bad guy' that kills a family and runs away. I wanted them to understand an unfaithful character, as Paul, and to find out that a former drug addict can be a good mother.

ALEJANDRO GONZÁLEZ IÑÁRRITU: I wanted to make a film that's even more intimate and raw. I wanted it to be as direct as possible, and not at all stylized. Rodrigo and I wanted to disappear so people felt that there was no source lighting. I wanted the people to feel like they were looking at some images from a documentary, things that were captured in real time in a real way. I think that with this film Rodrigo touches your heart with every frame. He also really helped me to narrate the tale by pointing out details that proved to be extremely important. This is deliberately a very quiet and subtle film compared to the neurosis of *Amores Perros*. Fortunately there's more than one minute that I like in this film, especially in the performances . . . One of them is the moment where Sean Penn is asking the doctor if he is going to die after his new heart fails, because Sean's performance is remarkable. He expresses such fragility. Paradoxically I was really afraid of shooting the doctor scenes – and there are quite a few of them – because they are always so hard to get right and are frankly mostly unbelievable. Another moment is when Naomi Watts throws Sean out of her house after discovering the truth. Every time that I watched this scene I was moved by it. Naomi's range and honesty is unbelievable. I also like Benicio's simplest moments, such as his arriving home from gaol and kissing his little boy or at the end of the film when he's in the rural clinic asking Naomi for forgiveness just by looking at her.

I wasn't worried about the chronological order of the facts, but rather the emotional order of the events. I like that this film obligates you to judge again the same fact that you already saw before, and revise your prejudice. The editing phase was a very experimental and psychological time.

The people I work with are my family and my partners. It's an organic work and I hope that I can work for ever with these people. That way, you develop continuity and are able to grow together. I have been working with Rodrigo [Prieto] and Brigitte [Broch] for the last ten years and with Martín Hernández for twenty years. Memphis was like a Mexican invasion. Fortunately, after *Amores Perros* all of us continued to grow and learn more about our craft by working with others. Brigitte worked on various projects and Rodrigo worked with Spike Lee and Curtis Hanson on *The 25th Hour* (2002) and *8 Mile* (2002). Martín did the sound design for *City of God* (2002) and Gustavo Santaolalla and Aníbal Kerpel have just completed the music for Walter Salles's *The Motorcycle Diaries* (2004). When we all got together again, they were able to bring me the things they had learned and we returned to our roots.

RODRIGO PRIETO *cinematographer*: From the start we talked about the colours and what differences we could achieve. One thing we were struggling with is that we found that in America the colours weren't as vivid in terms of the interiors of houses as the colours they are painted outside. We had to adapt. In *Amores Perros* you see houses where the interior walls are very vivid blues and greens and this is the way that houses are in Mexico. We were struggling to keep strong colours in *21 Grams*, especially with the bleach-bypass process that produces colour. I used a little more colour in the

God's lonely man: Benicio del Toro as Jack Jordan in *21 Grams*

lighting this time. Paul's world is a little bluer to express his loneliness and his melancholy. His wardrobe was also designed to accentuate this and in the night lighting I use mercury vapour lights that are blue-green in hue. In Jack's world, where we went for more yellow and red tones, for the night lighting I used sodium-vapour type of lamps that give a very characteristic street lighting. Christina's world was more golden with a little red. When she goes back to her previous life of drugs we really pumped up the colour, with the lighting emphasizing amber, red and green.

Again, all of it was hand-held. Sometimes we used sandbags on top of a dolly. As with *Amores Perros* we wanted to have that breathing feel. The hand-held takes away the mechanical part of the camerawork to make it feel a little more organic. Also, in terms of the actual way that you work on the set, this way is much less obtrusive. You don't have obstructions such as a big dolly or tracks. You just light it, walk in with a camera and are ready to go. It's very helpful for the actors as well. As a cameraman, working hand-held is much more intuitive, there are no intermediates that you need to signal when you wish to move in for an extreme close-up.

BRIGITTE BROCH *production designer*: There was also a lot of Memphis reality. There is a lot of suffering still lingering in that city. The blues was born there and there are still clear racial and economic problems. We also wanted to capture the abandoned buildings and the exuberant vegetation that reminds you of sweat and passion. We looked at books by William Eggelston, juke joints, broken landscapes, and photographs by local artists.

RODRIGO PRIETO: I felt that we were initially trying too hard to make it not look like Memphis. When we were looking for locations within Memphis Alejandro would often feel loath to use somewhere that was too character-istic. We were feeling uncomfortable with that and I finally told Alejandro that we should embrace it. More and more we started accepting locations that had a very specific Memphis feel and texture without also trying to be too obvious about it. There were also some places that looked amazing that we didn't use because we thought that it was a bit much. It was a question of striking a balance.

The prison scenes were also very difficult because the space was so tight and enclosed. The actors and myself could barely all fit in the cell. Alejandro certainly likes to make me work hard. There were several other locations like this. When we shot in the bathroom in Paul's apartment I had to sit in the bathtub and then leap out at the moment Paul looks into the mirror. To get light in this sequence so that I was not then reflected in the mirror was very challenging but I really like this kind of challenge. When you are uncomfortable it probably means that it is a better shot.

On 21 *Grams* Alejandro pretty much continued what he'd done on *Amores Perros* in terms of casting the actors and rehearsing with them. He doesn't choose actors dependent on their ability to help bring finance to the movie, or for their likely contribution to the box office. And I think the main reason Alejandro did 21 *Grams* in the States was because of the actors: to tell that story, he wasn't sure that he would get what he had in his mind from only Mexican or Spanish actors. He approached it in a very similar way, taking his time and being very specific in terms of what he wanted from the performances and from each piece of dialogue.

It is amazing to watch Alejandro work; it is of an intensity that is almost spiritual. There is a deep respect for the actors, the emotions and for telling the story among the whole crew so I've learned to also get into this mode. With a camera you are so close to the actors and having to respond to them that you almost become an actor as well. It is very exciting. There becomes a point where you become a spectator and your job is a real privilege. Operating the camera you really are the first one to witness the performance and from the best angle. The camera is the best seat in the house. This feeling of privilege has happened to me on many occasions where you get a great ticket to see these incredible performances.

GUILLERMO ARRIAGA: I always describe this film as one about hope and love. How can someone overcome the deepest abyss? How can hope be found in the darkest places? I see this movie as the journey of three characters from hell to heaven and back to hell and then their struggle to come back. Jack comes from the hell of gaol and abuse, Christina from the hell of drug addiction and Paul from the hell of bad health. When they think that heaven has arrived, Jack through Jesus, Christina through her family and Paul with his new heart, circumstances throw them again to an even deeper hell. This is the theme of 21 *Grams*: how can these characters find hope inside darkness; how can someone fight for life in a moment when death is striking with all its strength?

ALEJANDRO GONZÁLEZ IÑÁRRITU: I was interested in hope and I sincerely wish that I were able to convey this, as it is, I admit, a very intense and heavy film. I did struggle a lot in the editing and could see the film getting heavier and heavier. It was as if I were the pilot of a jumbo jet that was in danger of never taking off. I really tried to make the point that despite the intensity the characters were brave enough to confront their amazing losses.

My wife and I lost a baby two days after he was born. I dedicated *Amores*

Perros to Luciano, the son that we lost. *21 Grams* I dedicate to my wife. The presence of the absence is heavy.

I can tell you that there is no bigger loss than the one that Naomi's character suffers in the film. Some people have said that this is too much, but I say to them that life is like that. A friend of mine just recently lost his father and his sister to cancer. They died just two days apart. To put this in a film would feel as if you were making some terrible soap opera, but life is sometimes like that. There was a critic in Mexico who didn't like *21 Grams* and I told him that the reason he didn't like it was because he had nothing to lose. He has no wife, no children, not even a photograph of a dog or a plant. I feel that anybody who has something to lose or has already lost something can connect with this film.

I think that in the end I have an obsession and probably I will be repeating myself in different ways and times, but I definitely have a shadow that I project and I can't escape from it. The main difference between *Amores Perros* and *21 Grams* was that *Amores Perros* was three stories that intersected in an accident and *21 Grams* is only one story told from three different points of view. All these people reach a point where they stop living and merely begin to survive. How can you return to your life after such a moment? I think that redemption is not the end or an infinite state once you reach it, as many people believe. I think that it is just a temporary state, from which to begin again the strange cycle of life.

I would love to shoot in Mexico again. What has always helped me in my life is that I don't always know what I'm going to do, but I have always known what I am definitely not going to do. I can't imagine myself working to orders or the authority of another voice. In fact, I have a problem with authority, full stop. When somebody tries to interfere even a little bit in my process, it's very hard for me, so to submit to this machinery is not in my character. But you should never say 'never', because there could be some great novel's rights in the hands of the studio . . .

* * *

Guillermo del Toro enjoyed a big US hit in 2004 with Hellboy *(the film grossed over $60 million in the US alone). Based on the graphic comic by Mike Mignola, it concerns a demon raised from infancy by kindly surrogate father (John Hurt) after being conjured by and rescued from the Nazis; he grows up to become a defender against the forces of darkness. Photographed by Guillermo Navarro and starring Ron Perlman as the eponymous hero, the film is distributed worldwide by Columbia TriStar/Sony Pictures. Del Toro has just announced plans to direct a sequel in 2006.*

BERTHA NAVARRO *producer*: *The Devil's Backbone* really liberated Guillermo in terms of his being able to discern between personal projects on the one hand and studio assignments on the other. Interestingly, *Hellboy* is a real synthesis of both. It's a really personal project, but one made within the Hollywood structure. It's amazing that they let him do this very personal film with a huge budget but no stars. Guillermo is very happy with it.

GUILLERMO DEL TORO *director*: I work where I am allowed to – be that Spain, Prague, or the US. Wherever I go, however, I am a Mexican film-maker, and that is a fact that gets lost on the people who make these criticisms. They believe – in what is a form of ultimate racism – that if you leave then you are no longer 'one of us' and you're not going to come back. Well, Alfonso and I came back. Alfonso stayed and did *Y tu mamá* while I was rejected and went to do *The Devil's Backbone*. I was then rejected again, because even though *The Devil's Backbone* was half Mexican in terms of finance the authorities decreed that it was a Spanish film.

BERTHA NAVARRO: *The Devil's Backbone* opened things up in Hollywood for Guillermo. He was very at ease with himself after making this film, as it was very personal to him and that gave him the confidence to tackle a big-budget franchise with *Blade II* without striving to make it into a personal film.

Previously, del Toro's Spanish-language works had represented his more personal approach to film-making while the bigger-budgeted American studio projects – for one reason and another – saw the director mostly struggling to stamp his own personal vision on genre pictures. Hellboy, however, muddied these waters.

GUILLERMO DEL TORO: The only movie that truly blurs this line is *Hellboy*. This is really a combination of both.

  Blade II was a very joyful experience. It was the opposite to *Mimic* in that I didn't have any aspirations to making a personal film and just wanted to give a personal touch to a movie that was unequivocally commercial. I was in total agreement with the producers and the studio on the movie we were making. On *Mimic* we were making two different movies. On *Blade II* I was very aware of what I was making and thoroughly enjoyed every minute of it. I was very afraid of fucking around with the screenplay too much because I understood that the franchise had its own rules.

  The main thing was that I felt that I could exercise some muscles that I was going to need on *Hellboy*. Also, I have all my life made mid-term plans. When I was a kid I decided to study make-up so that I could set up my own

© Columbia Pictures

Giving evil hell: Ron Perlman (and 'friend') as the eponymous *Hellboy*

make-up company to allow me to do the effects for my own movie. After *Mimic* I said, 'I'm going to do my Spanish movie first and then I will do an American commercial movie and the two together will get my *Hellboy*.' Just like *The Devil's Backbone* was sixteen years in the wanting. I can tell you right now that my two favourite of my own films so far are *The Devil's Backbone* and *Hellboy*. I love them both and I could die a happy man just knowing that somewhere there are others who also like these two movies too.

The way I see the movies that I have done is that to me they are all one big movie that says, 'Hi, I'm Guillermo del Toro and I'm kind of ugly and disenfranchised.' *Hellboy* is ultimately what I think an atomic adventure-book movie could be and is very different from the other comic-book franchise and has a huge heart and a lot of beauty in the horror. It also has a lot of beautiful horror and very beautiful creatures and it's a celebration of otherness and being different. It is a Beauty and the Beast story where at the end they kiss and they both turn to beasts.

Some directors are very good at shooting dialogue, like Woody Allen or Quentin Tarantino, and I admire them, but when I do it it's so painful for me. My ideal movie would have no dialogue; it would just be a camera implicating the viewer in the action. I try to use the camera as if it were a curious child, always tiptoeing and trying to get a better view, but it keeps being pulled away, like when your mother is pulling you away from the scene of an accident but you keep rubbernecking to try to catch the last glimpse of the victim. I love to use the camera in this way to play with perspective. This occurs in *Cronos* where Ron Perlman is beating the crap out of Federico Luppi in front of the billboard. The camera pulls back a mile away, so that you see the whole billboard with them very tiny. I like to play hide-and-seek with the moment and be dragging the camera away just as the worst is about to happen. I have a killing in *Hellboy* that is very much like that. I have the camera in a position and then move it so that you go, 'Whoa, did I just see that or not?'

8

The State of Things

MARTHA SOSA *producer*: I believe that we cannot afford to lose this momentum within Mexico, and that my responsibility – and also the responsibility of our famous actors and directors – is to ensure that the international media know that we regard culture not as a luxury but as a *necessity*. That way, maybe, our government will also get this message. If we are known in the world, it's because of our culture: our books, our films, our music, our food. This is the only way we can last as a culture. It's the responsibility of the successful – the lucky – ones, and at the moment this is quite an extensive list that includes Alfonso Cuarón, Diego Luna, Arturo Ripstein, Guillermo del Toro, Gael García Bernal and Alejandro González Iñárritu. These are the ones who have to really open their mouths – because, as you know, nobody listens to producers. And thankfully, they are doing it.

ALFONSO CUARÓN *director*: I hate it when people talk of all that is happening as part of the changes post Vicente Fox. It was all already going on, actually. Fox is merely a by-product of the changes that are going on in this country. He was chosen and elected not because of Vicente Fox, but because people were pissed off with the PRI, and Fox himself knows this. On the other hand, I don't have the perception that Fox is a crook, as opposed to our previous president. I don't think he's corrupt. Maybe he is and I'm being naive. But then I don't agree necessarily with the way he is trying to handle our country as if it is a corporation.

ÁNGELES CASTRO *Director,* CCC: I think we had expectations, perhaps *naive* expectations, regarding the Fox government. One of our main expectations was that in a cultural sense we would have the same level of support. At this time, culture is not a priority. Because the country is suffering terrible economic problems.

GUILLERMO DEL TORO *director*: To be honest, our current president is not unlike our other presidents in his lack of interest in culture.

We almost had a very sad epilogue about the Mexican industry when they were trying to exterminate IMCINE and the CCC. And I said to people that we had to all be united, or together as an industry we would all go to hell. Those events were a warning sign. I repeat again: we should be united to form a strong front and we should not underestimate the value of having all film-makers standing firm together.

I do not say this in the poetic way of 'I would like to teach the world to sing' but it really should be a much needed call to arms.

Vicente Fox initially appeared supportive of the film industry – a support that included the announcement of an initiative to boost local film produc-tion by applying a one peso levy to all cinema admissions, with the intention of channelling monies raised directly into local production. However, the initiative provoked outrage from Motion Picture Association President Jack Valenti and was swiftly withdrawn.

ALFREDO JOSKOWICZ *film-maker/Director,* IMCINE: The Mexican Congress passed a 1 per cent box office levy on ticket sales at the Mexican box office. In 2002 Mexican exhibitors sold something in the region of a hundred and fifty million tickets at an average cost of $3 so we expected to have $15 million dollars for our two funds, FOPROCINE and FIDECINE. The reaction of Motion Picture Association President Jack Valenti was immediate. He sent a letter to President Vicente Fox saying that they felt violated because the Mexican Congress did not consult with them over the decision. In January of this year the five major studios took legal action and issued the Mexican government with a lawsuit. It is currently going through the courts, but I do not think that the money will be coming. We in the film community are all outraged, but we have to follow the legal process, which is lengthy. So we are trying to divert our energies to finding other possible avenues of finance. It is interesting that in Brazil large corporations make tax contributions to national film production.

Fox's institutional overhaul then became much clearer on 12 November 2003. In an announcement to Congress that provoked howls of outrage both within the industry and throughout the international film community, Fox proposed plans to end the Mexican government's decades-long involvement with the industry by dissolving both IMCINE and the CCC and selling off the Churubusco Azteca studios. In an open letter to the govern-ment, artistic and intellectual commentators and film-makers including González Iñárritu, Alfonso and Carlos Cuarón and Salvador Carrasco vehemently opposed Fox's intentions. Fox's measures were subsequently abolished, with continued support pledged to all three institutions.

JOSÉ LUIS GARCÍA AGRAZ *director*: Although attributed to Goebbels, it was actually Hanns Johst, the Nazi head of the German Writers' Union, who said, 'When I hear the word "culture", I reach for my revolver.' In Mexico, though, we don't need bullets to threaten or demolish culture. You need look no further than the law itself for the means of exterminating, for example, an institution whose specific function is the promotion and dissemination of culture, or a school dedicated to the education of future Mexican artists. The means to do this are dissolution, liquidation, extinction, merger or expropriation.

As well as the institutes and funds that support cinematographic activity, the Fox government proposed the 'de-incorporation, liquidation, extinction or merger' of Notimex, the official news agency, the Colegio de Posgraduados de Chapingo which makes strategic studies of the Mexican countryside, the earth, etc., and of the Prónosticos para la Asistencia Pública, a public-health-authority research institute.

The proposal suggested that 'faced with a shortage of budgetary funds for the coming year', 'a series of measures as regards de-incorporation, rationalization, and budgetary austerity' be carried out 'in order to generate savings that allow the increase of expenditure destined to programmes of social and economic benefit that carry priority'.

IMCINE is the sole public body that still provides financial support for cinematographic creation and creators – an activity that has clearly moved to the private sector. That is how cold, insensitive and lacking in historical perspective managerial thinking becomes when it is not accompanied by the slightest interest in art and culture. In an ideal world, public servants would be both good administrators and people sensitive to artistic creation.

ALEJANDRO GONZÁLEZ IÑÁRRITU *director*: When it was suggested to Churchill that he should close the museums and stop the funds for every cultural project because the country needed money for the war, his response was that if we sell this and close that, then what we are fighting for?

Mexico is a country of miracles. In fact, it's a miracle that we're even still alive because there are so many things that have to be solved. Everybody is talking about the hot things that are happening in Latin American cinema, and in Mexican cinema in particular, and I feel ashamed about this because I know that *nothing* is happening. This is the problem. All these films that have been made by people such as myself, Alfonso Cuarón, Carlos Bolado or Carlos Reygadas are quite simply miracles that have exploded.

In poor countries such as mine, art is a secondary need; people should come first, and I agree with that. But if the money that we pay in taxes goes towards food, education, medicine and all of the things that they say the money is going towards, everything will be all right. But the problem is that our politicians are the shame of the nation. They spend millions of dollars in costly presidential campaigns they fight between one party and the other without any result, solution, ideas or straight planning for the country. By so clearly favouring the television industry over the cinema industry, these self-same politicians forget that the cinema industry can create a lot of employ-ment, exportation and very positive cultural and economic consequences. With just with 2 per cent of what they stole or 1 per cent of what they spend to promote themselves, we could have a powerful industry.

BERTHA NAVARRO *producer*: I do think that institutions such as IMCINE should be there to help film-makers, especially first-time film-makers. But the contradiction is that they are also producers, and I think that an Institute should nourish and help make films, but not itself be actively involved in making them – as they can only reflect the dominant ideology of the state. The increased freedom of speech in Mexico remains inextricably linked to the rise of the independent producer. Independent film-making is more open to freedom.

CARLOS CUARÓN *writer/director*: If you have a good solid project, then one of the private production companies is going to take it. The majority of the films that go through IMCINE become stuck in production: the pre-sales are not good, and on some the quality is not that good, and none of the private investors want to share the risk. As a film-maker, my point of view is that IMCINE should produce only short films or features by first time directors. IMCINE should certainly not produce beyond this, or even distribute.

What the state *could* do for cinema

GAEL GARCÍA BERNAL *actor*: According to the media, Mexico is one of the hottest spots right now talent-wise – but it is also one of the hardest places for film in terms of economics and indigenous industry. Other Latin American countries such as Brazil and Argentina are constantly introducing legislation to support their national cinema, and all despite their own fragile economies. This is very inspiring, and something I think that Mexico should learn from. Cinema in Mexico *can* be sustainable and it *can* be an industry and it *can* become a major source of revenue for the country.

ÁNGELES CASTRO: I think that if the state is not going to support cultural endeavours then it has to make law in order to stimulate private investment. Without this legislation, it is a huge risk for private investors to participate in cultural projects, because many of these projects have no way of recouping their investments, meaning that there's no reason to conduct business.

GUILLERMO ARRIAGA *writer*: It is all connected to the distribution of the peso at the box office. The exhibitors take a very large chunk; the distributors a chunk, leaving very little to return to the producer. To have a successful Mexican film for the producer, the box office must reach at least $7 million. That is a *lot* of money.

JOSÉ LUIS GARCÍA AGRAZ: For some years now, the various cinematographic sectors have wanted to undertake a full-scale restructuring of the industry. We want the institutions to function more efficiently. We want a new division of box-office receipts. The producer, the party that has taken the most risks, receives the least. That's why there are no producers who want to risk their money in such a disadvantageous manner. It means the only sectors that grow are the cinema owners – in their majority linked to American chains – and the distributors, Fox, Warner, UIP, Buena Vista, etc. And we all know what interests they respond to.

GUILLERMO DEL TORO: We are fighting trans-national companies, companies that are very aware that Mexico is an incredibly important market, and it is important that legislation changes at a federal level in order for our industry to survive. Mexico has an incredibly rich heritage and history of great movies in all genres, and to let our identity in cinema be lost would be a tragedy.

JOSÉ LUIS GARCÍA AGRAZ: What is required is a law like in France or Spain – and now in Brazil and Argentina – that gives incentives at the box office, that exempts films from tax, that displays an awareness of the importance of having a national film industry that is strong and competitive, which means having more freedom to create and incentivize national production. But everything indicates that the majority of this government's civil servants are ignorant of what art is, and that, among other things, it serves to satisfy needs that go beyond man's animal nature. And woman's. And children's.

As one of our great writers, Fernando del Paso, has recently pointed out:

We have a government that does not know what culture is. That does not understand it. That is unaware that the various manifestations of Mexican culture are – and have been for many years – the most valuable part of our exports. And the part that is the most precious and the most appreciated by people around the world.

We have a government that does not know – and if it does it prefers to hide the fact – that the Mexican institutions charged with promoting and disseminating our culture, within and beyond our borders, have paltry budgets, which, if eliminated, would make no real contribution to the savings the Executive intends to achieve, but would achieve this: paltry savings. But the cost, to the development of our cultural wealth, would be immense.

We have a government that does not understand – and if it does it prefers to say nothing – that these institutes and schools were not set up to generate profits. They are not businesses. They are not companies. They are not Coca-Cola. They are bodies for long-term investment, which is recouped, and richly so, when they carry out their functions properly. They invest in the talent of the Mexican people, and they are successful when this talent bears its fruit. On many occasions, as is well known, IMCINE recoups a good part of its financial investment. On some, everything. IMCINE's money is not given away lightly.

We have a government that intends to generate savings in order to increment expenditure destined for programmes of a social benefit, which have priority, but which ignores – or pretends to ignore – the fact that culture – like education – also represents a social good. Although I doubt that the majority of our government's functionaries have ever received the benefit of culture.

RODRIGO PRIETO *cinematographer*: Look at *Alexander* (2004). We have British, French and Dutch money, and it's because of the tax breaks that we are shooting in England and bringing money into the country. This is the kind of thing that should be happening in Mexico – not considering closing down IMCINE and the film schools. Why not instead give tax breaks and incentives to the producers, so that we can sustain what is a very important and obviously very creative industry? The industry, a major boost to culture, could potentially also give a major boost to the Mexican economy.

DANIEL BIRMAN *producer*: The main obstacles are the same as always; production costs are high and the sharing out of the income is much less favourable for the producer. Distributors and exhibitors really take the biggest share of the pie, but there is always a film or two that passes the 1 million attendance and makes a profit. My grandfather has always impressed on me the huge risk involved in producing, not only in Mexico but also worldwide. He says, 'If I knew what films would do huge business, I would leave the producing part, and just charge to give advice.'

ROSA BOSCH *producer: Japón* was actually very aggressively marketed internationally. But if we are talking of these more niche titles within Mexico, then no matter how in love with a film one may be, the reality of the matter is that rules and regulations don't ensure that these films get the exhibition support they perhaps deserve. There are legal protections that we as producers all want, and there is a very open-door policy that is the result of regulations being lobbied for by producers such as Bertha Navarro, to make sure that locally produced pictures do get a fair crack of the whip compared to more obviously commercial titles, American or otherwise. But look at the UK. Even with the various film bodies that exist here, particularly the Film Council, this doesn't necessarily provide a cinema that is entirely active and fully culturally diverse.

LEONARDO GARCÍA TSAO *critic/academic*: Like everybody else throughout the world, we in Mexico have been overtaken by Hollywood. The audience has been conditioned by Hollywood, so when we get films from Spain or Argentina the audience doesn't want to go and see them. Even Almodóvar isn't successful in Mexico. *All About My Mother* (1999) didn't do any business here. It comes down to the fact that Mexican audiences want to see only a handful of Mexican films and the rest of the time will watch films only made by Hollywood.

This is a problem of education and culture and if the official stance on culture is negligence then this is part of the problem. We also have several large television companies taking their cue from the rest of the world to produce mass-market reality TV shows that are in danger of rendering audiences brain dead.

ALFONSO CUARÓN: I believe in the responsibility of the government to support culture, and to fund and help IMCINE. The problem with Mexican cinema is the lack of continuity. When I raised this issue about the sustaining of a Mexican cinema industry six years ago, the bureaucrats at IMCINE told me that there was only one true film industry in the world and that is Hollywood; the rest are just film communities. I told them that I disagreed. You have France, you have Spain, you have England, you have India, and you have Hong Kong. What they wanted was to control the industry completely, not to regenerate it.

What is very encouraging in Mexico is when, as has happened, the biggest film of the year is not an American film, it is a Mexican film. That shows willingness.

ROSA BOSCH: Mexico is now one of the top three emerging countries in terms of cinema attendance, so the rate of growth of the whole audio-visual sector has been phenomenal and there has been an explosion in the number of cinema screens. Financial analysts can now see that, as a business, cinema in Mexico is becoming viable, which will inevitably trigger further private investment. This is, of course, in conjunction with a group of film-makers who have really been able to deliver the goods. By the same token, the film-makers have more energy and more imaginative scope to devote to their films because they are no longer subject to the pitiful funds available from IMCINE or any other bureaucratic organization.

ALFREDO JOSKOWICZ: So we are all fighting and discussing, especially right now as we have something like 70 per cent of our talent in Mexico without jobs. I am constantly, with the help of my minister, asking for production funds.

The demands of the Mexican audience

DANIEL BIRMAN: Right now there's a huge need from Mexican audiences to see Mexican cinema, and what they want to see is what they are living. I really don't think that it varies that much from class-to-class or region-to-region; the shared experience is often the same, and so these audiences are closely linked. There is a need for Mexican cinema to reflect our culture and our lives with all their various idiosyncrasies. That said – and I think this is universal and not just confined to Mexican films – people do not want to go to the cinema only to suffer. I think a very important aspect of film-making is to consider for whom you are making the films. I don't believe that a director should make a film only to satisfy their own views and desires. I believe you must be tolerant of the audience and differing perspectives, without sacrificing your own point of view.

HUGO RODRÍGUEZ *director*: I've always said to my students that if we don't devote at least a small part of our thinking to the person who will see our creation, we shouldn't complain afterwards when no one comes to the cinema to see our work. I believe in individual creativity and in experimenting, but you have to be a mature artist – and obviously I'm not speaking only in terms of age – to meet the challenges that these works represent.

*In 2001 Daniel Birman founded Arthaus Films. Prior to Arthaus, art-house
distributors were releasing only two or three 'specialized' titles per year.*

DANIEL BIRMAN: We implemented a strategy to tackle the lack of diversity
faced by Mexican cinema-goers. We founded Arthaus with this philosophy
in mind, and it worked. People are eager to see all kinds of stories, not only
action and special-effects films. I think the most important part of being a
distributor is to show the audience what they want to see. Unfortunately
there are many wonderful films out there every year that are almost impossible to market; therefore we are forced to 'sacrifice' many of them. But our
idea of bringing good-quality films was made, basically, because it was predominantly art and foreign-language pictures that were being sacrificed.

We have proved that there is a market for our films. And exhibitors have
also seen this. Therefore we've established special circuits of five to fifteen
cinemas in Mexico City, and probably another fifteen to twenty throughout
the rest of Mexico to show our movies. And it has turned out very well for
all of us. I believe that all Mexican films should be able to have a theatrical
life. That is one of the reasons I firmly opposed the plans to sell IMCINE. Even
though I believe that it's not the best distribution channel in Mexico, it is still
a distribution outlet for not-so-commercial films, and a valuable resource
through which these films can be screened in the traditional manner in movie
theatres.

The Latin American Spanish-language dimension

EMMANUEL LUBEZKI *cinematographer*: We have had such renaissances
before, and they have always died. I think that we have right now a great
talent pool of writers, directors, actors, cinematographers, production
designers, etc., but what we also have, and what we have not had before, is a
massive amount of people speaking Spanish who also happen to have
money. It's also important that the biggest minority in the United States
speaks Spanish and so now all of the studios are moving towards making
low-budget movies that can make millions of dollars in these markets. For
the first time in many years we potentially have a great business.

ROSA BOSCH: From a purely business point of view, I guess there's a strong
case for saying that this has happened against the background of Latin
America as a continent accelerating its growth in regard to cinema distribution, box office, and increased and improved screens. There is clearly

development throughout all of Latin America, not just Mexico. Plus, the rest of the world is really paying attention. Latin American cinema has not had this kind of attention for many years.

FRANCISCO GONZÁLEZ COMPEÁN *producer*: AltaVista has been reconfigured but I am still involved with the company through some of the projects that I originally began to develop there. I have started Draco Films, my own production company. I'm not so sure how we're going to do it, but we do want to break into the US market and are trying to develop films that could be marketed in America. There is the Latin way and the crossover way and I think that both ways should be explored very conscientiously.

BERTHA NAVARRO: We used to focus only on 'Mexican films', but now I am co-producing with Chile and Ecuador and I hope in the near future to also have a project in Argentina. I think that the goal now, and certainly with a film that I have just produced in Ecuador,[1] is to make the best Spanish-speaking films. It's not only Mexican films. This tendency of working with other non-Mexican director and actors is something that I think will grow for Latin American producers: it's a new way of enabling us to tell our stories, and also a way of making the Spanish-speaking market even stronger.

To achieve this, we need to have a wider distribution and to make sure we have presence at all the international markets. It is so difficult to do any film that is not in the English language. I think that we could be potentially the most important market. As a language Spanish is spreading beyond the Spanish-speaking countries, and we have a huge Latin community in the States. Also, throughout Europe there is an increased awareness of Spanish-language products. This is in part due to the status of prominent Spanish cinema auteurs such as Pedro Almodóvar. What is happening now is something that feels evolutionary and very natural. This is also reflected in the renewed pride that people in Latin American countries have for their cinema. This is very much the case in Mexico where audiences are once again watching Mexican movies and taking satisfaction from them. I also think that the Mexican audience is like any other audience in that there is a growing sense of fatigue when faced with the same Hollywood films. It is not

---

[1] Directed by Sebastián Cordero, *Crónicas* screened to great acclaim at the 2004 Cannes Film Festival. The film concerns the star of a sensationalistic Miami news show who travels to the Ecuadorian coastal village of Babahoyo to cover the story of a serial killer who hunts children. When his personal ambitions gets out of hand, tragic consequences ensue.

just Mexican films that are being more widely shown in Mexico but distribution is also opening up for Spanish and other European films. This was not the case four years ago.

Producciónes Anhelo is the production company Cuarón set up with business magnate Jorge Vergara.

ALFONSO CUARÓN: We created this company to do *Y tu mamá* and in the process of doing the film we talked about putting together a company in the States, which we now have called Monsoon. It was actually Jorge's initiative, saying, 'You are forgetting about Latin America', and 'Though you have it easy there are a lot of people who don't.' So we said, 'Let's go for it.' The idea is to not only do Mexican films but also films in Spanish. We will develop Mexican projects but we also want to be open, just like they did in Asia, so that it was not only about Hong Kong cinema but also about the areas around. We also have something that is priceless that even the Asians don't have: a shared language. If we can create a circuit of films from Mexico, Argentina, etc., then it is going to be healthier for everybody. That doesn't mean to lose the individual or national voices – I hate the word 'national' – but certainly the individual voices from each culture.

Mexicans in Hollywood/globalization

ÁNGELES CASTRO: I have been thinking a lot recently about globalization. It would be better, I think, to view it in a positive way rather than bemoaning it. It is good that Mexican directors and film artists can leave to work in America, but most do come back. Look at Alfonso Cuarón and Emmanuel Lubezki and *Y tu mamá también*. Cuarón is also developing another project to be shot here in Mexico. Look also at Alfonso Arau and Luis Mandoki, who are both going to be shooting pictures here.

CARLOS CUARÓN: OK, Alfonso [Cuarón] made *Harry Potter and the Prisoner of Azkaban*; Alejandro [González Iñárritu] made *21 Grams*; [Guillermo] del Toro made *Hellboy*; so Carlos Reygadas is the only one working in Mexico City. But after *Harry Potter*, Alfonso is coming back to Mexico because we have other projects.

EMMANUEL LUBEZKI: Because we have often worked in an environment where there is no supporting industry, it's easy to develop your own distinctive voice. In the States that's more difficult, because there is such a strong industry, and it has certain standards, and consequently there's a fear of experimentation. Working in the States, I have less chance to experiment. It's just more difficult for an author to find a voice in America than it is in Mexico. In the States you don't have any freedom but, on the other hand, you have everything else. In Mexico it is very different. You, the film-maker, are very poor, almost to the extent that you don't have the tools to do the job. What you *do* have is complete freedom, and this freedom is undoubtedly a big plus.

ROSA BOSCH: The current level of craftsmanship and talent in Mexican cinema is astonishing. One can perhaps be unfair to Arturo Ripstein's generation, because they simply didn't have this level of technical excellence; and they certainly didn't have casts of the calibre of Gael García Bernal, Diego Luna and Salma Hayek, actors who are able to get even the major studios excited.

Felipe Cazals has made only one film in eight years. Paul Leduc hasn't made a feature in something like ten years. The only one who has had a wider output is Arturo Ripstein. And, in a way, Ripstein was at a very interesting, if you like, blossoming moment in Mexican cinema with *Profundo carmesí*. Since then he seems to have worked mainly in video. These directors have simply been overtaken. Ripstein and Leduc would consider themselves *auteurs* in the sense that, for example, Theo Angelopoulos is an *auteur*. And this perhaps can be a dangerous thing. Though their films have screened at international festivals, they haven't had the same kind of sustained publicity enjoyed by films directed by Cuarón, del Toro and González Iñárritu. Those directors have their films released commercially on a massive global scale, and this obviously sustains their reputation and increases their exposure. In some ways it's sad to say this, but inevitably there has been a takeover – not a handover, a takeover.

BERTHA NAVARRO: The pressure you have as a film-maker now is how to make sure that your films are more commercial and can be appreciated by a wider audience.

But I must also add that it's my belief that you should be able to make any film you want. If there is a healthy industry, it should sustain the *auteurs* and those making more personal expressions. Not every film should be made because of its potential to generate box office. But the circumstances, the economics and the general market are so against us that you have always to have an eye on commercial success.

ALFONSO CUARÓN: It's so important that though Guillermo, Alejandro and myself can now work anywhere in Hollywood, we still are able to find our individual voices. There are other film-makers who have continuity and make a film year after year, such as Ripstein. I mean, you may not like the films but ultimately they have an audience, even though there is no pretence of their regenerating the industry. And yet ultimately Ripstein is a film-maker with an undeniable international presence. Ripstein is not reaching out to audiences and probably couldn't care less about audiences. It is about having an eloquence that is accessible. It is important to differentiate between the industry and cinema, but we must never forget that the healthier the industry the more possibilities for cinema.

JOSÉ LUIS GARCÍA AGRAZ: There are extraordinary Mexican film-makers who don't yet have a worldwide reputation. Ignacio Ortiz Cruz is a director from Oaxaca and a graduate of the CCC, writer and director of *La Orilla de la tierra* (*The Edge of the Earth*, 1994) and *Cuento de hadas para dormir a los cocodrilos* (*Bedtime Fairy Tale for Crocodiles*, 2002).

BERTHA NAVARRO: I think this is a really interesting period for women directors in Mexico. There is an amazing documentary film [*Recuerdos* (*Remembrance*, 2003)] made by Marcela Arteaga, a first-time film-maker and graduate of the CCC. There was also *Perfume de violetas* (2001) by Marisa Sistach. This was a lower-budget film but it was very hard hitting in its depiction of rape and it didn't have the luxury of a huge marketing campaign or a recognizable soundtrack and yet it still managed to find a very good audience.

LEONARDO GARCÍA TSAO: *Perfume de violetas* was quite successful. The film is very much in the league of hard-hitting films about the under-privileged classes and is, I think, Marisa Sistach's best work to-date.

GUILLERMO DEL TORO: In 2001 Alfonso Cuarón – with *Y tu mamá* – and I – with *The Devil's Backbone* – were both hoping our movies would be selected to represent Mexico in the Foreign Film category at the Oscars. I was confident that Alfonso was going to get the majority of the vote, and he felt that I was going to. We spoke the night before the decision was to be announced to wish each other luck, and I told him that if he got it, I would be as happy as if my film had been selected. Of course, the next morning we realized that neither of us had got it.

CARLOS CUARÓN: Marisa Sistach's *Perfume de violetas* was the film they selected, and actually Alfonso and I always said that *Perfume* was in many ways the better film. But, you don't send the best movie to the Academy –

© IMCINE

Ximena Ayala and Nancy Gutiérrez in Marisa Sistach's *Perfume de violetas*

you send the one that they're going to like and that has a chance of winning.

ROSA BOSCH: It's the same everywhere – behind all of these great guys is a great woman. Remember also that women have not just been behind the scenes. Mexico has produced great women directors, such as Marisa Sistach, María Novaro, and Dana Rotberg. That said, I don't want to be led down the feminist route. Women producers and directors have not had it easy in Mexico, but there is sexism everywhere, and in Mexico 'the boys' have also had a tough time directing and getting their films made. What I will say is that all those years of feminism have given women the right to have a family and a career, whereas before they had to choose between the two. The truth of the matter is that in terms of the roles women perform, there have always been fewer women directors than producers, and I really don't know why. I think it's fair to say that within the film industry the majority of roles performed by women are in either PR, marketing, distribution, line producing, or as heads of production in arts and crafts departments. I think that women make very good producers because, in a way, what we are essentially doing is babysitting – both financially and artistically.

The year 2003 saw Gael García Bernal take lead roles in Walter Salles's film about the young Che Guevara, The Motorcycle Diaries, *and Pedro*

Almodóvar's Bad Education. *Bernal can make an economic success of a Mexican project. He also has acquired a spokesman-like status for Mexican cinema in general.*

GAEL GARCÍA BERNAL: It's a tough ride, but it really allows me to reinvent the rules of the game, and often for good. For example, being an actor from Mexico, I perhaps have a freedom that an actor in Hollywood might not have. I'm able to make surprising and uncompromising choices. I do feel an intense responsibility, but I also feel a responsibility towards enjoying my position – and to also being grateful for it. It's a drive, for me, to do the films I want to do, not only because of the consequences that may arise because of them but to also reaffirm why I originally wanted to act.

MARTHA SOSA: Gael is a bona-fide superstar; I would put him in the same league as Marcello Mastroianni now. He's been offered lots of American films. Now he is shooting his first American film, James Marsh's *The King*, an independent feature. I have no doubt that 2004 will be both Gael's and Diego's international year as the films they have made will be seen everywhere. With both Gael and Diego I think it is a case of having waited for the right project to come without fear and working very hard. It has been important to them that they very carefully hand-pick the people that they are going to work with and they are both monitoring their careers very carefully and also have the benefit of having very good American agents.

Diego made *Frida* (2002), his first American studio project; he then made *Open Range* (2003) with Kevin Costner. Then he completed *Dirty Dancing: Havana Nights* (2004). He has also been shooting *Criminal*, a Steven Soderbergh and George Clooney production that is a remake of *Nine Queens*.[2] He has taken a very big step in a very short time. It was between *Open Range* and *Dirty Dancing: Havana Nights* that he made *Nicotina*.

Last words: future prospects

LEONARDO GARCÍA TSAO: I am pessimistic by nature, but Mexican cinema has survived the very worse of times. Think back to the 1980s. The situation was even bleaker than now and yet the cinema managed to survive. I have always said that Mexican film-makers are like cockroaches – not in a

---

[2] Directed by Fabián Bielinsky, *Nine Queens* (*Nueve Reinas*) is a gripping, stylishly shot heist thriller that could be considered to Argentinian cinema what *Amores Perros* is to Mexican cinema.

derogatory sense I must add, but in that they can survive anything. They have a very strong survival instinct. I think that emerging technologies such as Digital and High-Definition will be a salvation for Mexican cinema. We have seen a lot of films recently made digitally. Even Ripstein has done it.

BERTHA NAVARRO: These guys – especially the directors such as [Guillermo] del Toro, Alfonso Cuarón and [Alejandro] González Iñárritu – have very clear ideas of what they want to do and they will go where they have to go to do it. It is important to point out, however, that all three of these directors – and these three are undoubtedly the biggest director figures right now in Mexican cinema – have started producing, and use their influence to discover and nurture other young directors. This is their way of being linked to the Mexican cinema.

ALFONSO CUARÓN: To summarize everything, this 'wave' is an effect of what is happening in the arts in Mexico and not just film. It is a generation reclaiming its part in the world, and not only in Mexico – and this doesn't make you less Mexican. There is a big fear of the old guard, and there are a lot of criticisms of people such as myself and Guillermo that we are selling out and that we're not good Mexicans. I think that you can be universal and still be a good Mexican.

What I find very exciting about Alejandro, Guillermo and Carlos Reygadas is that what we are talking about is a generation and what I am talking about here is not age but minds. There are Mexican film-makers, artists, scientists, entrepreneurs who want to reclaim their position in the world, not only in Mexico.

CARLOS CUARÓN: The Mexican media speaks of a renaissance every six years. It's due to the fact that we change government every six years. IMCINE changes hands and new people make movies, but that's about it. There is no true renaissance. What is happening within Mexico is that there are four or five very bright film-makers, and now most of these are abroad. I am speaking of course of my brother Alfonso, Alejandro González Iñárritu, Guillermo del Toro and Carlos Reygadas, who is doing his specialized art films – actually, I think *Japón* is the best Mexican film in a very long time. It's a similar thing in terms of cinematographers. You have Chivo [Emmanuel Lubezki], Rodrigo Prieto, and maybe three or four others, and they are all now abroad. We also have a big problem with writers because we have never had a huge writing tradition in Mexico in terms of film-making. The ones that we had during the 1940s and 1950s – the Golden Age – were mostly Spaniards that came with the Civil War. Strong writers that are writing and writing also outside of Mexico City are probably only Guillermo Arriaga – for me the best – and then myself. The rest are suffering, and perhaps teaching, because it's very difficult to survive as a writer here.

MARTÍN SALINAS *screenwriter*: I've been involved in teaching, and I still am, though not on a regular basis: I travel a lot, so what I usually do is to get involved in one- or two-week labs or workshops. Being in touch with the new generation of screenwriters and directors from all over Latin America is an extremely nurturing experience to me. In many cases I have continued re-reading the new drafts of scripts that have been brought to that lab, and making notes for the writers up to the final draft. Although I do think that a good story is a good story no matter what the language or culture, I also think that we do need to work hard to dig within our own cultural background and language to explore our roots. My mother, who studied literature, would make me laugh with joy by reading fragments to me of *El Lazarillo de Tormes* and *El Quijote* by the bedside when I was a child, or quote Lope de Vega or Francisco Quevedo, with their sharp angles and notes on human nature. You'll never get something like that from a screenwriting manual published in LA . . .

CARLOS CUARÓN: I'm always optimistic. I believe in talent, so, even though I think we are in something of a crisis regarding talent, I do think there are kids either in high school or film school and even drop-outs who will contribute to film culture. I know this because I am already starting to meet some of them. With Jorge Vergara,[3] Alfonso has a production company here in Mexico and I work in the company as a creative producer. My role is to work very closely with the head of development, nurturing the young talent he finds. Most of these people are very young, and I want to believe in these people I have been meeting in the last two years.

GUILLERMO DEL TORO: The tragedy of Mexico is that we do have the human resources; we don't have the structure to support them. Alfonso, Alejandro and I are part of a panel of judges in a contest that happens every year on the radio. We basically award cash to short films on an annual basis. In those shorts, I have seen a lot of people who I am absolutely sure will eventually become very good film-makers. If you don't water your roots, then you will go dry. It is incredibly important that Bertha, Alejandro and I continue

---

[3] The producer of *Y tu mamá también*, Jorge Vergara is a visionary Mexican businessman who in 1991 founded Omnilife de Mexico SA, a company that creates products for healthy living.

producing. I was talking to Alejandro the other day and I said to him that we have to get together to produce something, to give something back. The key of life is flow, and if you don't make things flow, they die. You have to make your experiences go beyond yourself and count for other people.

ÁNGELES CASTRO: During the hardest, most barren periods of production – and amongst these periods I include the here and now – the film schools are the one sector making films. Some of them may be short films but, still, the schools are the only ones consistently producing. Thanks to the short film festival we organize, there are now many people making shorts, and there is an audience ready and willing to see Mexican short films.

I also think that we have so much that we will contribute to the future of Mexican cinema and in all fields: directing, writing, cinematography. And my hope is that there will be several cross-over breakthroughs of CCC students in the coming years.

GAEL GARCÍA BERNAL: I don't want to be too pessimistic. We have very good foundations in terms of talent, and little by little there are others coming through. The more difficult it is for new film talents to get through, quite often the stronger those talents are. Film may not be high on the agenda for the Mexican government right now – and remember that Vicente Fox's term finishes in a few years – because they see it purely in business terms. But, as a medium, film transcends this. It is through cinema that we learn about other countries and other cultures. And that, after all, is the reason that you and I are talking right now.

PART TWO

Introduction

Timing is everything. There are clear parallels between the writing of *The Faber Book of Mexican Cinema* in 2006 and the completion of this follow-up edition in 2020. As we entered the early 2000s, Mexican cinema was on a creative, critical and commercial roll, spearheaded by the emergence of Alfonso Cuarón, Alejandro González Iñárritu, Carlos Reygadas and Guillermo del Toro. In truth, and as Cuarón pointed out when I interviewed him for this new edition, himself and del Toro were actually connected to the previous generation of Mexican film-makers but the success of projects such as *Y tu mamá también* (2001) and *The Devil's Backbone* (2001) chimed perfectly with the emergence of Iñárritu with *Amores Perros* (2000) and Reygadas with *Japón* (2002).

There was also a surplus of creative talent in terms of composers, cinematographers and inventive private producers; the excellent film schools in Mexico, especially the Centro de Capacitación Cinematográfica (CCC) in Mexico City, continued to produce distinguished new voices at an alarming rate. The only dark cloud on the horizon was the coming to power of Vicente Fox Quesada, who served as the 55th President of Mexico from 1 December 2000 to 30 November 2006. There was a concern that Fox, who campaigned as a right-wing populist, would prove hostile to the funding of arts and culture. However, IMCINE, the Mexican Film Institute, survived, as did their various funding schemes to aid Mexican production.

As I began this book, Andrés Manuel López Obrador, in his third presidential campaign, took over as the Mexican President on 1 December 2018. Representing MORENA, the PT and the socially conservative right-wing Social Encounter Party (PES) under the coalition Juntos Haremos Historia, many in the arts in Mexico were waiting to see what approach this government would adopt in relation to arts and culture. However, if the past shows us anything, it is that Mexican film-making and Mexican film-makers will continue to flourish and survive.

As many of the interviews in this book attest – and this time round I limited myself to interviewing directors and screenwriters only – and as Cuarón's foreword to the book indicates, Reygadas, del Toro, Iñárritu and Cuarón himself did provide inspiration and sustenance to an entirely new generation of film-makers from Mexico. In fact, the quartet enjoyed unprecedented success on an international scale. Reygadas, who many within Mexico regard as the finest director of his generation, has become a permanent fixture at international film festivals, winning multiple awards. *Amores Perros* (Iñárritu) was Mexico's entry to the Academy Awards in 2000. *Pan's Labyrinth* (del Toro) followed in 2006 and *Biutiful* (Iñárritu) in 2010. *ROMA* (Cuarón) triumphed in the Best Foreign Language Film category in 2019. Whether one puts much store in Academy Awards – and many of the winning directors interviewed, though grateful for their victories, don't – what is undeniable is that in recent years Mexico has dominated the ceremony.

Iñárritu became the first Mexican director to be nominated for Best Director for *Babel* in 2006 (in 2019 he became the first Mexican director to be named President of the Cannes Jury). Cuarón won the Best Director award for *Gravity* in 2013, becoming the first Mexican to do so. Iñárritu won best director for *Birdman* in 2014 and for *The Revenant* in 2015, becoming the first Mexican director to win Best Director twice and only the third figure in history to win consecutive Best Director awards. Del Toro won Best Director for *The Shape of Water* in 2018 and then Cuarón won again for *ROMA* in 2019, also becoming the first person to win Best Director and Best Cinematographer. *Birdman* and *The Shape of Water* both also won Best Picture. There have also been Best Cinematography Academy Awards for Guillermo Navaro (*Pan's Labyrinth*, 2006) and Emmanuel Lubezki (*Birdman* and *The Revenant*).

What these victories do create is a strong sense of perception on an international level, the perception that Mexico, despite its myriad social and economic problems and its having to live in the shadow of the United States and suffer the contempt and vehement racism of Donald Trump, has the ability to produce a prodigious amount of incredibly gifted story-tellers and visual artists. If the work of these figures is not inspiration enough, then the recognition that their work receives perhaps provides further validation. It is also important to note that though Carlos Reygadas is the only director of the quartet to remain working in his homeland, del Toro, Cuarón and Iñárritu maintain very close links to their homeland and regard themselves as Mexican wherever they may be working. All of them return to Mexico for festivals such as Morelia and Guadalajara, both of which are also rising in profile, and following Cuarón's return to a Mexican production, Iñárritu is also apparently preparing a feature to be shot back in Mexico. It is important to note that del Toro, Iñárritu and Salma Hayek set up a fund to help support Mexican movie industry workers out of work due to the coronavirus pandemic. The fund has raised about $440,000 so far, and will go first to technical workers like set, costume, sound and visual employees. La Corriente del Golfo, a company founded by Gael García Bernal and Diego Luna, also contributed to the fund.

What is also clear is that no matter how hostile their environment or who is in power, the film-making community has remained solid, and just as established figures have acted as advocates for emerging talent – witness the support of Carlos Reygadas for Amat Escalante – so other figures to recently emerge have used their power and position to bring through others that wish to find their visual voice. The recent *Workforce* (2019) by David Zonana, produced by Michel Franco, is just one example. It's clear that recent Mexican cinema is also united in its desire to tackle the social and economic conditions within Mexico, including the dichotomy between the rich and the poor, and the fact that as Michel Franco points out: 'Mexico is a very violent society.' This willingness to focus on social issues through powerful and compelling human stories is what makes *The Chambermaid* (2018) by Lila Avilés so compelling and engaging, quite apart from the director's unique visual sensibility. A film that achieved worldwide acclaim, *The Chambermaid* was Mexico's 2020 entry to the Best Film in a Foreign Language category at the Academy Awards.

A final note on the figures interviewed in these pages. I wanted to try and convey the diversity in Mexican cinema and the huge range of voices. Mexican cinema is incredibly diverse in terms of tone and aesthetic, with many directors also working between narrative and documentary film-making. I wanted to include a number of film-makers who have excelled in documentary and also a figure like Nicolás Pereda, who is perhaps closest to the notion of an artist film-maker. Like many countries – in fact one could argue all countries – Mexico still has a way to go in terms of gender parity and the fact that the majority of these interviews are with men is representative of that. There were a number of other female film-makers I contacted to be interviewed and would have wished to include but work schedules proved immovable. It is very much hoped that as we witness the emergence of more film-makers from Mexico that an equal proportion of these are women.

As in 2006, Viva México!

Jason Wood

2020

I
Lila Avilés

Lila Avilés studied direction and performing arts with some of the leading theatrical figures in Mexico, including Martín Acosta, Sandra Felix and Juliana Faesler. Avilés also studied film writing with Beatriz Novaro and Paula Marcovich. Initially staring out as an actor, Avilés subsequently moved into directing. Her work as a director includes Gardenia Club, Microdermoabrasión *(National Theatre Award),* Antígona *and* The Chambermaid, *which would become the inspiration for her first feature. Avilés has also directed the operas* Così Fan Tutte *and* Alcina *by Mozart and Händel respectively.*

FEATURES FILMOGRAPHY:
The Chambermaid (La camarista) (2018)
Nena (documentary) (2017)

JASON WOOD: I wondered if you could begin by taking me through your journey into cinema. Prior to *The Chambermaid* (2018) you had acted in a short film (*Caminando las noches,* 2012) and produced and directed a previous short, *Déjà Vu* (2016). Did you study at film school, as Mexico is noted for its film schools?

LILA AVILÉS: I come from the world of theatre. I studied acting and since I left school I have ended up directing, producing and working mainly in theatre, but I always wanted to be a film-maker. Since I didn't study in a formal film school, the only way to produce my film was to do it myself, so I bought the simplest camera I could buy and started doing practice exercises. Not short films, formally, but exercises that were like a cinema school for me. Then I made a short documentary titled *Nena* (2017) that won a prize, and for a number of years I earned the money to help me make *The Chambermaid*. Right now, I'm proud to say that I'm already a film-maker; I found that I was able to unite the two things that I like the most in the world: photographs and humans.

JW: I understand that the film involved a number of production companies but also involved the input of FOPROCINE, the Mexican Film Institute's scheme for assisting lower-budget works. Was the support of IMCINE something which was of great help to you? And, more generally, do you feel that there is a structure in the Mexican film industry today to assist and support emerging young talent?

LA: In my case, I knew that I could not ask for funding from an institution to help produce my film because I didn't have any film CV. The only way to realise the film was by producing myself first, then asking for financing for post-production. That's how Tatiana Graullera, the other producer, and I managed to finish it. First we won The Gabriel Figueroa Film Fund for post-production from Los Cabos Film Festival; there we found our co-producers, and it was then I got support from FOPROCINE to finish post-production. It was almost like a marathon, because we had only one month to make a rough assembly so we could enter the competitions, and in the middle of everything there was a terrible earthquake in Mexico that caused me to move out of my apartment. It was a really crazy period.

JW: Did other figures in the industry – directors or otherwise – come forward to offer help, support or encouragement?

LA: Because I was an outsider I didn't know anyone in the industry, so I was relatively on my own. But I have a friend who is a cinematographer and we've known each other since we were fifteen years old. When I told him that I was going to direct a movie, he told me something that stayed with me. He told me that this film was going to be like a baby and I was the only one who was going to know how to raise it. He also told me to follow my intuition. I now follow my intuition every time. That was my guide when I was filming; it was like something linked with something bigger, something quite magical. There is something really powerful in cinema that makes you feel that you are connected.

JW: And how did *The Chambermaid* begin to develop in terms of both your original idea and your working relationship with co-writer Juan Carlos Márquez? Was the story of Eve and her co-workers in the high-class hotel one of which you had personal experience or was the narrative more directly born from your desire to explore the huge divide between the rich and the poor in contemporary society?

LA: This story began about eight years ago. The first seed was the 1981 book *The Hotel, Room 47* by the visual artist Sophie Calle, in which she

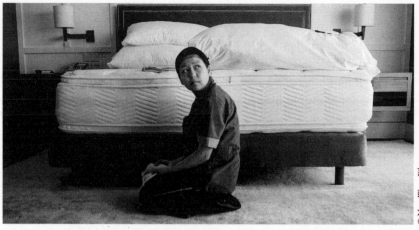

© New Wave Films

A life of servitude: Gabriela Cartol as Eve in *The Chambermaid*

disguised herself as a chambermaid in a hotel in Venice. When I saw that book, I was really curious about that idea and wrote a play that I wanted to present in a real hotel. So, I went to a real hotel and started following the chambermaids in their day-to-day work. I spent seven years of my life chasing them everywhere, but at some point there were too many stories. I'm sure you can imagine what happens in a hotel. It was like a jigsaw puzzle.

As soon as I met a chambermaid that I really liked – because of her particular attitude towards life and a humanity that was touched by tenderness and also a sense of solitude – from that moment the story began to emerge.

JW: The film takes an observational, almost documentary approach. One of the things I admired most was its restraint and economy. I get the sense that by keeping things relatively straightforward you were able to very articulately communicate the central themes of the film (inequality in society, the drudgery of work, the lack of resources lowly paid workers have in their everyday private lives . . .)

LA: Because I spent so much time shadowing chambermaids it was very important to me that the film felt alive and realistic. It had to have elements of their real lives, down to the slang that they use and the silences between them, so that the spectator can truly enter their lives and have a sense of real life. Half of the people you see are actors and the others are real workers at the hotel. I made some very strong relationships with these workers. Since the anchor of my film is a sense of absence, for me it was very important that there was congruence between the narrative and the way in which it was filmed, in terms of what you hear but don't necessarily see. I wanted to use a lot of single shots and keep things to a minimum to stress a sense of invisibility. For me, it has the feel of a poem.

JW: The wealthy guests are not portrayed as purely monstrous but in a more nuanced way. You have the egocentric man constantly demanding more amenities and the Argentinian woman with a newborn baby who, despite showing signs of kindness, is entirely ignorant of the kind of life Eve lives.

LA: I like to create characters with their own particular humanity. Neither the bad is the baddest nor the good represents absolute goodness. I like that duality between human beings. So, in that sense, I wanted to generate the feeling of cultural and socio-economic biodiversity. There are people of all nationalities and, at the same time, we are all humans. That subtle paradox was important to capture.

JW: Despite the hardships they endure and the little hustles they have going on to try and make ends meet, there is a kindness and camaraderie amongst the workers; in general, they help and look out for each other. What was it that you felt important to communicate to the viewer in this sense?

LA: Whenever I was in the working areas and in the basement, which was often without windows, I was aware that these Mexicans were very hardworking people. At the same time, I had the sense that they were also beautiful and kind and would give anything to help their families progress. This was an essential element that I wanted to communicate in *The Chambermaid*. In terms of the history of Mexico, not everything has to do with drugs or murders. There are also workers who work tirelessly to survive. This is very moving to me. Obviously, the situation in Mexico is really complex, but I wanted to talk about this other essence of my country.

JW: You offer a fully rounded portrait of Eve, informing the audience of her struggles and hardships and her kindness but also showing other facets of her personality. I am mainly thinking here of her determination to get the red dress and gain promotion but also of her awareness of her own sexuality (the scene where she undresses on the bed in front of her male co-worker who is outside cleaning the windows). Can you elaborate more on these moments and why they felt important to you?

LA: I was interested in generating a protagonist who would be in almost every scene and that protagonist was Eve. I liked the combination of her tenderness, her sense of solitude and her strength. While she advances in her work, she begins to create her own world, starting from objects and then imagining the lives of other people and how she may relate to them. I think this is something that we all do. This helps Eve to understand her own voice.

For me, that moment of the window is a search for identity – and a journey towards one's own femininity and the assumption of a sexual power free of prejudices and suppression. Pleasure is important. At the same time, the presence of the window suggests the world that is out there; for me it was very beautiful to generate a love story, where there is never an exchange of words and everything is through glass.

JW: As someone who has acted, you display a natural affinity for actors and all of the performances feel very naturalistic. Can you say more about your casting process, and perhaps about the incredible Gabriela Cartol (Eve) and Teresa Sánchez (Minitoy)? They form quite a combination.

LA: First of all, I was very interested in finding people who had confidence in my work and that there was also a chemistry. At the beginning of the project I had someone in mind to interpret the main character but when I met her I realised that there was no chemistry and that she was never going to let herself be directed. I looked at some other people with my casting director, Lucía Uribe, who is also one of my closest friends. I had already seen Gabriela Cartol in *La tirisia* (2014) by Jorge Pérez Solano and I really liked her face, which is a very beautiful combination of Mexican and Japanese. When I invited her to meet and talk with me, I knew immediately that she was the one.

Teresa Sánchez has appeared in a number of films directed by Nicolás Pereda. First of all, I auditioned her for a smaller part. Then Teresa sent us some WhatsApp videos. She immediately became Minitoy. I really liked her spirit and there was some malice but charm in her that suggested that she was perfect for the character. I could not have chosen better actresses and better human beings to accompany me on this trip.

JW: The film is composed almost entirely of interior shots. What we see of the outside world, which I presume to be Mexico City, is from the windows of the hotel and, particularly the striking view from the hotel room with its very own swimming pool. There is a sense that, despite the luxury, the women are imprisoned. Was this the feel you were going for and can you also talk about the challenges of shooting in a relatively enclosed film space? What kind of discussions did you have with director of photography (DoP) Carlos Rossini?

LA: From its initial inception I knew that I wanted to film everything in that location and that everything would happen in that contained space. We filmed in a very short time, just seventeen days. I needed a special crew with me because the hotel made it clear that if they needed the rooms we were staying in we had to clean them and move out. Exactly like a chambermaid crew.

Carlos Rossini has mostly worked in documentary, so for me it was very important to have that feeling of being alive, although there is also a precision to the image. We used almost no artificial lighting.

JW: And how have people generally reacted to the film? It won a major prize at Marrakech and I was at the world premiere in Toronto, where you seemed genuinely touched by the reception it received.

LA: For me, making this film is almost like having overcome a phobia. When you make a movie that means so much to you, but not knowing what it will mean to other people, and then you start travelling and see how the movie is not only being understood but it can mean something very different to each one of those people with their own personalities, culture and personal history – that is when you understand that your work is transcendent. That is the importance of cinema. It is not only something for entertainment, it is something as alive as a painting or a piece of music.

JW: Finally, what are your future plans? IMDb lists you as making another *Déjà Vu* ...

LA: My IMDb is a disaster. I need to put order in all of that stuff. I have already finished writing my next film, which I started developing when I was writing *The Chambermaid*. I need to polish it, but it's again a simple story but with layers.

2

Natalia Beristáin

Natalia Beristáin is a graduate of the Centro de Capacitación Cinematográfica (CCC). Beristáin's short film Peces plátano *(2006) was awarded Best Mexican Short Film in the Fifth Morelia International Film Festival and screened at the Cannes Film Festival as part of Critics' Week. In 2009 Beristáin co-founded the production company Chamaca Films, and from 2008 to 2010 she was the cast manager for the National Theatre Company in Mexico and for a selection of works by Thomas Bernard. A renowned casting director in films such as* El violín *(Francisco Vargas, 2005),* Abel *(Diego Luna, 2010), and* Machete Language *(Kyzza Terrazas, 2011),* No quiero dormir sola *(2012) marked Beristáin's directorial debut feature.*

FEATURES FILMOGRAPHY:
Los adioses (*The Eternal Feminine*) (2017)
No quiero dormir sola (*She Doesn't Want To Sleep Alone*) (2012)

JASON WOOD: I wondered if you could begin by talking about when you first became interested in cinema and what your tastes were. What specific films or film-makers interested you and did you pay particular attention to Mexican cinema, contemporary or historical?

NATALIA BERISTÁIN: In my case the saying that goes 'the apple never falls far away from the tree' is quite accurate: I come from a family of actors – everyone, and I mean everyone in my family, is or has been an actor – but even though theatre was my basic habitat, I had always been close to cinema. But I do remember being around fourteen years old, going to the Mexican Cinematheque and watching Tom Stoppard's *Rosencrantz and Guildenstern Are Dead* (1990) and getting out of there thinking I want to do that!

As I said before, I come from a family of actors. My grandfather – Luis Beristáin – had worked with Luis Buñuel on two of the films he made in Mexico, so I do remember watching his films and being mesmerised by

Film-maker Natalia Beristáin strikes a pose

them at a very early age. Also, I was and am a huge fan of the French New Wave cinema. Agnès Varda's *Cléo From 5 to 7* (1962) very much inspired my first attempts to tell stories in my first short films.

JW: Like many of the film-makers with whom I have spoken, you studied at the CCC. How important was this education in your own progression and, more generally, how pivotal is the role the CCC plays in developing talent and then providing a pathway to a profession and a career?

NB: For me, it was the beginning of everything. When I got out of high school I already knew I wanted to study cinema, but I wasn't quite sure where and so I decided to take a break from school and ended up back-packing in Europe for a year. I spent that time just working in whatever job I could get and meeting people from all over the world. And that experience helped me decide I wanted my education to come from my country. I wanted to be part of a generation of people who spoke 'my same language' – and not only in a literal way. I believed that being able to grow as part of a generation was important. To this day some of my closest friends and work partners are people I met during my CCC years because we have created the same references together. Besides being an amazing technical school, for me what CCC gives you as a film-maker is that without even realising it, you start to become a part of the industry. All your teachers are people who are currently working in different branches of cinema, so first you start visiting their sets, then you are working as a PA on some low-budget film, and there you meet someone else who calls you for a new project . . . and so on and so on. It's family.

JW: *Peces plátano* (2006) was a prize-winning short. What particular aesthetic were you seeking and did the look and subject of the film establish any sort of formative template from which you continued to work?

NB: That was the first work I shot with sound, or, to be more accurate, the first time the actors spoke, so in a way for me it meant it was the first time I really felt like a director. Being able to start a dialogue with the actors, and not only watching how ideas and feelings of my own became alive but, most importantly, how they were boosted because they were happening through and to someone else bewitched me. I do believe that made a mark. To this day that's the place where I feel most comfortable and sharp: directing actors.

JW: As well as working in cinema, you have also worked in theatre, both as a director and in a casting capacity. What were some of the reasons that you decided to work in another discipline and how, if at all, did this impact upon your work as a film-maker? I am thinking specifically perhaps of how you work with actors, but also more generally.

NB: As I said earlier, I come from a family of actors and this is more or less how I got involved in casting. By doing so I realised that I could make a living out of it and pay rent. This was amazing to me as I was in my early twenties. Then I realised that I really liked working in casting. I got to read scripts beyond my own and also gained an insight into what other directors liked and wanted. This made me start to think of things I wasn't aware of. I didn't take on a lot of projects. I only took on scripts that I liked and did all the casting myself. I became able to multi-task, giving the actors the response they needed, learning lines and also thinking about placement and positioning. I had to see ten or twenty people a day and encourage them to do the best they could for this casting process. This really helped with my directing skills. During the past twelve years I have been directing, I have been involved less in casting but I mentor someone who works with me in terms of how I like the casting process to be done. I'd like to think that I can always keep my casting skills on the side in case I need them.

JW: *No quiero dormir sola* (2012), your debut feature, dealt with the relationship between a young woman and her alcoholic grandmother. It's a tender and compassionate work that addresses both alcoholism and relationships between women of different generations. Was it important to you that the film have a strong female dynamic at its centre, and what wider social points, if any, did you wish to make?

NB: When I made the film I was perhaps unaware of its political statement. To have two women as the main characters was simply because it was the story of the film. I was interested in the contrast between women of a young age and women of old age and being able to know yourself and be comfortable in your skin in the way that perhaps I was not when I was a young woman. But as years passed and I made *Los adioses* (2017), which is also a film starring a woman, I realised how hard it is to make films as a woman. *No quiero dormir sola* made a mark on me in terms of how I wanted to keep on doing films. It's become really important to me to have female characters at the centre of my films. I may not continue to do it, but for the moment it does feel like a political statement. I am starting to work more and more with female creative heads. I have always liked to work with Dariela Ludlow, an incredible DoP. *Los adioses* had a crew of about 150 people and we managed to ensure that half of them were female. That was important. This certainly started with *No quiero dormir sola*, even though I wasn't perhaps aware of it at the time.

JW: You cast Adriana Roel in the role of Dolores (*No quiero dormir sola*). Roel's work in Mexican cinema is quite formidable and stretches back to the 1950s. Were you an admirer of her work and how did it feel to work with a veteran figure?

NB: I am a bit embarrassed to admit that I did not know Adriana from before. I got to know her when I was working as the casting manager for the National Theatre Company in Mexico. I worked there for two years, and at the time I was also working on the script for *No quiero dormir sola*, which I had originally thought of for my own grandmother but then she got really sick and was unable to make the film. Adriana and my grandmother were of the same generation and had even worked together. Adriana was amazing and was so eager to return to cinema. She had more energy than the rest of us. She was very open and genuine. Adriana, like all great actors, had her own opinions and perspectives, but she was also happy to be committed to the material that she had been given and to, where possible, seek a combination of the two perspectives. I'll always be grateful to Adriana.

JW: The film won, amongst other prizes, Best Feature at Morelia. How did this impact upon your career, and more generally have you found the industry within Mexico (festivals, funding bodies, film-making peers, critics) to have been supportive of your work?

NB: I myself have been on juries and on funding panels and know that here is a lot of work to be done. I have gotten into discussions where projects with very high budgets are awarded to male directors but when the funding bodies see a woman's name on the project they have doubts. Women directors, and not just in Mexico but around the world, remain a minority. Things are changing but I do want to state that I have been fortunate and privileged and this is not a position that most female film-makers enjoy.

JW: What were the circumstances that led to *Los adioses*? It's a film that charts the life of the feminist intellectual Rosario Castellanos, who though is now regarded as one of Mexico's most important literary voices of the twentieth century, fought to have her voice heard. What was it about her tale that touched you and how important was it to highlight the patriarchal nature of society? I ask the latter both in a universal sense and also in relation to your own country.

NB: In the beginning I didn't even know that I wanted to make a film about Rosario Castellanos. When I was wrapping up *No quiero dormir sola*, I started to think about my next project and knew that I wanted to make something around a couple's life and how easy it is to inflict pain on whoever you love the most. This works both ways. I was having different thoughts and doubts about maternity and how being a woman is usually marked by the time, the education and the culture she has been formed in. I was having all these ideas and couldn't really combine them until I found Rosario's letters to Ricardo Guerra Tejada, which were perfect for the story I wanted to tell. I hadn't read Rosario before. I read some at high school but she was not a writer I was particularly interested in. It was only after reading the letters and discovering that she was real flesh and blood and not the caricature she was often depicted as that I found someone that I could instantly connect with.

She was a very avant-garde figure and fell in love madly with the wrong guy – she couldn't make rice without burning it. That was what I could really connect with. It opened a way to talk about the difference between private life and public life, that in the end it doesn't matter how brilliant, educated and sensible you are, patriarchy is so hard and so pervasive. What I wanted to think about with *Los adioses* is that in a relationship there are always two sides and I didn't want to pick a victim and a victimiser, to have these roles go back and forth. What was terrible and which still happens today is that you had a woman with a brilliant mind but in the core of her own home she could not step away from what hurt her. That is patriarchy.

JW: I was struck by the function sound plays in the film, specifically in regard to the sound of the typewriter keys. Something of a motif. Could you say more about this?

NB: They are certainly a motif. The sound department and myself always thought that Rosario's work was both her tomb and her salvation. It was an important part of the story to have her surrounded by this sound.

JW: You have more recently worked in TV. A lot of directors are excited by the funding opportunities afforded by television and by the fact that the format is also more suited to experimentation in regard to narrative. Is this true for yourself? Do you plan more features and are financing and support for these features readily available? Other figures I have spoken to are waiting to see the position of the new government on arts and culture . . .

NB: I have been working in television for the last two years and it's been a really amazing opportunity – high-class projects that have enabled me to keep on directing and perfecting my skills and play around with formats. I also got the chance to do things that I hadn't had the opportunity to do in cinema. But unless you are a big name like Martin Scorsese, I'm not sure that television is offering quite as much opportunity as perhaps it could for the rest of us film-makers. For now, they are just aiming for the world-renowned director. I am not sure that the path is completely open. The project I am developing now has been submitted for federal funds and we are having to do it like artisans. I don't want to wait for the new government in Mexico. I voted for them and at least culture-wise I am surprised by the way they are dealing with things. They are treating artists as if they were all privileged snobs who cannot really give anything to society except for spectacle and fireworks. I'm really disappointed.

3

Mariana Chenillo

Mariana Chenillo studied cinematography at the CCC *film school, where she also taught courses on directing assistance, screenwriting and directing. Chenillo currently teaches screenwriting at the SAE Institute México. Chenillo's work, which spans shorts, features, documentary and television (including the entire second series of* Soy tu fan*) has participated in numerous festivals around the world and has won more than twenty national and international awards. Chenillo's first documentary short,* En pocas palabras *(2003) was selected for the Morelia International Film Festival, as was her short fiction film,* Mar adentro *(2004). Chenillo's debut feature,* Nora's Will *(2008) won the Morelia Audience Award and seven Ariels, including Best Picture, Best Screenplay and Best First Film.* La tienda de raya *was Chenillo's contribution to the portmanteau project,* Revolución *(2010). Chenillo's second feature,* Paraíso *(2013), was selected for the San Sebastián International Film Festival.*

FEATURES FILMOGRAPHY:
Paraíso (2013)
Nora's Will (Cinco días sin Nora) (2008)

JASON WOOD: Can you start by talking about how your interest in cinema began, the figures that influenced you, and at what point did you decide that you wanted to pursue a career in film-making?

MARIANA CHENILLO: I got into film school right after high school. I was really young. Eighteen. It was an abstract decision. Looking back, it's obvious that I was interested in story-telling. As a child I was an avid reader. My mum would tell me to stop reading and to play with friends. At high school I was also interested in physics and had no relationship to cinema or film-making at all, apart from watching the films in the huge VHS collection at the house of my grandfather. He was also a photographer, though not professional, and had been taking photographs his whole life. He had his own darkroom and showed us how to develop photos. The films I watched were by Tarkovsky, Godard, Fellini and Kurosawa. It was a very nice age to watch them: fifteen or sixteen. They impacted me in a very personal way. I was accepted at university to study physics but that soon became calculus, which I thought was boring. Then I thought that I should study philosophy. Studying film didn't feel concrete but then I made my first short film at film school. Your first short film is always horrendous. I remember thinking that I put all my effort and my intelligence into *this*? It was a very formative experience. I understood how difficult making a film is. Philosophy felt different. Everyone could be a genius because it was theory and there was nothing creative being made. Film school suddenly started to seem more appealing, and in a way, profound. I dropped philosophy after two years to concentrate on film school. Film school made me happy inside. I knew I would never go back.

JW: The film schools in Mexico, such as the CCC, seem so important. They produce talents in so many different disciplines and seem so supportive.

MC: There are more things being produced now. When I went to film school twenty-five years ago there were really only two schools and they were both financed by the government. We were funded to learn. Our teachers were also amongst the few film-makers that were working at the time. There were relatively few films being made in Mexico at this time, perhaps around a dozen, and they were being made by our teachers. That gave us a real link to the film-making industry. I think the growth of the Mexican film industry is absolutely connected to the schools. You could go back to the schools and ask for help and they would give you access to equipment and their studios. They sheltered an industry that needed shelter. We are all worried at the moment about what will happen with the new government because we have all been making our films with public funding for years. The film I have just shot is funded by one of the three funds that Mexico has for film-making and the funds work.

Now that television pays so well, it is harder to make a film because people prefer to work in television. For one reason or another making films in Mexico is hard. The public funds make it easier. With only private investors believing that they are going to get their money back, it would be impossible. The government also allows the film to be personal and for a vibrant arthouse cinema to flourish. There also are the films made on a larger budget, with a mix of state and private investment – an endless cycle of slightly bland and more mainstream romantic comedies.

JW: After making a number of shorts, your first feature, *Nora's Will*, emerged in 2008. The film tackles universal themes such as love, religion, family and infidelity, but it felt relatively unique to them in that it is set within a Jewish community in urban Mexico. This is a community rarely depicted on screen in Mexican cinema. What led you to it?

MC: My family. It's loosely based on a family story: the story of my grandmother and my grandfather. They did live across the street from each other and they were divorced for more than twenty years. I got the best years from my grandmother when I was young. She was taking lithium and was very stable. When my mother and her aunts and uncles were young, she was not so stable and tried many times to commit suicide. Her suicide attempts started when she was in her thirties and was pregnant. This was a family story that was hanging over all of us. When I was at film school, comedy wasn't really on the menu. My grandmother committed suicide when I was in the fourth or fifth year. It was a story and a theme that was always there.

My shorts that I produced as part of the curriculum were very serious. They also focused on suicide and depression. I remember the films not being good. I haven't watched them again and I wouldn't, but I recall that I thought that because the subject was so serious I could approach it as comedy. Film school was great, but getting out of it was also important. I felt like I was

Bright lights, big city: *All That Is Invisible*

free of something. Going to workshops with the screenplay for *Nora's Will* really helped me find the tone. The film changed my life, and the life of my family as it contained sadness but also irony and hope. It reflects life in that it is full of contradictions. If you talk about things with humour in cinema, you can often delve much deeper. It felt important for the film to be light. I didn't want audiences crushed by the weight of it.

JW: The film was well received, connecting at international festivals and in Mexico. It cemented your place in history when you became the first Mexican female to win an Ariel award for Best Picture. Can you talk about what winning the award meant for you in particular, and what it also meant in a wider sense for women working in Mexican cinema?

MC: Nobody told me I was the first. I only learned years later. The Ariels have gained in importance for our industry. We couldn't actually get a festival to premiere *Nora's Will* in the beginning. A lot of the Mexican films at the time revolved around poverty and violence and a lot of the international festivals were looking for something similar. *Nora's Will* didn't seem very representative. We opened in Morelia and won the Audience Award. Then for six months nothing happened. Nobody wanted the film, but then Miami took it and then a few other international festivals, but not the biggest ones. We started to win prizes everywhere. It was a bittersweet experience. My feet were very much on the ground because I was already working on other things. Audiences immediately connected with the film and were touched and moved by it. This was my main reward.

It was a difficult moment for women film-makers in Mexico but I think that things have changed a lot in the last ten years. The day after the Ariel award, I remember my mum commenting that my photo wasn't anywhere. If a man wins the award, it is on the first page of the newspaper. I think they actually showed a picture of the beautiful actress that presented me with the award. With my next film, *Paraíso* (2013), I had a much clearer understanding of what had happened. The award didn't take me to success. But it did enable me to continue working.

JW: After *Nora's Will* you worked for a time in Mexican television on *Soy tu fan* (2010–12). Was this something you undertook to ensure that you kept working?

MC: I think I was lucky to get *Soy tu fan*. It was a funny and intelligent project. The writer and producer, Constanza Novick, became a friend and writing partner. It was a transitional time for television. Of course there were bad projects being produced; it was before television as an art form was so widely accepted, before the recent period of innovation, but there was a sense that things were changing. I thought that it was a wonderful format. It offered a place to explore and it felt more immediate. You didn't have to wait five years to see the results of your work and you also have more space to develop your characters. You have to have all your tools sharpened because you have to shoot ten or twelve script pages a day versus three or four for a film. I have relished working in television and have learned a lot of new skills from it. I don't feel that it is particularly representative of my work, but that's OK. It is a good experience to work outside of your comfort zone. Not counting *Nora's Will*, which was a very personal project, I have always worked for hire. In fact, the first thing that I have done that wasn't for hire is the film that I have just shot. I was also a director for hire on *Paraíso*. I think it was also more difficult for me being a woman, but it's beginning to open up a little. There is Natalia Beristáin and three or four other women who are now taken into consideration when it comes to hiring someone for a project.

jw: And how did *Paraíso* come about? I understand that the producer, Pablo Cruz, originally only hired you to write the script. I note also that you changed the perspective in the story from the husband to Carmen, the wife.

mc: When I finished *Nora's Will*, I was invited by the production company Canana to direct a segment of the portmanteau project, *Revolución* (2010). My segment was *La tienda de raya*. My co-directors included Carlos Reygadas, Amat Escalante, Rodrigo Plá and Patricia Riggen, film-makers I admire. I was the last director to be invited to contribute to what was intended to mark the centenary of the revolution. I honestly enjoyed the experience of talking with the other directors and discussing the subject of the Mexican Revolution more than I actually enjoyed my film contribution. I had to shoot quickly without much time. But this is how my relation-ship with Canana and Diego Luna and Gael García Bernal started. Canana actually offered me a project before I got to make *Nora's Will* that was based around the thirty-two states that we have in Mexico. The short story that I read for this project, which never came to fruition, was by Julieta Arévalo and would become the basis for *Paraíso*. After I had made *Nora's Will* I was working as a continuity girl and it was then that Pablo asked me if I wanted to write a script from Arévalo's story. I had been directing for *Soy tu fan*, going on to do the entire second series, so by the time *Paraíso* was ready to be made I had qualified as a director. I was offered the chance to direct but I said that I needed to make it a bit more personal. I put a lot of myself into the script. I thought about my long-term relationship and about the nature of love.

JW:: The film deals with issues relating to body fascism, which feels like an increasingly important subject, especially in terms of expected ideals of beauty amongst women.

MC: I think today more would be made of the body shaming issue than it was when the film was released. At the time it may have felt strange for audiences but critics were also harsh on the film. Their attitude was that the woman is so fat that she should just be grateful to have someone. I don't think this attitude would be accepted today. The reviews for *Nora's Will* were excellent. For *Paraíso* they were not so good and I can't help but think that this was partly down to the reaction it provoked in terms of its depiction and presentation of a plus-size woman. I learned a lot from making the film, particularly about adapting a short story and trying to give the characters life and complexity.

JW: The film really thrives on the central performances of Daniela Rincón and Andrés Almeida.

MC: In both of my features, as well as the other projects I have been involved with, I have always enjoyed working with the actors. This was Daniela's first and really her last film as she seems to have not continued with acting after moving to America with her husband. She did speak out on body issues but never made another film. Andrés continued to work quite extensively. He is a very spontaneous and natural actor. We also used a lot of non-actors in the film. Most of the Spanish women in the film are my husband's aunts and their friends. When I saw how they gathered together to cook and sing, I thought well, why should I cast actors when I have them?

JW: There seems to be a really strong support network in Mexican cinema. Is this something you have noticed? For instance, you mentioned the work of Natalia Beristáin. Have you personally found this help and encouragement an inspiration? And do you feel a responsibility to nurture it?

MC: Absolutely. This goes back to my teachers in film school, especially Ignacio Ortiz and José Luis García Agraz – figures who survived the era when just six films were made every year. I learned all the basics with them when I was younger, but I also understood the concept of struggle. At a later stage of my career I was also helped by colleagues. I am a very slow writer and when I was writing *Nora's Will* people involved with the reading workshops were helpful and very encouraging. They helped me find the story. I've done the same with reading the screenplays of colleagues. There was another type of support and encouragement with *Revolución* because we were all film-makers travelling together. My latest project received invaluable support from Michel Franco and Gabriel Ripstein. Later I partnered with Humberto Hinojosa Ozcariz and Pablo García Gatterer – film-makers from my generation with whom I produced the film. So it changes really from the support of friends starting out to the support of more established film-makers and producers. I also get involved in projects, mainly assessing young women film-makers from film school in their final-year projects. I enjoy taking care of them, helping them with their work and, more generally, just encouraging them. I want to help them in the way that I got help when I was younger.

JW: You have referred to a project you are currently working on. What more can you say about *Guía para el viajero que no quiere preguntar*?

MC: It's a story that is close to my heart in a similar way to *Nora's Will*. Again, it's about family but it's also partly about going blind. When I was just starting film school my retina completely detached from one eye. I spent six months recovering. I then developed a hole in the centre of my other eye. I was always in fear of going blind. I was in a lot of conflict. I considered dropping film school, or even just being a producer. But when you are young, conflict can make you grow. I did lose a little vision but now I have grown used to it. I have to wear contact lenses and glasses and have regular appointments with doctors. It's a part-time job to keep my eyes in working order. I don't like melodrama at all, so the only other approach I felt was humour. It has to be funny because there is something slightly comical about it. It has taken a long time for the story to materialise and, unlike *Paraíso*, I knew that the main protagonist had to be male.

Vulnerability is different for men and women. Men have a harder time with vulnerability because they are expected to be strong. It was better for the character going blind to be male to take a total journey of vulnerability and acceptance. The film features Ari Brickman, who appeared in *Nora's Will*. We also wrote the film together. It's taken ten years to get the story to materialise. Our approach to the material quite naturally evolved. For instance, we both became parents, and this made us reappraise what it would be like to go blind if you have children. I would have loved to make this film five or ten years ago, but in a way we had to grow older. I am in the final stages of the editing. Hopefully it will be released next year.

4
Alfonso Cuarón

Alongside Alejandro González Iñárritu, Carlos Reygadas and Guillermo del Toro, Alfonso Cuarón acted as the inspiration and impetus for the original publication of The Faber Book of Mexican Cinema. *Since we last spoke, Cuarón, like his three aforementioned contemporaries, has gone on to be a hugely successful and influential figure on an international scale.*

Though working on international productions since the success of his breakthrough picture Y tu mamá también *(2001), a work credited, alongside* Amores Perros *(2000), as precipitating a renaissance in Mexican film-making and film-makers from Mexico, Cuarón has remained a passionate advocate for cinema from his homeland and has been widely supportive of the Mexican film-makers who emerged in his wake. If his dystopian sci-fi adaptation of P. D. James's* The Children of Men *(2006) brought critical acclaim,* Gravity *(2013), co-written with his son Jonás, took things to a whole new level, and saw Cuarón become the first Mexican director to win a Best Director Academy Award.*

Returning to Mexico to make the biographical ROMA *in 2018, Cuarón achieved even greater success, winning another Best Director Academy Award, as well as the Academy Award for Best Cinematography. The film was an unprecedented success globally, also winning BAFTAs for Best Film, Best Foreign Language Film of the Year, Best Achievement in Direction and Best Achievement in Cinematography. Moreover, the film proved a watershed moment in terms of film history, becoming the first Netflix-financed production to not only dominate the awards circuit but to also challenge the Netflix business model and secure a theatrical release.*

FEATURES FILMOGRAPHY:
ROMA (2018)
Gravity (2013)
Children of Men (2006)
Harry Potter and the Prisoner of Azkaban (2004)

Y tu mamá también (2001)
Great Expectations (1998)
A Little Princess (1995)
Sólo con tu pareja (1991)

JASON WOOD: We last spoke just before you started work on *Children of Men* (2006) and just after you completed *Harry Potter and the Prisoner of Azkaban* (2004). On a truly global scale the success and achievements of yourself, Alejandro, Guillermo and Carlos have been a tremendous boost for the cinema of Mexico. You became the first Mexican director to win an Academy Award as Best Director with *Gravity* (2013) in 2014 and repeated the feat with *ROMA* (2018) in 2019, for which you also won Best Cinematography. How important were these successes on a personal level and how important were they in terms of reminding the world of the talent and diversity in Mexican film-making?

ALFONSO CUARÓN: It's a matter of perception. There is a sense that our careers are stratospheric because of Oscars but this is just a perception. Don't get me wrong. I am very happy and very proud to have them, but at the end of the day Oscars don't mean anything because the only test of cinema is time. We have been having a great run, that's for sure, and we've been having a great run in the context of acceptance and audiences. It's unquestionable that these awards and all these media events put you in the zeitgeist of society. I also think that it is important to differentiate between Mexican cinema and Mexican film-makers. I am not so proud to say that only a little more than a third of my films are Mexican films and I would never dare to call *Gravity* or *Children of Men* a Mexican film. Those are films made by a Mexican film-maker. I could argue that they could only have been made by a Mexican but they are not Mexican films. I say this because it is important to make the differentiation, otherwise it is unfair on the Mexican film-makers making Mexican cinema in Mexico, among them Carlos Reygadas, Amat Escalante, Gerardo Naranjo and Alonso Ruizpalacios. They have been making Mexican films. And yes, I have made Mexican films as well. And I have just heard that Alejandro Iñárritu is going back to do a Mexican film, his first since *Amores Perros* (2000). I am very excited about this because I know what it feels like to go back to Mexico and to make a Mexican film. It's different. You can be a Mexican film-maker doing your film from the standpoint of who you are, but it is very different when you are surrounded by your language and cultural symbolisms.

jw: But even when you made *Children of Men* and *Gravity*, which is written with your son Jonás, you retained a Mexican identity.

ac: For sure. The teams are very Mexican. Emmanuel Lubezki, Jonás and myself. There is a Mexican madness to the method.

jw: But also a sensibility. These larger studio films still very much have your imprint. It strikes me that when yourself and Guillermo and Alejandro make films within the Hollywood studio system, you retain your signature styles.

ac: There is a shared cultural identity and a shared set of cultural influences. And to these film-makers you can add others, including Carlos. There is unquestionably a huge visual baggage in Mexico. I dare to say that there is something else and that is that we all share the sense that cinema has a language that is very related to the visual, the visual being one of the tools. You can do a film without sound and without actors and without music. You can do it without sets and without a screenplay, but you cannot do it without a camera. It is pretty much how cinema was born since the Lumières and Georges Méliès and how it has kept on going. It's a visual means to tell an experience – and I say experience as opposed to story.

Of course, the story is another tool, but I think all these film-makers have a strong faith in the notion of depicting experience and of using the visual as a means of expression. The pictorial art in Mexico is perhaps stronger than the narrative art. Of course, you also have incredible writers such as Juan Rulfo. There is a poetic aspect, I think, to Mexican art and culture. Again, I cite Rulfo and *Pedro Páramo*. There is a specific rhythm and, as film-makers, we come from the same nest in terms of how we think about how rhythm and images create meaning.

Even in school the narratives are very visual. I am sure that Guillermo, Alejandro and Carlos will tell you the same thing. And I think this will certainly be reflected in the work that we make. I am not comparing myself with these masters but when Antonioni goes and makes a film in the UK, it remains Antonioni. There are also film-makers that feel more at ease in other places and then there are film-makers that don't feel that comfortable. I think you can tell that Bergman did not feel comfortable or happy when making *The Serpent's Egg* (1977). You could possibly say the same of *Fellini's Casanova* (1976). And there are clearly directors who, wherever they travel, they remain themselves. Murnau is unquestionably one of them. You also had all the émigré directors in the early days of Hollywood.

Murnau is my favourite. He made films in Germany, in the US and then he makes *Tabu* (1931) in the South Pacific. He uses his environment to tell his experience. And the environment is not romanticised.

I find that a lot of European film-makers go to America and they romanticise Americana and American iconography. I think when the Mexican directors we have mentioned shoot abroad they make the elements part of their own understanding of the world. Guillermo can shoot films that take place in the real world or in a fantasy world but they always come from the point of Guillermo feeling at ease in those places. Alejandro has transitioned from a point where the environment was directly related to the social environment of the character to a place where it is much more internalised and the environment is almost a projection of the character.

JW: And how did the perception of the success we have mentioned help in terms of supporting a film industry and an infrastructure within Mexico? When we last spoke a new president was coming to power and a similar transition is now happening.

AC: I think the bottom line is that in Mexico – where you don't receive too much good news – any reports of a success, especially on an international level, is going to be in some ways inspiring. It would be disingenuous to think that the government supports and then directly helps the emergence of great art. It has a responsibility to art but art and artistic movements are created by people, and usually by new generations that are fearless. I am not going to defend or attack the films that Carlos, Alejandro, Guillermo or myself have made but we have perhaps been an inspiration for younger people to say, 'Oh shit. It's possible.' Guillermo and I were more connected to the film-makers of the previous generation than Alejandro or Carlos. We were part of the industry before we started directing our films. Pretty much the message you used to receive as an aspiring film-maker was that it's impossible. When I made my first film it was made very clear to me that nobody gives a shit about Mexican cinema. The person responsible for selling Mexican films around the world told me this directly. There was an entire psychology like this. So, when we began to have our success, even the people that may not have liked our films may have thought that perhaps it can be done after all.

I am not saying that there have not been good government initiatives but we have to remember that these initiatives were often pushed for by film-makers who held government or academic positions. All the good government policies in Mexican cinema were crafted by film-makers, and we have to be very grateful to film-makers and producers such as Jorge

Sánchez who, once they became bureaucrats, used their position and their power to make a difference. Sometimes there is more will than at other times from the government. There is also a tremendous sense of solidarity amongst the Mexican film community.

JW: As well as your close-knit bond with Alejandro, Guillermo and Carlos, you have also helped produce emerging Mexican talent such as Sebastián Cordero and also assisted your son Jonás with *Year of the Nail* (2007) and *Desierto* (2015). Carlos Reygadas produced Amat Escalante. Michel Franco produced David Zonana. Do you think it's important to use your position to nurture, inspire and encourage newly emerging figures?

AC: Beyond producing, it's the sense of support that is so important. Those who are a little further down the line in their careers should support and encourage. I remember that the first time I saw *Japón* (2002) by Carlos Reygadas I thought that he was a master. In Mexico there is a very horizontal relationship between film-makers. The industry has fluctuated, but the community remains. I think this sense of community is ingrained in the psyche but I worry a little bit now because of the explosion that is happening. It's amazing for the industry, but it's worrying for the community and the explosion I am talking about is the explosion in production, a great deal of which is from Netflix. The result is that there are no crews and when you come to make a film people are struggling to team up. You work under different conditions when you make a Mexican film. You may work for eight weeks on the film. But on a Netflix show you may work for six months. A by-product of this is that a part of the process is getting lost. As in any industry there is a learning curve. A DoP would go and assist other DoPs for a few shows. You can have an amazing eye but there are still little tricks of the craft that you can pick up, such as how you learn on a set and how you learn to communicate with other people on the crew. What is happening now is that anybody that knows a little bit becomes a head of department. I worry that we may be creating a disparity of quality and fracturing the community. Let's see what happens. I hope the community doesn't implode. I feel that it will remain, especially amongst those film-makers committed to the art.

JW: There seem to be even more voices emerging. Michel Franco, Lila Avilés, David Zonana. And they seem to be making films that are risk-taking and audacious in terms of their cinematic language and their aesthetic. These films may not be hugely populist but they are important.

AC: I think Carlos Reygadas has played a huge part in this. He completely took the rug of Mexican cinema and gave it a shaking. Carlos showed us that there are other ways to what Carlos may call the classic way. He has been a huge inspiration.

JW: I think we can place *Year of the Nail* by Jonás Cuarón in the same category.

AC: It's a very complex film. It's a fiction created out of the truthfulness of moments. The film has a tremendous sense of the passing of time even though you are watching still images.

JW: And how did you come to work with Jonás on *Gravity*?

AC: We had written a film that fell apart. Because of my personal situation I have to remain based in London and the other film was a road movie that went from the south of France to Scotland. We had even cast it with Charlotte Gainsbourg and Daniel Auteuil. We had all the locations but the project became impossible. On the evening we learned that the film wasn't going to happen we were bummed but decided not to just sit and lick our wounds. We decided to move on. We agreed to write another screenplay.

I wanted to do something that I could do from London and which was controllable. We decided to talk about films that we loved and we mentioned *Desierto* by Jonás, for which I had written an early draft. I liked the precision of the concept and the idea of a film that was a relatively straight line on which you could hang a lot of thematics. It is non-stop action from beginning to end. We then got to talking about a character confronting the void. So, we thought about a character confronting the void in space. This was the point of departure. That same night we had the basic premise. We also wanted to do something a bit different from other science-fiction films and set it closer to earth. We wrote the whole film very quickly. Maybe three weeks. We thought about films like Spielberg's *Duel* (1971) and *Runaway Train* (1985) by Andrei Konchalovsky, based on a story by Kurosawa. I love that movie. It's an existential film.

JW: And what led you back to working in Mexico for *ROMA*? It's obviously such a personal project.

AC: After *Children of Men* the sketches of *ROMA* began to appear but I was afraid and unsure how to handle it. Working with Jonás, we talked about the fact that I loved story-telling and film but that I cannot stand it when cinema only illustrates a story. I think of those films as being for lazy readers. Sometimes the illustrations are very pretty, sometimes they are flashy enough to make you believe that you are watching cinema, but with Jonás and I on *Gravity* we decided that language was going to convey everything.

I then wrote another script with my brother Carlos, who had co-written *Y tu mamá también* (2001) and directed films such as *Rudo y Cursi* (2008). We researched the screenplay for a year and a half but it proved to be too ambitious and too expensive. I also felt that I had done too much research and this had then guided the screenplay to too great a degree. But I realised that *Gravity* had given me an opportunity and if I was going to make a film like this then the time was now. I found myself faced with the means to do a film in Mexico the way that I would love to do a film. I would have the tools and the resources and so if I didn't do the film it would be a way of avoiding it and it may be something that I'd avoid the rest of my life. I decided that I'd better jump into it.

I started to work on it and used a protective safety blanket to keep a distance from a process that at the end was very painful for me. I told Carlos that I was going to do something but that I didn't know if it would have a narrative or even what it was going to be. I spoke with my family and started to go back into the period. This was aided by the fact that I have a very vivid visual memory of my childhood. I then started to base my research more on that. I paid particular attention to the movie listings in the newspapers. As a kid I was fascinated and I spent such a long time gazing at these listings. Each listing would have a different little poster inside. It was not about box office but about the weeks a film had run. '12 successive weeks!' I also liked revisiting the listings for the double and triple bills. And then, when I thought I had enough I spent one month writing.

I usually start with a structure and a timeline, but this time I just wrote. The rule I had was that I would write without questioning. As long as I was connected with my memory, any idea that came out would play. That's how I wrote the screenplay. When it was finished, nobody saw it. I gave each different location only the information they needed; this is the location; these are the actors and we need these materials. I was an AD [assistant director] so I broke the film down like an AD. I didn't read the script again. I knew that I was going to shoot in sequence. Every single day had a date and I gave these dates to the departments so that they could immerse themselves into researching what films were playing and what news was emerging on each specific date. If on that date in history the military were marching in the street, I included it in the schedule. There were pages and pages of schedules. It was so detailed to the extent of 'what day is it today? It's Tuesday. And what does the girl do today? She does sports.' And so, on Wednesday, it would be 'Today it's Wednesday, which is laundry day. So, what should the laundry be? It should be sports laundry.' It was also about replicating places that didn't exist any more. I always wanted to shoot in actual locations. One or two big locations we couldn't use because they didn't exist any more or they had been completely transformed. It was only when I finished this process that I realised how painful it was.

JW: Was it therapeutic?

AC: It was, but this particular therapeutic process was not joyful. It was about going through the pain. Sometimes on the set I was in a foul mood. It was nothing to do with the work that was going on. And this could be on any scene, even those not directly about me. In fact, most of the scenes are not directly about me. It became perverse actually. Spending six months in an exact replica of the home of my childhood surrounded by actors dressed and looking like my family when I was a kid. Only two people read the screenplay. One was Carlos. I asked him to read it because he understood the world. His response was, 'You said that you weren't going to do a narrative film. This is a narrative film.'

JW: Who was the other person you allowed to read it?

AC: An amazing Indian film-maker called Chaitanya Tamhane. We met on a mentor programme. I had to choose one film-maker and I saw his film *Court* (2015) and thought that it was amazing. He went to Mexico for a couple of months and I thought that if he was going to be involved then he should know what I am doing.

The narrative thing I realised was like a muscle and the muscle took care of the process. I knew what I was doing in every moment but I didn't know the film I was making. I had an intuition of the feeling that I had and how I wanted it to be. I didn't have the clarity of something like *Gravity*. I knew I wanted the moments to flow.

JW: *ROMA* has an incredibly realised aesthetic. You mentioned that you shot chronologically but can you talk about some of your other choices? Shooting yourself, shooting in black and white . . . It's intimate. But also feels on a big scale.

AC: I wanted to do a film about who I am and where I come from. In other words, what fucked me up. I didn't want to do it solely about me because

I was not interested. My own experience was a very insular, bourgeois and middle-class experience. And this wouldn't have allowed me to go where I wanted to go. I wanted to go through the kaleidoscope and the cacophony that is Mexico. The film had to be about the Mexico I grew up in as much as it is about characters and I wanted that Mexico to be constantly present. This was in the city, the sounds and the context. I also wanted to journey through the perverse relationship between race and class. And, to be frank, to do this only from my insular experience of a middle-class ten-year-old boy, it was going to be very limited. What was driving the film was something more abstract. The observation of time and memory – the mystery of time. I think that this is the difference I believe between cinema and narrative. Narrative is: and then, and then, and then. Cinema is: and now . . . The now may stretch or compress itself.

JW: The casting of Yalitza Aparacio as Cleo was very important in terms of the race and class that you mention and in terms of looking at how the children of the middle classes were often raised by lower-class women of indigenous origin.

AC: It was a very long casting process. The principle was that I was going to cast people that looked and felt like the real people. And that applied to everyone. The indication that I gave to the casting director, Luis Rosales, who is one of the heroes of the film, was do not limit yourself to actors. I didn't care if they had any experience as long as they looked and felt right. It took a while for him to start getting the feel of each of the characters. Cleo was going to be my lead. I was going to be following her. She was a woman I knew so well and a woman my film would know so well and I knew that I wanted her to be a woman of indigenous origin.

We searched in Mexico City and it was not happening. For people of indigenous background, if they were born or have lived in Mexico City it is a completely different experience. Luis starting going to other states. In the script I wrote that Cleo is from Oaxaca. I wanted to explore a Zapotec and so Luis started going to Zapotec communities. Luis interviewed thousands of women. The tape of Yalitza was just her talking and, straight away, I knew that I wanted to meet her. There was an intelligence and a very generous smile. When I met her, it was immediate. My heart started pounding because I also knew that she wasn't really interested. She only went to the audition in Mexico City because her sister wanted her to go. I was so happy when she had a friend, because I was looking for someone to play Adele. The friend was Nancy García García. I said, well bring her, but if she's your friend it's going to work. Nancy speaks perfect

A window to the world: Yalitza Aparicio in *ROMA*

Mestizo, which helped a lot as Yalitza's Mestizo was very basic. It's amazing. Yalitza had never acted before and she had to act in a language that was also new to her.

JW: Given the incredibly personal nature of the material were you surprised by the extent to which the film connected on a global scale?

AC: I thought that it might be for cinephiles. I was going the Reygadas route! When I was late into the editing process, I realised that it was less abstract than I thought and I started to feel the narrative rhythm. I then started showing the film and people started to give me advice. People commented that I didn't need the fire because it doesn't take you anywhere but I knew I was going to keep it. I could make the film forty minutes shorter and, in a narrative sense, nobody would miss anything, but that isn't what I wanted to do. I could cut heads and tails. But I didn't want that because I liked the pacing and the rhythm.

I had a great partner in David Linde and Participant Films. I love working with David. We worked on *Y tu mamá* and David was head of Universal when I did *Children of Men*. He paid for the development of *Gravity* and then he was fired from Universal and it moved to Warners, but he was involved in it. And now *ROMA*. I told David my idea for *ROMA* and he said, 'Let's do it.' I then told him that there were rules. I told him that it was black and white. He said, 'Good.' I told him that it was in Spanish. He said, 'Good.' I told him that nobody was going to read the script. He said, 'Not even me?' So, I said only you. But then I sent him the screenplay in Spanish. David saw the film and said that he felt that there was something there that I was not seeing. From the get-go he saw the bigger impact.

JW: The film won multiple prizes and people really connected with it, but it was also an industry game changer because it was made with Netflix. It brought them the prestige they desired but it also broke the mould by playing more widely in cinemas.

AC: It's a film shot on 65 mm with Atmos sound. It's made for the big screen. But at the same time, it's a black-and-white Mexican film in Spanish and Mestizo that is also very slow. David and I decided that we were going to shoot it and sell it after. When we came to sell it, it was very apparent that a new world was emerging. I initially rejected the Netflix idea and the notion of platforms and stuff. For me it was the equivalent of straight to VHS. But David convinced me of the reality that was going on. I am happy to hear that because of *ROMA*, the rules are changing. We did a presentation and I could see that even many of the good distributors and exhibitors that I love had concerns about the ambition for the film. They didn't think that they would have the budget for press and promotion. This felt in stark contrast to my last Spanish film, *Y tu mamá*. The arthouse sector seems to have become less international in their outlook. It feels like the edgiest they will go is a film by the Coen Brothers. And don't get me wrong, that is not a criticism of the Coen Brothers, who I love.

I was initially very reluctant about the Netflix thing. But I had known Scott Stuber [head of original films at Netflix] for some time and I could be very straight with him. I said this is only going to happen with a theatrical release and he said, 'Done.' We created a network of independent exhibitors to show the film. In Mexico there was even a *ROMA* bus that travelled around rural communities to show the film. It was challenging, but I am happy to hear now that because of *ROMA* – and to return to what we spoke about earlier regarding the subject of perception – international film-makers are having it easier to find a market for their films. There is also now a conversation about platform titles having theatrical runs. Everything, inevitability, will come to a balance. The studios are largely doing tentpole films as opposed to international films. The platforms are a reality. I am pleased and proud with what happened with *ROMA* but it was also a painful process. There was a lot of digging to make things happen.

JW: What, if anything, can you reveal about *Ascension*? It has only relatively recently been announced as a future project.

AC: I wrote a season with Carlos. I love working with him. Jonás doesn't want to work with me! He is doing his own stuff. I don't know if I'll be able to direct *Ascension* because it takes place in different places and I have to be in London now. But as a writer, I love it. I want to try and do a series. With a film, at the most interesting moment of writing, you have to take away. I enjoy shows. I feel that most TV is a narrative medium but I want to see if there is a way of challenging that. Challenging the 'And then, and then, and then', and making more the 'And now'. I like what Bruno Dumont did with *P'tit Quinquin* (2014). I do a film every five years at the moment. Maybe when my kids leave home, I will become more prolific. Life keeps you busy. But ideas come all the time. It becomes what you have to do. *Children of Men*, *Gravity*, *ROMA*, they were all like that.

5
Jonás Cuarón

An auspicious and remarkably assured debut for Jonás Cuarón (the son of Alfonso), Año uña (2007) started life as a photographic project documenting people as they went about their everyday lives. At the end of the assignment, Cuarón and Eireann Harper completed an installation in which they mounted the thousands of photographic images in one room, ordered in scenes composed of shots. Consistencies began to emerge. The film's narrative is completely fictional and can be summarised as an impossible romance between Molly, a twenty-one-year-old American, and Diego, a Mexican in the throes of puberty. The co-writer of Gravity *(2013), Cuarón's most recent work as director is* Desierto *(2015), a tale of immigration and racism starring Gael García Bernal.*

FEATURES FILMOGRAPHY:
Desierto (2015)
Año uña (*The Year of the Nail*) (2007)

JASON WOOD: Could you start by talking about the genesis of *Año uña* (2007)?

JONÁS CUARÓN: The summer when I began taking the photographs, Eireann had just finished writing an essay in which she explored the work *La Jetée* (1962) by Chris Marker. I had never seen this film before and was deeply inspired by it. We decided that we wanted to make a film in a similar format. In our approach there was one key difference from the work of Chris Marker. In *La Jetée* he wrote the screenplay first and then staged the photographs he took. In the case of *Año uña*, we wanted to capture the photographs from a candid reality and from those photographs construct a fictional narrative, blurring the line between fiction and reality. After a year of taking photographs, Eireann and I decided we wanted to do an installation in which we filled all the walls of a room in our university with the photographs I took. The idea was to give people the opportunity to approach all of the photographs and, by seeing them, construct their own narrative. When the installation was finished, I spent some time in the room, looking at the images and coming up with my own fictional narrative.

JW: How did the film then begin to develop and what themes and consistencies suggested themselves?

JC: Looking at the photographs, I began to see emerging patterns from which I constructed the narrative. The first thing that became obvious was that the people I photographed the most that year were my younger brother and my girlfriend, Eireann. I decided that they would have to be my main characters, and the story became about a platonic relationship between a twenty-one-year-old girl from the US and a thirteen-year-old Mexican boy. Even though the narrative is fictional, many of the themes explored in the film were things that I observed while taking the photographs, and because I was constructing a film out of still images, I knew that time would be an important theme for me. That year my brother hit puberty and I could not help but notice how he moved through that transitional moment in life. The summer when I began taking the photographs, Eireann came to Mexico with me, and I experienced through her what it is to be a foreigner, a stranger in a new place. That year my grandfather was diagnosed with cancer. The photographs of his surgery became an important backdrop through which I explored the concept of the passage of time and the impermanence of things.

JW: As I understand it, every image in the film was captured using a stills camera. To what extent did this allow you to capture people at their most honest and relaxed and did this technique enable those that you shot to forget about the camera's presence?

JC: The main concept of the film was to capture a very honest reality and later fictionalise it. I knew that the best way to approach this was with a stills camera since it would not intimidate my subjects. People are used to being photographed and after a couple of pictures they easily forget about the camera's presence.

JW: What other themes and subjects were you keen to tackle?

JC: The film explores the arbitrary boundaries that separate people from one another and which define us as individuals. In the film the boundaries are present in the age of the characters, in their culture, their nationality, and their language. Because the film is made with photographs, it inevitably explores the concept of time's passing. That is why the film is structured around a year of the characters' lives. The passage of time becomes very apparent in the character of the teenage boy, since adolescence is an age in which everything moves very fast. And it is also felt in the grandfather's illness and death.

JW: The casting is also very significant on this film given its background and the manner in which it evolved.

JC: Part of the concept of the film was to capture the essence of the people I photographed, of my family, so it was important for me to record the voices of the people seen in the photographs instead of casting actors to do the voice-overs. Unfortunately, my grandpa could not speak after his surgery and I was never able to record his voice. I am lucky that my brother, Diego Cataño, had previous acting experience. For him this was a very interesting and different experience because he had to re-envision himself and give his character life only through voice.

JW: Mexico is blessed with skilled and very creative technicians and the sound design from Martín Hernández is tremendously important to *Año uña*. How closely did you work with Martín and what contribution did you want the audio to make to what many may mistakenly see as a purely visual work?

JC: From the moment I ventured into this project, I knew that the sound design would be crucial to giving the film life. When I had the first cut finished I showed it to Martín Hernández, who I admire greatly, and he immediately decided to support the project. We worked together in creating a sound design that would allow the images to 'move'. A common response people have to the film is that when they look back on it they remember it as if it had movement. I believe this effect is achieved thanks to the sound design. It was also important to create levels of sound to show variation between dialogue and inner monologue, which allows the narrative to move in and out of the characters' heads.

JW: The production notes for the film make reference to the novel *Elsinore* by Salvador Elizondo.

JC: Salvador Elizondo was my grandfather, who plays a very big part in this film. Many of the themes explored in *Año uña* are echoes of themes that he explored as a writer. He himself made a short film constructed out of still images called *Apocalypse 1900* (1965).

JW: I'm struck by the translation of the film's title, *The Year of the Nail*. Could you just explain its significance?

JC: A central theme of the film was the passage of time, so it was important for me to include in the title the concept of 'the year'. Another very important theme is the boundary of language. That is why I decided to create a title with the letter 'ñ', since it is a letter that does not exist in English. '*Año uña*' is a tongue twister, and it is a title that is really difficult to pronounce for anyone who speaks English. When I had to give the film's title an English translation, I decided to use a literal translation to include the concept of time, and Diego's ingrown toenail bookends the year.

6
Fernando Eimbcke

Fernando Eimbcke's anticipated follow-up to the well-loved coming-of-age stoner tale, Temporada de patos (Duck Season) *(2004), which was 'Presented' by Alfonso Cuarón, the enigmatically titled* Lake Tahoe *(2008) similarly charts the difficult journey to adulthood. A film that also incorporates the theme of grief, it does so with grace, subtle humour and maturity. Eimbcke's most recent work is* Club Sandwich *(2013), the tale of a mother and her adolescent son on a summer vacation. The film continues the director's interest in youth and issues of communication. This interview took place prior to Eimbcke's completion of* Club Sandwich.

FEATURES FILMOGRAPHY:
Club Sandwich (2013)
Lake Tahoe (2008)
Temporada de patos (*Duck Season*) (2004)

JASON WOOD: *Lake Tahoe* marked your second feature following *Temporada de patos* (2004). What experience were you able to bring to this project and what differences, if any, do you see between the two films?

FERNANDO EIMBCKE: When I finished *Temporada de patos* I thought I had learned something about screenwriting, actor's direction and how and where to put the camera. But when I wrote and shot *Lake Tahoe* (2008) I found myself like a first-time film writer-director and I would like to continue like this. I don't want to be a 'pro'. I want to make every film with the fears and doubts I had first time round. Those fears and doubts propel my creativity.

Both films are melodramas with a slight farcical tone, but in *Temporada* this tone was heavier. The protagonist in *Lake Tahoe* deals with a stronger conflict than the *Temporada* characters. *Lake Tahoe* is also a road movie of sorts, while *Temporada* is like an anti-road movie.

JW: *Lake Tahoe* won the FIPRESCI Prize at Berlin. How much did this award mean to you on a personal level and, in terms of enhancing your reputation outside of Mexico, how significant do you consider the award to be?

FE: On a personal level a prize means recognition of the work of all the crew that worked on the film. And as director I feel very proud and thankful. A prize helps the film to get attention, and that's invaluable with an independent film with unknown actors. A prize can help you to find funds for your next film, but at the end I find the prize system kind of strange. I mean, to decide which film is better than another? We're not talking about football where two teams play to demonstrate who's better; we're talking about films. I don't think a film is better than another; they're just different. But when you apply to a festival you accept this prize system. But also, when the film wins a prize I turn into the happiest person.

JW: Critics are quick to compare you with Jim Jarmusch. Is the reference flattering and are there other directors from who you draw inspiration?

FE: I grew up in a non-cinematic family; I didn't go to the movies so often, but I remember that on Sunday mornings I used to see Laurel and Hardy on television. That sense of humour, that simplicity and the melancholic black and white made a deep impression on me. All my friends were into *Star Wars* (George Lucas, 1977); I never saw *Star Wars* until I was thirty years old. When I was in film school a friend of mine showed me *Stranger Than Paradise* (Jim Jarmusch, 1984) and I found in the film a sense of humour, a simplicity, and a melancholic black and white that transported me to those Sunday mornings. Then I had the chance to see Ozu's *Tokyo Story* (1953) on 35 mm, and the feeling I experienced in that screening is the reason why I make films. The other film that inspired *Lake Tahoe* was De Sica's *Bicycle Thieves* (1948). I wanted to make a film where the objective was really simple like a bike or a car but the meaning behind that object was really deep.

7

Amat Escalante

A self-taught film-maker, Amat Escalante spent the first years of his life in Guanajuato, Mexico, and began working in film when he was fifteen. Escalante made his debut as a film-maker with his short fiction film Amarrados (2002). Escalante's debut feature, Sangre (2005), won the FIPRESCI Prize at the 58th Cannes Film Festival, France, in the Un Certain Regard section, and the Silver Alexander award at the 46th Thessaloniki International Film Festival. The film listed Carlos Reygadas as an assistant producer, Escalante having worked as an assistant on Reygadas's Battle in Heaven (2005). The pair have continued to collaborate and support each other, and in many ways, represent the vanguard of arthouse cinema in Mexico.

Los bastardos (2008) is characteristic of the sensibility of Escalante in its measured and calculated look at violence (and its aftermath) and the relationship between the United States and Mexico. A contributor to Revolución (2010), Escalante's third feature, Heli (2013) won the Best Director award at the 66th Cannes Film Festival and the Best Director award at the 56th Ariel Awards.

A mix of Lovecraftian science fiction, social commentary and Andrzej Zulawski's Possession (1981), Escalante's most recent film, The Untamed (2016), won the Silver Lion at Venice, as well as five Ariel awards, including Best Director.

FEATURES FILMOGRAPHY:
The Untamed (La región salvaje) (2016)
Heli (2013)
Los bastardos (2008)
Sangre (2005)

JASON WOOD: You are American from your mother's side and though raised in the Mexican city of Guanajuato you spent your youth oscillating between Mexico and the US. How did this inform your view of the world, and especially the relationship between Mexico and America, which you depict very specifically in *Los bastardos* (2008)?

AMAT ESCALANTE: The way in which I grew up has always been an influence, especially in regard to viewing these two countries and the way in which they are stuck together. I travelled from one side to the other and it makes you appreciate what is good and bad about both countries. This gives a deeper appreciation, I think, than if you had only grown up in one of the countries. I feel at times that I didn't belong in any place, because I was half from one and half from another. I learned to accept this very quickly in my life and tried to reap the benefits of being an outsider in both countries.

I wrote *Los bastardos* with my brother Martín, who also has this dual identity and experience of having an early childhood in Mexico and then moving to the United States and going to high school there. We were very aware of the differences between the countries, both in a concrete sense and in terms of practicalities but also in a more visual way. Even in the plane and looking down I was able to see when Mexico turned into the United States. I felt that this experience enriched me actually. There is a crisis that is constantly happening, both now and forever, and it's curious to see both sides and experience their crises.

JW: I understand that you had artistic parents. Your father was a painter and musician and your mother also played music. Did they play a part in your introduction to culture?

AE: For sure. On my father's side there are many musicians, artists, writers and poets. My mother was also attracted to that and when she was in the United States she was doing long-term research for the University of San Francisco, but based in Los Angeles, and she interviewed a lot of people that were at high risk from sexually transmitted diseases. When I first arrived in the US she had a job where she would speak on the phone and I would hear her asking all these interesting and raw questions. Mostly to women and gay men. She would ask about their sexual habits. This would influence *The Untamed* (2016). My father would paint, often in the kitchen, because we lived in small apartments. My mother would always ask him what his paintings meant and he wouldn't know. I say this in a good way. I think this way of thinking and an open approach to interpretation also influenced my way of thinking. I liked the notion of not necessarily having to explain certain images, and not having to worry about that too much.

JW: You moved to Austin in Texas. What was it about Austin that inspired you and did you make discoveries at the Austin Film Society? I understand that figures including Chantal Akerman, James Benning, Fritz Lang and Stanley Kubrick were favourites.

AE: My parents separated and I moved with my mother to Long Beach, California. This would have been around 1994. I was in a difficult high school where there was a lot of racial tension and violence. Like many teenagers I didn't like high school. It was at this time that I started to really get into movies. I became obsessed with *A Clockwork Orange* (Stanley Kubrick, 1971). It was shown on television and I recorded it on VHS and would watch it over and over again. I was in a very violent environment and I think I found myself reflected in the character of Alex. It was this film that I thought of as my salvation. I then saw *El Mariachi* (1993) by Roberto Rodriguez and I started to think that maybe movies could be something I could do. Rodriguez of course was also from Austin. I then saw Richard Linklater's *Slacker* (1991) on the Bravo channel, which was then a channel for independent films, and I saw Austin, Texas for the first time. I watched *Slacker* many times and thought that the place where the film was set looked great. It was very relaxed and everyone talked about movies. By chance, my father, who was still in Mexico, then moved to Austin, Texas with a girlfriend. I decided to go and live with my father for a while. I was convinced that I knew Austin.

I went when I was sixteen, having dropped out of high school, and got a job in a fast-food place. I lived for two years in Austin. For the first year I had almost no contact with anybody. I used this time to go to the Union, which was the film theatre associated with the University of Austin. My father had an interest in what we would call arthouse films. He liked Herzog and Tarkovsky. I started to get into them too. I first saw them on VHS but then thanks to the university I got to see them projected. I then started to make my own discoveries, film-makers that really impacted me. The impact perhaps wasn't felt at that moment but I was really soaking it in. I would go every Tuesday, and sometimes I would also go to extra screenings that they would put on. The screenings on a Tuesday were free. I saw Benning's *Landscape Suicide* (1987) and it really impacted upon me. I felt lucky to have seen it at a young age. It taught me to appreciate that there were other types of movies. Akerman's *Jeanne Dielman, 23, quai du Commerce, 1080 Bruxelles* (1976) also stood out for me. It was difficult to watch. I forgot about it but the images stuck with me. When I was preparing *Sangre* (2005) I went back and revisited it. I liked exploring why it had affected me.

I wasn't interested in academic studies but I loved being able to take in movies without anybody telling me to. It was important that I could discover them for myself. The first year I was like a monk. Isolated. And devouring movies. In the second year I started to meet more people. I never got to speak to Richard Linklater but I did get to see him present a few films. I am shy. But I was even more shy then. It was in my second year in Texas that I started to write *Amarrados* (2002), my short film. Working in menial jobs for three years I raised enough money to shoot the film.

I have to stress just how important it was to see the films projected on a big screen. I think both *Landscape Suicide* and *Jeanne Dielman* were shown on 16 mm. I saw Tarkovsky in CinemaScope at another cinema and I also saw Nick Ray's *Bigger Than Life* (1956). Fassbinder's *In a Year of 13 Moons* (1978) was another important work I saw projected. This was my education. I would read the programme notes at the screenings but then also go to the library at the university and read publications such as the *New York Times* to experience some of the critical thinking around the films. I guess this was my own form of academia.

JW: *Amarrados* was shot in Guanajuato with a small crew and it chronicles the life of a young glue-sniffer. How much did this production establish a template for your future work?

AE: There basically wasn't a crew. I shot it myself, using the same camera model as Rodriguez, and also did the sound with my brother. An actor friend, Kenny Johnston, also helped out. I was very inspired by Buñuel's *Los olvidados* (*The Young and the Damned*, 1950). I wrote *Heli* (2013) outside of Mexico when I was living in Istanbul, Turkey, and I wrote *Amarrados* when I was living in Austin, and yet they are very Mexican movies. They could only be in Mexico. I think I am more inspired to write about Mexico when I am outside it. *The Untamed* was written in Mexico. It still feels Mexican but is probably my least Mexican movie. Being outside of Mexico you romanticise it a little.

At this moment the idea of working with non-actors was not something I had formulated. I just wanted to shoot with whatever was around and felt logical. I was really interested in Alejandro Jodorowsky and I knew that one of the actors from *Santa Sangre* (1989), Zonia Rangel, lived in Guanajuato and I met her and managed to get her to appear in my short. As a gift she gave me her shooting script from *Santa Sangre*. I shot the film for ten days but I sent the film off to the lab without the money to pay for processing. If you leave it too long without processing, it can affect the stock, but I had to let them keep it until I could find the money for payment. I shot, and didn't see anything of what I was shooting.

JW: Can you talk in a general sense about the process by which you arrive at your ideas? In an interview in *Film Comment* you spoke about the fact that your inspiration tends to come from a single pictorial image or something you think about when living your everyday life. Can you give specific examples of how this has manifested itself in your features?

AE: Yes, that's true. I have made relatively few films so I like to think I am just starting out but a starting point for each of my movies has been an image. The exception would be *The Untamed*, which was from a news article. The image that acted as the impetus for *Sangre* ended up not actually being used in the movie. I got the idea for the first idea of *Sangre* watching *Blood Feast* (1963) by Herschell Gordon Lewis, in which somebody is being dismembered in a bathtub. There are some traces of this in *Sangre*; there is a bathtub at least and we see a character buying a saw to dismember someone. From a single image things start to grow, like a plant or the branches of a tree. In *Heli* the first image was of a countryside at night and a young man looking for his father with the lights from a pick-up on him. That image isn't in the film but again there are traces of it. With *Los bastardos* the starting point was the experience of living in the US and an image of an empty street in the suburbs. I remember walking in such streets and being stopped by the police because they were suspicious that there was somebody in the street in the middle of the day. I'm a light-skinned person and not dark-skinned or African American but even then it felt clear that America was not as free as it was sold to be. That was the seed for *Los bastardos*. Benning's *Los* (2001) was another inspiration.

JW: And what were the articles that helped inform *The Untamed*? The film deals with ideas of otherness and patriarchy but also sex and sexuality.

AE: With *The Untamed* there were articles and these were based on things that had happened in a town that I then discovered more about through the newspapers. Well, actually, one is a newspaper, another is more of a magazine that shows pictures of local murders and tragedies. These publications are very popular in Mexico. A situation occurred where a woman working in a bar accepted a lift to the mountains which are a drive away from Guanajuato. The driver tried to rape her but she fought back. They beat each other up quite badly. She escaped and ended up in hospital. The man also had to go to hospital and they ended up being put in the same room. When the family of the man came to visit him and discovered her she was taunted by them. During the trial, presided over by a female judge, the woman was blamed for accepting a ride with the man. So the woman posted pictures of her wounds on Facebook and the story was picked up by a national newspaper and became major news.

The other inspiration occurred when I was walking in the street and I saw a picture in a paper of a man who had drowned face down in a stream. The headline read, 'They have drowned a little faggot.' I recreate this image in the film. The way that the news was sold and the way people consumed the news spoke to me a lot about the society and the atmosphere here. The first version of the screenplay didn't have any science fiction element. I started to mix the story up so that you had the guy that doesn't really like women but who has to pretend that he likes women so he cheats with his gay brother-in-law. I was looking for something that was a little bit shallow. The prejudice against gays and against women is in its own way very shallow and so after two drafts of the film screenplay I found it uninteresting. I couldn't get to the heart of the hatefulness. When the idea came of having something that wasn't from reality to represent the confusion that some people have inside it felt very liberating. The creature saw me through a script crisis. I had a similar crisis with the script for *Heli*. There are some traces of it still in *Heli* with the conversation about an alien. I've seen a lot of science fiction films and films dealing with things that are not of this world and liked a number of them. It's an interesting and liberating way of representing elements of reality. Guillermo del Toro, who almost always works with creatures, does something similar. His films can seem like they are far from reality but actually they are often even closer to it.

JW: I wondered if you could speak about your approach to CGI and the very anti-traditional decision to reveal the creature quite early in the film.

AE: This decision was actually made in the later phase of the editing process with Fernanda de la Peza and Jacob Secher Schulsinger. We were struggling because the film is a hybrid film and it was difficult to make it work because it wasn't a fully genre film, it was something else. It felt dishonest how we were approaching it with showing the creature toward the end so we decided that we had to establish very quickly the world of the movie. We did this by showing the creature at the beginning. Straight away the audience knows the kind of world it is going to enter. The sound design was also very important. Towards the end of the post-production it became clear that it was key, as was the music. This is in fact the first film I have made for which a score was composed. I just re-watched David Lynch's *Blue Velvet* (1986) and for me the opening scene clearly sets up the kind of world the film is going to take you into. I was also inspired by *Blue Velvet* when I was making *Heli*.

JW: Could you say more about the score for *The Untamed*?

AE: Lasse Marhaug, member of the Norwegian band Jazkamer, produced the score. The composer and the musician is Guro Moe, who is a member of the band MoE. Jazkamer did do some music for *Heli* and they did compose credit music for *Los bastardos*. My brother is really into music, as well as being a screenwriter, and he was into what might be termed extreme music. I shared his interest. We started with figures like John Zorn. I heard a record by Jazkamer around the time of *Los bastardos* and I contacted the band and Lasse happened to also be a cinephile. We became friends. Jazkamer introduced us to MoE and then came to Guanajuato and have actually became quite popular over here. This was actually Guro's first experience of composing for the cinema; she had though worked on a composition for the theatre. It was a really great experience to work with Lasse and Guro. In fact I edited part of the film in Denmark and also visited Norway when we were recording. My brother was instrumental in the international co-ordination of all this. The voice of the creature is actually performed by Jenny Hval. Lasse and Guro recorded her in Norway.

JW: You use sound design in a really interesting way throughout your work. It's obviously something you pay real attention to. Televisions often feature in the background of scenes – specifically in *Los bastardos* – and in *Heli* there is the audio of the video game that the kids are playing during the torture scene. How do you approach sound? Carlos Reygadas has a similar approach, regarding sound as being equally as important as the image.

AE: I took a long time to work with music because I felt that I wasn't ready to work with music. I knew that I had to use the elements without music first. From the very beginning, and my first short film, it was a revelation how much you could do with sound. For my first short I mostly recorded without sound as the camera had no sound. I added the sound in the edit. And I had to re-create a lot of the sound, which was an interesting learning experience. I learned that you could affect the image with really good sound. I haven't mentioned Robert Bresson yet but he is another of the film-makers that I have learned from. I learned from his book (*Notes on the Cinematographer*) and his films. His very specific use of sound was very important to me. As was the use of sound on Fritz

Lang's *M* (1931). It was relatively restrained in terms of its use of sound but the whistling is the thing I remember most about the movie. *Blue Velvet* was also very important in its use of sound. Design too, of course. The apartment of Dorothy Vallens would not be the same without the sound textures. The way that James Benning uses ambient sounds was also very influential for me.

I worked with Carlos on *Battle in Heaven* (2005) and I saw the dedication that he had to recording sound and to see him be so obsessed set a good example to me. I talk to younger film-makers when they are starting out and one of the things I tell them is don't forget the sound. You can get obsessed with the camera but don't forget the sound!

JW: You have worked regularly with untrained actors. Is this a search for realism/authenticity of naturalism?

AE: I started working with whoever I had. Then I started to discover other films and these included documentaries. I wanted to make documentaries actually at one point with real people in life. I wanted to capture their experiences. I wasn't able to do documentary films as I just felt that it wasn't for me but I always stayed with the idea of trying to film real people. I wanted their faces and their mannerisms. A good actor can use their face or their mannerisms but I didn't always have access to good actors. There is also something exhilarating about seeing someone on screen that you haven't seen in anything else. This is another reason why Carlos Reygadas is so important to me. To see *Japón* (2002) and recognise that there was a film-maker in Mexico making a film like the ones that inspired me was very important. *Japón* of course uses non-actors. If I had known Mexican actors featured it would have taken it to another universe. At this time in Mexico there were relatively few really good actors and you would of course immediately recognise them from another movie where they were doing something similar. For me it was completely logical that *Japón* could be made only with non-actors. The non-actors are surrounded in the film by very raw landscapes. This may well have thrown an actor who had grown up or learned their trade in Mexico City. It would have broken the harmony of the film. Throughout history there have been a lot of great films with non-actors. There are of course also lots of great films with professional actors. In my next film I want to use an actor as she would be playing a celebrity so it would feel right, but she will probably be surrounded by non-actors. It feels logical for the piece. Carlos is pretty strict re: working with non-actors; I am not that strict about it. Also, and like Carlos, I don't live in Mexico City and a lot of Mexican films that are made seem to be made specifically for Mexico City. I am interested in showing other aspects of the country.

JW: And what is this film? I read that you were interested in tackling a literary adaptation.

AE: I have a few things in the States that I am waiting on. I have had a manager there for a few years and there are a few projects that I am attached to. I did direct *Narcos* (2015–18), which was quite a radical thing for me. Lots of famous actors.

JW: After the renaissance in Mexican cinema kick-started by directors such as Alfonso Cuarón, Alejandro González Iñárritu and Guillermo del Toro, there also emerged a more experimental arthouse form of film-making, cinema with an arthouse sensibility. Is it important for there to be this space? A space for personal, distinctive and less commercial cinema?

AE: I think you could say that Carlos Reygadas was the first of a new generation to emerge after del Toro, Cuarón and Iñárritu. These three were also inspiring and very important. It is interesting how this trio were only really appreciated by the Mexican Film Institute after they had been successful outside of Mexico. I guess this is normal. When Carlos came out with *Japón* it was very important. The consequences of that are still very much in the air and tangible. It suggested a new way of making movies.

Something wicked this way comes: *The Untamed*

It was also an independent way of making movies. This was important. It showed me, and film-makers like me, that it could be done. You didn't need to have an uncle in the film industry.

I wrote to Carlos after seeing the film and he was very generous in his response, helping me to make *Sangre*. This still happens actually and is very important for film-makers in Mexico, this sense of trying to help and support each other. In other industries I think it is much more competitive. There can be a philosophy of 'if they succeed, I may not so let's not help them succeed'. I don't think this attitude exists so much in the film industry. You find a lot of film-makers who help and support each other. This is also something that del Toro, Cuarón and Iñárritu have continued to do. I have had support from them. Especially after Carlos told them about me. They read an early screenplay of mine and they all took the time to feed back and offer advice. These three film-makers have helped not only in a personal way but they have also helped to show Mexican film-making institutions what can be achieved and as a result these institutions have helped that little bit more.

I did my first and second films before the introduction of a new state funding scheme called EFICINE. After EFICINE was introduced there was a huge increase in production. It went from something like thirty to fifty films per year to around 130. There has been a radical change. Bad movies still get made, of course, movies whose aim is purely commercial, but there have also been films made with artistic and cultural ambition. Carlos just went out with a small crew to tell a story and to show people that hadn't been seen before. This was a very important example to a lot of film-makers, including myself and others such as Michel Franco, Gerardo Naranjo and Natalia Beristáin. It may be getting to the end of it as there is always a threat to state support with the introduction of a new government and there is a threatened austerity toward culture. If the EFICINE tax incentive scheme is taken away it will be a major blow to the film industry. Fewer movies will be made. A lot of less bad movies, but a lot of less good movies as well.

There are many film festivals which also play a part; there is one in my town in Guanajuato starting in a few days and we have Brillante Mendoza coming. Morelia is a very important film festival, especially in regard to its section for Mexican films. Governments like to be associated with success. I found it hard to get invited to Mexican festivals in 2005 with *Sangre* but then it was invited to Cannes. There had been Mexican films invited to Cannes before of course – *Cronos* (Guillermo del Toro, 1993), *Amores Perros* (2000), *Japón*, *Temporada de patos* (2004) – but it was still then relatively rare. Once Cannes invited *Sangre*, suddenly the government wanted to help. They had to support it. They had to at least pay for the flights. They couldn't not be part of it, especially with *Battle in Heaven* also screening. But as a first-time film-maker I was forced to make the movie without them. I found funding from IFFR Rotterdam and the Hubert Bals Fund rather than from the Mexican Film Institute. Now it's different. There is more support. There are also many more women making movies, which is tremendously important.

8

Michel Franco

As a director, screenwriter and producer, Michel Franco is a prolific fig-
ure in Mexican cinema. Daniel & Ana *(2009), Franco's debut feature as*
director, premiered at Cannes and established him as a film-maker with
a forensic eye for detail and character. Franco is also incredibly attuned
to contemporary issues in Mexican society, in this instance the rise of
underground pornography. The winner of the Un Certain Regard award
at Cannes, After Lucia *(2012) continues the director's interest in fractured*
family lives and how technology can act as a powerful and poisonous tool.
A los ojos *(2014), a collaboration with Franco's sister Victoria, adopts a*
documentary aesthetic to explore the ends to which a parent will go to
protect their child, whilst also examining how little we can ever really
know someone, a theme similarly explored in Franco's subsequent fea-
tures, Chronic *(2015), the director's first film made outside of Mexico, and*
April's Daughter *(2017), which won the Cannes Jury Prize.*

FEATURES FILMOGRAPHY:
New Order (2020)
April's Daughter (Las hijas de Abril) (2017)
Chronic (2015)
Through the Eyes (A los ojos) (2014)
After Lucia (Después de Lucía) (2012)
Daniel & Ana (2009)

JASON WOOD: Can we start by talking about your route into cinema? Were
you formally trained? You have multiple skills?

MICHEL FRANCO: I didn't go to film school so I had to start shooting short
films without any guidance or training. I used common sense and trial and
error. I realised that if I was going to direct something then I was going to
have to write and produce it myself. I learned the basics at a summer workshop and then started making short films right away. I started showing them

to people and sending them out to festivals but I was pretty much self-taught and without realising it I was trying to do different things such as write, produce, direct, edit and shoot without being really conscious of this fact.

JW: Has being able to work across different disciplines been a huge benefit? Has it enabled you to retain control over your work?

MF: Yes. It has been the only way actually because I am producing very personal films. Everything I write has to be delivered in a very specific way and I am not sure that there are too many producers that would fully understand my work. Or at least I was never able to find one. We also have to consider that we are not going to be able to do these movies for tons of money, especially my first two or three movies. I had to shoot them on very small budgets and the only way to do this was to apply the money where it really mattered. Producers would keep saying 'No' to everything because they wanted security and to do everything in a traditional or classic manner. This is not my approach to cinema. For me to be my own producer is an absolute must.

JW: Are there film-making figures you take inspiration from? Those especially with a singular vision perhaps.

MF: I like most of the usual big names: Bergman, Buñuel, Fellini, Jean-Luc Godard, Andrei Tarkovsky. Lars von Trier is one of the more recent directors that could be said to have been an influence. I'm also a huge fan of Korean cinema. My work is often compared to Michael Haneke, and I do like and admire his work. With Haneke, if I don't mention the name others tend to.

JW: And any works by Mexican directors?

MF: *El callejón de los milagros* (*Midaq Alley*, 1995) by Jorge Fons was a film I saw when I was young and that stayed with me. I saw it when I was fifteen or sixteen. I liked the way it was constructed but, to be honest, when I started making my short films I wanted to get as far away as I could from Mexican cinema. I didn't feel close to it. Films like *Amores Perros* (2000) and *Japón* (2002) felt important because they showed that a different type of film could be made in Mexico but I wouldn't say that they directly influenced my work at all.

JW: How did your debut feature *Daniel & Ana* (2009) come about? I read it was based on a real case.

MF: That's true. I came to know about it via a therapist that had worked on the case who thought that I would be interested in it. I didn't have direct access to the victims but I did have all the details about the story. I also had

Radical empathy: *Chronic*

to fill in the blanks with the dialogue etc., but the actual structure and the story pretty much reflected reality.

JW: You approach the material in such a way as to put the spectator in the position of the two central protagonists. We feel their fear and we also feel their trauma.

MF: I wanted the viewer to feel the emotions of Daniel and Ana, the brother and sister in the film, and to understand the psychological stress they endure, but I wanted to do it without resorting to the usual tricks. I wanted to avoid music and I wanted to avoid close-ups. I wanted to avoid the type of typical film language that tells you what to think and how to feel. I wanted to give people space but at the same time to make it as effective as possible. I think my choices were also partly a reaction against Mexican cinema as entertainment and heightened melodrama.

JW: The release of the film also contributed to the notion of an emerging arthouse approach to cinema emerging from Mexico.

MF: When it was released ten years ago people would tell me that it didn't look or feel Mexican and, if I am honest, I took it as a compliment. Things have changed now, but back then it did have more of a European sensibility. I'm not sure how deliberate I was in trying to get away from what was traditionally thought of as Mexican cinema, but I was certainly trying to do a lot with as little as possible.

JW: The film, like much of your work in general, does take a look at specific issues in Mexican society. *Daniel & Ana* looks at underground pornography in Mexico.

MF: We live in a very violent society in Mexico and we sadly have become used to it. The film was partly a reaction against that.

JW: *After Lucia* (2012) shares an affinity with *Daniel & Ana* in that it again deals with members of the same family who find themselves in a distressing situation.

MF: It's interesting for me to explore how violence affects people that are closely linked and this of course applies to the family unit. I am also interested in how a violent or shocking event changes the dynamic within a family. And as I said, violence is a natural part of our daily lives in Mexico. Every time somebody is kidnapped or robbed you just have to carry on in the aftermath and there will be a psychological price to live with.

JW: Your film-making style is very specific and precise. There is very little that is superfluous and this extends to the fact that you rarely show violence on screen. This is certainly true of *After Lucia*.

MF: My films are economical in every sense and I want to not show too much violence because I am not really interested in the shock value of depicting violence on screen. If a film is more violent than it needs to be I think that you lose your audience. They stop thinking and feeling because they are too shocked to think and feel. It shuts you down when you are exposed to too much violence. I think that it is better to rely more on the imagination of the spectator. What is happening off screen may be even more violent, but they can imagine this for themselves. I also want people to think about the violence and the act of the violence and its inevitable consequences.

JW: *A los ojos* (2014) is different to your other work in some ways. It's co-directed with your sister Victoria, who has a background in documentary. How did this project evolve and how did the collaboration affect your aesthetic approach?

MF: This was actually supposed to be my second movie, but the shoot lasted more than a year and we had to keep going back to the editing. The reason for this is that we shot without a script. We had an outline and we worked with real people. The main character, Mónica, played by Mónica del Carmen, is real. These people and their lives were all documented by my sister and she shot them for over a year, taking a strict documentary approach. I only shot for about two months. We had to keep going back to the editing to find the final story. Whilst making *A los ojos* I also managed to make *After Lucia*. I am fond of *A los ojos* because of the fact that it was made in an entirely different way.

JW: The central character, Mónica, is very interesting. We think we know her and her nature, but then the film reveals that we do not really know her at all.

MF: She is a social worker but she isn't wealthy and the minute her son has a medical emergency she turns into a desperate mother that will do anything for her child. Money can't solve her problems. So she has to resort to other means.

JW: *Chronic* (2015) is again interested in the family unit but this time it is more the idea of the surrogate family. It is however again a departure because it sees you working for the first time outside of Mexico and in English.

MF: It was a challenge to make a film in Los Angeles with Tim Roth. I now count him as a friend but back then we had just met. I had another film that I was going to shoot in Mexico about a palliative carer with a female protagonist but then *After Lucia* won Un Certain Regard in Cannes and Tim Roth was a member of the jury; he said turn the carer into a man and I'll do it. Tim wanted us to work together and I regard him as one of the best actors in the world. It was a challenge not to lose my voice and my identity because I was shooting in the States. I was also producing the film. Another challenge.

JW: How did the central idea for the film come to you and how deep did you go in terms of research? Palliative care is such an interesting and emotive subject and to this you add the notion of a human being who, in order to make himself feel, sort of plugs himself into the suffering of others.

MF: The answer is very simple. My grandmother was sick. She suffered a brain stroke, which left her bedridden and unable to communicate. She had a series of caregivers who helped her. The first or second day I watched how the caregiver cared for her, analysed her and began to develop a relationship with her. I was intrigued and began to think that there was a movie there. Throughout the months, until the final death of my grandmother, I developed a relationship with the carer myself and we talked a lot. This is where *Chronic* was born.

JW: You reveal the details of the suffering at the heart of the character Tim Roth plays in increments.

MF: I had to invest weeks and months to understand who this nurse was. It was a natural relationship and I didn't want to rush it and serve it up to the audience as a pill that they could simply swallow. I didn't want it to be straightforward. I hate it when I go to the cinema and everything is delivered within the first five minutes – who is good, who is bad and exactly what is going to happen. I think that's a lazy approach to cinema. In this instance, they are very specific people, caregivers I mean, and for me the interest of this movie is to understand them slowly and to take our time.

JW: The family members are slowly usurped in their grief, and realise this too late. Roth is like an emotional sponge.

MF: Yes, and I think because he is deeply depressed. That's what takes him to the job. I didn't want to reduce it to the fact that he had lost a child himself, but, of course, there is a clue there. The title of the movie is also a clue to his depression, and that's why he behaves the way he does.

JW: It's an incredible performance from Tim Roth.

MF: It's a film that I know he is very proud of. It's a very complex role. Most of it was there in the script but Tim certainly offered his own take on the character and his perspective. He also worked for months with patients and became a caregiver himself.

JW: You had produced *600 Miles* (2015), which also starred Tim Roth, directed by Gabriel Ripstein. How did the two projects interact?

MF: We were shooting *600 Miles* with a different actor and we had to let him go because he was a pain in the neck. We were stuck with a production without an actor. We were in Tucson, Arizona, and with a first-time director and I was a first-time producer for a film directed by somebody else. Tim and I were prepping *Chronic* and he decided to also get involved in *600 Miles*. When we shot *Chronic*, Gabriel Ripstein became one of the producers. So, we kept the actor but Gabriel and I switched roles.

JW: You've enjoyed numerous screenings in Cannes, winning Un Certain Regard for *After Lucia*, Best Screenplay for *Chronic* and Un Certain Regard Special Jury Prize for *April's Daughter* (2017). How important are these awards in terms of profile and raising finance?

MF: I think we need to make a distinction between the festival where the film is launched for the first time and then the subsequent festival life of the film. If it is launched in Cannes, Berlin or Venice, then you get a lot of attention. I premiered four movies in Cannes and the fate of the movie is pretty much determined on those first screenings. I have had largely positive experiences, mainly I think because I never expect everybody to like a movie of mine. I'm very thankful to Cannes. I don't think it helps that much with funding, perhaps to a small extent. The movie that helped me most to finance my next movie and to help finance the films by other directors that I produce was *After Lucia*. It won a big prize in Cannes but in Mexico it sold over a million tickets. In France it sold 120,000 tickets and was shown in schools. I don't think prizes get people to see a movie.

JW: When you announced *April's Daughter*, which shares *Chronic*'s interest in mortality, you mentioned that it was aimed at a broader audience.

MF: That would apply to every movie I make. You could say that making a movie in English was a way of reaching a broader audience but then with *Chronic* I made a very bleak movie. One shouldn't care about audiences. By that I mean we should make the movie for people to watch, clever audiences. But I'm not looking to make a crowd-pleaser.

JW: The film presents three takes on women, of different ages and characters, and was viewed by critics as a more feminine film. Was this a deliberate approach on your part? Emma Suárez is terrific in the central role.

MF: I actually prefer exploring female characters to male characters. Tim's part in *Chronic* was originally written for a woman. When writing the script for *April's Daughter*, I did try to look at women of different ages who all represent something different. Some are alone, without family, some are surrounded by family.

JW: And how did you approach telling the story from different points of view? It's shot in a very intimate style and sometimes almost has the feel of a documentary in terms of the use of POV . . . It reaches back a little to *A los ojos*.

MF: I think there are elements of it in *Chronic* too. *A los ojos* really was a documentary. My sister shot on the streets for months and then we made a fiction out of that material. Subsequent projects were fully scripted but hopefully something of the feeling remains. I want things to feel real. I want the audience to sometimes forget that they are watching a movie, if that's possible.

JW: Amongst your recent credits as a producer is David Zonana's *Workforce* (2019). I thought this was an incredible work that really looked at power, privilege and class. Can you talk about what attracted you to the project, about working with David and about the projects you are looking to bring to the screen through your production company?

MF: To be honest I only produce the movies of friends of mine. They have to be close friends and people I have known for years. It's a very intimate thing to make a movie with someone. David Zonana had been working on my movies for seven years as an apprentice. He learned on the job and became a collaborator. I produced his short films *Sangre alba* (2016) and *Brother* (2017) and then he showed me the script for *Workforce*. I liked it. With Gabriel Ripstein and Lorenzo Vigas, who directed *From Afar* (2015) and *The Orchid Seller* (2016), it is different as we have been friends for fifteen, maybe twenty years. We switch roles. I produce them, they produce me. We help each other and try to find what is best for each movie that goes through my company. Lorenzo and I are trying to support projects that we like through the company.

JW: You mentioned earlier that Mexico is a very violent society. *Workforce* also looks at the fact that it is a very unjust one in terms of wealth and power.

MF: I was more interested in the way the script seems to be going in one direction but then turns into a totally different thing. At the beginning it looks like it is going to be about a worker who cannot find justice but the second part of the movie turns into something else, a look at the dynamic inside of the house that the worker establishes. It didn't feel predictable and this excited me as I felt that I hadn't seen this specific movie. I would never produce a movie that I felt I had seen already. I would also never produce a movie that felt like a crossover from other movies. I hate that approach to film.

JW: And what projects are you working on at the moment?

MF: We are into post-production on two movies. One directed by Lorenzo Vigas and my own movie, which is called *New Order*, although the title might change. The film looks at Mexico and the way that it is going. I wrote it three years ago but there is a strong coincidence between what is happening not only in Mexico but also in Chile and Hong Kong. Lorenzo's movie is a more intimate work set in the north of Mexico, which is one of the most dangerous areas of the country. It's a collaboration with our regular technical crew. The film is called *The Box*, but I think the title will change.

JW: And any plans to work again with Tim Roth?

MF: We are prepping a movie actually. Something I wrote specifically for him.

JW: You should persuade him to direct again. It's been a while since *The War Zone* (1999).

MF: He should! We talk a lot about it.

9

Cary Joji Fukunaga

Like Daniel Graham, Cary Joji Fukunaga is not a director born in Mexico (he was born in California to Japanese/Swedish/American parents) but he is included here because his formative work, the short Victoria para Chino *(2004) and his feature debut,* Sin nombre *(2009), relate very much to the Mexican experience and were partly Mexican productions. Both films deal with social injustice, violence and the search for a better life, subjects that can be found at the heart of much contemporary Mexican cinema.*

Following Sin nombre *Fukunaga went on to achieve huge international success. At the time of writing he is completing* No Time to Die *(2020), the latest in the James Bond franchise, having replaced original director Danny Boyle following a disagreement over script-related issues. Fukunaga also directed the first season of* True Detective *(2014).*

FEATURES FILMOGRAPHY:
No Time to Die (2020)
Beasts of No Nation (2015)
Jane Eyre (2011)
Sin nombre (2009)

JASON WOOD: Could you talk about *Victoria para Chino* (2004) and how that fed into *Sin nombre* (2009)?

CARY JOJI FUKUNAGA: *Victoria para Chino* was my second-year film at film school. We had a time limit of ten minutes – which I still went over – but other than that we could do whatever we wanted. It was the first time I really got to experiment with dialogue and music and the first time I got to shoot in colour as well. I wanted to do something based in reality, and something about an important subject, but I didn't have a specific idea. I'd been interested in doing a child soldier movie for a long time but that's not easy to accomplish when you're living in New York and you have a very limited budget.

Then, at the end of my first year in May 2003, I read about the refrigerated trailer in Victoria, Texas, and about the immigrants that died inside it. Whilst doing research, I decided that I wanted to do a film that was almost entirely dark, a sound film. My tutor said no pretty quickly. My inspiration was Alejandro González Iñárritu's contribution to *11'09"01 – September 11* (2002), which was a soundscape piece. This concept seemed fascinating to me. I was previously known for being attentive to cinematography, so I wanted to prove that I could tell a story with no cinematography at all. Ultimately, that changed, and now in the film we have only a two-minute segment where it's all blackness, but there is that segment, it remained in the end. I wanted to try different things and still make it about something important, so that all the effort that went into it wouldn't just be some story about two people talking about their relationship in a café. I did not expect it to be a film that started my career by any means.

I ended up shooting *Victoria para Chino* in January of the next year, and then it took a year for me to finish because I was doing other stuff for school, and helping a friend shoot a documentary in Africa. I finally finished it in the fall and sent it off to Sundance. It was accepted and ended up winning a Jury Prize. From there it just kept on picking up prizes. Suddenly, I was in a position where I had the opportunity to make a feature film and that's when I went off and began writing *Sin nombre*. When that door of opportunity opens, you have to go through it.

Written on the body: *Sin nombre*

239

JW: You've been very clear that *Sin nombre* could not have been made without extensive research, and visits to Chiapas and Tapachula. How did these experiences bleed into the fabric of the film?

CJF: The news articles that I was reading beforehand were so sensational that it was hard for me to decipher what the real scenario was like. I needed to go there myself. What they were writing made it sound like a war zone; to the point where you're afraid to set foot in Tapachula, and you get to Tapachula and it's just like any other town. Even some of the anthropological professors in Tuxtla Gutiérrez, the capital of Chiapas, had been doing their own docs on immigration and the gangs and they warned me that it was best to shoot covertly, because if I went out and filmed in public I would be robbed and shot. We go there and it's totally fine. Originally, we were escorted by State Security, who were armed with heavy machinery, and every time we showed up, people would just disappear and walk away. We couldn't get any interviews, so we thanked the security officers and the next day went to the same places to film without them. It was a completely different experience. We ended up just hanging about in the train yard for two weeks, and in between we went back to the river where the crossing takes place and did the interviews. We also got a feel for the environment by visiting the prison shelters for immigrants injured on the journey. It was just so fascinating in Tapachula, especially in that train yard, that I considered writing something about just the yard itself and all the transients that gathered there.

The original intention was that the friends who travelled with me and a couple of people that had helped produce *Victoria para Chino* were going to write the script together and then undertake the train journey together, but after two weeks of seeing what happened in the yards and getting a feel of what happens on the journey, they decided against taking the journey with me. The project became a solo mission. I think they now regret not having taken the train and been a part of the experience.

JW: Isn't the journey approximately twenty-seven hours long . . .?

CJF: Yeah, until your first stop. You stop in Arriaga, and there's another train that then goes to Oaxaca, because Arriaga is about fifteen minutes from the Oaxacan border, and this Oaxaca section is infamous, a lot of oil goes back and forth. Then another train goes from there to Medias Aguas in Veracruz, then from Medias Aguas it goes up to Tierra Blanca, where it stops again, then across the mountains to Puebla and from Puebla to Mexico City. From Mexico City you can go in many different directions.

JW: How did you attempt to reflect the danger and the camaraderie of the journey?

CJF: Actually, I couldn't bring in as much as I wanted. The camaraderie definitely, but there's one element that I really wish was in the film that I didn't get right, and that was the humour. It's a very dark humour but it's there. I wanted to replicate Danis Tanovi⬚'s *No Man's Land* (2001). This really captures the humour that exists in the bleakness of war. There's the great opening line where the Bosnian soldier is reading a newspaper and comments, 'My god. Do you hear what's happening in Rwanda?'

On the train there were some real characters and jokers. I had a few shots of them and it was like a comedy show. I got a note from the studio saying it looked like people were having too much fun. I couldn't find a way of using the script to show that amidst bleakness you can make humour. In my next project I will definitely try to infuse that gallows humour; I guess balancing the tone is an ongoing development.

JW: *Sin nombre* could be said to correspond to a number of genres. It has road movie elements but is also an epic romance and a gangster drama. There are also traces of the western.

CJF: I don't think I've started to try and master any genre, or to try to really figure out what are the components of each one. Specifically, this story, the reason why I felt that this story was a western was because of the very basic elements of trains, bandits, gangs and immigrants. But I definitely did not want to treat it like a stylised Sergio Leone film, rather something that was more naturalistic and consciously removed from the style of *City of God* (Fernando Meirelles and Kátia Lund, 2002) or *Amores Perros* (2000). These are both films I love, but we've now had almost ten years of bleached cinematography. I was really keen to do something else. John Cassavetes's films of the 1970s were a major influence in terms of the look and feel I wanted. I especially looked at *A Woman Under the Influence* (1974). I really liked the natural lighting, warmer cinematography and longer edits.

When I was writing, I really wasn't that conscious of genre but was more interested in using basic story-telling structures to explore very real themes. I guess also that in the chase element and the somewhat doomed nature of some of the characters there are parallels with film noir, but I was much more focused on allowing the audience to feel the adrenaline of riding the train and sharing in the situations and experiences of the characters. I was also, to be frank, keen to not be too experimental with the structure as this is a film that I want as many people to see as possible.

JW: Can you talk about the casting process? The performances are very naturalistic.

CJF: The casting was difficult because I really wanted a lot of unknown actors and real people. Because of the number of people I needed, the street castings weren't as successful as I wanted them to be. In the Mexico sequences it's a bit of a mix of unknowns and more established performers. Because of this, their acting styles really contrasted, so one of the hardest parts was just getting them in the same film. The benchmark for that would be the character of Willy 'El Casper'. Because of his range, Edgar Flores just had to do what he knew how to do for that role, and everyone else had to basically get to his level. Basically, after we cast, my role was to try to bring a lot of the guys down, and get them as settled as possible – that was the work every take.

I workshopped a few scenes at the Sundance lab and, to be honest, I was apprehensive of how well I would be able to work with actors. Sundance threw in a couple of actors, which was my first time working with young pros. It was amazing, actually; when someone acts well your job as director becomes much easier. Having worked with non-actors where the majority of time is spent getting them to deliver a line just the way it is needed, I then went to talking to actors to whom I could give a certain amount of information about a scene and then they would take it in ten different directions.

Luis Fernando Peña [El Sol] now is a pretty well-established actor, even though he was cast off the street. If Luis was five or six years younger I could've cast him as Casper, but he was just too old for the role. But he's done enough work now that I could just be like, 'This time you know he's lying to you' and then he does it, and does it different, and it was so cool to watch. With some actors I could talk to and give them directions, some actors I had to bring them down, some actors I had to antagonise, like I was constantly antagonising Edgar Flores to get that intensity.

JW: In terms of aesthetics, you really capture both the brutality and the beauty of the landscapes. Were you keen to express this dichotomy?

CJF: I was travelling through Cambodia right after college in 1999, and Cambodia was still wild in the farther-out cities. In the small towns on the coast, there were no tourists at all and when I walked down the streets people would come out of their houses and follow me. I was taking pictures of these old French villas that were basically rotting away, and this kid came out, and in impeccable English asked, 'Why are you taking pictures of this stuff?' I said, 'What do you mean?' He responded, 'Why are you taking pictures of our city falling apart?' I didn't have an answer for him. There was an obvious aesthetic value, like paintings of old Roman ruins; there's something aesthetic about decay and entropy. But I don't think I really found an answer, even while I was making the film.

I have thought about it more in connection to the beauty aspect. You can't really frame a shot to be ugly; you frame a shot to what you think it should be scope-wise, and also, once you get there, what elements and lines you're going to include in the frame. I think the reason that decay is so beautiful is because it reminds us of our own mortality; that nothing is forever. It's like putting a mirror up to death, and in that way it wasn't a conscious effort to show beauty and hardness; it's just those were the locations, that's what they look like, and I tried to put the camera exactly where I thought it suited the moment. The violence was, in some ways, actually toned down in the film. At least I thought it was until I saw the film with an audience, but when I was doing my interviews I saw much more violence, and I didn't want to lose my audience in the first shot of the film.

JW: The Mara gang sequences feel especially authentic. Did you manage to obtain the input of gang members and what was their involvement?

CJF: A couple of guys – both active and non-active – really helped out in the dialogue part of the scripts. We'd write very basic street-style dialogue, get the reaction from the gangs, and they would laugh at it and say, 'No, we'd say it like this.' But, why would people talk to me? It was pretty hard at first; basically, the prison authorities would sit them down in front of me, and often they'd just sit there and stare. They would then either refuse to answer my questions or exaggerate completely and fabricate stories. It was a hard process trying to find people that I thought were honest and would tell me the truth and bring a little more to the gang portrayal.

What especially interested me was the domestic stuff, to see how that House functioned, because in all the interviews, all they talked about were the exploits of the gang and the violence of the gang, and not really about how it functioned on an interior level. The way a gang works in southern Mexico is not the same way the Mara works or a House works in LA, where the work of the gang started. So I would ask them questions concerning basic domestic arrangements, such as who buys the toilet paper, and this threw them a little. I was curious as to how a guy covered in tattoos goes and buys Mr. Clean in the local market. Hygiene and cleanliness are obviously important; the Mara see themselves as far superior in these terms to their gang rivals.

JW: Is there a sense that everyone in the film, gang members included, are yearning to attain a sense of belonging, to feel a part of a family unit?

CJF: Definitely, and the idea of what a family could mean when you don't have a family, and what the idea of a family means when you have a family, but it's not the family you wanted. It's all about recreating a family in the absurd and violent world of a rebel unit. It still fascinates me, the idea of tribalism and families and how they function, and human bonds, loyalty and betrayal and all those things that happen in a family. I think it will be a subject that I will always come back to.

JW: Were you keen that the film convey to an audience the immigrant experience and also give an insight into a world of poverty and a culture of fear and violence?

CJF: Definitely, and that started with *Victoria para Chino*, and trying to place the audience inside the trailer so that they would walk away feeling the fear and the claustrophobia. That is what I wanted to do – have the audience really partake in the experience. I don't think I could've really changed minds. Politically, if you're one side of the fence, you're not going to be different after. Maybe you'll come away with a little more empathy, but I think that's a lot to ask sometimes. You could write as many news articles about something, but unless someone has an emotional experience, they'll always feel intellectually detached. Giving them this emotional experience was a primary goal.

JW: Reaction to the film from Sundance onwards has been universally positive. What do you think people are responding to?

CJF: I don't know what individual people react to, because I'm sure it's probably different things. If people have children, they're watching Smiley, so it probably affects them on that level. For those who are immigrants, it really doesn't matter if you're an immigrant from Bangladesh, or if you're an immigrant from South America, there's a commonality to that experience. It was paramount to me that the film is made for an audience. There are directors that make films for themselves, but I always aspired to be the kind of director that made films for people to see and connect with. From the actual making of the film – and for the 150 people I work with for whom it's also their livelihood – through to its completion, I see it as a fully collaborative process. For me, film is an inclusive experience and that's what is so great about it as a medium. At the end of a film you can have a conversation with someone else about what you just experienced and discuss whether or not you felt connected to the story or the characters. You might even want to discuss whether you felt any connection to the person telling the story.

10

Everardo González

One of the foremost documentary film-makers in contemporary Mexican cinema, Everardo González has worked extensively across film and television, producing numerous acclaimed feature-length and shorter pieces. Graduating with a degree in social communications from Universidad Autónoma Metropolitana in Mexico City, González also studied photography at the Escuela Activa de Fotografía and film at the Centro de Capacitación Cinematográfica (CCC). Devil's Freedom (2017), the director's most recent feature, is an incredibly potent investigation into the phenomenon of Mexico's 'disappeared' from the perspectives of those bereaved by, and those responsible for, some truly barbaric acts of kidnapping, torture and murder. The film premiered at the Berlin Film Festival, where it won the Amnesty International Film Prize. Devil's Freedom was also awarded a Silver Ariel for Best Documentary Feature.

FEATURES FILMOGRAPHY:
Devil's Freedom (*La libertad del Diablo*) (2017)
El Paso (2016)
Drought (*Cuates de Australia*) (2011)
El cielo abierto (2011)
Old Thieves: The Legend of Artiego (*Los ladrones viejos. Las leyendas del artegio*) (2007)
Pulque Song (*La canción del pulque*) (2003)

JASON WOOD: You have been widely recognised as one of the most important voices in Mexican and Latin American documentary film-making. Could you begin by saying something about the formal training you received in film-making as well as what ignited your passion for documentary?

EVERARDO GONZÁLEZ: I don't know if your description fits me, but for sure I've tried to be consistent, if not persistent. I was trained first as a photojournalist and after that as a cinematographer, but in those days as a film student, there was a film that defined my path. It was Peter Brosens's *The State of Dogs* (1998). That film shocked me and showed me that narrative film-making and reality didn't have to go their separate ways.

JW: The first film of yours that I saw was *Pulque Song* (2003). This struck me as a very important work as it looked at a specific aspect of Mexican culture and at a very specific tradition. Was it your intention, at least initially in your career, to focus on subjects that had Mexico and Mexican culture at their heart?

EG: I saw that a bar like *la pulqueria La Pirata* was, in a way, a mirror of our huge migration process from the fields to the *urbes*. I wanted to show how this place was a universe of encounters between those who carry on their backs the benefits of a modern society but are always marginalised. I wondered who were the ones losing something with the extinction of a culture and, of course, it was mainly the marginalised. This was a tribute to them.

JW: *Devil's Freedom* (2017), like a number of your works, was widely screened at international festivals and won numerous awards, including Ariels. How important is this international exposure in terms of connecting you with an international audience and in terms of accessing finance for future projects?

EG: Unfortunately, Mexico has a history of cultural domination. We are always in need of recognition outside to have a value here. International exposure is always good for film-makers because it provides an opportunity to see what is happening in the wider world.

JW: A look into the stories behind the headlines in the battle against drug crime in Mexico, *Devil's Freedom* is an incredible achievement. You tell the tale from both sides, including testimonials from both victims and perpetrators. Was it important to you to have this dual perspective? It certainly highlights how systematic violence holds everyone in Mexico in a death grip.

EG: Systematic violence is now in our daily life; it is everywhere and we are now living with limited freedom. For me, it is important to recognise violence and to learn where it comes from. I genuinely wanted to listen to what both sides had to say.

JW: The film also shows how this culture of violence has become an accepted part of everyday life in Mexico. It's the most harrowing indictment of just how pervasive death and killing has become. It seems to be a cycle that is looking almost impossible to break in a society governed by fear and insecurity.

EG: It can be broken but it won't be soon. I believe we've lost three or four generations, at least. The culture of violence is deep rooted in our society, but justice can bring us peace. Impunity is the main problem here.

JW: 'What do you get when you kill someone?' a voice asks off screen. 'Power' is the reply from a Mexican gangster who committed his first murder at the age of fourteen, still in his school uniform. This, for me, is perhaps the most powerful moment in the film. Were you shocked by this revelation whilst filming it?

EG: I was shocked during the making of this whole film – and on multiple levels. Not only recognising that killing brings power to someone, but also knowing that fear is the main reason for committing atrocities.

JW: Can I ask about your use of masks in the film? I also understand that you used a mirror at the time of interviewing so that the subjects would see themselves. What was your intention with this technique?

EG: I needed to show testimonies supported by truth. The mask is something that reveals that truth. The use of a mirror was because I needed eye contact between the characters and the audience; that is where empathy resides. The mirror also brought the characters an opportunity to make a self-confession. When we see the film, we are actually witnessing a confession.

JW: I read an earlier interview with you prior to your attending a three-day documentary workshop at IFF Panama. You stated that 'Film-makers often confuse documentaries with journalism and social anthropology, and this takes people away from cinemas. Everyone forgets the importance of plot. My main task is to try to help people find the plot, and find the dramatic force in reality.' Would you describe this as an apt encapsulation of your philosophy regarding making documentaries?

EG: I don't always achieve that but I'm always seeking to achieve it. I understand that documentaries carry a heavy stigma. They were made to instruct us; I prefer story-telling.

JW: You also spoke at IFF about a new project, *El vientre yermo* (*Sterile Womb*). The project returns to your earlier *Drought* (2011) but is more global in scale, looking at the hidden life in ten deserts around the world. Where are you shooting and what have your experiences included so far?

EG: *Yermo* will be the name of the film. It was a great opportunity to learn from reality but also to learn from our own exoticism. The end of the film became that: the chance to be watched by those who are usually the characters of a film.

JW: Was the project also a way of escaping *Devil's Freedom*? This must have been a harrowing and psychologically tough assignment.

EG: It was exactly that. I needed to keep a distance from cruelty.

JW: In general, how would you describe the state of documentary film-making? To the outsider, it looks to be in good health through a combination of a new generation of film-makers and festivals such as DocsMX and companies such as Ambulante.

EG: It's in great health but always facing the complexities of the market and the industry. I'll always be thankful to those who believe in documentary, including Ambulante and DocsMX.

JW: Are there particular contemporaries whose work has especially impressed you?

EG: Asif Kapadia, Tatiana Huezo, Jorge Caballero, Talal Derki, Lola Arias and many more have impressed me with their work. They deserve huge exposure.

Daniel Graham

Daniel Graham has made several short films in Australia and France. He was the line producer on Carlos Reygadas's Post Tenebras Lux *(2012). Reygadas would go on to associate produce Graham's debut feature,* Opus Zero *(2017). A very distinctive feature, the film is evocative of Antonioni in its use of landscape. The interview below also provides an interesting insight into Mexican funding initiatives. Graham is currently editing his second feature,* The Obscure Life of the Grand Duke of Corsica (2020).

FEATURES FILMOGRAPHY:
The Obscure Life of the Grand Duke of Corsica (2020)
Opus Zero (2017)

JASON WOOD: Can you begin by talking about how your idea for *Opus Zero* (2017) began and then developed?

DANIEL GRAHAM: The first inkling of an idea I had was upon listening to the completed version of Mahler's Tenth Symphony as constructed by the great British musicologist Deryck Cooke in the mid-1960s. Despite being a remarkably uncanny invocation of the inimitable Mahler style, there was something fundamentally missing from it as a listening experience. It certainly sounded convincing but it just wasn't Mahler. What was missing was the sense of imminent mortality that Mahler was experiencing at the time of its composition, having recently been diagnosed with a fatal heart disease that would kill him two years later. This is something that no musicologist or subsequent composer, no matter how brilliant or intuitive, could ever convincingly capture. However, to be fair to Deryck Cooke, who was an utterly brilliant and innovative musical thinker (author of *The Language of Music*), he never claimed it was a definitive work but was academic in nature and should be taken as such.

Nonetheless, it got me thinking as to why it was an unsatisfactory listening experience despite the obvious appetite amongst Mahler fans to believe it was just like the real thing. This led me to concoct the first half of the script, in which an American composer arrives at a small, remote and foreign village where his father had recently died in order to settle his affairs. Whilst sifting through random objects and memories without context, he is somehow drawn back into the completion of an unfinished symphony written by a fictional, early twentieth-century composer (a hybrid Mahler/Sibelius-type figure). That seemed a good start, but it was clear that I needed a second act, and indeed a third.

After watching an Italian documentary one evening, the idea came to me that this American composer should come into contact with a gormless documentary crew wandering around aimlessly looking for inspiration amidst precisely nothing, not realising that you don't find inspiration, it finds you, something the American composer attempts to tell the documentary film crew in an extended interview, using coded language to test their skills of detection and interpretation – a master/apprentice-type scenario, albeit implicitly so.

There followed a very long period of development whereby the script was eventually transformed from something overly conceptual and intellectually impenetrable to something that I hoped would be more concise and precise, yet dense with meaning and connections. I might even be as pretentious as to suggest it was very much how I imagine sculpting to be. You start with a slab of marble and an 'idea' as to what the final shape will be like, but it is only when the 'concept' becomes the 'doing' that the real shape begins to reveal itself to you. This was very much the case with the script of *Opus Zero*. I might also add that at a late stage of the writing process I read the works of the Italian modernist composer Luciano Berio, specifically a series of lectures he gave on music called 'Remembering the Future'. His thoughts on the nature of art and authorship became immensely influential on my thinking and I hope that some of it made its way into *Opus Zero*.

JW: How was the film funded and how did you come to shoot in Mexico?

DG: Originally the script was set in Ariège, a department in the far south of France with which I had become quite familiar. Despite having Willem Dafoe and Michael Nyman (who later left the project abruptly) attached from an early stage, I failed to engage any real interest from over sixty different producers in France I had made contact with over a two-year period. It seemed an impenetrable industry to make your way into as a foreigner. Finally, it was Carlos Reygadas who suggested I try some producers he knew of in Mexico, one of whom eventually boarded the project. This was Julio Chavezmontes. I then had to consider how I would adapt the very French nature of the script into a Mexican landscape and culture, one that I had very little exposure to. Would we shoot interiors in studios and find exteriors that resembled France? This seemed highly improbable, so I instead looked on a map at dozens of small villages in Mexico for a sub-stitute to the very special nature of Ariège until I came across the *pueblos magicos* of Real de Catorce.

What at first seemed a bumpy transition from France to Mexico actually turned out to be a blessing, as the strange and beautiful nature of Mexico illuminated the script in a way that shooting in France probably would have rendered it an intellectual dead end.

JW: What support did you receive from Mexico?

DG: IMCINE financed about 75 per cent of the film so they were absolutely instrumental in getting it made, although the individual most responsible for this was the producer, Julio Chavezmontes. Before Julio, however, there was Carlos Reygadas, who inspired me in more ways than you can imag-ine. Not only did he introduce me to Willem Dafoe, he helped me in many other ways.

Carlos is a genuinely unique man, not only in the world of film-making but as a human being. He is an extremely rare example of a true artist working in cinema. I say an artist as opposed to a craftsman or an expo-nent, meaning his fail rate might be higher than someone who plays it safe, someone content to make the most beautiful and comfortable chair imag-inable as opposed to questioning why we'd want to sit down when could instead stand up.

JW: Where did you shoot and how did you find the experience of working in Mexico as a non-Mexican? It has proved a source of inspiration for directors such as Buñuel, Welles, Peckinpah and Eisenstein.

DG: Dafoe and I were the only foreigners on set, so yes, there was a feeling of being on someone else's home turf. Having said that, the crew could hardly have been more welcoming and friendly. I said many times during the shoot that I wish I'd gone to Mexico right from the beginning rather than spending two years looking for producers in France. Mexico is a truly exceptional country, which I think is reflected most immediately in its people. I made some good friends on the film and found the atmosphere on set, especially for a director who was making his first film, to be one of utter professionalism and optimism. That's not to say it was an entirely smooth ride, however. Things became heated at more than one point, but anyone who's worked on a film will know what kind of pressure you're under. It's very much a matter of money squeezing art and vice versa – a rocky marriage can still produce a beautiful child.

We shot in the village of Real de Catorce, which has a long history of film production. It's a 'one off' sort of place. Anyone who visits it cannot fail to be affected by its strangeness and otherworldly feeling. It's the kind of village which seems to be brimming with the dust of lives past. We were spoiled for choice on locations and the script was certainly influenced by that. For maybe twelve months after I left Real de Catorce, I carried around the feeling of the place within me, unable to shake off its residue.

JW: Can you say more about how you came to cast Dafoe . . .?

DG: After working for Reygadas on *Post Tenebras Lux* (2012) in Sheffield in November 2011, I wrote the first draft of *Opus Zero*. I sent it to Carlos, who responded enthusiastically. As I recall, I talked with him about who could play the lead role, mentioning two possible names. One of them, Willem Dafoe, Carlos happened to be friendly with, so Carlos offered to email him about the script. Willem took Carlos's suggestion and called me. We spoke over the telephone and he certainly seemed interested. There followed a very long period of time during which I struggled to find a producer. Willem remained interested during this entire time as the project went through many different incarnations. Finally, when financing was secured, we were off to the races. It was Willem's participation in the film that finally got it made and that lifted the entire thing to a level of almost effortless artistry that I could never have achieved without him. Our first one-on-one read-through took place during a brutally hot Rome bank holiday weekend. On the first day of reading, Willem started immediately to rewrite his part with the memorable declaration of 'If you want your dialogue performed word for word then you're going to need a better actor.' I was rather taken aback by this but quickly realised what he was doing. He was tailoring the suit that I had created for him, making it fit more comfortably, and thank God he did because had he performed the role word for word it would have resulted in perhaps the most tedious character in cinema history. What Willem did was to vivify what I had written, which was too intellectual in nature and too academic in execution. He could see what it was I was trying to capture, so by editing the dialogue he was effectively doing two jobs at once, that of co-writer and lead actor. This carried on over two blistering days in Rome, punctuated by glorious meals and rather a lot of wine (drunk mostly by me). We also got to know each other a little better, which became, I suppose, something of a friendship over the coming months. To say I learned a great deal from Willem would be an understatement. I could write a book about the experience but one of many memorable experiences was the day we went into a sound studio to record his voice-over for the film, which was extracts from Lucretius' *On the Nature of Things*. Being the professional he was, we nailed his voice-over in about forty-five minutes flat out of a two-hour booked session.

Wanting to make the most of the time we had him for, I quickly scrambled through the rest of Lucretius' book and highlighted some additional passages for Willem to cold read, effectively. I was worried this was asking too much of him but, yet again, he nailed it in one or two takes with no direction. That was a real eye-opener, that an actor could do a cold read on a rather tricky text and deliver something of utterly compelling gravity.

The collaboration with Dafoe wasn't always a smooth one but then what artistic collaboration ever is? Without struggle and conflict you'd probably have a very dull end result. Much like *Avengers Assemble* (Joss Whedon, 2012), for example.

JW: And what about other key casting? And also the rest of the technical crew?

DG: The two most important actors in the film after Willem were Andrés Almeida and Cassandra Ciangherotti, who play Daniel and Fernanda. Originally the character of Daniel was accompanied by a cameraman and soundman, no producer, but after discussions with Julio and rehearsals with the actors it became apparent that the character of Daniel would work best if there was an opposing force in his scenes. This became the role of Fernanda, his producer. The really marvellous thing about working with actors as talented as Andrés and Cassandra is that they help you understand the characters you've written in the world. Of physical behaviour and, yes, motivation.

© Somos Piano

Motion and emotion: *Opus Zero*

As the writer I may know why they do the things they do, but as actors they need to understand it in their own way so they can believe in what they're doing, to understand how and why they got there. There was also the character of the cameraman, Gilles, who was in fact named after my friend Gilles Laurent (soundman on *Post Tenebras Lux*), who was going to do the sound on *Opus Zero*. Very tragically, Gilles was killed in the Brussels Metro terror attack of 2016, only a few months before we started pre-production. In the end we were very fortunate to have Raúl Locatelli do sound, who is an artist in his own right, a terrifically debonair and charming man and a quite brilliant technician.

I was very fortunate to have an exceptionally gifted DoP on *Opus Zero*, Matías Penachino, who understood very early on what kind of look I wanted for the film and how to achieve it. The first conversation we had after he'd read the script was about films like *Nostalghia* (Andrei Tarkovsky, 1983) and *Ulysses Gaze* (Theodoros Angelopoulos, 1986), so it was apparent we were on the same wavelength. What I said to Matías was that I didn't want the film to look like a sunny desert movie, something of a challenge given we were shooting in the middle of Mexico. I wanted the camera to be constantly, yet imperceptibly, moving by using sequence shots rather than the more conventional, and safer, approach of coverage.

For the exteriors, I wanted morning or later afternoon light and for the interiors I wanted a chiaroscuro look whereby the characters would be moving in and out of large swathes of darkness. One could draw all sorts of intellectual parallels here but I just like how it looks and thought it appropriate for the script. If I was shooting a musical then I suppose it would've been lit up like a Christmas tree. Matías was also instrumental in evolving my own visual language as a director. Being my first feature film, I was still thinking in terms of what could be done on a short film scale, meaning you shoot and run, shoot and run. Here, we had more time and more resources to really find the best possible solution to the problem. I would rate Mati as probably one of the most gifted young cinematographers in the world today.

The other person I learned most from was the editor, Yibran Asuad. Yibran taught me the importance of continuing to find ways to better assemble the film, to really understand what it is you're saying and how best to present it. As we shot mainly sequence shots, apart from the amphitheatre scene, it was a question of chronology rather than building the inner tension of scenes through cutting. Yibran is also an accomplished scriptwriter so he brought an advanced narrative sensibility to the job, which was essential. He really drummed into me the importance of exposition.

JW: And what were the key visual ideas that you wanted to communicate? I wondered also if you drew on any specific influences, other than those you have already mentioned.

DG: My script was very dialogue heavy but not necessarily in the matter of exposition, rather of ideas, which provided ample material for artistic headache. In other words, how the fuck do we shoot this crap? But if we are talking visual language, I would again refer to the DoP, whose artistry and understanding was largely responsible for what you see on screen in its final form. We worked together really well in that I started with a very basic idea as to how the scene would be covered, which he then expanded upon, bringing art to the purely mechanical. I might then make some alterations to it and finally we would arrive at a conclusion that satisfied us both.

There was also the decision to shoot in the ultra-wide ratio of 3:1. I was against the idea at first as I could see no justification for it. After all, we weren't shooting a Roman epic. When we visited Real de Catorce to scout locations, I came to realise that the more we could capture in the frame the better. 3:1 brings with it a responsibility to fill the frame with something meaningful or necessary, but in fact, the wide-open spaces of Real de Catorce, and Paul's drifting yet magnetic presence within it, illuminated many of the ideas of the script in a way that a more conventional aspect ratio wouldn't have. There was also the marvellous production design of Claudio Ramírez Castelli, which bore the ultimate quality of being invisible as well as utterly appropriate. It was so convincingly crafted that at no point in the film are you aware of it being production design. It simply seems to exist on its own, as though it was always there and always will be.

Before we started work proper, I sent him a photo I took of Van Gogh's *Two Crabs* painting of 1889, which is predominantly green and orange but is mounted on a light grey wall. And so, it was muted green and grey that ended up informing the palette of the film. What I found most fascinating and rewarding was how a handful of very basic and conceptual starter points blossomed into what became the fabric of the film to the point where stylistic influences illuminated the root idea of the film.

JW: What music did you use?

DG: The remarkable blues song 'Last Kind Words', which was recorded in 1930 by Paramount Records. I wish I could take credit for having found this song but, in fact, it was Sebastian Hoffman who brought it to my attention. I had never imagined in a million years that a country blues song like this would fit the world of *Opus Zero* but the second I saw it in the promo reel I was immediately hooked. Very little is known about Geeshie Wiley and most accounts are wildly contradictory, although she was considered by some to be the greatest of all female blues singers from the South. When you listen to her hard-won singing voice, her loping, rhythmic guitar playing and her emotionally excoriating lyrics you understand why. Even seasoned blues musicians I've talked to about this song are taken aback. It's like a cyclone of pain, dignity and suffering that is impossible to not be moved by. The lyrics couldn't have been more appropriate for the film.

12

Jorge Michel Grau

Jorge Michel Grau studied communication at the National Autonomous University of Mexico (UNAM), film-making at the Centro de Capacitación Cinematográfica (CCC) in Mexico City, and film directing at the Film and Audiovisual School of Catalonia (ESCAC). He received a scholarship from the National Fund for Culture and the Arts (FONCA) in 2004, formed part of the Workshop for Young Producers Morelia Lab at the third Morelia International Film Festival (FICM) and participated in Guadalajara Talents 2008.

Grau's incredibly visual shorts, Ya ni Pedro Pablo *(2003),* Mi hermano *(2005) and* Kalimán *(2006) were all presented at the Morelia International Film Festival.* We Are What We Are *(2010), Grau's debut feature, premiered at Cannes and was subsequently exhibited at more than sixty international film festivals. A political horror film about a poor Mexican family turning to cannibalism in order to survive, the film also looks at how patriarchy is privileged in Mexican society.*

Grau has subsequently worked in television and contributed segments to The ABCs of Death *(2012) and* Barbarous Mexico *(2014), and worked in the US on* Big Sky *(2015). Grau has just completed* Perdida *(2019), a remake of the Colombian film,* The Hidden Face *(2011).*

FEATURES FILMOGRAPHY:
Perdida (2019)
7:19 (2016)
Big Sky (2015)
We Are What We Are (Somos lo que hay) (2010)

JASON WOOD: Could you begin by talking about how your passion for cinema started? Were there particular films or film-makers, Mexican or otherwise, that ignited your interest?

JORGE MICHEL GRAU: Growing up at the end of the 1970s and at the start of the 1980s, my father had a business where he rented films on Beta and videocassette players – long before the monster called Blockbuster existed. Little by little, and with Televisa's entry in that business, my father's video store went bankrupt and so dozens of boxes full of movies ended up in our living room. We had days and days of shows with all the neighbouring children: nights of terror, drama days, western weekends. My parents, during their separation process, left us alone, so we took advantage not only by watching movies but also replicating them as plays. We had no money for a camera but we had the ingenuity to make theatrical productions of the movies, turning our house into a mansion of terror with the theme of the movie in turn. We saw all the American movies of the 1970s and also a lot of Italian horror. Mario Bava, Dario Argento, Sam Peckinpah, Stanley Kubrick, John Carpenter, Sydney Lumet, Martin Scorsese, Francis Ford Coppola, Steven Spielberg, Akira Kurosawa and Brian De Palma were key directors. Key American films included *Star Wars* (George Lucas, 1977), *Apocalypse Now* (Francis Ford Coppola, 1979), *E.T. The Extra-Terrestrial* (Steven Spielberg, 1982), *Krull* (Peter Yates, 1983), *The Goonies* (Richard Donner, 1985), *Back To The Future* (Robert Zemeckis, 1985) and *Stand By Me* (Rob Reiner, 1986). Pedro Infante's filmography was also our bread and butter.

A *Clockwork Orange* (Stanley Kubrick, 1971) and *The Godfather* (Francis Ford Coppola, 1972) also marked my life. I saw them obsessively again and again. I have to add *Cronos* (1993) by Guillermo del Toro, *Canoa* (1976) by Felipe Cazals and *Rojo amanecer* (1989) by Jorge Fons to the great works that made me understand what I wanted to do for the rest of my life.

JW: There seems to be a strong horror element to your work. Is this a genre that particularly excites you?

JMG: Indeed, all the Italian horror movies, trash cinema, slasher, gore and everything else contained in my father's video club boxes made me love the genre. However, New Hollywood and the films of the great Mexicans (Felipe Cazals, Jorge Ripstein, Arturo Fons) showed me how to use film as a vehicle for social commentary.

JW: You studied communication at the National Autonomous University of Mexico (UNAM) and then film-making at the exceptional CCC Film School in Mexico City. The CCC has been a foundation for many of the Mexican film-makers who emerged in the post-*Amores Perros* (2000) renaissance in Mexican cinema, and it has continued to nurture new film-making talent in numerous fields and disciplines. How formative was studying at the CCC for you and why do you think there seems to be such a depth of talent in your homeland?

JMG: I don't have any family members working in movies; neither my parents nor anyone close to me is dedicated to that (except my brother, who is an actor). Everything I know about film I owe to the hours and hours I took refuge in the cinema during my parents' divorce and the CCC. I didn't know about its existence until I finished my degree and then tried to get in a couple of times before they accepted me. After that, the CCC became my home, my family, my den. The CCC gave me the technique, the trade and the exercise of reflection that makes films flourish. Although there are many ways to get to making movies, the CCC was a direct pathway to film. I had great teachers there and now, proudly, I am a teacher at the school that trained me.

Mexico is a country with a huge magical imagination, full of legends and traditions that allows us to be extraordinary story-tellers. Not only great narrators in film, but literature as well. Mexico is a country of stories, fables, monsters and virgins. But above all, a brutal, voracious and violent reality that forces us to look for a mirror where we see ourselves, and understand each other. Mexican cinema is powerful because of that.

JW: Prior to your debut feature you made a number of highly regarded shorts, including *Ya ni Pedro Pablo* (2003), *Mi hermano* (2005) and *Kalimán* (2006), all of which I believe were presented at Morelia. Two questions here: how important has the role of Mexican film festivals been – Morelia, Guadalajara – in supporting emerging Mexican film-makers, and did you always see shorts as a route to directing features?

JMG: Festivals are the main exhibition tool for us. We get to not only show our work, but know the work of other film-makers. Morelia and Guadalajara are the festivals with the greatest penetration and best film selection. Thus, a career's construction and the merits that allow you to continue filming are built by participating in festivals. In summary, the commercial theatre circuit has been kidnapped by superhero movies and simple and poorly made comedies. This forces Mexican film-makers to find alternative exhibition circuits, in addition to cine clubs and independent theatres. Festivals are extraordinary for that. In addition, there is no circuit in Mexico for exhibiting short films, forcing film-makers to use festivals as a way to show their work.

Short film seems to me to be a short-term exercise that forces the film-maker to be accurate, precise. It's the prelude of the great narrator. As an academic tool it is a thermometer to get to know the director, understand tone and genre. The short film is, in itself, a great oeuvre.

JW: How did the opportunity to direct your feature debut, *Somos lo que hay* (2010) arise? Also, was it a project that benefitted from state funding, through either the IMCINE FOPROCINE or FEDICINE schemes? The Mexican Film Institute strikes me as being very supportive of film-making in Mexico, even if it is, like all national funding bodies, subject to political circumstances.

JMG: *Somos lo que hay* is part of the CCC's First Feature project. It's an incentive that debuts film-makers graduated from the school. Students who have finished their studies with the degree (a short film) and have participated as a social service in some other first feature have the right to submit a feature film project. In addition, as a requirement, the main positions of the film (DoP, direct sound, producer) must be debuting, also having social service students in the crew. The contest is open to all CCC graduates and is supported by the Mexican Film Institute through FOPROCINE. Thus, the film is funded by the school and the IMCINE. No private investment or co-producers allowed. The movie belongs to the state.

In sum, there is no censorship or political line, although there are, depending on the incentive, certain criteria. Most of the time the director is respected.

JW: The film was immediately embraced internationally, and enjoyed invites to numerous prestigious international film festivals, including Cannes, Montreal and the Gérardmer Fantasy Film Festival in France. Why do you feel the film chimed with international critics and audiences? Like many of the best horror films, it brilliantly balances an ability to terrify with astute social observations. I was reminded of George A. Romero's zombie trilogy in this regard. Can you also talk in more detail about what you wanted to say with the film in terms of making social and perhaps political observations about not only contemporary Mexico but about Mexican society in general? It's a film in which austerity is quite literarily driving people to desperate measures – to eat each other.

JMG: I think the success of *Somos lo que hay* is the city. Mexico City is a living and active character in the film; its violence, its loneliness, its arrogance. Mexico City is the environment where this family decomposes, disintegrates and has to learn to survive. Mexico City is the family's risk and refuge – a family that has had to reinvent itself after the death of the patriarch, the provider, the leader. In Mexico, families suffer from an almost automatic disintegration. Being Mexican, in many cases, makes you grow up without a father. Killed by the Narcos, migration, or because of normalised infidelity, the men leave their families, forcing the family to find dynamics of survival; underage children taking care of families, mothers needing two or three jobs and a long list of other ways not to perish. The Mexican crisis, its inequality, the normalisation of violence, the murders of women (nine women every day), and an endless number of daily nightmares that force us to seek to survive, leads us to a war of 'all against all', of 'every man for himself'. In this sense, marginalised classes are the least able to survive; prostitutes, street children, homeless are the weakest social classes and the easiest to prey upon. The great metaphor of the film is that man is the wolf of man; we are a society structured around class; we are racists, giving skin colour a supreme value; we are governed by pigment, so a family has to devour marginalised classes to survive.

The film has a high social content well above its genre; the story has many edges and many layers that, I think, make it interesting in the eyes of foreigners.

JW: The film also has a lot to say on the subject of family dynamics and patriarchy and matriarchy. Were these subjects that were very close to your heart when devising the film?

JMG: In fact, the beginning of my exploration was to talk about family dysfunction, about disintegration. I come from a family of divorced parents, all my aunts are divorced, my whole environment comes from separated parents, I am divorced myself. The construction of the story is based on the family without a father and how mothers have to reinvent family dynamics.

JW: The opening sequence sets the tone for the film perfectly. It's incredibly disturbing. Were you aware of the need to grip the viewer from the very beginning?

JMG: Of course, the tone, conventions and history are seen in the first minutes of a movie. I think that the most honest approach as a narrator can be given in the first minutes, in the first shots; knowing how to summarise the story, the plot, the topic in a few shots comes from in-depth knowledge and investigation of the theme. The initial scene shows the death of the patriarch, consumerism and depredation of lower classes, the death of someone in a lower class is inconsequential, sales must continue.

In addition to this, the initial scene is a nod to connoisseurs of the subgenre of cannibalism. The death of the father, his black vomit and his apparent madness, are symptoms of a disease called kuru. A disease that only occurs if a person eats human flesh. It's basically the same disease that killed thousands of cows in England, the 'mad cows'.

Thus, the beginning of a movie contains the tone, the plot, the theme and the secret.

JW: This scene occurs in broad daylight, but as the film develops it becomes a more subterranean work, often taking place at night or in interior sequences. The visual aesthetic of the film matches the darkness of the subject. How did you work with your technical team to achieve the look (and sound) you desired?

JMG: The neighbourhood where the story takes place is the neighbourhood where I come from, where all my family lives and where I grew up. I know those mazes and walkways like the palm of my hand. I am each of the characters, in several dimensions, so the approach to the aesthetics of the film was very near to me – it was my childhood day by day; I just sought to reproduce it. With Santiago Sánchez, the DoP, and Alejandro García, production designer, we designed the city's underworld, those nights as dark as our theme. We wanted to make the desolation felt, and that was achieved in that intricate system of caged streets. My two collaborators perfectly understood where I wanted to navigate and where I wanted to take the public. I wanted to get into the darkest of the nights of Mexico City and its inhabitants.

JW: It's also incredibly well cast, especially in regards to the mother and Paulina Gaitán, who had emerged the year before in *Sin nombre* and who then went on to star in *Narcos*. How easy was the casting process, especially given that you were looking to replicate a family unit?

JMG: One of my obsessions was that the family looked like a family – physically, yes, but also in attitude. I looked for two months for actors of the age range I needed. First came Paco Barreiro, who, although he was a few years older than I needed, I knew him for his work in theatre and a couple of films by Nicolás Pereda. In addition to his extraordinary work as an actor, he has an incredible resemblance to a character in a Mexican documentary concerning a character that was a parricide who had killed his entire family; in fact, the costume design is very similar to the Santa Martha prisoners' uniforms, where the murderer is incarcerated. Having him, I started looking for the brothers. First, I found a fantastic actor, then a student who looked like Paco, and decided to cast the third brother together with them. That's how I met Alan Chávez, now deceased, who was running late to the casting and the actress had to leave. I was missing an actress to help me in the casting and that was when Alan told me that Paulina Gaitán was in the cafeteria having breakfast. I didn't know her, so it was Alan who asked for her help

© CCC and FOPROCINE

Long live the new flesh: *We Are What We Are*

and then it happened. I saw my family together for the first time. It was magical and instant. I had to talk to the actress I had previously selected and explain to her that I had found someone else (perhaps the saddest moment of my career was to break that actress's heart). It took me much longer to find the mother since many, and I really mean many, actresses read the script and they refused to even try out. The day I met Carmen Beato and she told me about her character proposal, I knew I had a movie in my hands.

JW: The film was subsequently remade in the US by Jim Mickle as *We Are What We Are* (2013). What was your involvement with the remake and were you in favour of it?

JMG: When they approached me for the rights for the remake, I thought it felt fantastic to let go of the story and for it to go beyond the border, to be told in another voice. I was very excited about the idea and sold the rights. It was the first Mexican film to have a remake. I sent Jim and Nick Damici all my research and all drafts of the original script. We had several sessions where we discussed many important aspects for the original film and how they could pass them on to their version. In the end, I think Jim made a great movie.

JW: Finally, can you bring us up to date on current projects? There were subsequent features such as *The ABCs of Death* (2012) and *Barbarous Mexico* (2014). Has it been relatively easy to continue your career? Have you found a strong support network within Mexico?

JMG: A while ago I premiered *7:19* (2016), a feature film inspired by the 1985 devastating earthquake (now on Netflix), and in January 2020 I will release my most recent movie called *Perdida* (2019). I'm currently looking for financing for my next new horror movie. I'm also showrunner of a Latin HBO show.

To tell the truth, I've been having a hard time financing new movies; it's not easy finding money for movies like the ones I like to shoot, but there is nothing that will make me give up.

13
Alejandro González Iñárritu

A passionate advocate for Mexican cinema who in the wake of the success of Amores Perros *(2000) has brought a singular vision to a raft of ambitious international projects examining the fragility of human relationships and the ever-present nature of mortality, Alejandro González Iñárritu has worked on increasingly broad canvasses (partly set in Mexico,* Babel, *2006, also encompasses Japan and the United States) and on an epic scale. Working with a close-knit team of creative collaborators (directors of photography Emmanuel Lubezki and Rodrigo Prieto, composer Gustavo Santaolalla and editor Stephen Mirrione), Iñárritu has nonetheless retained a sense of intimacy.*

Winner of Best Director Academy Awards for Birdman or (The Unexpected Virtue of Ignorance) *(2014) (which also won Best Screenplay and Best Picture) and* The Revenant *(2015), in 2019 Iñárritu became the first Mexican director to preside over the Cannes jury. An endlessly engaged and inquisitive figure, the director has recently begun to employ the cutting-edge technology of virtual reality to depict the terrifying plight of migrants attempting to cross the border from Mexico into the US with* Carne y arena *(2019), which saw him receive a special Oscar from the American academy.*

FEATURES FILMOGRAPHY:
The Revenant (2015)
Birdman or (The Unexpected Virtue of Ignorance) (2014)
Biutiful (2010)
Babel (2006)
21 Grams (2003)
Amores Perros (2000)

JASON WOOD: We last found time to speak after the release of *21 Grams* (2003). A lot has happened since then, both in your own career and in terms of Mexican cinema. How do you see the current landscape, both

266

in terms of emerging talent, the continued success of the film schools and support from the government for Mexican cinema?

ALEJANDRO GONZÁLEZ IÑÁRRITU: We are living in a paradox. On one hand, there is an immense opportunity for young film-makers that has never been seen before. Technology and streaming services have changed the game in a sense of how fast, easily, economically and immediately your film, short or documentary can be distributed and seen around the world.

The laws in Mexico still allow the private sector to invest in films with a nice tax rebate and there are more than 150 films being produced in Mexico each year, although, sadly, only a few find a way to be distributed and seen in Mexican theatres. There are more film schools and film workshops than ever before and the interest of young people to express themselves through images and sound is ebullient.

On the other side, this same interest, easiness, speed and enormous demand for more 'content' (as some studio or streaming executives call it) have created a very difficult landscape not only to be relevant but also to be seen in such a vast new digital ocean of material being offered. The challenge or discussion should not be about if the films should be seen in theatres, on TV, on an iPad or even on an iPhone. My generation saw most of the classics on TV or VHS or DVD. Bergman, Kurosawa, Tarkovsky, the Italian Neo-realists, for example. Besides some projections that the Mexican Cinematheque or some cine clubs did, you did not have more options than seeing them that way.

For me, the challenge and the danger with what is happening now is that, because most of this material is being made and conceived directly for TV, the visual grammar and the cinematic language have been eroded and affected forever. It's inevitable for the substance to get distorted by the medium it is exposed and made for. There is a huge difference between the TV and the cinema experience.

When musical instruments became available to everyone in the seventeenth century, everybody started to play piano or guitar. Music classes boomed. That was great. Everybody thought that by consequence there would be many Mozart-type talents around the world. It was clearly not the case. It will, as it always has been, be about the music. What I am trying to say is that it is great there are such good and numerous new opportunities for young film-makers, but the quantity does not necessarily mean that the quality has improved or will improve proportionally.

JW: On a truly global scale the success and achievements of yourself, Alfonso Cuarón, Guillermo del Toro and Carlos Reygadas have been a tremendous boost for the cinema of your country. Since 2014 yourself, Alfonso and Guillermo have dominated the Academy Awards, with you winning two Best Director awards for *Birdman* (2014) and *The Revenant* (2015) and also winning a special award for *Carne y arena* (2019). How important has this success been, both on a personal and on a more collective level?

AGI: An award is always a gesture and a recognition for your work, not for yourself. It means that your work has touched a group of people or jury members at a certain festival, the members of a union, or a vast amount of people around the world. That is a gift that I have never taken for granted and have always received with humility and gratitude. You never know if your next film will be a disaster!

The good thing about an award, like an Oscar, which is seen in the media around the world, is that it makes it easier for you to finance your next movie and it solidifies the freedom and independence you need in order to create your next film.

And if besides this, it inspires, makes happy and gives confidence to younger Mexican film-makers, then that award becomes a bigger reason of happiness because it's useful and shared with many.

JW: Last year you were selected as the first Mexican to be President of the Jury at Cannes. How did you find the experience? I know that you are a voracious and passionate cinephile and like to keep up to date with current developments, both in terms of world cinema and in terms of technological and aesthetic advancements.

AGI: It was actually a very pleasant experience. It has to do with the fact that eight out of the nine jury members were directors, and also that the calibre of film-makers I was surrounded with couldn't be better.

I delineated four simple rules to make our jury experience easier: 1. To not lose time destroying films. That's easy. Let's instead try to focus better on articulating and defending what we like and passionately love. 2. Nothing else besides the merits of the film itself should be taken into consideration when voting for it. No nationality, gender, country circumstances, political, religious or ideological views should be considered. The film should speak by itself. 3. Do not make any decisions the same day you saw a film. Let the film rest and grow (or disappear) inside us for as long as possible. 4. Do not read any reviews during the whole festival. Do not let any exterior hype or opinions influence or put pressure on you. This is not a popularity contest.

Because most of us were directors, we were all departing from the same interests or point of view and that made things easier since the discussions were framed in the same universe and experience. Elle Fanning, who I directed when she was seven years old in *Babel* (2006), was the only actress (with more than fifteen years of making films!) and the youngest jury member ever in Cannes. It was so great to have her. She brought a really smart, young and fresh counterpoint of view to the table to the much older and grumpy directors . . . Ha ha. The sessions after each film were really fun and passionate.

Hearing everybody's thoughts, perception and emotional experience after each film with a glass of rosé at hand was actually very nurturing and a learning experience too.

JW: As well as your own works you have acted as a producer or executive producer on projects such as *Nine Lives* (Rodrigo García, 2005), *Toro negro* (Carlos Armella and Pedro González-Rubio, 2007) – which I thought was terrific – *Rudo y Cursi* (Carlos Cuarón, 2008), *The Land of Silence* (Carlos Armella, 2014) and *Los ojos del mar* (José Álvarez, 2017). Can you talk about your passion for producing the work of others and bringing it to the screen? You have been particularly supportive of Rodrigo García . . .

AGI: I liked Rodrigo García's script [*Nine Lives*] a lot and it was a pleasure for me to collaborate with him on that project. The same with José Álvarez, who has been a friend of mine since we were seventeen years old; he has shown an enormous sensitivity on his documentaries. But I have to confess that producing a film is not the part that I enjoy the most. When it's a film of mine, I do not have a choice and I need to produce them. But to produce other films is actually less enjoyable. Not only because I do not have time or room to do it, considering that each film of mine takes around three to four years to make, but because I respect enormously the way a director wants and needs to express himself, even with the mistakes included in his process.

What I mean is that I find myself tempted to suggest or influence something that I consider can or should be done a certain way, and at the same time I struggle to say it or do it because I am not sure that my way is necessarily the best way. I mean, it's possibly better for me but not necessarily for the director of that film. Sometimes the best things that can happen in a first film are the mistakes, the things that are raw and that reveal the true voice, soul and view of an artist. And when you produce something, you tend to 'avoid' mistakes or shape things that sometimes can be helpful, but some other times you just hurt the way things should be. And on top of that it's just an endless problem-solving dilemma without enough creative rewards.

JW: We have spoken previously of course about *Amores Perros* (2000) and *21 Grams. Babel* shares similarities with these films in that it is a film that operates on a truly global scale and features numerous interlinking narratives. Did you feel in any way that with *Babel* you had taken this approach as far as you wanted? *Biutiful* (2010) feels like a much more intimate work, though it certainly retains your distinctive approach to sound and vision. It was also a return to working closer to home and in the Spanish language.

AGI: Yes, after *Babel* I thought enough is enough and the only next step possible in this direction was to expand and create a multi-cosmic story in space with different planets! Ha ha . . . Actually, I was satisfied with the narrative exploration, but I was too tired of it. It began to feel a little bit formulaic. Once I feel I have put my arms around something and it is already familiar and easy, I need to move on and learn and challenge myself. So yes, to write and direct a linear film like *Biutiful*, even when that is the traditional way to do it, was a real challenge for me.

JW: Thematically, though, *Biutiful* shares some abiding themes. Notions of mortality, characters facing difficult moral choices and a central protagonist caught up in an intricate web of events over which he ultimately has little control.

AGI: Yes, *Biutiful* carried some of the themes that have been chasing me all my life and at that time, since I was going through a difficult period in my life. My father was struggling with cancer and living in Barcelona, one of the richest cities in Europe. I felt and sensed the pain, disparity and invisibility of the big number of immigrants from Africa and China who were locked in a tiny ghetto. I spent a lot of time with them through a friend of mine who opened the door to me to that world and it all just came together. There were just difficult stories with very little oxygen on it.

JW: How did you come to *Birdman or (The Unexpected Virtue of Ignorance)*? It was originally based on a play by Raymond Carver. Was the play the impetus for the project?

AGI: The short story of Raymond Carver, who is one of my favourite American writers, came later. I first started identifying my own annoying voice and then I started to think how I could make a film about somebody, as all of us do, struggling with his own internal voice called 'ego'.

JW: *Birdman* saw you retain your collaboration with editor Stephen Mirrione, but saw you working with cinematographer Emmanuel Lubezki,

Leonardo Di Caprio confronted by a mountain of skulls
in *The Revenant*

© 20th Century Studios

who would also shoot *The Revenant*, for the first time. What is the process by which you choose your key technical collaborators?

AGI: During my first four films I basically had the same collaborators, almost like a family. But in *Birdman*, I was deliberately attempting and exploring a new different genre and style and I thought it would be great to experience and collaborate with a whole new team too. That way, the risk and the adventure would be completely new and exciting. I knew and had worked with El Chivo [Lubezki] almost thirty years ago since we both were living in Mexico. He and Rodrigo [Prieto] are my favourite DoPs and how lucky I am to count them as my old dear friends too. Stephen Mirrione edited my first American film, *21 Grams*, and since then we have been working together.

jw: One of the most notable elements of *Birdman* was the central performance of Michael Keaton. He was perhaps not at the best point in his
career but *Birdman* reminded us all of what a great actor he is. Was he
always your first choice for the role of Riggan and what particular qualities
do you feel he brought to the part?

AGI: Michael was always on my mind as a choice. But it was challenging
because for almost two years, nobody wanted to give me money for this
film. Nobody believed in it. Every studio or financier was absolutely scared.
A comedy film in one take? With only drums? With Michael Keaton??
Iñárritu directing a comedy? It all sounded like a perfect disaster. And it
could have been a disaster, of course. I knew it, and that was exactly what
excited me. But fortunately, in the end, I was clear that Michael was not
only, as you said, a great actor. He had been out of the system for a while but
he was the absolutely right person for this project; he added a meta-reality
to the character. After reducing the script and finding a way to shoot the film
in nineteen days, I got just enough money to make the film.

jw: On a technical level, it's an incredibly audacious and ambitious work,
shot in a single take and featuring an incredible 'flight' sequence. Do you
like to challenge yourself with each project in regard to what you can
achieve with the medium? This sense of challenge and of pushing the possibilities of cinema further is also very much present in *The Revenant*.

AGI: To make a film without fear is a banality. To be carried away by fear
is a banality. To make a film is an act of love. Fear must be used as an ally.
Only when you have something to say does the possibility of failure exist.
Only when you accept and own that risk will you gain the right to direct. I
may probably be a masochist but while I am working, in order to be awake,
fully present and giving the very best of me, I need to be challenged and
uncomfortable. When I am writing or imagining a film, my imagination
is wild and vast and unstoppable. The problem is when those things you
imagine have to be taken into the universe of reality and be executed. I
then sometimes regret how far and irresponsible I was by imagining certain
things which I then recognise I may probably have the capacity to dream
but not the capacity to make them happen. But once you are there, you
have to figure it out and try your best shot. Even failing is better and more
fun than the other way around.

jw: The film does riff on some of the themes I associate with your work and
which I have already mentioned, but it does also have a slightly less solemn
tone and is comedic. Did you want to do a project that was lighter on tone?

AGI: Absolutely. It was the first time in my life I found myself laughing out loud on a set and I loved it. I did not know it could happen.

I have a very good sense of humour in real life. But on my sets, I find myself submerged and concentrated under difficult circumstances or intense dramatic scenes where humour would sometimes come with my crew and actors, but there was not much of it.

In *Birdman* I wanted to liberate myself and I really had fun watching Michael and Emma [Stone] and Edward [Norton] and Zach [Galifianakis]. I was laughing with the crew while we were shooting, and I thought that if we were laughing and enjoying it there then it was a good sign.

JW: You return to the dark with *The Revenant*, which is a punishing watch. What elements of the novel by Michael Punke appealed to you? You chose to not film the novel to the letter. What elements did you particularly want to expand and build upon?

AGI: I was invited by my dear friend Steve Golin to participate on this project in 2010. There was a script already written by Mark Smith based on the novel by Punke. More so than the script, I responded to some of the elements and opportunities it presented that could be explored. Hugh Glass's story is more a myth than a real story. There are no actual historical facts that can be checked so the legend has been and can be interpreted depending on the angle you are interested in exploring. And that's what got me excited about it. I did not read Michael Punke's novel. Instead, I read an enormous number of history books and essays from that period, and journals written by the trappers at that time. I asked for Golin's and Mark's permission for me to rewrite the script with some of the themes I wanted to explore, and they agreed. This period in the US was a remarkable and painful time when the values and relation between men and nature were set, and are very sadly still very much present until today. Savage capitalism.

'Kill every buffalo you can. Every buffalo dead is an Indian gone.' That was the motto and famous line of a US army colonel. There were around twenty-five million buffalos in the US in the sixteenth century. By the end of the nineteenth century, there were just one hundred buffalos left. This madness of selling pelts and tongues almost drove this species to extinction. Indian tribes, as we know, were also almost extinct and millions of trees and forest were devastated in the name of prosperity and capitalism. French, English and American white men were in the middle of a vast land with native people who had taken care of this same land with a different cosmogonic vision. Many of them, who had no racial, religious or ideological attachments, mixed, married, procreated and became one with them. But they paid a price. And that is what I was interested in exploring. Not only the physical survival tale but the spiritual one.

JW: Can I ask about working with Ryuichi Sakamoto on the score? It's incredible.

AGI: Ryuichi Sakamoto has always been one of my favourite musicians. He generously gave me, without a cost, a theme that I used for the ending scene in *Babel* and we became friends. Working with him on *The Revenant* was a dream come true. He was dealing with cancer treatment at that time and despite it, he was all in and passionate with the project. He did massive soulful movements with minimal notes. He is a genius. I have to say that Carsten Nicolai (Alva Noto) and Bryce Dessner's collaboration on the score was extremely important too.

JW: The film, which was incredibly well received by audiences and critics alike, is one of the most visceral and primal film experiences I can recall. Was it important that this tale of survival feel authentic? The authenticity also lends the film a mythical quality.

AGI: As I said before, the anecdote of Hugh Glass was just an opportunity to explore the context where all this supposedly happened. Westerns tend to naturally be tales of revenge. And I found myself conflicted because, for me, revenge is such a dead end, a cul-de-sac, a fruitless enterprise. So, my challenge was figuring out how to do a western that explores revenge from a different angle, more like a reflection on our human nature than an answer or a device for entertainment. I do not know if I succeeded but at least that's what I intended to do.

JW: I also wanted to ask about the treatment of race in the film. It deals explicitly with notions of xenophobia and, though it never feels didactic, this element has powerful connotations with Trump's America and a move to a right-wing political philosophy.

AGI: Xenophobia is part human nature and not exclusive to any country or race. It's a stone-age characteristic of our still primitive brain, in which our survival mode sends us a panic signal saying that anything different from us can or is actually dangerous. Just the colour of the skin will be enough for that distorted part of our brain to declare war to kill the other. That's why Americans, still in this digital age, are obsessed with carrying guns. In Mexico, my country, the discrimination towards the indigenous people who form more than 10 per cent of the population is still terrible. I have dark skin; I am a Mestizo. In my country, where most of us are mestizos, dark skin is still something that can determine and deteriorate your possibilities to grow and be treated differently from the whiter mestizos. I found this just infuriating.

JW: I also wanted to ask again about Lubezki and the cinematography. One of the things I most enjoy about your films is the way the settings and landscapes become incredibly intrinsic elements of the film. You present the wilderness as harsh and unforgiving but also show nature as being almost spiritual and transcendent in its beauty.

AGI: The director of photography on a film is your right hand, your closest ally, and partner in crime. Rodrigo Prieto and I became brothers working together for almost twenty years. Working with El Chivo on my last two films has been a real joy too. He pushed me to work not with 18 mm or 16 mm lenses but with 14 mm or 10 mm lenses where everything can be seen, felt and breathed. He has challenged me, and I love it. It has been a very fruitful collaboration because when I direct, I like to be surrounded by people who make me grow and learn. El Chivo is a great person and an artist of his own and I appreciate that.

JW: Finally, can you reveal anything about what your next plans might be? I know you have been travelling a lot but I imagine you are already hard at work on your next project.

AGI: I have been working on two projects simultaneously during the last four years and both of them are almost ready. They both follow different interests of mine with different reasons. I'll be happy to do whichever one of them comes first.

14
Gerardo Naranjo

Raised in the small Mexican town of Salamanca, Gerardo Naranjo moved to Mexico City, where he started the film club Zero for Conduct and wrote film reviews. After making his first short film, Perro negro *(2001), Naranjo was invited to study at the American Film Institute in Los Angeles. His thesis film,* The Last Attack of the Beast *(2002), won the Directors Guild of America Directing Award.*

The features Malachance *(2004) and* Drama/Mex *(2006) followed, the latter seeing Naranjo work in Mexico for an Acapulco-set tale of two inter-linking stories that unfold over a single day.* I'm Gonna Explode *(2008) brought Naranjo to wider attention. A road movie about two troubled teenagers that bears the influence of the French New Wave, the film won the FIPRESCI at Thessaloniki and three awards at Guadalajara, including the MEZCAL Award for Best Film.*

After contributing a segment to Revolución *(2010), Naranjo further enhanced his reputation with* Miss Bala *(2011), the Tijuana-set tale of a beauty queen who witnesses drug-related murders and police collusion. The film was re-made by Catherine Hardwicke in 2019. Naranjo has subsequently worked widely in television, including directing the pilot for* The Bridge *(2013) and episodes of* Narcos *(2016) and* The Walking Dead *(2016).*

FEATURES FILMOGRAPHY:
Miss Bala (2011)
I'm Gonna Explode (*Voy a explotar*) (2008)
Drama/Mex (2006)
Malachance (2004)

JASON WOOD: I wondered if you could begin by talking about how you originally became interested in cinema . . .

GERARDO NARANJO: I grew up in provincial Mexico and would go with my father and my brothers to watch the films of Peter Sellers. We laughed a lot.

JW: I understand that you obtained a Master's degree in directing from the American Film Institute (AFI) in Los Angeles. How did your studies contribute to your understanding of cinema and inform the kind of projects that you wanted to undertake as a screenwriter and director?

GN: I went briefly to CUEC (Centro Universitario de Estudios Cinematográficos), the film school of Universidad Nacional Autónoma de México (UNAM). When I was there the students decided to strike. I was not involved in the strike and so decided to leave. I applied to the AFI and much to my surprise, I was accepted. Even my friends were surprised. Everything changed.

JW: How did the opportunity to make *Drama/Mex* (2006) come about?

GN: We had a film co-operative called REVOLCADERO and we managed to make the film. It was then invited to Critics' Week in Cannes and we found partners in IMCINE and Gael García Bernal and Diego Luna, who became executive producers for Canana.

JW: And how did the story of the film evolve? It's a choral drama that plays out over a single night in Acapulco and which deals with relationships, crime and corruption, and the divide between those with money and those without. Did you want it to function both as a relationship drama and as a social commentary on Mexico?

GN: To be honest, I was just desperate to make a film. I didn't have that much clarity regarding its functioning as social commentary.

JW: I read that the film was shot very quickly (around twenty days) and on a low budget. How did this influence some of your aesthetic choices? Unless I am mistaken, you worked with a cast of both first-time and non-professional actors and using mainly handheld cameras (working with DoP Tobias Datum, who would also shoot *I'm Gonna Explode*, 2008).

GN: We were all friends. There was no payment involved. We found a way to get a hotel that belonged to a friend and we would work and then we would party. We did this for the entire twenty days. It has never been this simple and carefree again to make a film.

JW: The film was well received and invited to festivals such as Thessaloniki, Rotterdam and Cannes. It also received an Ariel award. How did the reception to the film help your career and was there a different reaction to the film in Mexico as opposed to other territories?

GN: Yes, the film did well but I remember a big fight against all aspects of the industry. It was hard to find audiences, as they seemed to be expecting a rather facile comedy. To some extent this is still what they expect.

JW: *I'm Gonna Explode* felt so fresh and exciting. It had traces of Godard but also took a highly original approach to the young-lovers-on-the-run narrative beloved of both road movies and teenage thrillers. What were some of your original aims and intentions with the film?

GN: I was young and felt I could get away without following the quality dogmas of the arthouse film-making industry. I was simply keen not to repeat the arthouse formula that we all know so well.

JW: The film looks at society through the prism of those with money and those without. Román has a father who is a prominent politician and so comfortably off, whilst Maru is from a much harsher background. Were you again commenting on Mexican society, but also using the structure of a love story/road movie?

GN: The aim was to do many things at once. Another aim was for the film to reach as wide an audience as possible.

Love's young dream: *I'm Gonna Explode*

JW: The casting is essential as in part it relies on the chemistry between the two leads. How did you find Maria Deschamps and Juan Pablo de Santiago? Did you sense immediately that they would smoulder together?

GN: Casting the film was one of the best aspects of making it. A good friend and a great director, Emiliano Rocha Minter, who would direct *Tenemos la carne* (*We Are the Flesh*, 2016), was a friend of the actors and helped bring them to the attention of the casting director. They were all so young!

JW: The film is quite frank in terms of sex and sexuality in regard to teenagers. Did this present any complications for you?

GN: This was very much my decision, though I was a little unaware of how complex the terrain would be. I wanted to show more but also had to be very protective of the young cast. DoP Tobias Datum was a very important figure in terms of giving us a sense of moral guidance. We all trusted him.

JW: Can you say something about working with Daniel Giménez Cacho? He's a formidable actor and one of the finest Spanish-speaking performers.

GN: Daniel loves to act but also has fun when he is doing it. He is also quite an intense person. I will always remain grateful for what he brought to the film.

JW: If anything, the film made even more of an impact than your debut feature *Drama/Mex*, and was again invited to numerous major international festivals and racked up international sales.

GN: I really want to believe your words, and perhaps looking at it from the outside it may have seemed that way, but the film didn't feel a success to me in those terms. It felt like an ongoing battle, a battle that continues.

JW: Your next project was a contribution to the portmanteau film *Revolución* (2010), alongside contemporaries such as Amat Escalante, Fernando Eimbcke, Carlos Reygadas, Diego Luna, Gael García Bernal and Patricia Riggen. Is there a sense that, as with the likes of Guillermo del Toro, Alfonso Cuarón, etc., that there was at that time – and perhaps still is – a new wave of Mexican film-makers that supported and nurtured each other?

GN: I was fortunate that I got to know all those directors. Fernando Eimbcke was a big idol of mine and it's amazing to me, having been a fan of *Temporada de patos* (2004), that I would get to collaborate on a project that he was involved with. I love the humour of his work. Amat is someone else I very much admire. Perhaps all together we will form the next generation.

JW: *Miss Bala* (2011) felt like a higher-profile project. Canana, IMCINE and CONACULTA were involved, but in an international sense, there was also Fox International Productions. Did you approach the film in the same way as the 'smaller-scale' productions you had previously worked on?

GN: No, I wanted to do something new. I had grown bored with taking what could be considered a 'real' or 'natural' approach. I wanted to do something unexpected.

JW: It deals very explicitly with drug wars and corruption at the very highest levels.

GN: I wanted to locate the criminals and the authorities within the same moral ground. I wanted to depict them as being very much the same as the lead character, who is different to them in a moral sense, as being very much 'alone'.

JW: I know that the narrative of the film revolved around a beauty contest but it was interesting to see a female protagonist. Was this another factor for you when conceiving of the film and did you seek to look at the roles afforded women in Mexican society? Laura Guerrero is very much viewed as an object by the men in the film.

GN: My co-writer Mauricio Katz and I were clear from the beginning that we wanted the recipe of a thriller with a smart lead character. This was, of course, before the #MeToo movement.

JW: The film was to prove a breakthrough for Stephanie Sigman and it's a role that must have required total commitment.

GN: She is great person and actress, and a very good friend.

JW: You adopt an incredibly visceral shooting style, with lots of close-ups of Laura, especially as her ordeal escalates. Was the intention to put the viewer very directly in Laura's position? The film achieves the very difficult task of being a very effective action thriller whilst also acting as a biting social commentary and portrait of a society living under siege.

GN: Well, we live in the age of POV [point of view]. Editor Mátyás Erdély was a great partner. The film language was thought out in a very detailed manner by Mátyás.

JW: The film was warmly received at international festivals but I do remember some reviews citing the notion of the film as far-fetched. Was this amusing to you given that a) you didn't present it in a documentary style; b) it was based on a real-life incident; and c) an estimated 47,000 people have been killed since President Calderón began deploying the military against the cartels in 2006.

GN: After *Miss Bala*, many things evolved; we were not the first nor the last film using the theme, but the *Narcos* style did explode. What is incredible to me is how Mexico still adores the killers. The criminals are seen like super-humans by many in Mexico. I think it's a shame that series like *Narcos* don't portray how miserable the crime world is. I guess there would be less money in that . . .

JW: How have you generally found the experience of working outside of Mexico and also how do you consider the current climate for Mexican film-makers? Has the trail you have blazed helped other emerging figures to achieve success in their homeland and abroad?

GN: I am not sure. I don't think so. I am not sure this is the best time for films and for narrative.

15

Nicolás Pereda

Born in Mexico City, Nicolás Pereda holds a Master of Arts in film directing from York University (Canada). Pereda has made films and videos for several interdisciplinary plays, operas and dance pieces that have been performed in Mexico and throughout Europe. His first feature film, ¿Dónde están sus historias? (Where Are Their Stories?) (2007), won the French Critics Discovery Award at the Toulouse Latin America Film Festival.

Working across shorts, documentary and fiction, Pereda's work explores the everyday through fractured and elliptical narratives. Another facet of his work is a sense of community and collaboration, including the casting of Gabino Rodríguez and Teresa Sánchez, who have appeared in the majority of his work, earning Pereda comparison to Tsai Ming-liang. Rodríguez and Sánchez play the same mother and son captured at different moments in time, or perhaps in subtly shifting realities.

Pereda has been the subject of more than twenty retrospectives worldwide in venues such as Anthology Film Archive, Pacific Film Archive, Jeonju International Film Festival and TIFF Cinematheque. He has also presented his films in most major international film festivals, including Cannes, Berlin, Venice, Locarno and Toronto, as well as in galleries and museums like the Reina Sofía in Madrid, the National Museum of Modern Art in Paris, the Guggenheim and MOMA in New York, and in television stations such as HBO, Turner, MVS, Netflix and I.Sat. In 2010 he was awarded the Premio Orizzonti at the Venice Film Festival.

FEATURES FILMOGRAPHY:
Tales of Two Who Dreamt (documentary) (2016)
Minotaur (Minotauro) (2015)
The Absent (Los ausentes) (2014)
Killing Strangers (Matar extraños) (2013) – co-directed with Jacob Secher
    Schulsinger
Greatest Hits (Los mejores temas) (2012)
Summer of Goliath (Verano de Goliat) (2010)

Todo, en fin, el silencio lo ocupaba (All Things Were Now Overtaken by Silence) (2010) (documentary)
Perpetuum Mobile (2009)
Together (Juntos) (2009)
¿Dónde están sus historias? (Where Are Their Stories?) (2007)

JASON WOOD: I wanted to start by asking about your background. You were born in Mexico but have lived in Toronto. I am interested in this because when I spoke to Amat Escalante, who was raised and has lived in the US, he disclosed that this had a huge effect on how he saw the world and how he saw his own country. Is this something that you can relate to?

NICOLÁS PEREDA: I have thought about this quite a bit, of course not always in relation to my films, but to my life in general. I left Mexico when I was nineteen and have lived in Toronto, Vancouver and New York since then. I am sure my films would be different if I had not left, but it's difficult to say in what way. Perhaps one thing I can say is that when I started making films, Mexican cinema was not a reference, and neither was the Mexican film community. Unfortunately, I lack an education in Mexican Cinema, but perhaps to my advantage was that when I started, I was not immersed in the formal trends of contemporary Mexican cinema, but instead I was making films drawing influences from all over the place.

JW: And what was your entry to film-making? Did you receive formal training? Many of the directors I have spoken with for this project went to the CCC or other film schools. Carlos Reygadas is something of an exception and Amat Escalante also received very little formal training.

NP: I studied film-making in Toronto. Perhaps the best thing about my formal training was a couple of my fellow students. I became particularly close to Luo Li, a Chinese film-maker who had a great influence on how I was shaping my interest in cinema.

JW: One of the things I find most interesting about your work – apart from the fact that it is so distinctive – is that you take an approach much more evocative of an artist film-maker, or an artisan figure. In the UK I am thinking of people like Andrew Kötting, Ben Rivers and before those Derek Jarman, in that you work across various disciplines. Many directors start with making shorts and then move to features. You move fluidly between features, shorter projects, mid-length pieces such as *Minotaur* (2015) and documentary, with *Summer of Goliath* (2010) being a hybrid of fiction and documentary. Is it a question for you of whatever format best suits what it is that you wish to achieve?

NP: I am excited about making work that surprises me, and while many of my films have elements that repeat themselves, I try to always come up with radically new formal elements – at least new for me. This drive is what makes my work a bit freer, perhaps. Since I hardly make films with large budgets, and the grant organisations that fund my work are meant for artists, most of the time I don't have to make work that fits a particular mould. In fact, almost all my short and medium-length films were meant as features, but in the editing I figured that they worked better as shorter pieces.

JW: I also notice that there are projects that overlap. *Todo, en fin, el silencio lo ocupaba* (*All Things Were Now Overtaken by Silence*) (2010) evolved from your shooting an educational programme for television. *Interview with the Earth* (2008) exists both within and outside the overlapping *Summer of Goliath*. Are you inspired by this notion of connectivity? It strikes me as one of the central elements of your work.

NP: Connectivity between the works comes naturally. I make a lot of work, so when I am shooting one thing, the previous work, and sometimes the work that is coming up, are all in my mind. *Interview with the Earth* was a kind of rehearsal for *Summer of Goliath*. I was trying out some new things, and one weekend I decided to go with a friend to shoot the short. We went with only a handful of ideas and shot it in a two- or three-day period. Ironically, I think it's better than the feature, which involved funding and more people and so on. But my work is sometimes also connected to the work of my collaborators. For example, some of the footage that I didn't use in *Greatest Hits* (2012), Gabino (now Lázaro; he just changed his name) Rodríguez used for a play he directed about his family. Some of the ideas of the film overlapped the ideas in his play. There was a scene that didn't work in the film, where he and his dad go find the tree where they had scattered his mother's ashes. Unable to find it, they pick a random tree and pretend it's the one they are looking for. He used that footage and projected it as part of the play.

JW: Your first feature, *¿Dónde están sus historias?* (*Where Are Their Stories?*) (2007), established your working relationship with the actors Gabino Rodríguez and Teresa Sánchez, who have appeared in a number of your works. What is it about working with Gabino and Teresa that interests you and can you say more about how you work with them? They play different characters from project to project but there is something very knowing about the way that you use them.

NP: I like to do formal experiments in my films. I'm interested in finding new forms of representation. In order to be able to keep track of these experiments, it helps me to keep some things relatively constant. Gabino and Teresa give me a sense of home, and I can do anything once they are there. They mostly play mother and son, and while their relationship does vary from film to film, there is something that remains similar – perhaps it has to do with their idiosyncrasies. In any case, the cast of my films is a constant in an otherwise ever-changing cinema exploration.

JW: Some have suggested that they are the same mother and son captured at different moments in time, or perhaps in subtly shifting realities. Is there any credence to this reading? It would fit perhaps with the intriguing balance between flux and stability that I see in your films.

NP: I think I'm trying to construct various possible mother and son relationships altered by circumstance. So, maybe they are the same mother and son in all the films, but they behave differently with one another depending on their circumstances. They seem to have a very distant relationship in *Summer of Goliath*, while in *Greatest Hits* they behave like best friends. However, they don't seem to change that much. It's just that in *Goliath* Gabino plays a poor soldier from a rural town who hates spending time

Apocalypse now: The documentary/fiction hybrid *Summer of Goliath*

at home, whereas in *Greatest Hits* he lives in the city and seems happy to never move out.

JW: I am always reluctant to ask directors, especially those whose work is so aesthetically distinctive, to talk about their cinematic influences, but I wondered if this might be something that you are prepared to do. In your portrait of families and in your favouring of long takes over rapid cuts, Tsai Ming-liang has been mentioned in comparison. I know that you have said in the past that you are more interested in what is happening in your own life than in what you might find in films or other art forms ...

NP: I do recognise several key influences and Tsai Ming-liang is one of them. Others are: Robert Bresson, Béla Tarr, Hong Sang-soo, Apichatpong Weerasethakul, R.W. Fassbinder, Derek Jarman, Chantal Akerman, among others.

JW: I spoke to Carlos Reygadas just after the release of *Our Time* (2018) and he was perplexed by the constant attempts to categorise the film as in being in some way influenced by reality and representative of an attempt to capture reality. How interested are you in the notion of reality? I ask because this is something that people often also talk about in connection with your work.

NP: In this respect I tend to disagree with several film-makers that I admire. I see cinema as a total construction. I don't think the screen is a window to reality. I don't think cinema is capable of capturing reality. I don't think reality is something you can capture. However, I'm interested in the misconception. In films like *The Palace* (2013), or *Interview with the Earth*, the actors are representing themselves, but at the same time the whole thing is a construction. I play with the audience's expectation of the real. There is a strange perverse excitement in knowing that the thing/person you are watching exists in the world exactly as you see it on the screen. It's a total delusion.

Now, while you cannot capture reality as a whole, you can capture fragments of reality that can be enlightening. I believe these fragments have little to do with plot, narrative or character. Perhaps they are fragments of the formal, or even the sensorial elements of a film.

JW: I read an interesting conversation between you and Gerardo Naranjo where you talk about an audience member's reaction to *Together* (2009), complaining that it was a film in which nothing happens. As you pointed out, this is a film in which during a short period of time, less than a week, the protagonist loses his dog, his girlfriend leaves him, he finds himself in a fight with his cousin and things go wrong in his apartment. This is quite a lot of action. You responded to the audience member that your film just creates the sensation that nothing happens. Can you expand more about this? Your work does have a contemplative style and feel, which many tend to categorise as 'slow cinema'.

NP: I am simply interested in human experience. I think film is a good medium to observe, like one does in the everyday, to explore the passage of time. Time is key to the representation of human experience. We often tell our experiences in terms of information, because nobody wants to hear long-winded descriptions of the leaves on the trees of your last vacation. So, when we talk about what's going on in our lives, we talk in terms of bits of information that create a narrative. However, cinema has the possibility to engage with something closer to most of our experiences. While, of course, what is happening in our lives is important, how it happens, and how we experience it, is something that is often left behind when we focus on bits of information – narrative and plot and character. So, 'slow cinema', as I understand it, refers to the slow delivery of information, if there is information to be delivered at all.

Or perhaps I can propose another answer: we are used to a cinematic language with many cuts or camera movements. When we are confronted with a framing that doesn't change, we feel the passing of time. And once you become aware of time, you tend to regard it as slow.

JW: Is there a traditional route by which you raise finance and then distribute and exhibit your work? It could be described as existing within an arthouse world as opposed to a mainstream or commercial cinema world. Does this mean that you have to be quite inventive in terms of how you fund and then disseminate it? *Perpetuum Mobile* (2009), for example, received post-production funding from France . . .

NP: *Together* cost $500. We were very young and nobody got paid. In later films I've raised money from the FONCA (Mexican arts council) and the Canada Council for the Arts, and I've gotten money from the Hubert Bals Fund in Holland and from île-de-France. In general, I don't need that much money to make films, which is very liberating, because I can make films whenever I want.

JW: Finally, many of the other directors I have spoken with have been very complimentary about your work. I have the feeling that amongst Mexican film-makers there is a sense of shared empathy and struggle, be it the high-profile figures such as Alfonso Cuarón, Alejandro González

Iñárritu and Guillermo del Toro, but also with the less commercially well-known figures such as Escalante and Reygadas. Is this something you have experienced?

NP: Yes. I feel there is a sense of empathy and camaraderie. However, I don't share a sense of struggle. I share a sense of privilege. Most Mexican film-makers come from the middle and upper classes. All the film-makers that you have mentioned in your questions have lifestyles that most Mexicans don't even dream of. There is a ton of funding for film-making in the country. In fact, I've argued elsewhere that there is perhaps too much funding. It's not a popular position, but I believe our modes of production have been imported from first-world countries, and are not sustainable in our economy.

16

Carlos Reygadas

Carlos Reygadas studied law in Mexico City and later specialised in the law of armed conflict and the use of force in London. After quitting the Mexican Foreign Service, he made four short films in Belgium before filming Japón *(2002), which was presented at the Rotterdam and the Cannes film festivals. At Cannes it received a special mention for the Camera d'Or.* Battle in Heaven *(2005) premiered in competition in Cannes. Reygadas was awarded the Cannes Jury Prize for* Silent Light *in 2007 and the Best Director award for* Post Tenebras Lux *in 2012.* Our Time *(2018), the most recent film from Reygadas, premiered at Venice.*

Reygadas is one of the most distinctive figures in contemporary world cinema. Exploring the relationship between narrative and documentary film-making traditions, the work of Reygadas is bold, personal and compelling. His work signalled a new direction in Mexican cinema, and drew admiration from colleagues and contemporaries. An inspirational figure for a new generation of film-makers from Mexico, Reygadas has a long-time producing association with Amat Escalante.

FEATURES FILMOGRAPHY:
Our Time (Nuestro tiempo) (2018)
Post Tenebras Lux (2012)
Silent Light (Luz silenciosa) (2007)
Battle in Heaven (Batalla en el cielo) (2005)
Japón (2002)

JASON WOOD: You prefer to work with non-trained or non-professional actors. Did this come from a love of Bresson?

CARLOS REYGADAS: It really came from the work itself. It was not a dogmatic decision. I actually did try to cast a Mexican actor for the part of Ascen, played by Magdalena Flores in *Japón* (2002). I realised that a trained actor could probably very well play a rural peasant woman but then the next day

I would travel through the Mexican countryside and see an actual peasant woman and think why not just hire her? Why have someone give an interpretation? I realised that it is not about performing. It's about presence. I also realised that I enjoyed being with an actual peasant woman more than I enjoyed being with an actor playing a peasant woman, so why not put this on screen and make it part of the experience itself? I think the medium of cinema is not necessarily for acting. Acting is not necessary to build characters in cinema. Presence is far more important. I try to not fail in the casting, which I have done sometimes. I think theatre is more for acting. Whoever I cast has to give off an energy and the character will be built or developed though this and the rest of the cinematic language: the text, the light, the distance of the camera. I do differ from Bresson in that he wanted the people appearing in his films to also shed their personality or any show or display of emotion. I like to keep whatever the people are; if they want to smile or laugh I let them.

JW: You have continued to work in this way. Is this a gesture also towards replicating a kind of reality?

CR: Well, I have some doubts about that. For me it is about presence rather than reality. It isn't about signification. I think that most of what we think of as cinema is actually literature. Cinema for me is more equivalent to music, painting and photography. What matters is the presence. With literature it is about representation. I am opposed to structuralism, and the ideas that developed in the 1950s about photography being representation rather than reality. My idea is that the way you use photography is how it represents. Photography is truthful. The camera opens up to what is in front of it and repeats it. And I have the same philosophy when it comes to cinema. I am not into representation. I am into presentation. With *Our Time* (2018) everyone asks me how real the film is. Is it reality or is it fiction? Well, it's just about presence. For me the difference between fiction and documentary is less important.

JW: *Our Time* doesn't abandon the notion of fiction. What you depict is fictional, even though the people, including yourself, in the film are recognisable. From *Japón* onwards, all of your films have had a narrative, even if an existential narrative.

CR: That's right. I don't abandon fiction at all. I want all of my films to be connected to life. Life exists chronologically. We have a sense of time. This conversation we are having now exists in time. I therefore do not renounce the building of fiction. Cinema incorporates time. My mother, who is a Jungian therapist, introduced me to Jung at a young age and I liked that Jung didn't renounce the ego consciousness of the Western mind but also understands the passivity of the Taoist experience of life. I think that through recording sound and image cinema captures existence. I don't want to stop at this point but to build something else with that. I want to show part of my subjectivity and to share it. I don't see my cinema necessarily as experimental cinema, but I don't see it as mainstream entertainment either. Landscapes, mountains, packs of dogs – I realise that I am talking about nature – are right in front of us. They are molecular realities; these things also signify something in our subjectivity. Art can be concrete and objective but it can also be a vase for us to fill with our own subjectivity and personalities.

JW: You used to work a lot with the music of composers such as Arvo Pärt and John Taverner but in your most recent work you have moved away from that. Why?

CR: I felt that it was becoming too much of an effect. At a certain point I found it too directive and less and less part of the cinematic language. *Our Time* uses music again, but it isn't to direct or orchestrate but to signify presence. You also discover these things in the making of the film. I did intend to have music at the end of *Silent Light* (2007) and actually had conversations with Sigur Rós, but then when editing I realised that there was nothing better than the sound of nature itself. Music would have been an obstacle.

JW: Do you re-watch your own films?

CR: Never. Absolutely not. You work so hard on every single frame. It's in the past. Forget it and move on. Film is not a fixed form of language. It is always evolving and moving on in the history of time but also in the history of the artist. The idea of how to make a film, the idea of a perfect film, the idea of a film school teaching exactly how to make a film and the notion of critics who want directors to always work in a pre-defined and pre-established pattern is absurd. Art evolves endlessly. But I do re-watch films made by other people.

JW: *Battle in Heaven* (2005) is a much more urban film than your other works. How did this affect how you approached shooting it? The final scene, involving huge crowds, must have been a challenge logistically.

CR: I am from Mexico City but spent most of my weekends and all of my holidays in the country. For more than a decade I have lived in the country.

Field of dreams: Carlos Reygadas and Natalia López in *Our Time*

But for me the city and the countryside are more or less the same thing. I don't ascribe to the view that life in the country goes more slowly or anything like that. Actually, where I live has more neurotics per capita than anywhere else. Cities have nature. It gets dark. It rains. There is wind. That is nature and it still manifests itself. There is rain at the end of *Battle in Heaven*. I didn't treat the Zócalo, where the film ends, any differently to how I treated the valley in *Japón*.

JW: There is a genre element to the film; it was considered to have been your most political film and the one that took the pulse of your nation. I get the impression that you won't ascribe to this view.

CR: I am certainly not blind to it. Every decision I take is taken to a set of values or ideas that constitute my thoughts, but considerations such as how does this reflect my society always must be a by-product. The films of the *Nouvelle Vague* show you what life in France was like but I am sure that this was not the sole purpose of those films. If you are loyal to a vision then other elements, such as politics etc., naturally reveal themselves, but it has to be a by-product, otherwise you run the risk of making propaganda. I was always a little disappointed with the representation of working-class people in Mexican TV and cinema and I was keen that if I were to represent them then their presence had to feel real and authentic. I was accused of making a freak show. They are not freaks. These are the people that you see there. It is also another reason perhaps why I don't want to use actors. I never liked the cinema of Mexico's Golden Age because you would go to the village and the Mestizo would be played by a beautiful, white famous woman. I always reacted against this.

JW: Is there a spiritual sense to your work? And I say spiritual as opposed to religious.

CR: I have to be loyal to what I see. I don't think that Mexico is a particularly religious society, but I do think that it is a very superstitious and ritualistic society. With *Battle in Heaven* I did want to incorporate this, but to also incorporate the crime and the killing that goes on there. I prefer the term consciousness to the notion you mention of spirituality. When you realise that there are beings, beliefs and nature in the world this is consciousness and not necessarily spirituality.

JW: There is candour to the way you present sex. You show it as sometimes ugly and uncomfortable. I find this refreshing. It's almost opposite to pornography.

CR: I like to see the ordinary. Sex can be ordinary. So don't manipulate it. Just capture it. It isn't about being candid or honest. It's just how I think it is. I don't understand why there is anything controversial about it but people always seem to want to talk about it. Almost everybody has sex, or sexual wishes. I think it's about refusing to codify. When you code things in a way that is acceptable in mainstream cinema it is less of a problem. Quentin Tarantino can make a film in which lots of people die but when Amat Escalante shows a scene in *Heli* (2013) in which a character has his testicles burned, everybody freaks out. 'Oh, it's so hyper-violent.' The media wants to maintain these codes in the name of entertainment, and once you refuse to operate within these codes you are vilified. In *Our Time* I act in the film. I do this for many reasons. The American press labelled me narcissistic and self-indulgent. I really don't understand it. I think they think that I want to show that I can ride a horse and wear a hat. The character I play is a poet and so the inference in the reviews was that I saw myself as a poet of the cinema. When they see a western with Clint Eastwood they don't assume that he is riding a horse and shooting people in real life. *Our Time* is set on a ranch and so everybody assumes this is my house. It's what happens once you leave the code. They don't see that there is irony, there is distance.

JW: You have used your position to help other directors, such as Amat Escalante.

CR: It is a kind of duty when you think that someone has a special vision, and this is the case with Amat. I worried his films would not be financed and, having seen his shorts and read what he wanted, I felt that his features should be made.

JW: For you, sound is as important as image.

CR: Before, I'm not sure I knew why. But now I think I do. Presence always has sound. Everything you see is either surrounded by sound, if it's an object, or produces sound, if it's a living being or a landscape. Film-making requires observation and listening so that all living matter can be captured. I think cinema is truly born when sound is present. Sound is an essential part of cinema.

JW: You have also pushed the boundaries as to what cinema can look like – filming on Super 16 mm and using vintage cameras to produce strange visual effects. The example that most comes to mind is what became known as the 'milk bottle' sequences in *Post Tenebras Lux* (2012).

CR: I think we've mastered how to capture images. We seem to now be content to re-produce them. A lot of these images are very seductive and, in entertainment cinema, also spectacular but they are renders. It's like how architects work. I have the feeling that these images take all of your energy and push some of the deeper reactions and receptions away. It's as if you were kidnapped whilst watching. I like the idea of peripheral vision; in terms of architecture, it was something embraced by the Finnish architect Juhani Pallasmaa. An architect friend who turned me on to the work of Pallasmaa commented that *Post Tenebras Lux* reminded him of Pallasmaa. Pallasmaa used to write in his books about how much Scandinavians enjoyed walking in the forest and how because there was so much to take in – sounds, images and other sensations – that you were not kidnapped by one particular thing. I realised that images had to be re-interpreted. It's similar to what happened to painting in the middle of the nineteenth century. Capturing faces, skin tone, etc., had been mastered so painters had to change the way they interpreted. The Impressionists were derided at first. People initially commented that it looked like the paintings had been done by the blind. J.M.W Turner was hated. These painters began to see something beyond just reproducing images. I don't want you to think that I use vintage cameras as some sort of affectation. I also wouldn't want to use black and white. It would be regressive and we have to go forward. Vision goes forward. I like to re-interpret, to see differently.

JW: You also like to shoot with natural light.

CR: It's also sometimes about making a virtue out of necessity. I like to shoot over a long time, with a small crew and with the least equipment possible. I realised very early on as a film-maker that there is no need to enhance light, unless you are shooting in extreme circumstances. If you want your film to be like an advertisement, which many films frankly are, then you need them, but if not you really don't; you can do something much more interesting if you just observe and wait for the right time. If you don't have a huge crew and don't need to work super-fast to reduce costs, a lot can come out of just waiting. I usually only shoot two shots per day: one in the morning and one in the afternoon.

JW: Location is also key. Location and community. *Silent Light* was shot within a Mennonite community. What challenges did this bring? As with working with non-actors, I imagine establishing a sense of trust was key. And, of course, in *Silent Light* they were also speaking in the Plautdietsch dialect.

CR: On and off, I spent five years with them. I went to watch them in the fields and at weddings and took meals with them. I tried to get to know them. Some, of course, kept their distance. But I didn't become an expert. It was not necessary. What was necessary was getting to know the actual people that are working with you on the film. I needed to get to know their feelings and the way they would behave. As I mentioned in regard to casting, you have to adapt the character to who these people really are so you have to get to know each other really well. One of my favourite moments from my own films occurs in *Silent Light* when the couple are in the car talking about their early relationship. All of the energy came from the performance of Miriam Toews. Her lines were taped to the interior of the windscreen. Toews is actually Canadian and didn't speak Plautdietsch very well. I don't think she even understood what she was saying. And neither did I. She may very well have been saying, 'This director is an idiot.' I actually didn't subtitle the dialogue to correspond always with exactly what was said and some Mennonites attacked me for that, but I think that it is absolutely fair. It isn't documentary. It isn't fiction. It's THIS thing. I think similarly about sound and vision. It's really just one thing and our mind conceives of these elements also as just one single thing. A lot of this also comes from writing. For me writing is also visual.

JW: *Post Tenebras Lux* is an allusive work but it also has at its heart a consideration of a number of universal themes: the fragility of childhood, sexual ennui, the complex union of marriage and the beauty of nature. How did you seek to offer such a personal take on themes and issues that have been discussed countless times in cinema and in culture in general?

CR: When I decide what it is that I am to immerse myself into, rather than talk about or communicate, I do not consider at all if these have been discussed or not. I do not think that the purpose of cinema is necessarily to discuss or even to just tell stories. We'd just repeat what has already been told. What I try to do when I make cinema – and this is the same with cinema that I enjoy to watch – is to communicate or show a point of view: to show a vision or individual consciousness, to show what existence is or means to an individual human being. We all are original by definition; our faces, our tones of voice, our fingerprints are all unique. I never need to ask myself why, but rather I just let intuition guide me.

This is the way that internal vision can come out. We are not engineers designing a plane. Some of the themes that you mention go back to some of the earliest Greek writers – the idea of narrative, the idea of character, and the idea of events serving a purpose. But this tradition has been overcome by a lot of literature but also by a lot of cinema. And cinema is different to literature. But film schools, financiers, producers still talk about the motives, character construction, development of events, etc. People talk of cinema as if it were literature rather than an art of presence.

JW: When making the film did it feel like you were breaking new ground? It certainly seems a very natural progression from Post *Tenebras Lux* to *Our Time*, so I wondered if making the film was liberating for you in some way, both as an artist and as a human being.

CR: I honestly never thought about breaking new ground or achieving something specific. But I have always felt very close to the idea that we are all unique and that we have access to who we are with the least possible codes and the least possible codification, so we can build our own houses and our own pyramids. Each one of us will choose our own path and feel and hear in his or her own ways. I do understand that there is something that I am building. The language of cinema isn't permanent. This is the same with art, music and theatre. In literature, if you think of Vladimir Nabokov or T. S. Eliot, then this is very clear. In music if you think of John Taverner or Pierre Boulez, then you also easily understand that these people are developing for ever. They are part of a big movement. They move the language around all the time by using it. If James Joyce were to have lived for three hundred years, he would have been moving on and changing his language.

Unfortunately, when it comes to discussing film, it seems to me that there is a belief that it should be some rigid, fixed language, as if it were an instruction manual. People think that Orson Welles or Alfred Hitchcock achieved the task of making the perfect film. I am really against this approach and this way of thinking. It's a mechanical way of viewing art. Film should not be like a perfect Swiss clock, never losing a millisecond throughout centuries. People perhaps see cinema this way, as something that needs to be perfect, because as an art form it is still so young. Some people, like Peter Greenaway, have claimed that cinema is dead. I think the exact opposite. I think that it is just being born.

JW: Can you also say something about *Post Tenebras Lux* in terms of its technical specifics? You always use equipment in an interesting way to achieve a certain aesthetic.

CR: I only used available light and worked with a crew of less than ten people. In this film I used MicroPrime lenses and state-of-the-art microphones as opposed to vintage ones. I did want to go beyond capturing images just as technology allows you to do it. I didn't want images like those we now see on phones or increasingly in mainstream cinema: hyper-defined and hyper-clear. When images are imperfect, if you want to put it that way, then they can penetrate on a deeper level of consciousness. In *Post Tenebras Lux* we used images to break this idea of hyper-definition and perfection.

JW: I know that you are repeating yourself but could you expand upon Pallasmaa in terms of the similarities in your approaches. He seemed interested in both the imagination and the power of nature.

CR: I also like to build houses and a friend of mine who recommended Pallasmaa did so because he knows how much I dislike computer renders. Pallasmaa in his writings also wrote about the problem with perfect images and how they didn't leave any room for the experiences of those viewing the images. Pallasmaa wrote about how people in Finland would go on walks to the forest, and how in the forest because of the branches, and the leaves etc., there is nothing that acts as an obvious focal point, nothing on which you have to set your eyes. Pallasmaa wrote about how relaxing these walks are and how they have such an effect on the person enjoying them. He saw it as a form of peripheral vision, and I relate very much to it in architecture and in film.

JW: Nature is very central to the film and to your films in general. European audiences shuddered at the proximity of the children to cattle and dogs. They had a sense of dread or horror at these moments.

CR: Nature is very important for me. I live in the countryside and I enjoy it. It is part of my natural atmosphere. Perhaps the most interesting way to answer this question is to talk about the fact that I want to make what I would term bi-lateral as opposed to uni-directional cinema. Rather than having someone that comes and delivers a film in which you just passively receive the plot, the characters and the situations, with their moments of fear and elation, as in a Hitchcock film, for example, I would rather make a film where the audience has to engage. Just as you have to do when you are living life. You must relate to what you see rather than just having something simply present itself in front of you. As a film-maker I try to emulate this. I don't want to be some sort of master of ceremonies whose role is to entertain the public. Art shouldn't be purely entertainment. It should also be about paying attention to what is in front of you. But yes, some European audiences did feel a dread because they are not used to dogs or [other] animals. Others felt a sense of peace and beauty.

JW: Was it interesting to you how different people experienced the film?

CR: Of course. I'd describe it as filling up a vase. You fill an empty vessel and then give it to someone to experience. It is there where we see that we are all one species but that we are also individual beings that feel their own way. What we feel may be influenced by the society in which we live, but perhaps not determined fully by it. Each interpretation of my film is just one more interpretation. You have to believe me when I say that just because I made the films it isn't necessarily that I have all the answers or have sovereignty in terms of how they may be interpreted. Because they are made with intuition, I often really don't know how they will be experienced or interpreted. As with so many things in life, and not just art, you just really don't know. If you think of the end of *Silent Light* – when Esther re-awakens – people ask me 'is she really waking up or is it imagination?' They want to know the answer to the riddle. For me, there is no riddle. What you see is what there is. You have to relate with your own ideas. My own opinion is just one more opinion only.

JW: Like all of your previous work, the film was screened to some acclaim at Cannes and earned you a Best Director prize. Does a prize such as this have greater meaning? Your cinema resists the mainstream and easy categorisation.

CR: You can talk about this on two levels. On one level, it means nothing. Festivals need to create prizes in the hope that people will pay more attention. It's like sport. Prizes really mean nothing to me at all. On another level, on a practical level, they do carry weight. It's a financing and marketing tool. The Americans are obsessed with the term 'Award-Winning Director' but winning awards does not mean you are any good or have any talent or not. We all know that some of the best directors never win awards and so many mediocre ones do. It's absurd. But, on a practical level, it does unfortunately help. It earns financing. And it earns respect. You are never as good as your prizes, and you are never as bad as your critics think you are. They certainly can help people make films that perhaps have limited commercial appeal or which are not purely for the purposes of entertainment. I have had this opinion for years but I must say that in the last two or three years my vision is becoming darker. These festivals and these prizes feel less and less important. They have been largely overridden by the dominance of entertainment. Films that are not made primarily for entertainment are increasingly marginalised. It feels like dark times. Freedom of thought, freedom of expression and freedom of conduct are out of fashion.

JW: *Our Time* is another work that credits the audience with having the intelligence to make their own decisions. You don't give answers. You allow for interpretation.

CR: Absolutely. The thing I hate most in contemporary cinema is the notion of morality and of being told what to think and feel. I don't like this as a viewer so I don't do it as a film-maker. I don't think that I am asking the audience questions necessarily, or if I am, I don't know what the questions are; I am presenting elements of life.

JW: We have spoken a lot in this conversation about presenting and your desire to present in terms of sound and image. How is this desire impacted by your decision to appear in *Our Time*, along with your wife and family? It has led to some people misreading the film as biography.

CR: I insist that what I want to do with cinema is use the camera and the sound recording device to capture presence rather than just being tools to transfer information for narrative purpose. This is a method. It's a way of understanding the medium of cinema and of using its main devices. This means that it is irrelevant if I or my family are in front of the camera. A stone, a chain, a tree, a cloud, a human, myself, my children, a lake are all the same for these inventions that are at the centre of film-making: the sound device and especially the camera. I am not presenting what actually happens in life, but building a construction with elements in life. The elements in *Our Time* are myself, as a body and as a pack of energy. There is also the energy of my children and my wife. But it is not our personal lives or our stories. This is the amazing quality of cinema, that you capture molecular life – let's call it that so as not to repeat the term presence – in its time, and with it you now have real life, which becomes the filmic material with which you will compose and construct something. Something that is not the real life of the things or the people giving their energy to the film. It is not autobiographical but quite the opposite. Think of someone like Karl Ove Knausgård and his writing. He is drawing from real events, but then writing them in what is – whether he likes them to be described this way or not – fiction. Even when he is being 'real', he could still be fictionalising as it is passes through memory. What I am doing is the opposite – I am drawing from imagination and not from the way I remember the past. It is an invention of the mind. It's a construction of imagination. I then use the real to make it possible. Instead of out of fiction, it is out of reality. Fictionalised reality.

JW: The film asks some sensitive questions: how do we distinguish love from possession? Fidelity from sexual exclusivity? How do a couple survive an irreparable fracture? What is it about some of these issues that most interests you? They are at the basis of most relationships and sexual relations and so seem to me to be very universal in a way that is totally at odds with the accusations of narcissism that some critics saw in the film.

CR: I'm not that keen to get into this because, even though as a film-maker I talk about these things and think about these things, I am not an expert in these issues the way a psychologist or a sociologist would be. What I can do as a film-maker is build stories and emotional situations from them. This is certainly true of *Our Time*. There is no system that is better than the other. The idea is that each person finds the situation that is best for his or herself and his or her partner. The important thing is that you find your system authentically; that it is not a previous system organised by somebody else.

I genuinely do not understand the accusations of narcissism from critics. I genuinely think that some of them don't understand how cinema works so they project their own intentions as if they were themselves film-makers. They seem to think that I want to show off that I am good at riding a horse or that I want to take advantage of the fact that I am a film-maker to be an actor. This suggestion is totally absurd. I don't understand how they can interpret exposing issues in such a light as narcissistic. I am simply using my energy and my body to build a character. This is the same for the rest of the people in the film. It is the same as the way a farmer would work with his family. I am an artisan and not a professional or industrial film-maker. Secondly, they think I want to pretend I am an internationally renowned poet. They have completely missed the irony. When my character delivers a masterclass on poetry in Madrid, there is an audience of only twenty people and some of them are sleeping. The whole lecture is also partly about superficiality and artificiality. I then show my character doing things that display the kind of weakness that exists within all of us. They then talk about my character as if he were a lowlife. Perhaps these critics live like St Francis of Assisi. I also don't understand why they have considered the film a form of family therapy, as if they actually believe that everything they have seen is real. It's absurd. Immediately after a take, we would be talking about food and what we are going to eat. The perfect example is the Kuleshov effect. It's a construction. The people in the film must not feel the emotions of the character. This would be theatre. Cinema is the opposite.

JW: You employ much more dialogue than you have in your previous work but still retain a sense of time passing and a presentation of nature. Was it a challenge to combine these elements?

CR: This film is about a couple going through conflict, and dialogue is a basic element of the story. It's about how we take a subjective view of events. We think that we remain loyal to the events but we put our own perspective on these events. And then we externalise these events and we talk. My character is a writer so he probably has an even greater need than the woman to expose his thoughts in words. Language is the expression of thought, to a limited extent, and this is what the characters are trying to do – to explain how they think and relate. As humans both of them have different approaches to reality. They want to solve things in his or her own way, but both also know that the other wants to solve things in his or her own way. They are trying to achieve a balance. Love is a sacrifice of oneself. There needs to be dialogue but that doesn't mean that the film is about narrating with dialogue. The dialogue here is like the wind, or a kiss or horse riding in the fields. It's an important element, but it's just one more element. It is also about the time, the place, the beings and time unfolding. The dialogue is, if you like, the face to their bodies.

17

Alonso Ruizpalacios

Alonso Ruizpalacios trained as an actor at the Royal Academy of Dramatic Arts (RADA) in London. Previously, Ruizpalacios studied directing in Mexico City with the renowned Polish director Ludwik Margules. Initially working in television, he directed several fiction and non-fiction shows, including Ideas Planet *for Discovery Channel,* Expedition 1808 *for National Geographic Channel and the award-winning drama series* XY *for Channel 11 Mexico. Ruizpalacios has also directed many stage plays in some of Mexico's most prestigious theatre venues, including Chekhov's* The Kiss, Rock 'n' Roll *by Tom Stoppard,* The Kitchen *by Arnold Wesker and Shakespeare's* The Comedy of Errors.

In 2008 Ruizpalacios wrote and directed Café paraíso, *which earned him the Mexican Film Academy's Ariel for Best Short.* Güeros *(2014), his first feature, won the Development Grant from Fundación Carolina and Casa de América (Spain), as well as the National Fund for Film Production (FOPROCINE), with which the project was green-lit by the National Film Institute of Mexico (IMCINE).* Güeros *won Best First Feature at the Berlin Film Festival and had its UK premiere at the London Film Festival. Expanding on the theme of stunted youth explored in* Güeros, *Ruizpalacios also looked at cultural patrimony in his follow-up feature,* Museo *(2018), which debuted at the Berlin Film Festival.*

FEATURES FILMOGRAPHY:
Museo (2018)
Güeros (2014)

JASON WOOD: You studied at RADA and also have had huge success as a theatre director on productions by Chekhov, Stoppard, Wesker and Shakespeare. At what point did you begin to gravitate towards cinema and what form of study or training did you undertake? I read that you studied under Ludwik Margules.

ALONSO RUIZPALACIOS: I trained as an actor and theatre director at RADA and then here in Mexico, but I was always interested in ending up in film. In fact, I think theatre was a detour for me. I originally wanted to study cinema and started making little movies with my cousins as they had a movie camera. I didn't. This would have been when I was around ten or twelve years old. We used film as if we were performing magic tricks, leaving the camera whilst we removed an object that was previously there and then using a jump cut as if the object had disappeared. I also remember watching *Who Framed Roger Rabbit* (1988). This was the first time that I was conscious that there was a director behind what was being put on screen. My parents are both doctors, but a mother of a friend was a photographer and she led me into the world of art. She took us to see *Who Framed Roger Rabbit*, and I remember leaving the cinema and telling her that I wanted to be the one who made the movies. Her name was Patricia, and she is the sister of Guillermo Arriaga, the writer of *Amores Perros* (2000) and *Babel* (2006). It was a very artistic family and I gravitated towards them from an early age.

I went to a school where there was a lot of Shakespeare and putting on plays, and this is really how I ended up working in theatre. I still have a passion for Shakespeare and a fantasy of doing Shakespeare on film. Margules was at the school. I think it would be fair to say that theatre seduced me, but cinema was always my first love. Now I am split between the two; I still direct theatre and have an independent theatre company here in Mexico City. As a film-maker I am entirely self-taught. I read a whole bunch of books and during my time at RADA in London I really watched a lot of movies, especially at the National Film Theatre (NFT), the Institute of Contemporary Arts (ICA) and the Ritzy in Brixton. It was during this period that I became immersed in what would be called arthouse films. There was a Godard retrospective at the NFT and myself and a couple of friends from RADA saw the whole thing.

JW: Prior to *Güeros* (2014), you directed shorts including *Café paraíso* (2008) and *The Cu Bird's Last Song* (2010). Both these films won Ariel awards and were screened at international festivals. How did the experience of making the shorts and their success prepare you for your feature-length debut?

AR: It's quite logical that short films are regarded as a stepping-stone to making your first feature. In a way, making the shorts was my film school, although I did work for a couple of years at a TV company in Mexico working on a kids' programme. I learned about cameras and lenses and also a little about film grammar.

I did regard short films as a medium in themselves and not just the bas-tard child of feature films. When I went to the wonderful Claremont-Ferrand International Film Festival – the Cannes of shorts – with *Café paraíso*, it was eye-opening to see that there was a world of short films that I didn't know existed. I also discovered that there were people that made only short films. It's comparative to the writing of short stories and the writing of novels; they are two disciplines that are related but not the same. I still regard short films like that. I have a great respect for the short film format. They contain things that you couldn't get away with in a feature. They are also slightly free from the constraints of commerce in that they are not being made purely to be sold.

JW: *Güeros* was made with support from IMCINE, including production funding from FOPROCINE. Did you always feel supported within Mexico in terms of being able to achieve your vision and were there other figures, particularly other directors, who provided advice and encouragement?

AR: My generation of film-makers in Mexico are very lucky because the funds have allowed an industry to flourish. They have also allowed auteurs to flourish and for people to develop their voice beyond one film. I really cel-ebrate that and continue to fight for that. There is the threat that these funds will disappear and we are putting up a fight to keep them alive. The previous generation wasn't as lucky as we are. Only a handful of directors got to make films and they held on to their relationship with the Mexican Film Institute. These directors, and there were about five of them, were like sacred cows. There was no openness to new voices and the people at IMCINE changed the rules little by little, and in doing this they did a great thing as they allowed cinema in Mexico to flourish. The Mexican film-makers of my generation need to acknowledge and to continue to fight for the freedom we now have. It's at a fragile point right now, the point where this bubble can burst and go back to the Mexican cinema that we had in the 1980s, or it can consolidate itself and go on to become a stable industry.

I never had an older mentor, apart from Margules, who passed away many years ago. Margules did love cinema, but it wasn't really his thing. I did have some influential teachers also at RADA and I still carry what they taught me into film. Joe Blatchley was a great teacher but I'd hesitate to label him a mentor as I'm not still in touch with him. I sometimes fantasise about having a mentor. I'd love to have one. But he's never shown up. The encouragement and advice has come from directors of my own generation. There is strength in numbers. I talk a lot with Amat Escalante; his work is very different to mine but I like to talk with him about film and to show him my stuff. I also talk with Alejandra Márquez, who I admire a lot and who is both very smart and very clear about things. My editor Yibran Asuad, who is also a director, is perhaps who I talk to the most, he is a great interlocutor.

JW: The film fuses two genres, the road movie and the coming-of-age drama. What particularly interested you about these genres and how did you wish to respond to them?

AR: The road movie is a genre I fell in love with after seeing the films of Wim Wenders. *Güeros* wasn't originally a road movie but I always had this idea about making a trip inside Mexico City. My friends were on the strike in UNAM [National Autonomous University of Mexico] that the film is based on and they used to get into a car and drive around when the strike was on. They just drove with no destination. It became a game to stop in new places and try to get into trouble or to find cool places to drink. I went with them a couple of times. Then we had the idea to make a road movie inside Mexico City. It's so fucking huge that it's like a country in itself. You can drive around it and not finish; you will drive for hours and you'll still be in Mexico City. I also like the structure of road movies. They are very free. They say that Homer's *The Odyssey* is the first road movie and I suppose that, in a way, it is. It's not a three-act structure. I also really like deviations in stories so it's a genre that appeals to me. Once I discovered the road movie as a thing, I began to watch loads of them. *Vanishing Point* (Richard C. Sarafian, 1971) and *Two-Lane Blacktop* (Monte Hellman, 1971) are amongst my favourites. And the early Wenders, especially *Alice in the Cities* (1974). The road movie is also suited to the theme of coming of age. The steps along the road represent the steps involved in coming of age. This also appeals to me in narrative. I have always drifted towards that. *The Catcher in the Rye* is a kind of road movie without cars and the stops along the way being New York etc. I also admire *The Savage Detectives* by Roberto Bolaño, which is both a coming-of-age story with a lot of road movie to it.

JW: One of the secrets of the success of the film is the casting. How did you come to your teenage leads, Tenoch Huerta, Sebastián Aguirre and Leonardo Ortizgris? The rapport between them is palpable.

AR: I met Tenoch when I was looking for an actor for *Café paraíso* and then we worked together on some ads that I made. He's a fun guy to work with on set and we became friends. I think he's a great actor and has a great face for cinema. The camera just loves him. Leonardo is another friend. He's from my theatre company and so it felt natural to cast him. Sebastián I saw by accident on assistant director Lucero Quiñones's computer. She was showing me some faces for a character and his face came up and I thought that he instantly had a face for cinema. He was fourteen when we shot *Güeros* and there was still something childish and innocent about him. I think the film captures that beautifully. The film really captures him changing. It was crazy really because originally the character was written for somebody who was dark-skinned and who looked like Tenoch, but when I saw Sebastián my producers told me that it wouldn't work and that we would have to make up a backstory as to why they were brothers. But then the fact that one of them is dark-skinned and one of them is fair-skinned became an important part of the film. This happens a lot in families in Mexico. The darker-skinned kids tend to be more left out. When I hit upon that notion it became really interesting. We filmed some tests and the results were fantastic. Sebastián was a little in awe of Tenoch and Leonardo and then during our prep they began hanging around and building this relationship of brothers. Tenoch taught Sebastián to drive and taught him to drink a little bit. By the time we started shooting he really looked up to Tenoch.

JW: The music in the film and the figure of Epigmenio Cruz suggests the need to talk about Mexican culture and its resonance and relevance. Was this also foremost in your mind?

AR: Only in as much as the film is set in Mexico and I wanted it to speak about Mexican culture and to be a genuine expression of the Mexico that I know and love. The rest followed from that basic principle. I did discuss this with my co-writer Gibrán Portela and we said let's try to make a movie that is not what all the other movies being made are like. We wanted to make something that was celebratory about Mexico and to stay away from clichés. I hope that we achieved that. We did a lot of research. The location aspect of the film was very important; we worked really hard on that. This film also gave me the opportunity to get to know Ana Álvarez – she wrote a book that was a guide to some of the curiosities of Mexico City; it's basically a provocation to walk through all of Mexico City, a kind of anti-tourist guide. Ana was a researcher on the film; I'd contacted her after I bought her book and she drove us around Mexico City. We also walked it a lot when we were prepping the film. It was wonderful to discover parts of Mexico City that I didn't know before.

As for the music, I'm a huge Bob Dylan fan and I wished that we had someone like Dylan in Mexico. Maybe we do and I just haven't heard it. This is why I made up Epigmenio.

JW: In many ways the film – which is bookended by two objects falling from the sky – is also about breaking cycles and travelling from adolescence to adulthood, even though the trio are essentially on a road trip to nowhere. Can you talk about structure in this regard? The 1999 student strike also feels to me an essential – and personal – element and also acts as an impetus for change.

AR: The water balloon thing was something that I used to do as a kid a lot. I'm sure this is very common. The brick incident was something that actually happened to me once, when I was working on the kids' TV programme that I mentioned. A brick suddenly smashed into the production car. We were on the outskirts of the city and ended up chasing after the perpetrator. I like the idea of how these accidents make you end up somewhere completely different. I always wanted to make a movie that started like an episode of *The Simpsons* – they always start with a story that they completely abandon by the third minute. But it hooks you in. I like deviations and coming into a place through the back door. The physical journey also dictated the structure as well. We used a physical map to chart the physical journey. This is common in road movies. The physical journey often also dictates the spiritual journey.

With the student strike, I was interested in the journey from stasis to motion. I started writing this film in London after RADA so it was after the strike, but I was remembering the period of the strike and my days after graduation stuck in a flat all day with my roommates with no job and nothing to do. I kept journals which I used to observe the roommates and how they would find ways to kill time. The strike is a metaphor for stasis. When you are a student and study is taken from away you, suddenly you have no purpose in life and find yourself in an existential crisis. This was intended as a journey out of that crisis. They achieve that by moving.

JW: Can you speak about your cinematographic choices? Beyond the black-and-white 4:3, the camera maintains an interesting balance between formal, composed still frames, frenetic handheld and push/pulls.

AR: I always try to find a code when I am shooting, a code that is logical to the story that I am telling. I work a lot with my DoP Damián García, who is a great collaborator. He's taught me a lot. We do shot lists and storyboard scenes. In our effort to find the code for *Güeros* it came from the first third of the film, which covers life in the apartment. It's stillness and the camera is mostly on sticks. It's kept stable to emphasise the stasis that the kids are in. When they have to leave the apartment – because they are being chased by the angry neighbour they have been stealing electricity from – the camera literally snaps from the tripod. We have this shot for a while. We then continued into movement and jump cuts. The film goes freestyle and follows the characters into every area of the city. I also wanted to honour the landscape and to try to create the mood that the landscape dictates.

JW: *Güeros* also had international success, winning Best First Feature at Berlin, Best Cinematography at Tribeca and screening at the London Film Festival. Was the film similarly embraced in Mexico? I know it won multiple Ariels and the term *güero* is, of course, quite specific to Mexico and Mexico City . . .

AR: It was a failure commercially. It wasn't a big success. But it became a kind of cult movie and I love that about it. I say this without any pretension. I still get people writing to me about it and lots of film students like it. It's become embraced. I went to a projection of it about one year ago at the Cinematheque, where it was a success. It was amongst their most popular films of that year. But the numbers here are small compared to elsewhere. At the recent screening – which was outdoors and it was raining – I thought that nobody would turn up. But it was full and it was lovely to see people watching the film. And the organisers told me that they could see the audience and that it was not their first time watching the film.

JW: Praised by critics for its insight and portrait of slackerdom, many also noted the spirit of Jarmusch and figures from the French New Wave. Were these figures important for you or did you draw upon other film-making influences?

AR: You can't escape either of the above when you shoot in black and white. I did re-watch *Stranger Than Paradise* (Jim Jarmusch, 1984) and *Down by Law* (Jim Jarmusch, 1986) but more than that I went back to Fellini. He's one of my favourites. His joy of film-making and his unexpected use of close-ups; I love that about him. He also creates a tremendous atmosphere. *La Dolce Vita* (1960) and *8½* (1963) are the films that I watch before I shoot anything. Fellini is a much bigger influence on this film than the French New Wave. Even though it may not seem that way.

JW: Can you say more about the robbery at the Museum of Anthropology and how this acted as an inspiration for *Museo* (2018)? Was it something you clearly remembered?

AR: I came into this project via a friend. I had never done anything like this before and I doubt I'll ever do anything like it again. And not because I regret it. I think it turned out pretty well. It's just a different way to get into a project. The project was started by my co-writer Manuel Alcalá. He had a script and was trying to get it produced and my friends told me about it. Manuel had seen *Güeros* and so he asked me to direct *Museo*. I agreed but I wanted to re-write the script. Basically, we started from scratch and it took us two years.

History revisited: Gael García Bernal in *Museo*

I remembered that there had been a robbery in 1985 but that's as far as my memory went. Manuel was closer to the incident because his father was a reporter and he kept all the newspaper cuttings and videos from when it happened. He was obsessed with the events. It was instantly fascinating to me when I got involved. Many Mexicans had an idea of what happened but few really knew what had gone on. This is also what gave us the freedom to depart from the real story. Nobody really knows what happened.

JW: *Museo* shares some similarities with your debut, from the laid-back central characters, the period setting and a look at Mexican society. The year the film is set – 1985 – is important for other reasons too. It was the year of an earthquake, and with the robbery there was the sense that the cultural heritage of the nation was endangered. How did the 1985 setting work as a springboard for you in terms of exploring the past and present of your country?

AR: I'm only interested in stories about the past in as much as they can tell us about the present. I'm interested in what we can learn from history as opposed to just fetishising it. Yes, 1985 was a key year and the theft was like adding insult to injury. It was the final slap to the Mexican cheeks. People felt very betrayed. In moments of crisis you often develop a sense of national identity and pride. Sometimes these crises tend to forge identity. Certainly in

Mexico, we tend to feel Mexican only when we are in deep shit. I was looking for intentional anachronisms. This is true actually of both my features.
The film I am writing currently will also be set in an uncertain time. This
appeals to me. A time period can become like a straightjacket and be very
constraining. You have to depart from the historical frame to allow the story
to breathe. The historical frame is only good in so far as it gives you a framework. I didn't want to make *Museo* a parade of quirks and kitsch hairdos.
My DoP and I were certain about that. It was tough to tie the hands of our
designers in hair, make-up and wardrobe. We had to tone it down. This also
makes it more truthful. We looked at a lot of pictures from the year and most
people dressed normally. Not dissimilar to how people might dress now.

JW: In both *Güeros* and *Museo* there are these mythical figures from pop
culture: in the former it was a musician and in this new film a cabaret-style
singer known as a vedette. Why do you find these popular icons curious or
compelling?

AR: I do find them compelling because they are unsung Mexican heroes or
characters on the fringes of culture. You find these people a lot in Mexico;
they have yet to be Instagrammed or hyped. The vedette is based on a real-
life character, an Argentinian starlet who did soft porn-type movies but
avoided graphic stuff. They were more like sexy comedies. The vedettes
would also dance in nightclubs.

JW: When the art goes missing, people are more interested in visiting the
museum to see the empty cases. How does this relate to the quote at the end
of the film from writer Carlos Monsiváis?

AR: When he was interviewed about the heist, Monsiváis did use those
words. People were shocked to hear him say that. The notion that there
could be value in the crime and the idea that you don't know what you have
lost until it is gone is true. One of the things I found most heartbreaking
when I was researching this film was the photograph Manuel showed me of
people queuing to see these empty displays. This actually happened. I found
it tragic and so telling of Mexicans and who we are. It's like Instagramming
something rather than seeing the thing that you are Instagramming.

JW: You were given permission to shoot the exteriors at the National
Museum of Anthropology, but had to recreate the interiors and the artefacts. How arduous and painstaking was this process?

AR: It was incredibly arduous and all credit goes to the art department, led
by Sandra Cabriada, the production designer. Sandra did her job so well.

She wasn't nominated for anything, which I think is really unfair. I think people genuinely thought that we shot inside the museum. We didn't. When we first heard that we were not going to be able to shoot inside the museum, I became very negative. I just thought, 'Fuck. If we don't have that then we don't have a movie on the budget that we have.' Sandra proved me wrong, and even knocked it out of the park. We shot at Churubusco, where all the classic movies have been done, and even when Gael García Bernal arrived – and of course he has been in some big movies – he was like, 'Whoa.' The prep started a long time before. I insisted that we shoot the pieces that were stolen and Sandra hired people from the museum to replicate the pieces. They also did an amazing job. In many cases they used the real material. Real gold and real jade. They made 150 pieces. They were all so precise. It was actually fun to design the layout of the museum interior with Sandra. We had to decide whether to go with the current exhibition hall set-up or the original one as the two were very different. In the end we went for a mix. A lot of our decisions went unquestioned.

JW: There is a power imbalance between the two thieves and their friendship, which can be affectionate but also often volatile and sometimes abusive. Was this power dynamic always present in the script or did it evolve more slowly?

AR: It was one of the strongest reasons to re-write the original script. In the original script there wasn't much of a relationship. We needed to root for them but also sometimes be repelled by them so the dynamic had to evolve little by little. It was very much laid out when we got to shooting. Our actors made it stronger and fleshed it out more. They really got the hang of where we were going and what we were trying to do.

Perhaps as a result of my work in theatre, I really rehearsed a lot with the actors. I do this as much as I can. I do a lot of improv. Those of us that come from the theatre aspire to make a film like Mike Leigh. With Leonardo Ortizgris and Gael García Bernal I re-wrote elements that had evolved out of their improv and from the time that we spent together rehearsing. They both really understood what it needed to be. Friendships often are abusive.

JW: You had worked previously with Leonardo but for the first time with Gael. How did you find this experience? Bernal, along with Diego Luna, has been a real force for Mexican cinema and seems very game here in terms of the jokes about his height.

AR: I was a little surprised about that! Gael read the script but never mentioned it. I am also really short so he was able to take the piss out of me.

I had never worked with Gael but knew him from before. He had also been in England. We'd wanted to work together for some time. When I was writing the character, who had to be short, charming but also an arsehole sometimes, I knew that Gael could cover all this. He was totally game. It is different working with a star and the first weeks take some adjustments and considerations as we got together in the workspace. Gael is very respectful. He's also a director too and knows that cinema is considered a director's medium.

JW: How did you come to work with Simon Russell Beale? I understand that his character was originally written for an American . . .

AR: Simon Russell Beale saved my life. He saved the film. The producers wanted a big-name American actor and we started looking for one but then I decided that I wanted a good actor as opposed to a very famous one. The producers started doing their search and I also started doing my own secret search. I contacted a friend at RADA and asked her to send me a list of top actors that she thought would be game for this part in an independent arthouse Mexican movie. Simon was the first name on her list. I had seen him pay Hamlet and Vanya in London and I was 'Yes.' My friend had done a play with him and gave me his number and I just called him up. He was incredibly sweet and I can't stress enough what a joy it was to work with him. I hope that one day soon I get to work with him again. He came for just one week and it was such a pleasure.

Before he came, Simon went to see the Mayan objects at the British Museum, objects that were stolen from us, and did his own research to come up with things that he thought his character would know, such as handling the artefacts. He came up with the idea of licking the piece. He read that they did that to test temperature and mineral composition. The scene Simon is in is very theatrical. It could be on stage. It's just four characters in a room talking, taking part in a sub-textual mental chess game. I knew that Simon would do it really well. We rehearsed a whole day without shooting. The second day we shot it. Simon begged me to let him use his English accent as opposed to an American one. The English steal from everywhere, so having him be an English character felt fitting.

JW: You also have the great Chilean actor Alfredo Castro. How did his participation transpire?

AR: It wasn't dissimilar to Simon Russell Beale's participation. We were looking for actors and I didn't really find a Mexican actor that felt right for the part. The doctor is partly based on my father, who was a doctor. I had the part very clear in my head and knew that I needed a very good actor.

Again, it was a friend who had worked with Alfredo who suggested him. I got his number and called him up. He read the script and liked it. Working with Alfredo was also great fun and straightforward. Alfredo was wary of improv at first, even though he comes from theatre, but as soon as we started, he really got into it. The scenes with the Christmas dinner had to be authentic as to feel like a documentary and this was partly down to the ability of all the actors to improvise. Alfredo became an expert at knowing when to pitch in and when to hold back and to just listen.

JW: A multiple award winner, this film is also significant in a wider industry sense in that it was the first Latin American feature to enjoy a release as part of YouTube Premium. What benefits do working with streaming services offer film-makers and was it important to you that the film also have a theatrical presence?

AR: The film was paramount to me. The rest was the producer's decision and I had very little say in that. We shot the film on 35 mm and I am a huge fan of the theatrical experience. I still believe that it is the best way to watch a movie. Something else happens when you go to a big dark room and suspend your life for two hours with a group of strangers. A film doesn't ever get that kind of attention elsewhere. It suffers when it is streamed. I see this every day. Even when I am watching something that I really want to watch. There are endless interruptions. Of course, there are advantages to streaming, but I would also question the argument that it is a democratic process. You still have to pay for it and there are many areas in Mexico that are still without the Internet. I'm all for the film experience. I spent a lot of time on the sound design and the sound mix to add to this theatrical experience. This is all lost when you watch it on a computer or on a phone. The theatrical experience will never die, even though it may feel threatened. I see the theatrical experience as a cure for how isolated we have become with our technology.

JW: Finally, you mentioned that you are currently shooting in Mexico City. Are you able to reveal any details about your most recent project?

AR: Not too many! I am making a documentary about the Mexico City police. It's an experimental documentary. I'm also writing a new feature that I hope to shoot next year.

18
Guillermo del Toro

Alongside compatriots Alfonso Cuarón, Alejandro González Iñárritu and Carlos Reygadas, Guillermo del Toro emerged as one of the most visible and distinctive artists in modern Mexican cinema. A major contributor to the critical and commercial renaissance cinema from Mexico enjoyed on an international scale, the universal acclaim generated by Pan's Labyrinth *(2006) (which won a BAFTA and was nominated for an Academy Award) placed del Toro firmly at the forefront of contemporary film-makers. A superlative visual stylist closely associated with horror and fantasy genres, del Toro's work frequently examines the nightmares of the past, using history to eloquently speak of the often-traumatic passage from childhood to maturity.*

A director equally at home in Spanish language features or working on big budget Hollywood productions such as Hellboy *(2004),* Pacific Rim *(2008) and* Crimson Peak *(2015), and imbuing them with his own distinctive vision, the book emerges at a time when del Toro's artistry and profile reached new heights with his most recently completed work,* The Shape of Water *(2018). The winner of the Golden Lion at Venice, the film went on to triumph at all the major international awards ceremonies, winning two Golden Globes for Best Director and Best Original Score (Alexandre Desplat); three BAFTAs (including the David Lean Award for Direction) and four Academy Awards, most prominently for Best Picture and Best Achievement in Directing.*

Del Toro is something of a workaholic and once he has committed to a project he is fully *committed. Currently completing filming a remake of Edmund Goulding's* Nightmare Alley *(1947), he has also embarked on a long-cherished version of* Pinocchio *with an emphasis on the darkness of the material.*

FEATURE FILMOGRAPHY:
The Shape of Water (2017)
Crimson Peak (2015)

Pacific Rim (2013)
Hellboy II: The Golden Army (2008)
Pan's Labyrinth (2006)
Hellboy (2004)
Blade II (2002)
The Devil's Backbone (El espinazo del diablo) (2001)
Mimic (1997)
Cronos (1993)

JASON WOOD: How is life in lockdown?

GUILLERMO DEL TORO: I like it. It's a time to read and a time to watch movies. But this pandemic has caused a mini apocalypse for the arts. And it's happening in slow motion.

JW: COVID-19 caused production on *Nightmare Alley* to be postponed. I just wondered if you were able to just say a little bit about that production. I know at the moment it's on hiatus. I'm a big fan of the original film by Edmund Goulding (1947), and I know the novel. I just wondered if you could say a bit about the production and your attraction to that project.

GDT: I first found out about it through Ron Perlman in 1992. Back then, Ron wanted to help me create a screenplay for him to star as Stan. He was probably thirty, thirty-five or something like that. We found out that the rights were at Fox, that it was a library title, that they wouldn't sell the rights. I read the novel back then. I told Ron what I thought about the novel, which is that it was much more sexual, more political, more grimy. A lot more about the underbelly. I think Stan, in the novel, was very sociopathic and a complete narcissist, where I think in the film adaptation, probably because of the mores of the day, it was different. We couldn't go that far with sexuality; we couldn't go that far with some of the darker, more nihilistic aspects. I enjoyed the first movie by Goulding very much. I'm a huge fan of Tyrone Power and I think it's a great setting of the novel. But I thought that there was an occasion for another version because when stories come from a literary source you can version them differently. It's different when a movie is the origin. Then it's a remake and that does not attract me. But when there is a common source – *Dracula, Frankenstein, Moby-Dick, Day of the Locust,* whatever it is that has the literary source, the book will always hold little nuggets that somebody didn't mine.

Kim Morgan and I went about adapting it into a screenplay that spoke to some elements that were more surreal, a little darker perhaps. Before the lockdown we had shot approximately 45, 50 per cent. When we stopped, the material that we generated I've seen time and again, and I think with a little bit of love we'll start one day and finish it. At this point, at this exact moment in the pandemic and the quarantines and all that, nobody really knows when.

JW: The film continues your collaboration with Dan Laustsen, who obviously shot *The Shape of Water* (2017) and, I believe, *Crimson Peak* (2015), and his photography just seems to suit your sensibility so beautifully. I just wondered if you could say something about that, because I'm really impressed with his work as a cinematographer. It does seem the perfect fit for you.

GDT: For so many years I worked with Guillermo Navarro and I have with him one of the deepest friendships and the deepest cinematic collaborations. But I think that Dan is an equally good match in a different way. He's not so . . . It doesn't have a history, an origin. But we work in shorthand creatively. We started on *Mimic* (1996) and we were a perfect match. My relationship with cinematographers is one in which I can relax absolutely about the light, but if I see something in the light I can say it. I can say, whatever this, whatever that, and they can relax on the choice of composition lens, the mechanics of the camera, which are all things they choose, because I orchestrate the dance between the actor and the camera. But at the same time, likewise, if they see something that could be different they have the room to say it. It is only when you have this complete mutual confidence that you can have a great and repeated collaborator.

JW: It's interesting that you mentioned light. I saw *The Shape of Water* at the Toronto International Film Festival straight after it blew everyone away in Venice, and I remember seeing that film and seeing the way that light was used. But also I remember seeing that film – I'd known you a few years – and knowing immediately how it was going to connect. Why it was going to connect with audiences and win the Golden Lion at Venice, two Golden Globes, three BAFTAs, four Academy Awards. It just felt that was the moment everything was going to click. Did you have that same sense? You've made other films before that have been tremendously successful, but this was the one that just won everything and won every heart.

GDT: I think there were two things that happened. Number one, I didn't know. Because as far as I was concerned, when some people say, 'Of course it was going to connect with the Academy', I had no idea of that. It was a bizarre project, as bizarre a project as you can have on paper. My proposal was to shoot *Creature from the Black Lagoon* (Jack Arnold, 1954), so to speak, through the eyes of Frank Borzage. Or in my opinion it was a Douglas Sirk melodrama. The colours were very influenced by Douglas Sirk, Michael Powell, Emeric Pressburger. The saturation of *The Red Shoes* (Michael Powell and Emeric Pressburger, 1948). It was a completely bizarre formulation. I had no idea. I remember when we were shooting, Richard Jenkins and I, I turned around to Richard and I said, 'Look, I don't know if anyone is going to like this, but I love it.' To me there are moments in the sequels of *Creature from the Black Lagoon*, and in the original, that are quoted exactly in the movie. There are shots that are exact quotes of the creature emerging from the water, the feet touching the ground, and I thought, this is a monster that I fell in love with when I was a kid. Madly. The creature of *Frankenstein* and the creature of the Black Lagoon. I had an almost apoplectic reaction as a child. I would go into almost a Stendhal syndrome trembling trance when I saw these creatures, these characters. To this day I cannot explain why my connection is so deep.

JW: *Creature from the Black Lagoon* is the first horror film I ever saw. I was always obsessed with creatures that lived in water because of that.

GDT: It is such a beautiful design. Milicent Patrick, who designed that and a few others, was a genius. There is something sensual about the creature, because it was designed by a woman, I believe. There was an element of majesty. I had no idea that it was going to connect until Venice. I've been on every crucial screening of that movie and I can tell you that every reaction, almost mechanically, to the point of repetition, was exactly the same. People were very swept by it. The idea for the movie was to make a song of images and sound. To make it a song. To make it, like you could almost hum along with the movie. The Venice screening, the credits started rolling and they started the applause, and the applause didn't stop until we left the projection. I knew then – I thought, 'Oh my God, this really connects.' Then we went to Telluride and it was projected during a hailstorm on the tin roof, and still the reaction was a beautiful reaction. Little by little I saw it connect with the old Academy members, I saw it connect with the European audiences, I saw it connect with UK audiences. It was a movie that had such a clean spirit that I felt that connection was very pure. As pure for me as *Pan's Labyrinth* (2006) was.

JW: The other thing with *The Shape of Water*, and you said that you'd mentioned to Richard Jenkins, 'I love this movie, but I don't know who's going to see it.' It's a very personal film, but it's also a film which is like all of your work, very political. It deals with the ideas of monsters who are considered monsters because they're different. It deals with gender and sexuality. There's a racial element to the film. It looks at the way people are persecuted, and the way people abuse power, and it also hits that sweet spot of horror and fairy tale. It's interesting that the film was almost a summation of all the things that you love and all the things that you do. It is still a very political film, and yet it still connected. Was that satisfying, that you didn't have to distil your vision or distil what you wanted to say with the picture?

GDT: That's the second thing that happened. The second thing that happened, curiously enough, is that for anybody paying attention this was the perfect synthesis of twenty-five years of story-telling. You could see strands of it in the character of Hellboy, you could see strands on the girl in *Pan* grown up in the character played by Sally Hawkins, you could see strands of the politics of *The Devil's Backbone* (2001). But it was all happening lovingly at once and it was a love letter to cinema. It was a movie that was in love with the idea of cinema. The woman lived above a cinema, watched movies, loved musicals, dreamt herself Ginger Rogers dancing with Fred Astaire. The other thing that is beyond political for me is that the creature reveals itself to be the humblest of all the characters; it reveals itself to be a god, and she reveals herself to maybe also be one. She was not human completely. She was an other to the other of him. She may have been born in the water with gills, and she has forgotten, and the

The look of love: Sally Hawkins and Doug Jones in *The Shape of Water*

character played by Richard Jenkins makes her remember. These are all connections that are rhyming and that is very powerful. All my movies are very
odd, even the big ones, and all of them have a strange tangent. I'm definitely
on the side of the Other. I think it was right – somebody said, 'What a timely
movie.' But of course, we started planning it many years before. What I think
is sad is the spectre of intolerance, and the spectre of trying to destroy the
Other, always looms above our head as humans. I don't know why.

JW: I think the scene in the pie shop is incredibly powerful, where Richard
Jenkins goes in and the guy tells him not to come back any more once he
makes a pass at him. It's those moments in the film which really, for me . . .

GDT: Yes. The guy says, 'Don't come back, this is a family restaurant.' You
just saw him be a motherfucker to African Americans. And then Richard
understands, I don't want to side with this guy. He may be attractive, but he
is a monster. I'm going to side with Sally and with the creature. It's for me a
beautiful moment for him. I had originally written a big speech for Richard
and we shot it. It was a good speech; it was nice on paper. But then Richard
grabbed a napkin, spat the pie on the napkin. I said, 'OK, that's the speech.
I don't need the speech any more.'

JW: Sally Hawkins is wonderful in the film.

GDT: I saw everything she did and to me, it was a tailor-made part. It
was either Sally or there was no sense in making the movie. I think it
was that from the start. I told her many years before we shot that I was
writing this for her. In the same way that I wrote *Pan's Labyrinth* for
Sergi López. Completely different, but I could not imagine Sergi López's
character being played by anybody else. This all comes – my apprenticeship as a very young film-maker was under one of the most brave and
political film-makers, which was Jaime Humberto Hermosillo, who made
not only independent cinema, which was very, very much forbidden in
a way by the government in Mexico at that time, but also managed to
produce one of the first if not the first openly gay comedies and feature
films in Mexican history which went on to be a great success with *Dona
Herlinda and Her Son* (1985). All the foundations of indie cinema were
there. I was production manager and I was just a kid and my mother,
who had appeared in many of my short films, she appeared in the leading
part because Jaime liked her in many of my movies. Many of my room
decorations, the house, because I would tell my mum, 'Can I borrow your
dining set? Can I borrow this flowerpot?' The shoot was produced for
less than $5,000.

I was twenty-something and I had to do production budgets, deal with the shooting schedule staying on time, food, passports, equipment, timetables, permits, all of that. I came out of working on that movie very prepared to tackle my first movie and Jaime Humberto gave us three years of screenwriting, Mexican cinema history and we created the festival in Guadalajara, and the school, the cinema school in Guadalajara.

JW: And they're both still going strong. Something that always impressed me with Mexican cinema is the way that when figures reach a certain position of power and influence they use their achievements to help others; it seems very natural that yourself, Alejandro González Iñárritu and Alfonso Cuarón would help new emerging voices. A few weeks ago I know that you all collaborated in an open letter to the Mexican government asking for support for the arts due to the COVID-19 pandemic. You've done that on a collective scale, but you've also individually helped new film-makers coming through by acting as spokespersons and producers. Do you feel it's important to do that given that Mexican cinema, for so long, was kind of out of the spotlight? Now it's very much in the spotlight, but do you think it's a responsibility on yourself to use that position to help others and to help your industry?

GDT: After what is called the Golden Age of Cinema, the unions were closed for many, many years, because the unions were isolating themselves to quote unquote 'protect' the job pool. That led to a stagnant cinema. Then in the 1970s a new generation was able to enter the unions. Arturo Ripstein and Felipe Cazals, for example. But at the same time, that generation, not all of them built bridges. Some of them did, Humberto for sure. Then there was a middle generation between them and us that was sort of lost. José Luis García Agraz, Gerardo Pardo were from a generation that was barely able to make movies. But they were very, very generous with us coming up. García Agraz basically godfathered Luis Estrada, Estrada godfathered Alfonso Cuarón and Cuarón godfathered me. It was because we felt, I believe we felt, that Mexican cinema was really close to being extinguished. During the government of José López Portillo, in which the Cinematheque burned and basically all the money from the state goes to *Campanas rojas*, Sergei Bondarchuk; instead of going to productions in Mexico they co-produced with Europe. And the scandalously lavish way whilst Mexican movies didn't get funding. We all felt that it was a matter of all joining together and making movies against that frame. To give you an example, in Guadalajara, people used to say with great pride, 'We don't see Mexican cinema.' This is going to sound really scandalous, but some of the people in charge of selecting films to propose to Cannes or Berlin or Venice, the big festivals, in Mexico they only selected one or two or three names over and over again. Mostly the big festivals were very closed against Mexican cinema. We couldn't occupy a place in the panorama of world cinema. Little by little, the thing that our generation did, and we did it not with a Magna Carta or a big agreement, we just wanted movies to look better, sound better, look technically as proficient as any movie in the world, and tell stories that were different. That were not only enthralled with catastrophe and tragedy, but that could play in other genres. We wanted to attempt a noir, a comedy, a horror movie. A caper. Different directors tried different things. But the movies started to have a quality, technically, that was far superior. They looked better, they sounded better, they were technically orchestrated better, and a new generation of actors came out. They all emerged, and this consolidated a new Mexican cinema. The first movie to win in Cannes, after thirty years, was *Cronos* (1993), which won Critics' Week. Then a few years later *Amores Perros* (2000) wins the same prize. It was a change. These things broke the stasis. And Alfonso Cuarón with *Sólo con tu pareja* (1991) became the most successful Mexican film of all time for a while. It had stellar screenings everywhere. Alfonso got a job immediately in a series on HBO called *Fallen Angels*. These were things that were unheard of. A little time after he did *A Little Princess* (1995), which, to me, still is one of his best movies.

JW: The situation now is that in the last eight years there have been multiple Academy Award wins for yourself, Alfonso and Alejandro, and multiple Academy Awards for Mexican cinematographers. Mexican cinema has really seemed to be at the forefront again internationally. Did this not make the institutions in Mexico realise what a jewel they had? They'd gone through periods before of not supporting the film-makers. Is it still very difficult for films to get made?

GDT: Mexico is a country that reinvents itself every six years. The change of government is a reinvention. For example, when Luis Echeverría came up, the cultural apparatus got fortified very strongly. With Vicente Fox or Felipe Calderón, no it didn't. But during Carlos Salinas's time the cultural system became very strong. It goes up and down. I remember, *Cronos* was incredibly difficult to make. It was made basically against the grain because the institutions mostly financed dramas and tragedies. They disliked it. They said, 'We don't finance that. You should look for private money.' I kept saying, 'But it's an art movie. I think there's art and there's beauty in the genre.' It was very difficult; it was not supported when we went to Cannes. I think

I told you this story. Nevertheless it won so many awards in Mexico, it won at all the festivals all over the world, different prizes. Immediately after that I gave them the screenplay for *Devil's Backbone,* and they wouldn't finance it. It was a different version of *Devil's Backbone*, but they wouldn't finance it. They said, 'You should find private money.' Once again. I didn't think there was such a learning curve in the Mexican institutions, but we have been in conference with the senators for the funding twice. I think we are successfully managing to try and preserve that. We're hoping it's preserved because they're cutting a lot of funding for many things and we made a case. I had been in the phone calls, the Zoom conferences twice, they last about two to four hours, and we made a plea publicly. We're very actively hoping it is preserved. Culturally I don't think it's foremost on the agenda. These are very difficult times for the arts. It's not coincidental that it's happening all over the world. Governments tend to be divisive and dogmatic. They instinctively want to repress art and culture because these are two very powerful tools for independent thought.

JW: Despite the challenges, new figures in Mexican cinema continue to emerge. I was particularly impressed by *The Chambermaid* (2018) by Lila Avilés, and by David Zonana's *Workforce* (2019). I've always been a big fan of Amat Escalante. Are there film-makers whose work you're seeing that is still exciting to you?

GDT: Yes, of course. Only a couple of weeks ago I saw *I'm No Longer Here* (*Ya no estoy aquí*) (Fernando Frías de la Parra, 2019), which was financed by Netflix. It is a splendid movie and a completely unique voice. The amazing thing in Mexico is that we have an enormous percentage of salient and fabulous movies for the number of movies produced. We produce around two hundred movies and at least 10 per cent of those are extraordinary. Whereas to give you an example, in the US, thousands upon thousands of movies are produced, and maybe twenty or thirty or fifty are extraordinary. It's uncommon how much you find new voices in Mexican cinema because it comes out of need. Making cinema in Mexico, making movies in Mexico, is not prestigious, is not economically privileged. You don't become a millionaire. I remember I met once a billionaire that financed Carlos Reygadas. He financed *Devil's Backbone* and *Y tu mamá también* (2001). I said, 'Well, you're a billionaire. Mexican cinema will make you a millionaire!' Nobody compared to the first world, where you can have status, money, fame, power. Making cinema in Mexico is counterintuitively against those things. Most of the time, for example *Cronos*, I didn't make money. I was in debt close to a quarter of a million dollars, which I paid and never got back.

Making *Pan's Labyrinth* I got my salary back after the Oscar nominations, but I didn't make any more money than that. So making films in Spanish in Mexico, it comes out of a real need. There is this rage to tell the stories that all the young film-makers feel and articulate. That's why they are so ferociously independent.

JW: I wanted to ask a bit about one of the things that unites the work – I don't want to keep comparing you to your friends, Alfonso and Alejandro, but one of the things that also strikes me about your work is, when you work outside of Mexico in the American system, all three of you are able to make films that are still incredibly personal. You're a film scholar. You know that a lot of émigré directors that went to Hollywood had their personal visions flattened by the studio system. But you've been able to make films like *Hellboy* (2004), which I love, and *Hellboy II: The Golden Army* (2008), and *Pacific Rim* (2013), and *Crimson Peak*, which are every bit as distinctive and aesthetically and thematically Guillermo del Toro movies as *Cronos*, *Pan's Labyrinth*, *Devil's Backbone*. How do you retain that sense of your own identity? Is it on your part a determination? Is it an ability to get the executives on your side? It's quite a skill to be able to do that, Guillermo.

GDT: I think everything I needed to learn to survive creatively I learned, first, by going through the system in Mexico which already was a very oppressive, culturally oppressive system that dictated what type of movies were 'worth making', and what type of movies were not 'worth making'. Genre was a big thing. I still think that that goes – most people don't like or trust genre. Less and less that is the case. More and more people are starting to admit the artistry and beauty and poetic darkness of the genre movies. But I've been trying to get it to that place of respectability for three decades. What happens is, after surviving that in Mexico, then the second thing that I learned to survive with identity was doing *Mimic* with the Weinsteins. It put me through every situation and taught me to be very strong and firm in saying no in order to win the war, if not every battle. After that – there are two spaces in my filmography. Between *Cronos* and *Mimic* there are five years. Half a decade. Between *Mimic* and *Devil's Backbone* there's another five years. Half a decade. An entire decade I got offered different movies. I remember being a young film-maker after *Cronos* and I was offered a bunch of horror sequels. A lot. I said no to all of them. After *Mimic*, which ultimately did connect and was very successful on home video, it was highly successful on rentals and all that and created two sequels, I got offered almost every horror movie under the sun. I've always been very stringent. I don't take any project that I don't find has elements that speak to me in a very deep and personal way. I preferred to spend five years inactive, twice, which is a whole decade in a three-decade career – I'd rather stay inactive than do the wrong . . . I can do the wrong movie for the right reasons. I can survive that, because I have my own convictions. But if you do the wrong movie or the right movie for the wrong reasons, you get completely disoriented.

JW: I guess it's how people lose their way. You dedicate so much time to a film, you need to be passionate about it. I'm going to ask you one more question. It's interesting. We struggle to find time to speak; you're so busy and you work on so much. I'm looking at your current IMDb page. I never entirely trust IMDb but there are just two points I wanted to ask you briefly about which projects are further down the pipeline. I wanted to ask you a little about *Pinocchio*, which again features Ron Perlman, and also if you could tell me anything about *The Witches*, because I was lucky enough to count myself a friend of Nic Roeg, who was a hero to me. I'm interested to see about your connection to *The Witches*, which is probably the least Nic Roeg film of anything he ever made.

GDT: *Pinocchio*, for me, is an obsession that I've had since I was a kid. Recently I was co-creating the screenplay and co-producing for Gris Grimly to direct, because he designed a beautiful design for *Pinocchio* for his book. But we couldn't get it financed, so I said, 'Let me write a new screenplay and let's try again with me directing.' We tried it again and this time after years and years of rejection I finally managed to get the financing on Netflix. The difficulty is that it's not a children's version of *Pinocchio*. It's very dark. It's stop-motion. *Pinocchio* dies many times, many of them brutally. It's a metaphor for the rise of fascism and obedience in Italy. With *Pinocchio* rising when Mussolini is rising. It was only under Netflix that I found – I had a very big success with them with *Trollhunters* (2016–18), that series, and I'd been shepherding that series and other series for them for many years, and they knew they could trust me. They knew I could make something that was fun and beautiful and somewhat charming in spite of all those elements, and they gave me the chance to do it. I loved the Nicolas Roeg film, but I loved the Roald Dahl book more, especially the ending. For a long time I wrote many drafts of that screenplay which followed the book religiously. It was a very faithful adaptation of the book. I went to visit a gypsy house; I really wanted the Dahl family to approve. They approved the screenplay. Then I could not get it green-lit at Warner's, and they gave my screenplay to Robert Zemeckis and he changed it quite a bit. He added elements that are definitely different than the ones I thought – I think I'm still credited as co-writer, but it has very little if anything to do with my original intention. Structurally I think they are similar, but I think it's going to be a very different movie. For me, one of the great film-makers in my pantheon is Nicolas Roeg.

JW: Did you ever get to meet Roeg?

GDT: I spoke to him on the phone once, very briefly. But he knew I adored him. Anything, *Walkabout* (1971), *Don't Look Now* (1973), *Bad Timing* (1980), *Eureka* (1983). He's just one of the great deconstructors of time. His partnership with Donald Cammell ignited everything for me in terms of how you can do this fragmentation of being unstuck in time. It's not going to flash forward. It's really a rich tapestry of pure cinema.

19

David Zonana

David Zonana has worked with Michel Franco at Lucía Films on projects such as 600 Miles (Gabriel Ripstein, 2015), The Heirs (Jorge Hernandez Aldana, 2015), Chronic (Michel Franco, 2015) and April's Daughter (Michel Franco, 2017). Zonana's short films, Princesa (Princess) (2014), Sangre alba (Dim Blood) (2016) and Brother (2017), have screened at numerous national and international film festivals. In 2015, Variety named Zonana as one of the upcoming talents of Mexican cinema. The screenplay for Workforce (2019), his feature film directorial debut, was awarded prizes at the IX BoliviaLab and the XVI National Script Competition (Guanajuato International Film Festival) and selected to participate in the Sundance-Morelia Lab in 2018. As a work in progress, it won both main prizes at Los Cabos Film Festival in 2018. The film was premiered at the Toronto International Film Festival.

FEATURES FILMOGRAPHY:
Workforce (2019)

JASON WOOD: Prior to making your feature debut with *Workforce* (2019) you had both directed and produced a number of acclaimed shorts, such as *Princesa* (2014) and *Sangre alba* (2016). What was your route into the industry? Did you study cinema at one of the film schools and who were some of the influences on you when you were starting out? I'd also be interested to learn how your working relationship with Michel Franco came about. You were one of the producers on *Chronic* (2015) and Franco is one of the producers on *Workforce*.

DAVID ZONANA: Unfortunately, or maybe not, I didn't study film-making. My family background comes from the business world and, despite my interest in art in my late teens – I experimented with painting, photography, poetry and music – I never thought of seeking a career in art; my high school and family were very conservative. I did a major in finance, which didn't work out, and I dropped out a year short of graduation.

In every dream home a heartache: *Workforce*

Cinema wasn't really on my mind and I hadn't seen many films by that time. I think it was the only major form of art which didn't interest me in my teens, so when I dropped finance, at twenty-two years old, my idea was to move out of the city and make some music, kind of a hippie type of life.

Then, I met Michel Franco through one of my older brothers, which was the turning point. He invited me to work in his recently created production company, Lucía Films (now Teorema), which was interesting for me. I started working as his assistant and little by little earned more responsibilities. Meanwhile, he bought me around fifty classic films; if I wanted to work in his production company, I should know about cinema. It was then, watching those first films, that I realised that there was a new language in front of me, one that borrowed many of the traits of other forms of expression I had tried in my teens. My creative ambition was renewed and a year later I was shooting my first short, *Princesa* (*Princess*).

JW: I also wondered about the positives of having a producer who is also a director. Does it make some of the decision-making in terms of aesthetics easier and also lead to a strong support system?

DZ: Having a producer like Michel on board is the best thing that can happen to any director. He understands film language incredibly, and, at the same time, he is non-invasive (he went to the set only once and he barely commented on the script). So in a way, you know you have a top director watching your back in case you want to discuss anything about the film, but most importantly, he allows you to make the calls.

JW: What was the starting principle of *Workforce*? It asks a number of key social and economic questions regarding power, exploitation and class, but is also partly about what happens when the impoverished, if they suddenly enjoy some of the privileges of the rich, will automatically adopt their mores as well. Was this something you were keen to explore? It becomes a film about the subject of empathy, doesn't it?

DZ: I believe it is a moral problem, not an economic one. Regardless of your income, moral deficiencies such as voracious ambition, corruption and the incapacity to feel empathy towards others have permeated every economic system, at every level (blame the media, materialistic entertainment, politics or whatever you want). So regardless of each person's income level or political views, I think it is their individual battle against these moral deficiencies, rather than a macro-economic solution, that can take us out from this loop. *Workforce* is such a loop.

JW: Another key to the film is the absence of the foundations of a social democracy: state-regulated work insurance; access to reliable legal advice. Workers such as Francisco seem totally helpless when appealing against injustice. This is sadly common to third-world countries but seems to now be a first-world problem too. Did you want to analyse in a universal sense the repercussions of this system?

DZ: These kinds of precarious working conditions happen mostly in third-world countries, where the law is subjective and can be bent, via corruption, to the benefit of a few. Although, of course, there are similar situations all around the world. I would say that we live in an era with great social and economic disparity, violence, lack of empathy and shallow morality. All of this reflects, in my opinion, one of the darkest times in human history.

JW: I have noticed that in your work, and this applies also to *Workforce*, you adopt the technique of having many key plot moments occur off screen. Is this because you want the spectator to be able to construct details in their own head? I find it makes for a much more fulfilling viewing experience.

DZ: I'm interested in allowing the spectator to create their own mental images. Via this interpretation, they project their own personality onto the character, and the two blend in a way. I also believe it allows a ninety-minute film to feel longer in a good way. It allows you to dig deeper into the story without adding to the running time.

JW: In terms of your visual aesthetic, you seem to operate in quite an economical way. Your feature contains more frame movements than your previous shorts but there is still a sense of precision and control. Could you say something about this approach?

DZ: I've been inclined to make the camera a witness with no, or very subtle movement. I am trying not to distract the attention of the spectator from the story. Also, I didn't want to be intrusive with the non-professional cast, so that I could make them forget, as much as I could, that they were on a movie set.

JW: I'm also keen to learn more about your approach to casting. Carlos Reygadas and Amat Escalante prefer to work with non-professional actors, and when I saw the film in Toronto I heard an interview with you where you mentioned that many of the cast in *Workforce* are non-actors. Is this a quest for authenticity or realism?

DZ: Only the protagonist and another two or three secondary roles are actors. Most of the cast are real construction workers, their families and friends. I took the easy way; in my opinion, it was easier to direct real construction workers than to recreate the dynamics in the construction world with actors.

JW: Hugo Mendoza is very potent in the central role. There is an incredible intensity about him. Was this one of the qualities that led you to cast him?

DZ: He has a unique personality, being very sweet but toughened by life experiences at the same time; I needed someone with this characteristic. I think this is certainly captured on camera. Actually, he wasn't going to be in the film until three weeks prior to shooting. I initially cast him in a minor role because I had already cast the role he plays. But I ended up changing my mind at the last minute and gave him the role, which definitely was the correct choice. He is very talented and delivered a great performance.

JW: Mexican cinema has had periods of boom and bust but there seems to be a real momentum again at the moment with diverse film-makers emerging telling stories that resonate on both a domestic and international level. The films also seem determined to grapple with very pertinent issues, *The Chambermaid* (2018) being another recent example. As a film-maker and producer, do you see this as an exciting moment for cinema from Mexico?

DZ: I believe most film-makers and artists reflect their way of seeing the world and the problems surrounding them. So, it doesn't surprise me that there are several films in Mexico talking about economic disparity. Mexico's cinema has definitely positioned itself in the spotlight, but I don't think it is recent. We have seen a great increment in the amount of films produced since the 2000s, allowing the possibility of new voices to surface.

JW: The film has played very successfully at festivals worldwide, which must be very gratifying. What are your future plans in terms of projects, both as a producer and as a director?

DZ: I definitely intend to continue writing and directing films. I am in development on a new project, and it is starting from scratch again, but that's the best part. The success of *Workforce* won't guarantee anything. In my mind I'm making my first feature all over again, with the same ambition and excitement. The director's career is long, and I'm just starting.

Acknowledgements

There are so many people to thank for their help and generosity during the writing of both editions of this book that it is almost impossible to know where to begin. As good a place as any is with Will Clark and Danny Perkins, then of Optimum Releasing, the UK distributors of *Amores Perros*, *The Devil's Backbone* and *Duck Season*, who helped initiate the project. At the earliest stages of research – and during many of the later stages too – I would not have gotten by without the advice and assistance of Rosa Bosch. Rosa was also instrumental in the follow-up edition.

One of the greatest pleasures this book initially afforded was the opportunity to visit Mexico City to meet with a good deal of the people interviewed herein. During my time there, Bertha Navarro, Martha Sosa, Susana López Aranda and Claudia Prado were particularly accommodating, helping to facilitate meetings and establish new contacts. Prior to my departure, Paul Julian Smith provided a sense of local history and recommendations of the best (and cheapest) restaurants. Anna Marie de la Fuente was a further excellent source of industry connections.

I would, of cours, also like to express my sincere gratitude to all those interviewed in this book for so generously giving me their time and for taking an interest in my endeavours. Perhaps most of all I would like to thank Walter Donohue and Richard T. Kelly at Faber & Faber for their skill, patience and trust.

My thanks to all the directors who found time to be interviewed for both volumes of this book and who all committed wholeheartedly to the project. I am especially grateful to Carlos Reygadas. It is no exaggeration to say that without him this update would not have happened. My gratitude is also extended to: Nicky Beaumont, Robert Beeson, Alice Scandellari Burr, Karla Luna Cantu, Jake Garriock, Jessie Gibbs, Paul Baillie-Lane, Eréndira Núñez Larios, Daniela Michel and the Morelia International Film Festival, and Becky Thomas. I dedicate the book to Walter Donohue at Faber, who has always supported me.

Bibliography

Books

Arriaga, Guillermo, *Amores Perros* (original screenplay), Faber and Faber, 2001

—, *A Sweet Scent of Death*, Faber and Faber, 2002

—, *21 Grams* (original screenplay), Faber and Faber, 2003

Berg, Charles Ramírez, *Cinema of Solitude: A Critical Study of Mexican Film, 1967–1983*, University of Texas Press, 1992

Elena, Alberto, and López, Marina Díaz (eds), *The Cinema of Latin America*, Wallflower Press, 2003

Fisher, John (writer and researcher), *The Rough Guide to Mexico*, Penguin, 2003

Mora, Carl J., *Mexican Cinema: Reflections of a Society 1896–1988*, University of California Press, rev. edn, 1989

Paranaguá, Paulo Antonio (ed.), *Mexican Cinema*, BFI Publishing, 1995

Queirós, Eça de, *El crimen del padre Amaro* (novel), Carcanet, 2002

Shaw, Deborah, *Contemporary Cinema of Latin America, 10 Key Films*, Continuum, 2003

Smith, Paul Julian, *Amores Perros* (BFI Modern Classic), BFI Publishing, 2003

Articles

Archibald, David, 'Insects and Violence' (interview with Guillermo del Toro), *Guardian*, 28 November 2001

Barnes, Henry, 'How can we understand life without thinking about dying?' (interview with Michel Franco), *Guardian*, 18 February 2016

BOMB Magazine, 'Nicolás Pereda talks to Gerardo Naranjo', April 2012

Brooks, Xan, 'First Steps in Latin', *Guardian*, 19 July 2002

Brown, Colin, 'Children of the Cine Revolucíon', Screen International, 19 September 2003

Dale, Martin, 'Lila Avilés talks about her festival journey with *The Chambermaid*', *Variety*, 11 April 2019

Delgado, Maria, *The Chambermaid* (review) *Sight & Sound*, August 2019, Volume 29, Issue 8

Fuente, Anna Marie de la, 'New Mexico', *Screen International*, 22 February 2002

—, 'World box office focus: Mexico', *Screen International*, 7 March 2003

—, 'Thunder over Mexico', *Screen International*, 14 March 2003

—, 'Latin Revolution: Country Focus Mexico', *Screen International*, 19 September 2003

Hattenstone, Simon, 'Alfonso Cuarón on *Roma*', *Guardian*, 21 December 2018

James, Nick, 'Guillermo del Toro' (interview), *Sight & Sound*, March 2018, Volume 28, Issue 3

— 'Where the heart is', *Sight & Sound*, January/February 2019, Volume 29, Issues 1 and 2

Kuhn, Kimberly, 'What is a Ghost?: An Interview with Guillermo del Toro', *Cineaste*, spring 2002

Lodge, Guy, 'Guillermo del Toro's *The Shape of Water* is a much-needed ode to the "other"', *Guardian*, 30 November 2017

Macnab, Geoffrey, 'Revolution in the bedroom', *Independent*, 22 March 2002

Malcolm, Derek, 'Mexico lit up by dog's star', *Observer*, 7 April 2002

Martinez, Jose, 'The Other Conquest', Venice, April 2000

Matheson, Kristy, '"Somehow images are the perfect words": An interview with Amat Escalante', *Senses of Cinema*, March 2018

'Mexico's IMCINE is granted $14m budget', staff reporters in Los Angeles, *Screen Daily*, 28 January 2004

Pulver, Andrew, 'Carlos Reygadas: In defence of *Post Tenebras Lux*', *Guardian*, 14 March 2013

Index

Films and other creative works are filed under their title. Numbers are filed as as if they are spelled out. Where the middle name is a family surname, as in Alejandro González Iñárruti, the entry will be filed under that name. Illustrations are entered in **bold**.

Index

Index

Index